The Role of the Regions in EU Governance

Carlo Panara • Alexander De Becker
Editors

The Role of the Regions in EU Governance

Springer

Editors
Dr. Carlo Panara
School of Law
Liverpool John Moores University
John Forster Building
98 Mount Pleasant
L3 5UZ Liverpool
United Kingdom
c.panara@ljmu.ac.uk

Professor Dr. Alexander De Becker
Faculteit recht en criminologie
Vrije Universiteit Brussel
Pleinlaan 2
1050 Brussel
Belgium
alexander.de.becker@vub.ac.be

Universiteit van Amsterdam
Faculteit Rechtsgeleerdheid
Oudemanhuispoort 4–6
1012 Amsterdam
The Netherlands

ISBN 978-3-642-11902-6 e-ISBN 978-3-642-11903-3
DOI 10.1007/978-3-642-11903-3
© Springer Heidelberg Dordrecht London New York

Library of Congress Control Number: 2010937570

Cover design: WMXDesign GmbH, Heidelberg, Germany

Printed on acid-free paper

Springer is part of Springer Science+Business Media (www.springer.com)

Preface

The Treaty of Lisbon entered into force in December 2009 and is an extremely important step in the European integration process. This new treaty is not a full European Constitution, but it remains a further development in the ongoing process of creation of an evermore integrated supranational union. States were and remain the only "members of the club" (the Union) but the importance of sub-state entities is also recognised by the Treaty.

The concept of "multi-level governance" has grown in importance. This concept was originally developed to coordinate the action of the Member States (on local and national levels) with that of the EU. Coordination is more difficult to achieve in those Member States in which the government has a regionalised or decentralised structure.

During the last four decades, a number of Member States decentralised important powers of the central government to sub-national entities. At the same time, the Member States continued to hand a significant part of their powers to the supranational level. These are two parallel and simultaneous processes which, at first sight, seem to be contradicting one another. In reality, they complement each other and give birth to numerous and complex relationships.[1]

Initially, regional entities claiming further powers were not fully aware that the construction of the Union was absorbing both national and sub-national competences.[2] However, they became aware that all their obtained demands were in reality threatened by the transfer of powers made by the Member States in favour of the European Communities and, later, the European Union. Soon, the development of EC law and the increase of powers transferred to the Community and the Union, led to a change in strategy by regional entities. They began to claim participation in EU-related matters, especially when the EU law and policies involved

[1]Both processes have been highlighted in many EU Member States that have a federal or regional political system; see, in Germany, Ipsen (1966), pp. 248–264; in Italy, Caretti (1979); in Spain, Ruiloba Santana (1985), pp. 21–38; in Belgium, Velaers (2006), pp. 3–86.

[2]Portelli (1993), pp. 15–20.

subjects falling within their competence.[3] These observations indicate the complex evolution of the legal relationship between the European Communities (later the European Union) and its Member States.

The difficult balance between the exercise of powers of entities with certain legislative powers within the different Member States (called "regions" in the scope of this book[4]) and the European Union constitutes the subject of this comparative research book. The topics dealt with will be approached from two different angles: the EU level and the Member States.

Despite the supranational identity of the EU, recent treaties and regulations show some openness to the regionalisation and decentralisation process that took (and it is still taking) place in the Member States. The participation of the Regions in the meetings of the Council should be mentioned as an example. Additionally, the EU showed more awareness of the existence of sub-state regional entities through the growing recognition of the Committee of the Regions. One of the principal roles of this Committee is in the safeguarding of the principle of subsidiarity. Actually, the Committee is often referred to as the "subsidiarity watchdog".[5] However, the legal meaning of the principle of subsidiarity within the Treaty of Lisbon still needs to be clarified. On the other hand, the EU still remains "regionally blind" as to other aspects; for example, the locus standi of the regions before EU courts, which will be discussed in Chap.2.

On the Member State level, seven federal, regionalised and decentralised Member States will be discussed. It is the first time that so many national patterns form the focus of a comprehensive legal research project on the role of the Regions in the EU.

The following Member States are analysed: three federal States (Austria, Belgium and Germany), two regionalised States (Italy, Spain) and two major Member States that underwent a strong devolution (United Kingdom) or decentralisation process (France) in the recent past. Two other Member States with a regionalised or decentralised structure (Portugal and Finland) are not included in the book for two reasons. Firstly, the book aimed to address those federal, regionalised and decentralised states with the biggest impact on the EU. Secondly, regionalism in these

---

[3]Reich (2001), pp. 1–18; Lenaerts et al. (2005), pp. 533–534.

[4]For the purpose of this book, we call "regions" not only the regions in regionalised states. In a way which is consistent with the European primary law, we also call "regions" the level of government that, both in regionalised and federal settings, is at the intermediate level between the state and the local authorities. Accordingly, we refer to the German and the Austrian *Länder*, the Italian, Belgian, and French Regions, the Belgian Communities, the Spanish *Comunidades autónomas*, and the authorities with devolved powers in Scotland, Wales and Northern Ireland as "regions". In the case of Italy, the term "region" also covers the Autonomous Provinces of Trento and Bolzano which have powers very similar to those of the Regions.

[5]Among others, read the report pertaining to the 95th meeting of the Bureau of the Committee of the Regions, 7 July 2006, p. 5. Also read the press release of the Committee of the Regions of 4 December 2009 http://www.cor.europa.eu/pages/PressTemplate.aspx?view=detail&id=decfa388-ecd6-4cc0-9d0d-dc9ae2584112 (last checked on 15 June 2010).

two countries is rather limited in scope. In Portugal, it is limited to overseas regions. In Finland, regional authorities are not directly elected.[6]

To ensure uniformity throughout the book, the same topics are addressed for each of the analysed Member States. The authors of the national Chapters (Chaps. 6–12) were given the following issues to address:

(a) How does the transfer of powers of the Regions to the EU take place?
(b) The internal regulation of the forms of direct and/or indirect involvement of the Regions in the EU law- and policy-making.[7]
(c) The internal preparation of (European) Councils and how, or indeed if, it is guaranteed that internal agreements will be respected during the negotiations on the EU level.
(d) The judicial defence of the Regions' competences at national and European level in the case of an invasion of competences of the Regions by the EU.
(e) The fulfilment of EU obligations in the internal sphere.
(f) Main areas within which there is an overlap between the competences of the Regions and those of the EU.
(g) Representation offices of the Regions in Brussels.

The findings of the research have been thoroughly analysed and summarised in the Conclusion. The book has been updated until the end of April 2010. Where significant changes had taken place since, the texts were updated until the end of June 2010 and all the websites referred to in the footnotes have been accessed on that date.

Finally, we would like to make a number of acknowledgements. We wish to express our gratitude to the authors and to the publisher. Special thanks go to Springer Verlag's editor, Dr. Brigitte Reschke, for believing in this project from the beginning and for her continued support. Special thanks also go to our excellent Research Assistant Daniel Metcalfe for revising the English throughout the book. We wish him a very successful career. Special thanks are due to Dr. Mike Varney and to Joanne Maltby, who revised several chapters of the book, and to Frederic Eggermont, for updating the papers to the re-numbering introduced by the Treaty of Lisbon. Finally, thank you to our partners and to all relatives, friends and anyone not already mentioned who, sometimes unwittingly, contributed in keeping the editors' psychological balance relatively safe during the execution of this research.

Liverpool and Brussels
June 2010

---

[6]Prakke et al. (2004), pp. 229–231.

[7]Direct involvement concerns involvement at the EU level (e.g., regional participation in Council meetings). Indirect involvement includes legal mechanisms ensuring some safeguard of the powers of the regions to determine the position of the Member State on the EU level (e.g., negotiation of common positions in regional matters).

References

Caretti P (1979) Ordinamento comunitario e autonomie regionale. Contributo allo studio delle incidenze del Diritto Internazionale sui poteri delle Regioni. Giuffrè, Milano

Ipsen H-P (1966) Als Bundestaat in der Gemeinschaft. In: von Caemmerer E et al (eds) Probleme des Europäischen Rechts. Festschrift für Walter Hallstein. Klostermann, Frankfurt a.M., pp 248–264

Lenaerts K, Van Nuffel P, Bray R (eds) (2005) Constitutional Law of the European Union. Sweet and Maxwell, London, pp 533–534

Portelli H (1993) Aux origines de la décentralisation des Etats européens: l'absence de prospective européenne. In: Portelli H (ed) La décentralisation française et l'Europe. Editions Pouvoirs Locaux, Paris, pp 15–20

Prakke L, Kortmann CAJM, Van Den Brandhof JCE (2004) Constitutional Law of 15 EU Member States. Kluwer, Deventer, pp 229–231

Reich N (2001) Zum Einfluss des europaïschen Gemeinschaftrechts auf die Kompetenzen der deutschen Bundesländer. Europäische Grundrechte Zeitschrift:1–18

Ruiloba Santana E (1985) Repercusiones del ingreso de España en la Comunidad Europea sobre la constitución del Estado de las Autonomías. Aspectos generales. In: Coloquio de la Asociación Española para el Estudio del Derecho Europeo. Generalitat de Catalunya, Barcelona, pp 21–38

Velaers J (2006) In foro interno et in foro externo: de internationale bevoegdheden van de Gemeenschappen en de Gewesten. In: Geudens G, Judo F (eds) Internationale betrekkingen en federalisme. Larcier, Brussels, pp 3–86

Contents

Part I
Regions in the EU

Chapter 1
In the Name of Democracy: The External Representation of the Regions in the Council

Frederic Eggermont

The purpose of this chapter is to see whether the regions are involved, or even participate, in the decision making of the Council, which is, together with the European Parliament, the actual maker of EU law.

At the time of the establishment of the EEC, Germany was the only Member State which had a federal institutional structure; all other Member States were endowed with a centralised system, with the exception of Italy, a regional State according to its Constitution, where some regions with special autonomy and legislative powers were already in existence in the 1950s.[1] Today, the EU has several Member States with regional entities, namely Austria, Belgium, France, Italy, Spain and the United Kingdom.[2] The latter, for example, only started to become less centralised since the New Labour government's devolution plan of 1997.

Over time, the regions have seen their influence increased at the EU level. This is not merely a reflection of the declining normative authority of States and the increasing political importance of the regions within the Member States. It is also due to the insertion of the principle of subsidiarity in the EC Treaty. Also, the creation of the Committee of the Regions and the amendment of Article 146 EEC (current Article 16, par. 2 EU Treaty)[3] showed that the regions were given a more important role in EU policy making. This was all the more confirmed after the negative outcome of the popular referendum on the ratification of the Treaty of Nice held on 7 June 2001 in Ireland, when the Commission drafted a White Paper on European Governance in which it proclaimed that a stronger interaction with

[1] Art. 116 Italian Constitution.

[2] Seron (1998), p. 652.

[3] Previous Art. 203 EC Treaty which has been repealed by Art. 2, 190 Treaty of Lisbon.

F. Eggermont
Department Metajuridica, Vrije Universiteit Brussel (VUB), Pleinlaan 2, 1050 Brussels, Belgium
e-mail: Frederic.Eggermont@vub.ac.be

C. Panara and A. De Becker (eds.), *The Role of the Regions in EU Governance*,
DOI 10.1007/978-3-642-11903-3_1, © Springer-Verlag Berlin Heidelberg 2011

regional governments was one way to achieve better involvement of EU citizens in EU policy making and to work towards more openness.[4]

Many decisions taken at EU level have a direct impact on regional competences. It now has to be examined whether the regions really have been given a say in the EU decision-making process or if there has been a lack of respect for the issue of the regions in the EU,[5] keeping in mind that Europeanisation of regional competences moves the decision making "from *sub*national to *supra*national".[6] Besides, giving the regions the possibility to directly influence EU decision-making is a politically sensitive matter because the national States' (exclusive) competence to entertain the country's external relations is, in a way, ignored.

A. Composition of the Council

I. EEC Treaty

The EEC Treaty provided that the Council consisted of representatives of the Member States. Each government delegated one of its members.[7] The representatives therefore had to be members of the governments of the Member States, whatever their titles were (ministers or state secretaries).[8] Unlike with the Committee of Ministers of the Council of Europe, there was no deviation from this condition provided for in the EEC Treaty.[9]

It was up to each Member State itself to decide which representative met this requirement.[10] The Council was nonetheless of the opinion that each Member State had to be represented in that institution by a member of the national government, whatever the internal distribution of power within the Member State might have been.[11] An opening was provided by the Council Rules of Procedure which stated that "[s]ubject to the provisions of Article 5 on the delegation of voting rights, a member of the Council who is prevented from attending a meeting may arrange to

[4]White Paper on European Governance of 25 July 2001, COM (2001) 428 final, p. 4.

[5]See Storini (1997), p. 226.

[6]Falker (1999), p. 9.

[7]Art. 146 EEC Treaty; see also Art. 2 Merger Treaty.

[8]See van den Berg (1961), p. 3 *et seq.* and Falker (1999), pp. 131–132.

[9]Art. 14 Statute of Europe states: "Each member shall be entitled to one representative on the Committee of Ministers, and each representative shall be entitled to one vote. Representatives on the Committee shall be the Ministers for Foreign Affairs. When a Minister for Foreign Affairs is unable to be present or in other circumstances where it may be desirable, an alternate may be nominated to act for him, who shall, whenever possible, be a member of his government".

[10]Jacqué (2000), p. 131 and Houben (1964), pp. 125–127.

[11]Written Question n. 129/90 by Mr Marc Galle to the Council, O.J. C125/53 of 21 May 1990.

be represented".[12] Thus, where for one reason or another, it is impossible for the government of a Member State to delegate one of its members to a particular Council meeting, it is possible for that government to be represented by a person whom it designates. In that case, the substitute will intervene in the Council meeting on behalf of the Council member whom he represents, that is on behalf of the national government of the Member State in question.[13] Of course, this substitute can be a regional minister. In other words, the representation of a Member State by a regional minister in the Council was based on a flexible interpretation of the Council Rules of Procedure.

However, in such a case, the regional minister could not vote. The national minister did not have the ability to delegate his right to vote to the regional minister because the Council Rules of Procedure explicitly provide that delegation of the right to vote may only be made to another member of the Council.[14] The Member State which was represented by a regional minister would therefore have to delegate its right to vote to the national minister of another Member State, in order to be in conformity with Article 146 EEC Treaty. Obviously, in such a case, the regional minister would first have to communicate the Member State's position, adopted after internal deliberations between the central and regional governments, so that the designated member of the Council, who was to act in the name of that Member State, could vote in accordance with the latter's position. All the same, it has never been customary for a Member State to mandate another Member State to cast its vote. In the rule, if a minister cannot be present at the Council meeting, he is replaced by a colleague, a state secretary or the permanent representative. Moreover, in the rule, the Council President merely checks that a majority of ministers is present and that the opinions expressed make clear that a qualified majority is reached, without actually having a vote.

Until the entry into force of the Single European Act,[15] the European Council, composed of the Heads of State or Government, had to be considered a Council

---

[12]Art. 4 Provisional Council Rules of Procedure of 25 January 1958 and Council Rules of Procedure adopted by the Council on 24 July 1979 on the basis of Article 5 of the Treaty of 8 April 1965 establishing a single Council and a single Commission of the European Communities, O.J. L268/1 of 25 October 1979. Current Art. 4 Council Rules of Procedure adopted by Council Decision of 15 September 2006 adopting the Council's Rules of Procedure, O.J. L285/47 of 16 October 2006.

[13]Written Question n. 129/90 by Mr Marc Galle to the Council, O.J. C125/53 of 21 May 1990.

[14]Art. 5 Provisional Council Rules of Procedure of 25 January 1958 and Council Rules of Procedure adopted by the Council on 24 July 1979 on the basis of Art. 5 of the Treaty of 8 April 1965 establishing a single Council and a single Commission of the European Communities, O.J. L268/1 of 25 October 1979. Today, this article still stands, see Art. 11 Council Rules of Procedure adopted by Council Decision of 15 September 2006 adopting the Council's Rules of Procedure, O.J. L285/47 of 16 October 2006.

[15]Art. 2 SEA provided that the European Council is no longer merely composed of the Heads of State or Government, but also of the Commission President. Due to the fact that the Commission President is not a member of the Council (of Ministers), the European Council and the Council are, from then on, two separate entities.

while dealing with Community issues[16]; it continued being an informal gathering of Heads of State or Government while dealing with foreign policy (European Political Cooperation). It was possible for the European Council to sit as a Council before the Single European Act. Indeed, the Heads of State or Government are considered the highest representatives of the Member States. But, as provided by the 1974 Paris communiqué by which the European Council was established, only the Heads of State or Government were members of the European Council.[17] This of course excludes the representatives of the regions, although they can be involved in the preparation of the European Council meeting. For example, the Head of the Austrian Department for *Länder* and Regional Affairs is a member of the Austrian delegation at the European Council (and since 2000, at Intergovernmental Conferences).

II. Treaty of Maastricht

The EC Treaty, since its modification by the Treaty of Maastricht[18] states that the Council consists of a representative of each Member State at ministerial level, authorised to commit the government of that Member State.[19] The TFEU clarifies this by adding that that the representative may cast its vote.[20]

The wording of the EEC Treaty was changed by the Treaty of Maastricht at the request of Germany[21] and Belgium[22] to allow the participation of regional governments.[23] Due to this new wording, the EC Treaty was made in conformity with reality,[24] and there is no longer a discussion on the validity of the representation of a Member State by a minister of a regional government, as long as the representative may commit the Member State and cast its vote.

The minister of a regional government will no longer be merely able to participate in the Council as substitute for the minister of the national government but from now on he acts in his own right as regional minister.[25] The only formality that the regional minister has to perform is identifying himself before the General

[16]See Bramsen (1982), p. 631

[17]Communiqué of the Paris Summit meeting of 9–10 December 1974, Bull. EC 1974/12, par. 1104.

[18]Art. 146 EEC Treaty was amended by Art. G.43 Treaty of Maastricht.

[19]Art. 203 EC Treaty; repealed by Art. 2, 190 Treaty of Lisbon, and replaced, in substance, by Art. 16, par. 2 EU Treaty.

[20]Art. 16, par. 2 EU Treaty as inserted by Art. 1, 17 Treaty of Lisbon.

[21]Westlake and Galloway (2004), p. 29.

[22]Ingelaere (1994), p. 69.

[23]Hayes-Renshaw and Wallace (1996), p. 28.

[24]Storini (1997), p. 235.

[25]See Cerexhe (1995), p. 666.

Secretariat of the Council as the one who acts for the Member State.[26] The EU and TFEU are indeed concluded between the 27 Member States and not their regional entities. The representative at ministerial level therefore has to be able to commit the entire Member State, notwithstanding the fact that he is actually a minister in a regional government.[27]

B. Rationale for the Participation of Representatives of the Regions in Council Meetings

The current versions of the Treaties take into account the evolution in many Member States away from the "*unified national representation*" and, as such, the Treaties respect their internal organisation.[28] Regional authorities have undeniably received more and more competences in the areas of regional policy, social policy, transport, environment, research, technological development, culture, energy, tourism, employment, etc., and it is now up to the Member States to make sure that the regions can also have a say within the EU institutions. The Austrian *Länder* even made their approval of EU membership incumbent on their participation in the EU regulatory framework.[29] Otherwise, the European integration process could have the perverse effect that the competences of the regions are diminished because they cannot exercise them at the EU level (only the national state would be able to do so). EU integration would bring about a re-centralisation and re-nationalisation of competences within the Member States.[30] This is why the regions lobbied strongly for the introduction of the principle of subsidiarity in the EC Treaty to make sure that the EU would not perform tasks which the regions could perform, and for upholding the relevant provisions of their national constitutions.[31]

The principles of supremacy and direct effect of Union law would create problems if the regional entities of a Member State were not involved in the EU decision-making process. For example, it is established case law that a regulation is directly applicable[32] and has direct effect if its wording is "*clear and capable of direct application without difficulty*".[33] The Court of Justice furthermore ruled that it would be incompatible with the binding effect attributed to a directive by Article

26 Vasco (1998), p. 68.

27 Jacqué (2000), p. 131.

28 de Areilza (2010) and Etherington (2010), p. 108.

29 McLeod (2010), p. 6.

30 Biancarelli (1991), p. 526.

31 Art. 5 EC Treaty; current Art. 5, par. 3 EU Treaty as inserted by Art. 1, 6 Treaty of Lisbon and Van Ginderachter (1992), pp. 779–780, and Philippart (1998), p. 637.

32 Previous Art. 249 EC Treaty.

33 Court of Justice, case n. 31/64 of 11 March 1995, "De Sociale Voorzorg" Mutual Insurance Fund v. W.H. Bertholet, European Court Reports, 1965, p. 86.

288 TFEU to exclude the possibility that the obligation which it imposes may be invoked by those concerned. The *effet utile* of a directive, imposing the obligation to pursue a particular course of conduct, would be weakened if private parties were prevented from relying on it before the national courts and the latter were prevented from taking it into consideration as an element of Union law.[34] However, the provisions of the directive have to appear unconditional and sufficiently precise. In that case, the provisions may, in the absence of implementing measures adopted within the prescribed period, be relied upon as against any national provision which is incompatible with the directive or in so far as the provisions define rights which individuals are able to assert against the Member State.[35] Thus, even where the regions are competent for a certain issue, but the national ministers in the Council have adopted a regulation or a directive, it is possible that the courts do not put the regional act into operation because otherwise there would be a violation of European law. Going to the extremes, courts could even invoke directives of which the direct effect has been recognised, although the directive has not been transposed into regional law by the regional authorities because they do not agree with the directive's contents.

In addition, every national court is under a duty to give full effect to the provisions of Union law.[36] This means that the national court has to interpret the law – including regional law – in light of the wording and purpose of a directive in order to achieve the result it has in mind, even if it is the case that the directive has not yet been implemented in the Member State.[37] Often, the national law of a Member State also states that, when it has been admonished for non-compliance with its treaty obligations by one of its regions, the Member State, instead of the region, can execute the enacting terms of the judgment.[38]

The aforementioned principles of Union law make it possible that the competences of the regions are affected by decision making in the Council (and the European Parliament). This possibility was recognised by the *Bundesverfassungsgericht* (German Federal Constitutional Court) which stated in its judgment of 22 March 1995 that the federal government had infringed the rights of the German *Länder* by endorsing the Audiovisual Media Services Directive[39] because broadcasting is an exclusive competence of the *Länder*. According to the Court, the

[34]Court of Justice, case n. 41/74 of 4 December 1974, Yvonne van Duyn v. Home Office, European Court Reports, 1974, p. 1337, par. 12.

[35]Court of Justice, case n. 8/81 of 19 January 1982, Ursula Becker v. Finanzamt Münster-Innenstadt, European Court Reports, 1982, p. 53, par. 25.

[36]Court of Justice, case n. 106/77 of 9 March 1978, Amministrazione delle Finanze dello Stato v. Simmenthal SpA, European Court Reports, 1978, p. 629, par. 24.

[37]Court of Justice, case n. C-106/89 of 13 November 1990, Marleasing SA v. La Comercial Internacional de Alimentación SA, European Court Reports, 1990, I, p. 4135, par. 13.

[38]For example, Art. 16, par. 3 Special Act of 8 August 1980, *Belgian Moniteur*, 15 August 1980.

[39]Council Directive of 3 October 1989 on the coordination of certain provisions laid down by Law, Regulation or Administrative Action in Member States concerning the pursuit of television broadcasting activities, O.J. L298/23 of 17 October 1989.

federal government infringed the rights of the regions because it had not informed the *Bundesrat*, composed of members of the *Länder* governments,[40] about the results of the negotiations in the Council before taking a decision on the steps to be taken and because it had not tried to reach an agreement on the issue.[41]

The principle of subsidiarity, introduced by the Treaty of Maastricht,[42] cannot be restricted to relations between the EU and the Member States as advocated by Spain[43]; it also includes relations between Member States and regions, as suggested by the declaration of Austria, Belgium and Germany on subsidiarity, attached to the Final Act of the IGC which adopted the Treaty of Amsterdam, which states: "It is taken for granted by the German, Austrian and Belgian governments that action by the European Community in accordance with the principle of subsidiarity not only concerns the Member States but also their entities to the extent that they have their own law-making powers conferred on them under national constitutional law".[44] In this way, they wanted to make clear that, when regional competences were at stake, the regional authorities would intervene in the Community decision-making procedure.[45] Since the entry into force of the EU Treaty, it is provided that the EU respects the national identities of the Member States, inherent in their fundamental structures, political and constitutional, inclusive of regional and local self-government.[46] Before proposing legislative acts, the Commission moreover has to take into account the regional and local dimension of the action envisaged.[47]

The introduction of the principle of subsidiarity and the establishment of the Committee of the Regions[48] by the Treaty of Maastricht was, however, not sufficient. The regions had to be given the opportunity to defend their interests at the stage of preparation and adoption of EU legislation.[49] Therefore, the regions asked for and received the right to participate in the Council meetings. However, this does not mean that since the entry into force of the Treaty of Maastricht the participation

[40] Art. 51 German Constitution.

[41] German Federal Constitutional Court, 22 March 1995, 2 BvG 1/89, p. 57.

[42] Art. 3b EC Treaty (inserted by Art. G.5 Treaty of Maastricht): "In areas which do not fall within its exclusive competence, the Community shall take action, in accordance with the principle of subsidiarity, only if and in so far as the objectives of the proposed action cannot be sufficiently achieved by the Member States and can therefore, by reason of the scale or effects of the proposed action, be better achieved by the Community"; current Art. 5, par. 3 EU Treaty as inserted by Art. 1, 6 Treaty of Lisbon.

[43] Gutiérrez Espada (1998), pp. 12–13.

[44] Declaration by Germany, Austria and Belgium on subsidiarity, O.J. C340/143 of 10 November 1997.

[45] Seron (1998), p. 654.

[46] Art. 4, par. 2 EU Treaty as inserted by Art. 1, 5 Treaty of Lisbon.

[47] Protocol (No 2) on the application of the principles of subsidiarity and proportionality, O.J. C115/206 of 9 May 2008.

[48] Art. 263 *et seq.* EC Treaty (current Art. 305 *et seq.* TFEU). The Committee of the Regions was established by Art. G.67 Treaty of Maastricht.

[49] Van Ginderachter (1992), p. 778.

of the regions in the Council is now just taken for granted. The request of the Basque government to be able to take a seat in the Council is perhaps the reason why negotiations with the Spanish central government in 2002 on the *Concierto Económico con la Comunidad Autónoma del País Vasco* (Economic Agreement with the Autonomous Community of the Basque Country) did not go very well.[50]

In the end, the European Parliament also called on the Member States which have regions with exclusive legislative powers to facilitate the participation of representatives of these regions in meetings of the Council when matters falling within their competences are being considered.[51]

C. How Does the Participation of the Regions in the Council Work?

There are in fact two possible ways, which can be combined, to organise the involvement of the regions in the Council. First, the national and regional authorities assemble before the Council meeting to adopt a common position (internal participation). Second, the regional ministers are allowed to sit in the Council (external participation) and possibly even to represent the Member State.[52] The first form of representation will be the object of the chapters devoted to the single national patterns. The latter form of representation will instead be dealt with now.

I. Austria

The Austrian Constitution provides that, when a matter which also belongs to the competences of the German Regions (*Länder*) or which is of interest to them, is dealt with at the European level,[53] the federal government *can* (!) allow a regional representative to represent Austria in the Council. This representative will have to cooperate with the representative of the federal government. Of course, the regional representative, just as the federal minister, will then be bound by the common position of the *Länder* from which the federation may only deviate in certain specific situations ("*nur aus zwingenden außen- und integrationspolitischen*

---

[50]Olivar de Julián (2002), p. 16.

[51]Resolution on the participation and representation of the regions in the process of European integration: the Committee of the Regions, O.J. C329/279 of 6 December 1993, par. 11.

[52]Cantera Martínez (2002), pp. 451–452.

[53]Art. 8, s 1 Vereinbarung zwischen dem Bund und den Ländern gemaß Art. 15a B-VG über die Mitwirkungsrechte der Länder und Gemeinden in Angelegenheiten der europäischen Integration, BGBl 1992/775.

Gründen")[54]; the regional representative does not represent his region, but the whole Member State and all of its constitutive *Länder*. Until now, this provision of the Constitution has never been practised because it was never invoked by the Austrian regions, which means that the common *Länder* delegates were just members of the delegation as a whole.

In the permanent representation of Austria in the EU, there is, moreover, a Head of Department for *Länder* and Regional Affairs who can always participate in any Council meeting.

II. Belgium

The Belgian Special Act of 8 August 1980 states that the governments of the Communities and the Regions can represent Belgium in the Council.[55] The Cooperation Agreement further implements the relevant article and defines the possible forms of representation, namely an exclusive federal representation, a federal representation with an assessor of the Communities and the Regions, representation by the Communities and the Regions with a federal assessor and an exclusive representation by the Communities and the Regions.[56] In order to determine which Community or Region (Flemish Community, French Community, German speaking Community, Flemish Region, Walloon Region or Brussels Capital Region) will represent the country, there is a rotation system.[57] Furthermore, the Cooperation Agreement states that fisheries are an exclusive competence of the Flemish Region without rotation.[58] Also, in the field of agriculture, Belgium is represented by the Flemish and the Walloon Regions together with a federal assessor. The assessor has the rank of minister and assists the minister who represents Belgium. In doing so, he can deliver statements in the Council, in agreement with the actual representative.[59] The Cooperation Agreement

[54]Art. 23d, s 1-3 Austrian Constitution.

[55]Art. 81, par. 6 Special Act of 8 August 1980, *Belgian Moniteur*, 15 August 1980.

[56]Annex I to the Cooperation Agreement between the federal authority, the Communities and the Regions concerning the representation of the Kingdom of Belgium in the Council of Ministers of the European Union of 8 March 1994, *Belgian Moniteur*, 17 November 1994.

[57]Annex II to the Cooperation Agreement between the federal authority, the Communities and the Regions concerning the representation of the Kingdom of Belgium in the Council of Ministers of the European Union of 8 March 1994, *Belgian Moniteur*, 17 November 1994.

[58]Annex I to the Cooperation Agreement between the federal authority, the Communities and the Regions concerning the representation of the Kingdom of Belgium in the Council of Ministers of the European Union of 8 March 1994, *Belgian Moniteur*, 17 November 1994.

[59]Annex I to the Cooperation Agreement between the federal authority, the Communities and the Regions concerning the representation of the Kingdom of Belgium in the Council of Ministers of the European Union of 8 March 1994, *Belgian Moniteur*, 17 November 1994.

furthermore declares that the rules are *mutatis mutandis* the same for the informal Council meetings.[60]

III. Germany

Besides the possibility of the *Länder* attending the Council meetings as a part of the German delegation, the German Constitution provides that the rights of the Federal Republic of Germany are ceded to a representative of the *Länder*, appointed by the German Federal Council (*Bundesrat*), when the exclusive regional competences are definitely at stake in the fields of education, culture, radio and television.[61] The exercise of these rights by the regional representative has to be done with the cooperation of the federal government and with its participation (*Bundestreue*),[62] but it is the regional representative who defends the interests of the entire Member State.

The *Länderbeobachter* (joint *Länder* observer), appointed by the German regions, will inform the latter about the discussions in the Council when the *Länder* have not appointed a specific regional representative (the joint *Länder* Observer thus has a more subordinate role).[63] He attends the meetings of the Council and checks if the opinion of the *Bundesrat* is taken into account by the federal government in the negotiations without actually intervening in the meetings.[64] Unlike the Head of the Austrian Department for *Länder* and Regional Affairs, who has the quality of minister plenipotentiary, the German *Länderbeobachter* is not an integral part of the German Permanent Representation.

IV. Italy

The Italian Constitution proclaims that the relations of Italy with the EU are a matter wherein the state has exclusive legislative power, but the EU relationships of the regions are a shared competence.[65] The direct participation of the Italian regions means that they are represented in the Council ("*concorrono direttamente* [...] *alle attività del Consiglio*") by a regional representative when issues pertaining to their

[60]Annex III to the Cooperation Agreement between the federal authority, the Communities and the Regions concerning the representation of the Kingdom of Belgium in the Council of Ministers of the European Union of 8 March 1994, *Belgian Moniteur*, 17 November 1994.

[61]Art. 23.6.1 German Constitution.

[62]Art. 23.6.2 German Constitution.

[63]Cantera Martínez (2002), p. 456, footnote 14.

[64]Woelk (2005), p. 168.

[65]Art. 117 Italian Constitution.

competences are dealt with. The head of the Executive of a Region or of an Autonomous Province can even be appointed head of the delegation.[66]

V. Spain

Since the *Acuerdo sobre el sistema de representación autonómica en las formaciones del Consejo de la Unión Europea* of 9 December 2004, the autonomous communities participate in the Council meetings via a regional minister or his representative when matters pertaining to their competences are dealt with, although the principle of a single Spanish EU representation is still paramount. The regional representation is furthermore limited to the following Council formations: Employment, Social Policy, Health and Consumer Affairs, Agriculture and Fisheries, Environment, and Education, Youth and Culture. The autonomous regions can indicate that they want to be represented in the Council. The competent Sectoral Conference shall then appoint a regional minister who will be a full member of the Spanish delegation (for example, if the Council is to debate youth matters, the Sectoral Conference on Education and Social Affairs has to appoint the regional minister).[67] The appointment does not happen at will, but follows certain rules. For instance, in the Agriculture and Fisheries Council, the regional participant is designated via a system of six-monthly rotation on the basis of alphabetical order, while for the Environment Council there is a rotation for each Council session.[68]

When the Council discusses matters which belong to the competences of the autonomous communities, and in cases where they have adopted a common position, the regional minister will be allowed to speak when the head of the Spanish delegation considers it the best way to defend the country's interests.[69] It is interesting to note that this intervention does not have to be done in Spanish. At the Council (Education, Youth and Culture) meeting of 25 May 2007, the regional minister addressed his colleagues in Gallic, while at the Environment Council of 20 December 2007, it was done in Basque.[70]

---

[66]Art. 5, par. 1 Act n. 131 of 5 June 2003, G.U n. 132 of 10 June 2003; *see also* the Accordo generale di cooperazione tra il Governo, le regioni e le province autonome di Trente e Bolzano per la partecipazione delle regioni e delle province autonome alla formazione degli atto comunitari of 16 March 2006, G.U. n. 75 of 30 March 2006.

[67]Art. 1-3 Acuerdo sobre la Consejería para Asuntos Autonómicos en la Representación Permanente de España ante la Unión Europea y sobre la participación de las Comunidades Autónomas en los grupos de trabajo del Consejo de la Unión Europea of 9 December 2004, BOE of 16 March 2005.

[68]Ministerio de Administraciones Públicas (2010), p. 4.

[69]Art. 5.3 Acuerdo sobre el sistema de representación autonómica en las formaciones del Consejo de la Unión Europea of 9 December 2004, BOE of 16 March 2005.

[70]Ministerio de Administraciones Públicas (2010), pp. 15–16.

VI. UK

According to the UK *Memorandum of Understanding* on the matter, ministers and officials of the devolved administrations have to play a role in Council meetings at which substantive discussion is expected on matters likely to have a significant impact on their devolved responsibilities (Agriculture and Fisheries and Environment Council), but decisions on ministerial attendance at these meetings are taken on a case-by-case basis by the lead UK minister. It is he who takes the overall responsibility for the negotiations and determines how each member of the team can best contribute to securing the agreed policy position. This entails that the UK minister can consider it appropriate that the regional minister speaks for the entire country in the Council or that, even if the matter has a significant impact on the devolved regions, the regional minister should not have a role to play.[71] Most frequently, Scotland participated as an observer or, sporadically, as spokesperson for the UK, because its Executive has more resources than the Executives of Wales and Northern Ireland. Furthermore, it has more devolved powers than the other regions and Scottish participation in the Council was well established prior to devolution.

It has to be said that the discussion on the possible participation of the regions in the Council was one of the most symbolic and controversial of all discussions held concerning the introduction of devolution.[72] These concordats are, however, not legally enforceable but are binding in honor only[73]; they therefore have been referred to as "*soft law or 'administrative quasi-legislation' par excellence*".[74]

Regional representatives will now also be able to use Gaelic and Welsh in the Council meetings. For example, at the Council meeting (Education, Youth and Culture) of 20–21 November 2008, the UK representative, Welsh Minister for Heritage, Alun Fred Jones, addressed his colleagues in Welsh.

VII. Council Presidency

Article 146 EEC stated that the office of Council President had to be held for a term of six months by each member of the Council in turn. The Council President

---

[71]CM 5420, *Memorandum of Understanding and Supplementary Agreements between the United Kingdom Government, Scottish Ministers, the Cabinet of the National Assembly for Wales and the Northern Ireland Executive Committee* London: TSO, 2001, par. B4.12–14.

[72]Cantera Martínez (2002), p. 464.

[73]CM 5420, *Memorandum of Understanding and Supplementary Agreements between the United Kingdom Government, Scottish Ministers, the Cabinet of the National Assembly for Wales and the Northern Ireland Executive Committee* London: TSO, 2001, par. B1.2 (and B.2.2 for Wales and B.3.2 for Northern Ireland).

[74]Rawlings (2000), p. 258.

therefore had to be a member of the government of the Member State which held the Presidency. In other words, according to the EEC Treaty, it was impossible for a regional minister to chair a Council meeting.

Under the Treaty of Nice, Article 203 EC Treaty provided that the office of President was held in turn by each Member State in the Council for a term of six months in the order decided by the Council. This wording made it possible that a regional minister could preside over a meeting of the Council during the Council Presidency of his Member State.[75] Since the entry into force of the Treaty of Lisbon, the Presidency of Council configurations, other than that of Foreign Affairs,[76] is held by Member State representatives in the Council on the basis of equal rotation.[77] This new wording does not change anything about the situation which has existed since the Treaty of Maastricht.

Indeed, a regional minister has chaired a Council meeting. For example, the 2,380th and the 2,398th meetings of the Council (Research) held on 30 October and 10 December 2001 – during Belgium's Council Presidency – were chaired by the François-Xavier de Donnéa, the Minister-President of the Brussels Capital Region with responsibility for scientific research.[78] This move was openly criticised by France and considered by the Commission as an extra complication.[79]

VIII. Evaluation of the Effectiveness of Such Participation Rights of the Regions

With respect to internal representation, it depends on the constitutional arrangements as to how far the regions are able to influence the position that is to be taken by the Member State in the Council.[80] Internal representation entails meetings between the different levels of government to discuss EU matters in order to coordinate the different points of view. If consultation before every Council meeting is compulsory, then this gives the regions the opportunity to influence matters which do not belong to their competences, although this is not always the case. In Belgium, for example, the Communities and the Regions have always shown a reluctance to intervene in matters that fall outside their scope.[81]

---

[75]But according to par. 6.3 Gesetz über die Zusammenarbeit von Bund und Ländern in Angelegenheiten der EU of 12 March 1993, BGBl., 1993, I, p. 313 the German Länder cannot hold the Council Presidency, although they still have to be consulted by the federal government.

[76]The Foreign Affairs Council is chaired by the High Representative of the Union for Foreign Affairs and Security Policy, Art. 18, par. 3 EU Treaty as inserted by Art. 1, 19 Treaty of Lisbon.

[77]Art. 16, par. 9 EU Treaty as inserted by Art. 1, 17 Treaty of Lisbon.

[78]Press Release 12996/01 of the 2380th Council meeting (Research) of 30 October 2001 and Press Release 14888/01 of the 2398th Council meeting (Research) of 10 December 2001.

[79]Cañas (2001).

[80]Ingelaere (1994), p. 68.

[81]Philippart (1998) p. 640.

In relation to external representation, it first has to be established what matters will be discussed in the Council meeting and what entity (the national state and/or the regions) is competent for these issues according to the national constitutional provisions. Once established, the Member State can decide whom to send to the meeting (normally a regional minister for matters belonging to the competence of the regions). The representative in the Council can nonetheless be assisted by an assessor from the national or regional government. For certain Council formations, representation by the regions is very common because the matters dealt with are within general regional competences. This is very much the case for the Agriculture and Fisheries Council; for example, at the 2,860th meeting of the Council (Agriculture and Fisheries) of 17 March 2008, Belgium was represented by the Minister-President of the Flemish government and the Flemish Minister for Agriculture and Sea Fisheries, while the Spanish Minister and the UK Under Secretary were accompanied by the Minister for Agriculture and Fisheries of the Autonomous Community of the Canary Islands and the Cabinet Secretary for Rural Affairs and the Environment of the Scottish government, respectively.[82]

The participation of a regional minister in Council meetings can pose a problem concerning political responsibility. The representative in the Council has to assume political responsibility,[83] but while the regional minister is only responsible to his regional assembly, the entire Member State is bound by the position taken in the Council. Neither the other regional assemblies nor the national/federal assembly can exercise political control on the regional minister's acts in the Council.[84] This is, however, not the case in Austria. It is specified in the Constitution that when a matter dealt with in the Council belongs to the competence of the federation, the *Länder* representative is responsible to the *Nationalrat* (which represents the Austrian federation). But when the matter belongs to the regional competences, then he is accountable to the regional parliaments.[85] However, as already stated, this provision has not yet been used.

The regional minister should also make sure that he defends the position of his Member State and not only that of his regional entity. The issue of internal organisation of a Member State may belong to its national sovereignty[86]; the representative in the Council must be able to legally bind his entire Member State. This is why Article 16, par. 2 EU Treaty (previous Article 203 EC Treaty)

[82]Press Release 7508/1/08 of the 2860th Council meeting (Agriculture and Fisheries) of 17 March 2008.

[83]Ingelaere (1994), p. 68.

[84]Evans (2003), p. 24.

[85]Art. 23d, s 3 Austrian Constitution.

[86]Written Question n. 1390/90 by Mr Reinhold Bocklet to the Commission, O.J. C164/5 of 24 June 1991; *see also* Court of Justice, case n. C-302/1997 of 1 June 1999, Klaus Konle v. Austria, European Court Reports, 1999, I, p. 3099, par. 61–64.

explicitly provides that the representative must be able to commit the government of the Member State in question; this modification of Article 146 EEC by the Treaty of Maastricht was strongly inspired by France because it wanted to prevent any discussions on the ability of a representative to commit his entire Member State. It is therefore up to the Member States with regional entities to arrange the modalities by which a regional minister receives a mandate to represent the entire Member State.[87]

IX. Possible Limits and Drawbacks of the Participation of the Regions in Council Meetings

The participation of the regions in the Council's work is a noteworthy response to the criticism that the competences of the regions are diminished because they cannot exercise it at the EU level. This feeling of re-nationalisation is even more strengthened due to the effects of the principles of supremacy and direct effect of EU law in relation to regional law. It has to be taken into account that the more regions a Member State has, the less the opinion of a single region weighs in the formation of the country's stance and the more chance there is of not reaching a unified standpoint. In addition, the common position of the regions is, in the end, used to decide on the Member State's stance in the Council, but at that stage it is not sure yet that in the final stage this will be the opinion that the representative will defend in the Council. Nonetheless, internal representation is the most appropriate manner for a region to have its voice heard in the very first stage of the decision-making process. It is at that stage that the region can shape the Member State's stance to be taken in the Council to their benefit.

It is incorrect to think that the region in itself is represented in the Council. If a region receives the competence to be present in the Council, then there are two possibilities. On the one hand, it can merely be there to assist the national minister in representing the country when matters of regional interests are discussed. On the other hand, it can actually be the representative of the Member State, but then for the Member State as a whole and not just for the region which takes charge of the representation, even if the matter discussed is an exclusive regional competence.

Participation of the regions in the Council can nonetheless be abused. It is not impossible that a representative of a region with a government composed of political parties other than the national government makes use of its right to speak in the Council with the aim of attacking the national government. In that case, the access of regional ministers to Council meetings could be reduced.

[87]Ingelaere (1994), pp. 68–69.

D. Regions Within Coreper

The Coreper, consisting of the Permanent Representatives of the governments of the Member States, is responsible for preparing the work of the Council and for carrying out the tasks assigned to it by the latter.[88] It conducts a preliminary review of all legislative instruments before submitting them to the Council. It ensures the consistency of the Union's policies and actions, and sees to it that the principles of legality, subsidiarity, proportionality and providing reasons for acts, the rules establishing the powers of EU institutions and bodies, the budgetary provisions and the rules on procedure, transparency and the quality of drafting are observed.[89]

Representation of the regions in the Coreper is of importance because the vast majority of matters which appear on the agenda of the Council are "A" items. Normally, these items are approved in the Council without further debate. If the regions were not involved in the proceedings of the Coreper, they would not have any influence on the decision making concerning those acts which are not debated in the Council because they were approved in the Coreper. This is important, bearing in mind that it is far more complicated to influence the final stages of decision making in the Council (where compromises are made) than in the preparatory stage.[90] Nevertheless, it is the Member States that decide on the involvement of their regions in the Coreper. The regions can be invited by the Permanent Representative of the State concerned to attend the Coreper meetings; this is also the reason why there may be regional representatives in the Permanent Representation of a Member State. Nevertheless, the Member State's legislation or practice can restrict its representation in the Coreper and the concomitant right to speak to the Permanent Representative and the Deputy Permanent Representative. For example, although there are Scottish, Welsh and Northern Irish representatives in the UK Permanent Representation in the EU, they do not attend Coreper sessions. The Spanish Autonomous Communities are represented there when matters are discussed which belong to the regional competences.[91] This is also the case for the Austrian *Länder* and the German *Länder* when their interests are involved,[92] together with the joint *Länder* observer. However, the latter does not have the right to speak during the meeting, exactly like the representatives of the Belgian Communities and Regions who participate in the Coreper meetings.

---

[88]Art. 240, par. 1 TFEU as replaced by Art. 2, 192 Treaty of Lisbon.

[89]Art. 19, par. 1 Council Rules of Procedure adopted by Council Decision of 15 September 2006 adopting the Council's Rules of Procedure, O.J. L285/47 of 16 October 2006.

[90]McLeod (2010), p. 29.

[91]Art. 3.3 Acuerdo sobre el sistema de representación autonómica en las formaciones del Consejo de la Unión Europea, BOE of 16 March 2005 and art. II.4 Acuerdo sobre la Consejería para Asuntos Autonómicos en la Representación Permanente de España ante la Unión Europea y sobre la participación de las Comunidades Autónomas en los grupos de trabajo del Consejo de la Unión Europea of 9 December 2004, BOE of 16 March 2005.

[92]Par. 6.1 Gesetz über die Zusammenarbeit von Bund und Ländern in Angelegenheiten der Europäischen Union of 12 March 1993, BGBl., 1993, I, p. 313.

E. Regions Within Council Working Groups

Committees or working parties, composed of national civil servants, may be set up by, or with the approval of, Coreper with a view to carrying out certain preparatory work or studies defined in advance.[93] There are permanent and non-permanent working parties. In these working groups the preliminary discussions on Commission proposals are held before they go to the Coreper and then to the Council.[94]

Also, within the working groups, the representation of the regions is of importance because the majority of the matters on which the Coreper reaches an agreement are in fact arranged in the relevant working groups.[95] But, just as with the Coreper, the decision on the participation of the regions in the Council working groups rests entirely with the national level. Member States can allow regional representatives to take part in these meetings and even chair them when the matters discussed belong to the competences of the regions.

The regional minister who has been appointed by the Sectoral Conference to represent the Spanish Autonomous Communities, according to the *Acuerdo sobre el sistema de representación autonómica en las formaciones del Consejo de la Unión Europea* of 9 December 2004, can appoint an official who will participate in the working groups (including taking the floor).[96] Of course, the regions can only be directly represented in the working groups of those Council formations wherein the regions are allowed to participate, but the Spanish Permanent Representative or his adjunct may nonetheless decide that it may be useful to let a representative of the Autonomous Communities participate in other working groups.[97] Together with the joint *Länder* observer, the German *Länder* participate in the working groups on the same terms as applicable to their representation in the Coreper and thus under the lead of the federal government.[98] Also, the Italian regions[99] and the Austrian *Länder* can be present at the meetings. In the early years, there were precedents that regional participation had been refused by the Austrian federation,[100] but this does not seem to be a problem any longer. Representatives of the UK devolved regions also participate in the Council working groups.

---

[93]Art. 19, par. 3 Council Rules of Procedure adopted by Council Decision of 15 September 2006 adopting the Council's Rules of Procedure, O.J. L285/47 of 16 October 2006.

[94]Lenaerts and Van Nuffel (2005), p. 423.

[95]Vasco (1998), p. 69.

[96]Art. 3.3 Acuerdo sobre el sistema de representación autonómica en las formaciones del Consejo de la Unión Europea, BOE of 16 March 2005.

[97]Art. II.1-3 Acuerdo sobre la Consejería para Asuntos Autonómicos en la Representación Permanente de España ante la Unión Europea y sobre la participación de las Comunidades Autónomas en los grupos de trabajo del Consejo de la Unión Europea of 9 December 2004, BOE of 16 March 2005.

[98]Par. 6.1 Gesetz über die Zusammenarbeit von Bund und Ländern in Angelegenheiten der Europäischen Union of 12 March 1993, BGBl., 1993, I, p. 313.

[99]Art. 5, par. 1 Act n. 131 of 5 June 2003, G.U n. 132 of 10 June 2003.

[100]McLeod (2010), p. 13.

The representation of the Belgian Communities and Regions in the Council working groups follows the predefined system which applies to the representation of Belgium and its federate entities in the Council; this means that there are six possible categories of representation. In the first category (exclusive competence of the federation), there are often no representatives of the Communities and Regions present although attendance is possible when, for example, a matter of external relations which is of interest to a Community or Region is handled. In the second (federal representation with an assessor of the Communities and the Regions) and third (representation by the Communities and the Regions with a federal assessor) categories, representatives of the federate entities are almost always present. They can give information to and ask for information from their federal colleagues, and with respect to the third category, express themselves in the meeting. In the fourth (exclusive representation by the Communities and the Regions) and sixth (agriculture) categories, the representatives of the federate entities speak for Belgium, and in the fifth category (fisheries), the representation is always conducted by the Flemish Region. Beforehand, it is established which Community or Region will have to be present in the Council (and even represent the country, for that matter). For example, with respect to the third category and in particular research, the German speaking Community will participate in the first half of 2009 and the Flemish Community in the second half. Relating to the fourth category, in particular tourism, the participation will be taken care of by the Brussels Capital Region in the first half of 2009 and the Walloon Region in the second half.

Normally, the country's unified view has to be established before every working group meeting, and through preliminary coordination, the regional representative has to be informed as to the Member State's position and the positions taken by the national representative and the other regional representatives of the Member State at previous meetings of the working group. But because there are many meetings, it is at times difficult for a Member State to coordinate all the internal points of view. As a result, the regional representative may find himself in a position where he alone establishes the Member State's standpoint.[101]

F. Is Participation in Council Meetings Something the Regions Cannot Live Without?

Internal participation ensures that the standpoints of the regions are taken into consideration by the national representative in the Council. This already makes it more difficult for the regions to criticise decision making of that EU institution.[102] However, the commitment of the central government to consider the opinion of the regions is insufficient. In a time where solving the "democratic deficit" at the

[101]Olivar de Julián (2002), p. 18.

[102]Bulmer et al. (2006), p. 81.

European level is considered to be of paramount importance, representation by the entity which is closer to the citizens should be preferred to a system whereby national representatives decide on regional competences at the European level. It is logical that the entity which is responsible for the implementation of the decision of the Council is the same entity as the one which has actually participated in the decision-making process at the European level. If Member States want to give real autonomy to their constitutive parts, they have to be given effective representation at the EU level.[103] However, once the Member State has adopted a single position after (long and intensive) negotiations between the national government and the regional governments, then the regional representative in the Council has to abide by that position, even if "his" regional government has a different view. A change in the Member State's standpoint can only occur after internal negotiations where once more the regions have a say. As a result, the minister who represents the Member State does not have a lot of room for manoeuvre in the Council discussions because he has to stay within the scope of the common position adopted; otherwise, new negotiations between the national government and the regional governments have to take place. Especially in the Council (of Ministers), where the representatives always prefer to strive for consensus, this can pose a problem.

Having access to the Council, the Coreper and the working groups also provide the regions with access to networks of representatives,[104] which can encourage interregional cooperation in certain policy areas, such as mobility of the labor force between the regions of neighboring Member States or between a Member State and a neighboring region. Nonetheless, it can be understood that there are Council formations in which only the national ministers participate.[105] This is, for example, the case of the Ecofin Council, of which the Economic and Finance Ministers are members; the Belgian Cooperation Agreement provides that, in this case, there is exclusive federal representation[106] because the federal state is competent for economic and monetary union.

Not all regions are represented in the Council. The specific nature of UK "*cooperative regionalism*"[107] produces the result that it is uncertain who is now actually representing England in the Council. Are the interests of Wales, Northern Ireland and Scotland therefore better protected than those of England? Or does UK representation sufficiently ensure that English interests are taken into consideration? The UK *Memorandum of Understanding and Supplementary Agreements* merely proclaims that UK ministers and their departments represent the interests of

---

[103]Constantinesco (1989), p. 25.

[104]Kerremans and Beyers (1997), p. 53.

[105]The EC Treaty also made reference to the Council, meeting in the composition of the Heads of State or Government. This Council configuration is abolished with the Treaty of Lisbon.

[106]Annex 1 to the Cooperation Agreement between the federal authority, the Communities and the Regions concerning the representation of the Kingdom of Belgium in the Council of Ministers of the European Union of 8 March 1994, *Belgian Moniteur*, 17 November 1994.

[107]Bulmer et al. (2006), p. 90.

England in all matters.[108] But who will resolve a possible dispute between England and the UK? Until today, the Finnish autonomous Aland Islands have not participated in Council meetings, but the local Aland Government announced that it would not ratify the Treaty of Lisbon until it receives such formal right.

Participation of the regions in Council meetings (and in Coreper and Council working groups) enhances their democratic accountability because they become responsible, not only for the mere implementation of EU legislation but also for the actual promotion of regional interests at the EU level. Therefore, if a region desires to increase its authority at the EU and international levels, it cannot do so without external representation, not only in the Council but also in Coreper and Council working groups where the actual decisions are often taken. This explains why the European regions have always lobbied for having a representative in the Council. However, this does not mean that a region should shake off the central government when it is dealing with EU matters; only by seeking the support, and not the opposition of the central government, can regional involvement become effective.[109] One thing may not be forgotten: genuine regional interests are not represented in the Council, only national interests which may be intertwined with the interests of the regions.[110]

Selected Bibliography

Biancarelli J (1991) La Communauté européenne et les collectivités locales: une double dialectique complexe. Revue Française d'Administration Publique:526

Bramsen B (1982) Le Conseil européen: son fonctionnement et ses résultats de 1975 à 1981. Revue du Marché Commun:631

Bulmer S et al (2006) UK devolution and the European Union: a tale of cooperative asymmetry? Publius

Cañas G (2001) Un dirigente regional preside por primera vez en la historia un Consejo de Ministros. *El País*, 1 December 2001

Cantera Martínez J (2002) Crónica sobre modelos europeos en materia de participación y representación de las entidades subestatales en el Consejo de Ministros de la Unión Europea. Revista española de Derecho Europeo

Cerexhe E (1995) La Région wallonne et la Communauté française dans l'ordre international. Tijdschrift voor Bestuurswetenschappen en Publiek Recht:666

Constantinesco V (1989) Comunidades europeas, estados, regiones: el impacto de las estructuras descentralizadas o federales del estado en la construcción comunitaria. Revista de instituciones europeas:25

Ministerio de Administraciones Públicas (2010) Informe sobre la participación de las Comunidades Autónomas en el Consejo de la Unión Europea. Año 2007. http://www.map.es/

---

[108]CM 5420, *Memorandum of Understanding and Supplementary Agreements between the United Kingdom Government, Scottish Ministers, the Cabinet of the National Assembly for Wales and the Northern Ireland Executive Committee*. London: TSO, 2001, par. 1.

[109]See Sloat (2010), pp. 10–17.

[110]Woelk (2004), p. 86.

documentacion/politica_autonomica/Cooperacion_Autonomica/CCAA_Asunt_Europeos/parrafo/01/text_es_files/file2/Informe_CCAA_Consejos_UE.pdf. Accessed 15 Jun 2010
de Areilza J (2010) Sovereignty or management? The dual character of the EC's supranationalism – revisited. http://www.jeanmonnetprogram.org/papers/95/9502ind.html. Accessed 15 Jun 2010
Olivar de Julián JM (2002) La representación de las regiones en el Consejo de la Unión Europea. Unión Europea Aranzadi
Etherington J (2010) Nationalism, National Identity and Territory. The Case of Catalonia. http://www.tdr.cesca.es/TESIS_UAB/AVAILABLE/TDX-0621104-153930//je1de1.pdf. Accessed 15 June 2010, p 108
Evans A (2003) Regional dimensions to European governance. Int Comp Law Q
Falker G (1999) How pervasive are euro-politics? Effects of EU membership on a new member state. Max-Planck Institute for the Study of Societies, p 9 (discussion paper 99/4)
Gutiérrez Espada C (1998) La CIG de 1996 (o la crónica de una reforma anunciada). Noticias de la Unión Europea:12–13
Hayes-Renshaw F, Wallace H (1996) The council of ministers. Macmillan, London, p 28
Houben P-HJM (1964) Les Conseils des Ministres des Communautés européennes. Sythoff, Leyde, pp 125–127
Ingelaere F (1994) De Europeesrechtelijke raakvlakken van de nieuwe wetgeving inzake de internationale betrekkingen van de Belgische Gemeenschappen en Gewesten. Tijdschrift voor Bestuurswetenschappen en Publiek Recht
Jacqué J-P (2000) Le Conseil. In: Institut d'Etudes européennes (ed) Commentaire J. Mégret. Le droit de la CE et de l'Union européenne. Le Parlement européen. Le Conseil. La Commission. La Cour des comptes. Le Comité économique et social. Le Comité des Régions. La Banque européenne d'investissement. Le Fonds européen d'investissement. Université Libre de Bruxelles, Brussels, p 131
Jeffery C (ed) (1997) The regional dimension of the European Union. Towards a third level in Europe? Frank Cass, London
Kerremans B, Beyers J (1997) The Belgian sub-national entities in the European Union: second or third level players? In: Jeffery C (ed) The regional dimension of the European Union. Towards a third level in Europe? Frank Cass, London, p 53
Lenaerts K, Van Nuffel P (2005) Constitutional law of the European Union. Sweet & Maxwell, London, p 423
Maas HH (1960) Enkele opmerkingen over de Raad van Ministers in de Europese Gemeenschappen. Sociaal-Economische Wetgeving Europa:131–132
McLeod AJ (2010) Regional participation in EU affairs: lessons for Scotland from Austria, Germany and Spain. http://www.scotlandeuropa.com/PUBLIC%20SITE/Scotland%20Europa%20Papers/PAPER15-web.DOC. Accessed 15 Jun 2010
Ortino S et al (eds) (2005) The changing faces of federalism. Institutional reconfiguration in Europe from East to West. Manchester University Press, Manchester
Philippart E (1998) Gouvernance à niveaux multiples et relations extérieures: le développement de la 'paradiplomatie' au sein de l'Union européenne et la nouvelle donne belge. Etud Int:637
Rawlings R (2000) Concordats of the constitution. Law Q Rev:258
Seron J-L (1998) La mise en œuvre retardée du principe de subsidiarité. 423 Revue du Marché Commun et de l'Union européenne
Sloat A (2010) Scotland in the European Union: expectations of the Scottish Parliament's architects, builders and tenants. http://ec.europa.eu/governance/areas/group10/contribution_-scotland_en.pdf. Accessed 15 Jun 2010, pp 10–17
Storini C (1997) La homogeneidad como párame identificador interno y externo de la participación regional en la Unión Europea: una comparación entre Alemania, Bélgica, España e Italia. Revista Valenciana d'Estudis Autonòmics
Toniatti R et al (eds) (2004) An ever more complex Union. The Regional Variable as a Missing Link in the EU Constitution. Nomos, Baden-Baden

van den Berg WA (1961) De staatssecretaris. Samsom, Alphen aan den Rijn, p 3
Van Ginderachter J (1992) Le rôle des régions dans la construction européenne. Revue du Marché Commun et de l'Union européenne
Vasco G (1998) La participación de las Comunidades autónomas en los consejos de ministros de la Unión europea: jornada celebrado en el Palacio de Artaza (2 de julio de 1998). Instituto Vasco de Administración Pública, Bilbao
Westlake M, Galloway D (2004) The council of the European Union. John Harper, London, p 29
Woelk J (2004) A place at the window: Regional Ministers in the Council. In: Toniatti R et al (eds) An ever more complex union. The regional variable as a missing link in the EU constitution. Nomos, Baden-Baden, p 86
Woelk J (2005) Farewell to the 'unitary federal state'? Transformation and tendencies of the German federal system. In: Ortino S et al (eds) The changing faces of federalism. Institutional reconfiguration in Europe from east to west. Manchester University Press, Manchester, p 168

Chapter 2
The *Locus Standi* of the Regions Before EU Courts

Anne Thies

The Regions and other autonomous communities of the Member States arguably form one of the governmental layers of the constitutional legal order of the European Union. As shown by other authors contributing to this book, the transfer of Member States' powers to the supranational level has neither necessarily been accompanied by the provision of adequate forms of participation of the Regions at the EU level nor by the safeguarding of competences reserved for such entities by the Member States' constitutional order. The potential strengthening of the Regions' position within the Community (and later the EU) constitutional legal order has since been subject to extensive political debate and academic discourse. At the same time, questions arose concerning the Regions' access to judicial protection before the EU Courts, in particular with regard to the Regions' entitlement to directly challenge EU measures encroaching upon their prerogatives. Those prerogatives comprise, *inter alia*, Regions' legislative and executive powers allocated by their national legal system, their general interest in economic prosperity and territory, their interest in full judicial protection and the principle of subsidiarity.

This chapter assesses the standing of the Regions before the EU Courts and provides an overview of the potential impact of the Treaty of Lisbon on the current situation. The first section of this chapter analyses the Regions' direct access to EU Courts for challenging the lawfulness of EU measures in annulment actions brought under Article 263 TFEU (former Article 230 EC). The EU Courts have recognised the Regions' capacity to challenge EU measures neither as so-called privileged applicants, in order to enforce the EU institutions' compliance with EU law,[1] nor as

[1] C-95/97, *Région Wallonne* v *Commission*, Order of 21 March 1997 [1997] ECR I-1287; C-180/97, *Regione Toscana* v *Commission*, Order of 1 October 1997 [1997] ECR I-5245; C-406/06, *Landtag Schleswig-Holstein* v *Commission*, Order of 8 February 2007, paras. 3, 8 et seq. (unpublished). According to Article 263 (2) TFEU (former Article 230 (2) EC), the ECJ has jurisdiction in annulment actions brought by Member States and EU institutions challenging an EU measure "on grounds of lack of competence, infringement of an essential procedural requirement, infringement

A. Thies
School of Law, University of Reading, Foxhill House, Whiteknights Road, Earley, Reading RG6 7BA, UK
e-mail: a.thies@reading.ac.uk

C. Panara and A. De Becker (eds.), *The Role of the Regions in EU Governance*,
DOI 10.1007/978-3-642-11903-3_2, © Springer-Verlag Berlin Heidelberg 2011

"semi-privileged applicants" in order to defend their prerogatives independently from their Member States.[2] Hence, this section focuses on the Regions' standing as "non-privileged applicants", which requires applicants to be either addressed, or directly and individually concerned by the contested EU measure.[3] In its second part, the chapter provides a short overview of the Regions' capacity to access the EU judicature indirectly. The accessibility and scope of annulment actions brought by the Member States on behalf of the Regions, and the position of the Regions in preliminary ruling proceedings initiated by a national court and concerned with the regions' prerogatives impinged by EU measures, are subject to the procedural autonomy of the EU Member States' legal systems. Since an analysis of 27 distinct legal systems would go beyond the scope of this chapter, the issue is thus addressed only briefly by providing some examples actually brought before the EU Courts. After providing a summary of changes introduced by the Treaty of Lisbon, the chapter concludes with a critical evaluation of the overall scope of judicial protection provided for Regions by the EU legal order, i.e. by the Treaties and the EU Courts.

A. Regions' Direct Access to the EU Courts

According to the case-law of the EU Courts, Regions have no privileged status when challenging EU measures. In other words, regional authorities cannot – like national governments[4] – bring actions before the ECJ to challenge EU measures "on grounds of lack of competence, infringement of an essential procedural requirement, infringement of the Treaties or of any rule of law relating to its application, or misuse of powers"[5] without demonstrating the actual and distinct

of the Treaties or of any rule of law relating to its application, or misuse of powers" without further conditions to be met. According to the Court, Regions are not "Member States" in the meaning of this Article and do thus not belong to the group of "privileged applicants".

[2]According to Article 263 (3) TFEU (former Article 230 (3) EC), the Court of Justice has jurisdiction in actions brought by the Court of Auditors, by the ECB and by the Committee of the Regions "for the purpose of protecting their prerogatives". While with the entry into force of the Treaty of Lisbon, the Committee of the Regions was entitled to bring actions for the purpose of protecting its prerogatives, the Regions themselves were not listed as semi-privileged applicants, see further discussion below Sect. C.

[3]According to Article 263 (4) TFEU (former Article 230 (4) EC), "[a]ny natural or legal person may [. . .] institute proceedings against an act addressed to that person or which is of direct and individual concern to them, and against a regulatory act which is of direct concern to them and does not entail implementing measures".

[4]See for a detailed discussion of the "unlimited right of action of a Member State" Van Nuffel (2001), p. 874 et seq.

[5]See Article 263 (2) TFEU (former Article 230 (2) EC), footnote 1.

impact of the contested EU measure on their own prerogatives and legal situation. In 1997, the ECJ concluded in its Order in *Région Wallonne* v *Commission* that the immediate jurisdiction of the ECJ is limited to actions brought by a Member State or a Community institution.[6] The ECJ held:

> [I]t is apparent from the scheme of the Treaties that the term 'Member State', for the purpose of the institutional provisions and, in particular, those relating to proceedings before the courts, refers only to government authorities of the Member States of the European Communities and cannot include the government of regions or autonomous communities, irrespective of the powers they may have. If the contrary would be true, it would undermine the institutional balance provided for by the Treaties, which govern the conditions under which the Member States, that is to say, the States party to the Treaties establishing the Communities and the Accession Treaties, participate in the functioning of the Community institutions. It is not possible for the European Communities to comprise a greater number of Member States than the number of States between which they were established.[7]

Since Regions and other autonomous communities are not considered to be privileged applicants, their capacity to challenge EU measures affecting them is limited in the same way as it is for natural and legal persons. Accordingly, Regions have to address the General Court (the former Court of First Instance, CFI) instead of the ECJ, with a potential appeal to the ECJ challenging the General Court's decision on points of law.[8] When bringing annulment actions, Regions need to meet the conditions of Article 263 (4) TFEU (former Article 230 (4) EC), i.e. they need to have legal personality and be either the addressee of a EU decision or "directly" and "individually" concerned by a decision addressed to another person or a contested piece of EU legislation.[9]

---

[6]The Court referred to Council Decision 94/149/ECSC, EC of 7 March 1994 amending Decision 93/350/Euratom, ECSC, EEC amending Decision 88/591/ECSC, EEC, Euratom establishing a Court of First Instance of the European Communities, O.J. 1994, L 66/29. In Decision 94/149, the Council clarified that actions brought by natural and legal persons under (now) Article 230 (4) EC fall within the jurisdiction of the CFI.

[7]C-95/97, *Région Wallonne* v *Commission*, footnote 1, para. 6. The ECJ referred the case to the CFI, which dismissed the action as inadmissible; see T-70/97, *Région Wallonne* v *Commission*, Order of 29 September 1997 [1997] II-1513, paras. 21–24. This approach has been confirmed by the ECJ and the CFI since, see e.g. C-180/97, *Regione Toscana*, footnote 1, para. 6; T-214/95, *Vlaamse Gewest* v *Commission* [1998] ECR II-717, para. 28; T-238/97, *Comunidad Autónoma de Cantabria* v *Council*, [1998] ECR II-2271, para. 42; T-609/97, *Regione Puglia* v *Commission and Spain* [1998] ECR II-4051, para. 16; T-32 and T-41/98, *Nederlandse Antillen*, *Nederlandse Antillen* v *Commission* [2000] ECR II-201, para. 43. See Scott (1999).

[8]Articles 56, 58 of the Statute of the ECJ. According to Article 58 of the Statute, "[a]n appeal to the Court of Justice shall be limited to points of law. It shall lie on the grounds of lack of competence of the Court of First Instance, a breach of procedure before it which adversely affects the interests of the appellant as well as the infringement of Community law by the Court of First Instance".

[9]See for more detailed discussion of standing for natural and legal persons in annulment actions Craig (1994), Arnull (2001), Ward (2007), p. 284 et seq., Craig and De Búrca (2008), pp. 509–528, and Tridimas and Poli (2008).

There have been only a few cases in which Regions challenged Decisions addressed to them.[10] In several cases, Regions challenged Decisions addressed to another person, more specifically to a Member State,[11] or legal provisions of general application, which can in principle also be of direct and individual concern to certain applicants, even if not constituting a disguised decision.[12] The following sections provide an overview of the approach taken by the EU Courts in recent years with regard to the applicants' legal personality, and the contested EU measures being of direct and individual concern to the applicants.

I. Legal Personality of Regions

The aim of Article 263 (4) TFEU is to provide appropriate judicial protection for all persons, natural or legal, who are directly and individually concerned by acts of the EU institutions.[13] In the same way as private legal persons, a public legal person should enjoy a certain degree of autonomy under its own national legal order.[14] The EU Courts have recognised the legal personality of regional authorities after having referred to the national legal systems in question.[15]

[10]See, e.g. T-81/97, *Regione Toscana* v *Commission* [1998] ECR II-2889, paras. 21 et seq. In Joined Cases T-392/03, T-408/03, T-414/03 and T-435/03, *Regione Siciliana* v *Commission*, Order of 25 September 2008, paras. 27, 36 et seq., 46, the CFI considered letters addressed to the Region as either not producing legal effect (and thus not being challengeable under Article 230 EC), or being actually addressed not to the Region but the Italian Republic. In T-236/06, *Landtag Schleswig-Holstein* v *Commission*, O.J. 2008 C 142/25, the lack of legal personality under national law made the action inadmissible; the appeal is pending, C-281/08.

[11]See, e.g. Joined Cases T-132/96 and T-143/96, *Freistaat Sachsen* v *Commission* [1999] ECR II-3663; T-341/02, *Regione Siciliana* v *Commission* [2004] ECR II-2877, and C-417/04, *Regione Siciliana* v *Commission* [2006] ECR I-3881, para. 24 (concerning Commission decision closing the financial assistance from the European Regional Development Fund (ERDF) for the Messina-Palermo Motorway major project); T-60/03, *Regione Siciliana* v *Commission* [2005] ECR II-4139 (Commission Decision relating to the cancellation of the aid granted to the Italian Republic by decision concerning the provision of assistance by the ERDF as infrastructure investment, and to the recovery of the advance on that assistance made by the Commission – dismissed as inadmissible); on appeal the ECJ also denied "direct concern" in C-15/06, *Regione Siciliana* v *Commission* [2007] ECR I-2591.

[12]See, e.g. C-452/98, *Nederlandse Antillen* v *Council* [2001] ECR I-8973, paras. 51, 55; C-142/00 P, *Commission* v *Nederlandse Antillen* [2003] ECR I-3483, paras. 59, 64; C-445 and 455/07 P, *Commission* v *Ente per le Ville Vesuviane* and *Ente per le Ville Vesuviane* v *Commission*, Judgment of 10 September 2009, para. 42; T-417/04, *Regione autonoma Friuli-Venezia Gulia* v *Commission* [2007] ECR II-641, paras. 44 et seq., 52; T-37/04, *Região autónoma dos Açores (Portugal)* v *Council* [2008] ECR II-103*, Summ. publ., para. 39.

[13]See e.g. the summary of T-288/97, *Friuli Venezia Giulia* v *Commission* [1999] ECR II-1871.

[14]Van Nuffel (2001), p. 885, referring to the Opinion of AG Lenz in C-298/89, *Gibraltar* v *Council* [1993] ECR I-3605, 3628–3629.

[15]T-214/95, *Vlaamse Gewest*, footnote 7, para. 28; T-238/97, *Comunidad Autónoma de Cantabria*, footnote 7, para. 43; T-288/97, *Friuli Venezia Giulia*, footnote 13, para. 42.

II. Direct Concern of Regions

The Courts have considered a EU measure to be of "direct concern" to an applicant if the contested measure (a) "directly affect[s] his legal situation" and (b) "leave[s] no discretion to the addressees of that measure who are entrusted with the task of implementing it, such implementation being purely automatic and resulting from the [EU] rules alone without the application of other intermediate rules".[16] The Courts have acknowledged the applicant being directly affected where "it is possible in theory only for addressees not to give effect to the [EU] measure and their intention to act in conformity with it is not in doubt".[17]

1. Decision Being of Direct Concern

Many Commission decisions have been contested by sub-state entities, in particular Regions, in the areas of State aid and the Structural and Cohesion funds.[18] In order to attempt a later evaluation of the differences with regard to the Regions standing identified by the Courts in those areas, they are presented separately by providing some examples of recent case law.

a) State Aid

In *Vlaamse Gewest* v *Commission*, the CFI acknowledged direct concern where a decision "directly prevent[ed the Region] from exercising its own powers, which [...] consist[ed] of granting the aid in question, as it [saw] fit".[19] In *Freistaat*

[16]See e.g. Joined Cases 41/70 to 44/70, *International Fruit Company and Others* v *Commission* [1971] ECR 411, paras. 23–29; Case 92/78, *Simmenthal* v *Commission* [1979] ECR 777, paras. 25 and 26; C-386/96 P, *Dreyfus* v *Commission* [1998] ECR I-2309, para. 43; C-404/96 P, *Glencore Grain* v *Commission* [1998] ECR I-2435, para. 41; T-69/99, *DSTV* v *Commission* [2000] ECR II-4309, para. 24; C-486/01 P, *National Front* v *Parliament* [2004] ECR I-6289, para. 34; C-445 and 455/07 P, *Ente*, footnote 12, para. 45; C-501/08 P, *Município de Gondomar* v *Commission*, Order of 24 September 2009, nyr, para. 25; Joined Cases T-172 and 175-177/98, *Salamander and others* v *European Parliament and Council* [2000] ECR II-2487, para. 52; T-105/01, *SLIM Sicilia* v *Commission* [2002] ECR II-2697, para. 45; T-60/03, *Regione Siciliana*, footnote 11, para. 46.

[17]T-60/03, *Regione Siciliana*, footnote 11, para. 46; the CFI referred to C-386/96 P, *Dreyfus*, footnote 16, para. 44; see also, to that effect, Case 11/82 *Piraiki-Patraiki and Others* v *Commission* [1985] ECR 207, paras. 8–10; T-324/06, *Município de Gondomar* v *Commission*, Order of 10 September 2008, nyr in the ECR, para. 38; C-445 and 455/07 P, *Ente*, footnote 12, para. 46; and Gordon (2007), at 3.72, referring to C-298/89, *Gibraltar*, footnote 14, 3634, per AG Lenz.

[18]See for a list of cases submitted in the areas of State aid and Structural Funds by 2000 Van Nuffel (2001), p. 872 at notes 5 and 6.

[19]T-214/95, *Vlaamse Gewest*, footnote 7, para. 29. This was in line with previous cases concerning a decision affecting, *inter alia*, a region's power to grant state aid, in which the admissibility of the action had not been contested by the Commission, see Cases 62 and 72/87, *Exécutif regional*

Sachsen and Volkswagen v *Commission*, the CFI considered the Decision addressed to the Federal Republic of Germany to be of direct concern to the applicant, as the Decision had not left any discretion for Germany when communicating it to the Free State of Saxony.[20] As in *Friuli Venezia Giulia*, the CFI relied in this case on the fact that the decision required the Region to recover the aid from beneficiaries.[21] In 2000, the Region Sicily challenged a Commission decision which stated, *inter alia*, that the State aid established pursuant to a regional law in favour of undertakings operating in the agriculture or fisheries sector was incompatible with the common market and required Italy to withdraw the aid in question; the Commission did not contend the measure's direct and individual concern to the applicant, and the CFI held the action admissible after only assessing whether the applicant had met the time limit for bringing an action.[22] In many cases since, the whole question of admissibility of actions brought by Regions in the area of State aid was not even addressed explicitly by the Courts.[23]

b) Structural Funds

In 2003, the Region Sicily challenged another Commission Decision, this time relating (a) to the cancellation of the aid granted to the Italian Republic by prior Commission Decision, which had foreseen the provision of assistance by the European Development Fund (ERDF) as infrastructure investment, and (b) to the recovery of the advance on that assistance made by the Commission.[24] The defendant had not disputed that the contested decision was of individual concern to the applicant, so the CFI merely examined whether the applicant was directly concerned by the decision. According to the CFI, the revoking of the assistance in its entirety through the contested decision "has had the initial direct and immediate effect of changing the applicant's financial situation by depriving the applicant of the balance of the assistance (approximately EUR 39.8 million) remaining to be paid by the Commission",[25] and demanded the repayment of advances paid to

wallon v *Commission* [1988] ECR 1573, paras. 6, 8. See also Joined Cases T-127, 129 and 148/99, *Diputación Foral de Álava and others* v *Commission* [2002] ECR II-1275, para. 50.

[20] Joined Cases T-132/96 and T-143/96, *Freistaat Sachsen*, footnote 11, paras. 89, 90.

[21] Joined Cases T-132/96 and T-143/96, *Freistaat Sachsen*, footnote 11, paras. 84–86; T-288/97, *Regione autonoma Friuli-Venezia Giulia*, footnote 13 , paras. 31, 32.

[22] T-190/00, *Regione Siciliana* v *Commission* [2003] ECR II-5015, paras. 29–33 (dismissed as unfounded).

[23] See, e.g. Joined Cases T-228 and 233/99, *Westdeutsche Landesbank and Land Nordrhein-Westfalen* v *Commission* [2003] ECR II- 435; T-369/00, *Département du Loiret* [2003] ECR II-1789, and [2007] ECR II-851; T-318/00, *Freistaat Thüringen* v *Commission* [2005] ECR II-4179; Joined Cases T-211 and 215/04, *Gibraltar and the UK* v *Commission*, Judgment of 18 December 2008. Pending is T-394/08, *Regione autonoma della Sardegna* v *Commission*, O.J. 2008 C 285/52.

[24] T-60/03, *Regione Siciliana*, footnote 11.

[25] T-60/03, *Regione Siciliana*, footnote 11, para. 53.

the Italian Republic and passed on to the applicant; the CFI thus concluded that the applicant's legal situation must necessarily have been affected by the contested decision.[26] The CFI also stated that "the contested decision [left] the Italian authorities no discretion, its implementation being purely automatic and resulting from Community rules alone without the application of other intermediate rules".[27] As a consequence, the CFI acknowledged the contested measure being of "direct concern" to the applicant.

In its cross-appeal, the Commission contended that the CFI erred in law by starting its reasoning as to the admissibility of the action from the premiss "that the decision to grant puts the Regione Siciliana directly in the position of a creditor in respect of the assistance granted".[28] According to the Commission, the Region's ability to receive ERDF assistance was dependent on the autonomous decisions of the Italian Republic.[29] Without a provision or decision of national law the Region would never be a creditor of the Community assistance.[30] The approach taken by the CFI, so the Commission, "would have unacceptable consequences from the point of view of the judicial protection of recipients of the Structural Funds" as "any person or entity recognised by law which is an end-beneficiary of Structural Funds would be directly concerned by the Commission decisions regarding the funds granted".[31] According to the appellant, the Regione Siciliana, however, the decision "directly affected its legal position, since it went from being the recipient of assistance to a debtor required to pay back advances received by way of assistance"; "the Italian authorities enjoyed no discretion in implementing the contested decision".[32] Furthermore, the appellant stated that the annex of the contested decision referred to it as "the body responsible for the application for financial assistance" and pointed out that the decision had "prevented it from exercising its powers as it understands them", in particular the decision obliged it to "cease to apply the legislation on the project and to activate the procedure for the recovery of the aid from recipients".[33]

The ECJ reiterated that a measure is only of direct concern to a natural or legal person, if the measure "affect[s] directly the legal situation of the individual and leave[s] no discretion to its addressees, who are entrusted with the task of implementing it, such implementation being purely automatic and resulting from Community rules without the application of other intermediate rules".[34] The fact that the

[26]T-60/03, *Regione Siciliana*, footnote 11, paras. 47, 48.

[27]T-60/03, *Regione Siciliana*, footnote 11, para. 48.

[28]C-15/06, *Regione Siciliana*, footnote 11, para. 20.

[29]C-15/06, *Regione Siciliana*, footnote 11, para. 20.

[30]C-15/06, *Regione Siciliana*, footnote 11, para. 21.

[31]C-15/06, *Regione Siciliana*, footnote 11, para. 22.

[32]C-15/06, *Regione Siciliana*, footnote 11, paras. 24, 25.

[33]C-15/06, *Regione Siciliana*, footnote 11, paras. 26, 27.

[34]C-15/06, *Regione Siciliana*, footnote 11, para. 31, referring to C-404/96 P, *Glencore*, footnote 16, para. 41; C-486/01 P, *National Front*, footnote 16, para. 34; C-417/04, *Regione Siciliana*, footnote 11, para. 28.

Regione Siciliana had been designated as the authority responsible for the implementation of an ERDF project does not imply, according to the ECJ, that it is itself entitled to assistance; the Court held that nothing supports the conclusion that the Region was directly concerned within the meaning of Article 230 (4) EC [now Article 263 (4) TFEU] in its capacity as the authority responsible for the implementation of the project.[35] The Court concluded that the scope of regions' powers according to the national legal order cannot have any effect on whether the appellant is directly concerned.[36]

In 2007, the CFI held again in *Ente per le Ville Vesuviane* v *Commission* that the applicant was directly concerned by a Commission decision.[37] The applicant was a public-law consortium, comprising the Italian State, the Region of Campania, the Province of Naples and a number of municipalities, whose object is to protect and improve the complex of sites consisting of the Ville Vesuviane (the towns around Vesuvius) dating from the 18th Century. The contested Decision concerned the closure of financial assistance from the ERDF for Ente projects.[38] The CFI had identified differences between the situation in the *Regione Siciliana* cases and this case before concluding on the admissibility of the action.[39] First, the contested Decision had referred to Ente not only as the person responsible for execution of the project but also as beneficiary.[40] Secondly, the Italian State had already announced, prior to the Commission Decision, that it intended to require repayment and not to provide funds itself, it was thus irrelevant that the Decision had provided discretion to the State when deciding whether or not to require repayment of the assistance paid.[41] Thirdly, a right of action was necessary so Ente could ensure protection of its rights of defence.[42]

On appeal, Advocate General Kokott rejected the reasoning of the CFI and suggested to the ECJ that the CFI's decision should be set aside and the action brought by Ente should be rejected as inadmissible.[43] The ECJ followed this suggestion. According to AG Kokott and the ECJ, the differences between the *Regione Siciliana* cases and the present one do not support a different assessment of the applicant's direct concern for several reasons. First, only the Italian State was "entitled" to assistance under the Decision, while Ente was merely designated as the

[35]C-15/06, *Regione Siciliana*, footnote 11, para. 32.

[36]C-15/06, *Regione Siciliana*, footnote 11, para. 35.

[37]T-189/02, *Ente per le Ville Vesuviane* v *Commission*, not published in the ECR, information at [2007] ECR II-89*.

[38]D(2002) 810111 prot. 102504 of the Commission's Regional Policy Directorate General.

[39]See for this summary (available in English) Opinion of AG Kokott on appeal C-445 and 455/07 P, *Ente*, footnote 12, of 12 February 2009, para. 47.

[40]T-189/02, *Ente*, footnote 37, para. 43 (of the French version).

[41]*Ibid*, paras. 44 et seq.

[42]*Ibid*, paras. 51 et seq.

[43]C-445 and 455/07 P, *Ente*, footnote 12, Opinion of AG Kokott of 12 February 2009, paras. 48 et seq.

"beneficiary".[44] Secondly, while Ente was not entitled to the assistance under EU law, the issue was whether the decision affected the consortium's legal situation as beneficiary.[45] However, AG Kokott reiterated, there is no direct concern where the autonomous will of the addressee interposes itself between the Commission decision and its effect on the applicant.[46] The ECJ agreed with AG Kokott that the Italian Government was under no obligation to require repayment from Ente, and the "subjective announcement" of the Italian State was not binding, AG Kokott adding that it would be unconvincing to leave it to the Member State to decide whether to make the applicant "directly concerned" through announcement and thus decide on the applicant's standing before EU Courts.[47] Accordingly, the CFI erred in law in considering that Ente was directly concerned by the contested decision.[48] AG Kokott had added that the mandatory consultation provided with Ente before a decision on closing the financial assistance from the ERDF placed Ente in a stronger position than the applicants in the Regione Siciliana cases; however, this would not give the basis for an independent right of action against a decision on the merits where an applicant – as in the present case – is not directly concerned by the content of the decision.[49] AG Kokott and the ECJ reiterated that where the admissibility conditions of Article 230 (4) EC [now Article 263 (4) TFEU] are not met, effective judicial protection should be made available by the national legal systems in accordance with the principle of cooperation in good faith laid down by Article 10 EC [replaced, in substance, by current Article 4 (3) TEU] through access to national courts and thereby the prompting of national courts' reference to the ECJ for a preliminary ruling.[50]

c) Cohesion Fund

On 10 September 2008, the CFI dismissed by Order as inadmissible, because of the lack of direct concern, an application brought by the Município de Gondomar (Portugal) for the annulment of Commission Decision on the cancellation of the

---

[44] C-445 and 455/07 P, *Ente*, footnote 12, para. 51; Opinion of Kokott, para. 50.

[45] C-445 and 455/07 P, *Ente*, Opinion of AG Kokott, para. 51.

[46] *Ibid.*, para. 54, with reference to the Opinion of Advocate General Ruiz-Jarabo Colomer in C-417/04 P, *Regione Siciliana*, footnote 11, para. 76.

[47] C-445 and 455/07 P, *Ente*, footnote 12, paras. 52 et seq.; Opinion of AG Kokott, paras. 55, 64, referring to this effect, the Order of the Court in T-105/01, *SLIM*, footnote 16, para. 52, according to which an expressed intention of the Member State is not sufficient.

[48] C-445 and 455/07 P, *Ente*, footnote 12, para. 67; Opinion of AG Kokott para. 65.

[49] *Ibid.* para. 66.

[50] C-445 and 455/07 P, *Ente*, footnote 12, para. 66; Opinion of Kokott, paras. 67, 68, with reference to C-15/06 P, *Regione Siciliana*, footnote 11, para. 39, which refers to C-263/02 P, *Commission* v *Jégo-Quéré* [2004] ECR I-3425, paras. 30–32.

financial assistance granted by the Cohesion Fund for the Project concerning the Redevelopment of Grande Porto Sul – Subsistema de Gondomar.[51] The applicant brought an appeal before the ECJ on the basis that the CFI erred in law when denying the applicant's direct concern. According to the appellant, the Portuguese legislation giving effect to the Cohesion Fund left no discretion to the Portuguese Republic with regard to "whether or not to maintain the assistance allocated by the Cohesion Fund to the Município de Gondomar as the body responsible for the execution of the project, leading thus to the conclusion that the Commission's decision to cancel the aid granted by the Cohesion Fund is of an automatic nature, for the legislation concerned does not permit the bodies responsible for performance to be relieved of the duty to reimburse the sums overpaid"; by refraining from "making any reference to that question" the CFI erred in law; however, the ECJ rejected the appeal as unfounded in its Order of 24 September 2009.[52]

In an Order of 8 October 2008, the CFI rejected as inadmissible, because of the lack of direct concern, an action brought by the Community of Grammatikou (Athens, Greece) against the Commission Decision relating to the grant of assistance from the Cohesion Fund for the project "Construction of a Landfill Site at the Integrated Waste Management Facility of North-East Attica at the location 'Mavro Vouno Grammatikou', in the Hellenic Republic".[53] The applicant had claimed to be directly and individually concerned by the Decision "because it is a public body responsible for the protection of public health and the environment in the area where the project that is being financed is located".[54] No appeal was brought against this decision.

2. Legislative Measure Being of Direct Concern

In addition to those actions challenging decisions, the EU Courts have also dealt with cases concerning legislative measures of the Community. In 1993, the ECJ[55] denied the admissibility of an action brought by Gibraltar challenging a Council Directive provision that suspended the application of the provisions of the Directive (on the development of air services, etc.) to Gibraltar airport until cooperation

[51] T-324/06, *Município de Gondomar*, footnote 17, paras. 37–52.

[52] C-501/08 P, *Município de Gondomar* v *Commission*, see for Application O.J. 2009, C 19/18; Order of the ECJ, nyr.

[53] T-13/08, *Koinotita Grammatikou* v *Commission*, Order of the CFI of 8 October 2008, see O.J. 2009, C 32/35.

[54] See for Application O.J. 2008, C 79/29.

[55] The ECJ had jurisdiction over this case as actions under Article 230 (4) EC [now Article 263 (4) TFEU] had not been allocated to the CFI by Council Decision 94/149/ECSC, EC yet; see *supra* note 8.

arrangements for that airport agreed between Governments of the Kingdom of Spain and the United Kingdom had come into operation.[56] The Court held that there was thus an "obstacle of an objective nature to implementation of the directive"; "[i]n view of the differences between the Kingdom of Spain and the United Kingdom [...] concerning sovereignty over the territory on which Gibraltar airport is situated and the operational problems resulting from those differences, the development of air services between that airport and the other airports within the Community is conditional on the implementation of the cooperation arrangements agreed between those two States".[57] The Court concluded that the action was inadmissible.[58]

In 1998, the CFI denied the Comunidad de Cantabria (Spain) being directly concerned by the Council Regulation, in which the Council had laid down conditions under which the Commission was to approve state aid to shipyards. The applicant claimed to be directly concerned as the Regulation would lead to a restructuring of an important shipyard and to dismissal of the labour force.[59] Although Cantabria had been listed in the preamble of the regulation, the CFI held that the Region was not directly concerned as "the simple fact of adopting that measure cannot alone entail the consequences [...] which it alleges. The creation of such consequences necessarily supposes, first, the adoption of a decision by the Commission [...] and, secondly, the adoption by that shipyard of autonomous measures connected with that decision, namely making employees redundant".[60] In 2000 in *Nederlandse Antillen*, the CFI considered a regulation, being of direct concern to the applicant as it "contain[ed] comprehensive rules leaving no latitude to the authorities of the Member States".[61] On appeal, the ECJ did not need to address this issue as it had already denied the applicant's individual concern, which required the action to be declared inadmissible.[62]

3. Summary

In a nutshell – unless they had already denied the measure's individual concern to the applicant (see discussion in the next section)[63] – the Courts have taken the

[56]C-298/89, *Gibraltar*, footnote 14, para. 5.

[57]C-298/89, *Gibraltar*, footnote 14, para. 22.

[58]C-298/89, *Gibraltar*, footnote 14, para. 24.

[59]Van Nuffel (2001), p. 886.

[60]T-238/97, *Comunidad Autónoma*, footnote 7, paras. 51–53.

[61]T-32 and T-41/98, *Nederlandse Antillen*, footnote 7, paras. 60 et seq.

[62]C-452/98, *Nederlandse Antillen*, footnote 12, paras. 59 et seq.

[63]See e.g. C-452/98, *Nederlandse Antillen*, footnote 12, paras. 59 et seq.; T-37/04, *Região autónoma dos Açores*, footnote 12, para. 94; an appeal has been brought on 8 October 2008, C-444/08 P, and is still pending.

condition of the contested measure being of direct concern to the applicant seriously. Both decisions and measures of general application have been considered by the Courts to be of direct concern as long as they (a) directly affect the applicant's legal situation and (b) there is no discretion left with regard to their implementation.

The Courts have in principle considered decisions in the area of State aid to be of direct concern to Regions challenging those decisions in annulment actions [e.g. *Vlaamse Gewest* (1998) and *Freistaat Sachsen* (1999)], as long as the decisions had an impact on the exercise of power by the Regions. The Courts have been more reluctant to acknowledge Regions' direct concern where decisions relating to the ending or restriction of financial assistance or contributions previously granted under the Structural and Cohesion Funds. Although the CFI has recently, even in those areas, been more generous in recognising contested decisions being of direct concern to the applying Regions and has thus considered several actions admissible, the ECJ has taken a more narrow approach on this question. For example, in the *Regione Siciliana* cases (2005/2006), the ECJ denied direct concern: although the Region was responsible for the Decision's implementation, it was not necessarily the person "entitled" to financial assistance purely on the basis of the Decision; the Court emphasised that the internal division of power within the Member State would not have an impact on whether or not an EU measure was considered to be of direct concern.

In the context of an applicant being required to repay financial assistance received prior to the contested measure, the CFI in the State aid case brought by the Region *Friuli Venezia Giulia* (1999), and the ECJ in the ERDF case *Ente* (2009) brought by a public consortium, relied on whether or not the applicant's obligation either existed on the basis of the EU measure itself or could be presupposed because of a clear obligation for the Member State to ask the applicant for repayment.

In *Gibraltar* (1993), the ECJ denied that the contested legislative measure was of direct concern to the applicant as there was an obstacle to its implementation. The CFI followed this approach in *Cantabria* (1998), concluding that further implementation of the contested measure was necessary to create any consequences of it for the Region. In *Nederlandse Antillen* (2001), the CFI acknowledged the contested regulation being of direct concern to the applicant on the basis that no latitude was left to the Member States' authorities; after having already denied the applicant's individual concern, the ECJ did not need to assess whether or not the measure was of direct concern on appeal.

III. Individual Concern of Regions

In order to make an annulment action brought by a Region admissible, the contested measure also needs to be of individual concern to that Region. According to established case law, not only a decision but also a measure of a legislative nature can be of individual concern to some, and thus takes the nature of a decision in this respect, if it affects the applicants "by reason of certain attributes peculiar to them, or by reason of a factual situation which differentiates them from all other persons and thus distinguishes them individually in the same way as the addressee of a decision".[64]

As discussed above in the context of direct concern, it has often been relatively easy for Regions to show individual concern in the context of State aid decisions, even where the contested decision was addressed to the Member State.[65] In the context of the cancellation or restriction of financial assistance under the structural funds, such as the *Regione Siciliana* cases brought in 2003, the individual concern of the applicant has also in principle not been questioned.[66] It was rather the identified Region's lack of direct concern, which made the ECJ reject the action.[67] Where public authority requested the aid, it will be individually concerned by the decision even if addressed to the Member State.[68] In cases brought in the context of the cancellation of financial contributions, or granting to others, under the Cohesion Fund, the CFI did not need to address the issue of individual concern after having already denied the action's admissibility due to the lack of direct concern.[69]

In general, the "Community judicature has accepted the right of regional authorities to challenge Community acts which either prevent [sub-national entities] from adopting measures which they may legitimately adopt if there is no Community intervention or require them to withdraw those measures and to take certain action", for example where the contested decisions specifically concerned aid paid by the applicant local bodies, so that the lawfulness of that aid depended on the outcome of the proceedings.[70] The Court has also acknowledged individual concern of applicants challenging a legislative measure where the Commission had been under a duty specifically to take account of the negative effects that the regulations

---

[64]See, in particular, Case 25/62, *Plaumann* v *Commission* [1963] ECR 95, 107; see also C-358/89, *Extramet Industrie* v *Council* [1991] ECR I-2501, para. 13; C-309/89, *Codorniu* v *Council* [1994] ECR I-1853, paras. 19, 20; Case C-321/95 P, *Greenpeace Council and Others* v *Commission* [1998] ECR I-1651, para. 7C-41/99 P, *Sadam Zuccherifici and Others* v *Council* [2001] ECR I-4239, para. 27; C-50/00 P, C-50/00 P, *Unión de Pequeños Agricultores* v *Council (UPA)* [2002] ECR I-6677, para. 36; recently confirmed in the context of an action brought by regions in C-452/98, *Nederlandse Antillen*, footnote 12, para. 60, and T-417/04, *Regione autonoma Friuli-Venezia Giulia*, footnote 12, para. 52.

[65]See, e.g. T-214/95, *Vlaamse Gewest*, footnote 7, para. 29. See footnote 23 for reference to several State aid cases in which the admissibility was taken for granted.

[66]See discussion above in section "Structural Funds".

[67]C-15/06, *Regione Siciliana*, footnote 11, para. 32.

[68]Van Nuffel (2001), p. 887, with reference to C-213/87, *Gemeente Amsterdam and VIA* [1990] ECR I-221, and T-81/97, *Regione Toscana*, footnote 10.

[69]T-324/06, *Município de Gondomar*, footnote 17, para. 52; T-13/08, *Koinotita Grammatikou*, footnote 53.

[70]See T-37/04, *Região autónoma dos Açores*, footnote 12, para. 82, referring, to that effect, to T-214/95, *Vlaamse Gewest*, footnote 7, para. 29; Joined Cases T-346/99 to T-348/99, *Diputación Foral de Álava and Others* v *Commission* [2002] ECR II-4259, para. 37; Joined Cases T-366/03 and T-235/04, *Land Oberösterreich and Austria* v *Commission* [2005] ECR II-4005, para. 28.

in question might have on the economy of the countries or territories concerned.[71] The Court thereby recognised the prerogative of public authorities to defend their institutional rights granted by EU rather than national law.[72]

It is not clear, however, to what extent the EU judicature is prepared to take account of national law. The Courts have refrained from identifying individual concern on the basis of the division of legislative and regulatory powers within a Member State, which they considered "solely a matter for the constitutional law of that State and has no effect from the point of view of assessing the possible effects of a Community legal measure on the interests of a territorial body"; accordingly, it is in the EU legal order "for the authorities of the State to represent any interests based on the defence of national legislation, regardless of the constitutional form or the territorial organisation of that State".[73] The Courts have thus remained reluctant to recognise individual concern on the mere basis of powers conferred by the national constitutions.[74]

The Courts have concluded that EU measures which affect specific interests or groups important for the Region, or hinder the EU's political objectives, are not sufficient for establishing individual concern.[75] This has been of particular relevance where legislative measures were challenged. In *Cantabria*, the CFI held that "any general interest the applicant may have, as a third person, in obtaining a result which will favour the economic prosperity of a given business and, as a result, the level of employment in the geographical region where it carries on its activities, is insufficient, on its own, to enable the applicant to be regarded as 'concerned' within the meaning of the fourth paragraph of Article [230] of the Treaty [now Article 263 TFEU], by the provisions of the contested Regulation, nor, *a fortiori*, as being individually concerned".[76] A measure "capable generally of affecting socio-economic conditions within its territorial jurisdiction is not sufficient to render an action brought by that authority admissible".[77] This has been confirmed in several cases since.[78]

---

[71]Van Nuffel (2001), p. 888, with reference to T-32 and T-41/98, *Nederlandse Antillen*, footnote 7, paras. 50–57; T-310/97 R, *Nederlandse Antillen* v *Council* [1998] ECR II-445, paras. 33–37.

[72]Van Nuffel (2001), p. 889.

[73]T-417/04, *Regione autonoma Friuli-Venezia Giulia*, footnote 12, para. 62. This has has been challenged on appeal, C-444/08; see for Application O.J. 2008 C 327/15; the appeal is still pending. See also T-37/04, *Região autónoma dos Açores*, footnote 12, para. 82.

[74]See also Dani (2004), p. 192.

[75]Van Nuffel (2001), p. 887.

[76]T-238/97, *Comunidad Autónoma de Cantabria*, footnote 7, para. 49 (the contested regulation concerned State aid to certain shipyards); see also T-609/97, *Regione Puglia*, footnote 7, para. 21 (the contested regulation concerned production aid payable to producers of olive oil).

[77]T-238/97, *Comunidad Autónoma de Cantabria*, footnote 7, para. 50; T-609/97, *Regione Puglia*, footnote 7, para. 22.

[78]C-142/00 P, *Commission* v *Nederlandse Antillen*, footnote 12, para. 69; Order of the President of the CFI of 7 July 2004 in T-37/04 R, *Região autónoma dos Açores*, footnote 12, para. 118; T-417/04, *Regione autonoma Friuli-Venezia Giulia*, footnote 12, para. 61.

In *Região autónoma dos Açores*, the applicant had claimed to be individually concerned by a regulation in the area of fisheries policy as Article 299 (2) EC [now Article 349 TFEU] – i.e. "the obligation for the Council to adopt specific measures for the outermost regions, taking into account the special characteristics and constraints of those regions" – provided "specific protection under Commmunity such as to distinguish [the Region] from all other persons", in particular where it was not certain that the Member State would ensure that the prerogatives of the outermost regions were respected.[79] Also, the contested regulation would have more serious consequences for the environment in the waters of the Azores than in other areas affected, including Madeira and the Canary Islands, and the applicant's dependence on the fishing sector is greater than theirs.[80] The action was dismissed. The CFI held that the fact that a regional authority is entitled to specific protection under Community law is not sufficient to give it standing under Article 230 (4) EC [now Article 263 TFEU]; the Court concluded from the ECJ judgment in *Nederlandse Antillen* that, since it examined whether the regulations at issue were of direct and individual concern to the applicants, the protection granted to them under the Treaty or other provisions of Community law was not considered sufficient to show that the applicants were directly and individually concerned.[81] After assessing the effect of the contested provisions on marine environment, waters, fishing sector, control of fishing activities, research and conservation, etc., the CFI concluded that "the applicant has not put forward arguments which enable it to be held that the contested provisions will entail harmful effects for the fish stocks and for the marine environment in the Azores and, consequently, for the survival of the fishing sector in the region".[82] The appeal brought on 8 October 2008 is still pending before the ECJ.[83]

Many applicants have claimed that their actions, challenging legislative and executive EU measures, should be declared admissible on the ground that the only effective remedy is an action for annulment before the EU judicature. However, the EU Courts have consistently held that the requirement for effective judicial protection "cannot have the effect of setting aside the condition laid down in the fourth paragraph of Article 230 EC [now Article 263 TFEU] that an applicant must be individually concerned".[84] According to the Courts, the Treaties have established a

[79]T-37/04, *Região autónoma dos Açores*, footnote 12, para. 46, with reference to case-law.

[80]T-37/04, *Região autónoma dos Açores*, footnote 12, paras. 48, 49.

[81]T-37/04, *Região autónoma dos Açores*, footnote 12, paras. 54 et seq.

[82]T-37/04, *Região autónoma dos Açores*, footnote 12, para. 78.

[83]See for Application O.J. 2008 C 327/15.

[84]C-50/00 P, *UPA*, footnote 64, para. 44; C-263/02 P, *Commission* v *Jégo-Quéré* [2004] ECR I-3425, para. 36; Order in Case T-417/04, *Regione Autonoma Friuli-Venezia Giulia*, footnote 12, para. 67; T-37/04, *Região autónoma dos Açores*, footnote 12, para. 92; C-15/06 P, *Regione Siciliana*, footnote 11, para. 39; recently confirmed in C-445 and 455/07 P, *Ente*, footnote 12, paras. 65 et seq. See also Order of 24 September 2009 in C-501/08, *Município de Gondomar* v *Commission*, paras. 25 et seq., appeal against CFI Order in T-324/06, *Município de Gondomar*, footnote 17, in which the appellant claimed that the communication of the Commission's decision concerning the demand for reimbursement of financial assistance granted under the Cohesion

"complete system of remedies and procedures intended to ensure control of the lawfulness of the acts of the institutions by entrusting it to the Community judicature. In that system, direct control of the lawfulness of Community acts of general application is entrusted to the Member States and to the Community institutions".[85] Regional authorities are able "either indirectly to plead the unlawfulness of such acts before the Community judicature under Article 241 EC[86] [now Article 277 TFEU] or to do so before the national courts and ask them, since they have no jurisdiction themselves to declare those measures unlawful, to make a reference to the Court of Justice for a preliminary ruling as to lawfulness".[87] If a change was desired, it is for the Member States to reform that system in accordance with [now] Title VI TEU.[88]

B. Regions' Indirect Access to the EU Courts

The EU Courts have held that it falls within the responsibility of the Member States to provide full judicial protection to non-privileged applicants where actions are inadmissible under Article 263 (4) TFEU [former Article 230 (4) EC].[89] Member States have the possibility to bring cases concerning sub-national entities' interests before the EU Courts by either bringing direct legal actions on their behalf (Article 263 (2) TFEU, former Article 230 (1) EC), or by referring questions concerning the interpretation and validity of EU law, which allegedly conflicts with regions' powers granted by national and/or EU law, before the ECJ (Article 267 TFEU, former 234 EC). Although both possibilities are subject to the procedural autonomy of the Member States and can thus not be analysed in detail here, the following sections are meant to give a flavour of what sort of indirect access to the EU Courts Regions might obtain through the representation of the Member States under which legal order they exist.

Fund, "unactionable at domestic level", so an inadmissibility under Article 230 EC (current Article 263 TFEU) would be contrary to the principle of the right to effective judicial protection, see for Application O.J. 2009, C 19/18.

[85] T-37/04, *Região autónoma dos Açores*, footnote 12, para. 92.

[86] According to this article, the validity of legislative measures can be challenged in the context of other proceedings brought before the court.

[87] T-37/04, *Região autónoma dos Açores*, footnote 12, para. 92.

[88] T-37/04, *Região autónoma dos Açores*, footnote 12, para. 92.

[89] C-15/06 P, *Regione Siciliana*, footnote 11, para. 39; C-445 and 455/07 P, *Ente*, footnote 12, para. 66.

I. Annulment Actions Brought on Behalf of REGIONS

Some Member States have established procedures to assure the regional governments that Member States can take action to defend their interests before EU Courts where exclusive regional powers are at stake.[90] In Austria[91] and Belgium,[92] even an individual Region can require the federal government to bring such action. In Germany, the *Bundesrat* has the power to do so.[93] While it would go beyond the scope of this chapter to assess the legal position of the Regions within all Member States with regard to their representation before EU Courts, the examples introduced in the following paragraphs illustrate that there have been cases, in which Member States clearly represented interests of Regions before EU Courts in the areas of State aid, financial assistance under the Cohesion Fund and financial contributions under the ERDF.

In 2003, Portugal brought an action before the ECJ, in which it sought the annulment of the Commission's Decision regarding the fiscal regime adopted by the Azores regional government.[94] This Decision had been one among others by which the Commission had considered fiscal regimes adopted by regional

---

[90]Van Nuffel (2001), p. 881.

[91]Article 10 of the *Vereinbarung zwischen dem Bund und den Ländern gemäß Art. 15a B-VG über die Mitwirkungsrechte der Länder und Gemeinden in Angelegenheiten der europäischen Integration* of 12 March 1992. According to that provision, there is in principle an obligation for the federal Government of Austria (*Bund*) to bring an action before the Community Courts against Community measures concerning the legislative powers of a *Land* requesting such action. However, this obligation does not exist if another *Land* objects this request or in the case of "compelling reasons of foreign or integration policy" (see for full text of the provision: http://www.issirfa.cnr.it/3792,949.html?PHPSESSID=f770435324f14430cd7bc6e720b03913, last visited on 15 June 2010). Van Nuffel (2001), p. 881, refers in this context also to Schweizer and Brunner (1998), pp. 52–53.

[92]Van Nuffel (2001), p. 881, refers to Art. 81, § 7, *BijzondereWet Hervorming Instellingen*, and states that "in all matters that concern regional powers, consultation with the regions is required before the federal government can bring action. According to the *Samenwerkingsakkoord* (Cooperation Agreement) of 11 July 1994 on litigation before international and supranational courts in mixed disputes, action will only be brought when there is a consensus among the federal and the regional governments. However, if a region requests that action be brought in matters of exclusive regional powers, the federal government is obliged to initiate a lawsuit if no consensus can be found (Art. 81, § 7, second paragraph, *Bijzondere Wet Hervorming Instellingen*)". See also Van Nuffel (2000), pp. 551–552.

[93]See Article 7 EUZBLG (*Gesetz über die Zusammenarbeit von Bund und Ländern in Angelegenheiten der Europäischen Union*) of 12 March 1993 (*Bundesgesetzblatt Teil I*, p. 313, 1780), lastly changed through the *Föderalismusreform-Begleitgesetz* of 5 September 2006 (*Bundesgesetzblatt Teil I*, p. 2098) (see for full text also http://www.bundesrat.de/cln_099/nn_9740/DE/struktur/recht/euzblg/euzblg-node.html?__nnn=true, last visited on 15 June 2010).

[94]C-88/03, *Portugal* v *Commission (Azores)* [2006] ECR I-7115. See for a comment on this case Lindsay-Poulsen (2008); see also Kurcz (2007).

governments to constitute unlawful State aid under the then EC Treaty [current TFEU].[95] The ECJ acknowledged the possibility of sub-state entities exercising autonomous powers within its territory, as long as those are granted under national law and can be exercised without the potential intervention of the Member State.[96] However, the action was dismissed as unfounded. In 2004, not only the British Overseas Territory Gibraltar but also the UK brought actions before the CFI to challenge the Commission Decision on the aid scheme, which the UK was planning to implement as regards the Government of Gibraltar's Corporation Tax Reform.[97] The CFI joined the two cases and delivered its judgment on 18 December 2008, in which it annulled the Commission's Decision.[98] As in previous State aid cases, the admissibility of Gibraltar's action was not even contested and thus not addressed by the Court.[99] The Commission brought an appeal against the CFI's decision, which is still pending.[100]

In 2005, Greece brought an annulment action before the CFI to challenge the Commission Decision reducing the financial assistance granted under the Cohesion Fund for the project concerning the new Athens International Airport at Spata by a prior Commission decision; in November 2008, the CFI rejected the action as unfounded.[101] An appeal has been brought on 29 January 2009, claiming that the CFI had misinterpreted and misapplied Community law in several respects, that its judgment contained contradictory reasoning, and infringed the principle of proportionality.[102]

In 2007, Germany brought an annulment action to challenge the Commission Decision on the reduction of the period of the financial contribution of the ERDF granted to the Operational Programme under the Community initiative INTERREG II in the *Land* Saarland and the Lorraine and Western Palatinate areas in Germany. On 28 January 2009, the CFI dismissed the action as unfounded.[103] No appeal was brought against this decision.

---

[95]See, e.g. Decision 93/337 Basque Countries, O.J. 1993L 134/25; Decision 2003/442 Azores, O.J. 2003L 150/52; Decision 2005/261 Gibraltar, O.J. 2005L 85/1.

[96]C-88/03, *Portugal* v *Commission (Azores)* [2006] ECR I-7115, paras. 56–58, 62, 65–67.

[97]T-211/04, *Gibraltar* v *Commission*, O.J. 2004 C 179/8; T-215/04, *UK* v *Commission*, O.J. 2004 C 217/29.

[98]Joined Cases T-211 and 215/04, *Gibraltar* v *Commission*, and *UK* v *Commission*, Judgment of 18 December 2008.

[99]See footnote 23 for reference to cases.

[100]C-106 and 107/09 P, *Commission* v *Gibraltar and the UK*, nyr in the O.J.

[101]T-404/05, *Greece* v *Commission*, nyr in the ECR, see O.J. 2009 C 6/21.

[102]C-43/09 P, *Greece* v *Commission*, O.J. 2009 C 69/29.

[103]T-74/07, *Germany* v *Commission*, nyr in the ECR, see O.J. 2009 C 69/36.

II. The Position of Regions in Preliminary Ruling Proceedings

In addition to the Regions' capacity to bring direct legal actions against the Community themselves or through their Member State in the form of annulment actions, the EU Court in the context of preliminary rulings can also consider their interests. A preliminary ruling proceeding can or must be initiated by a national court if there are doubts with regard to the interpretation or validity of EU law, and a decision (by the ECJ) on the question is necessary to enable the national court to give judgment. Article 267 TFEU [former 234 EC] gives all national courts the option, and even compels those national courts against whose decisions there is no judicial remedy under national law available, to stay their proceedings and refer their questions to the ECJ.[104] Once a preliminary ruling is initiated by the national court, a regional authority can present its arguments about the EU measure in question to the ECJ.[105]

In May 2006, the Belgian Court of Arbitration [now Constitutional Court] referred questions to the ECJ, which concerned the interpretation of Treaty and EU regulation provisions and their compatibility with a care insurance scheme such as the one established by an autonomous community (Flemish Community) of a federal State (Belgium).[106] As the parties in the national proceedings were several federated entities – the Government of the French Community, and the Walloon Government on the one hand, the Flemish Community on the other – one could say that those entities' interests and rights under EU law were addressed before the ECJ in the course of this preliminary ruling procedure.[107]

In October 2006, the High Court of Justice of the Basque Country referred seven cases to the ECJ.[108] Those cases again did not concern the validity of EU measures in the light of regional interests as in the cases discussed in the context of direct actions brought by the Regions (see Sect. A). Instead, they had been brought before the Court by the Regions of La Rioja and Castilla y León and the trade union Unión

[104]See for a general discussion of preliminary ruling proceedings Craig and De Búrca (2008), pp. 460–501.

[105]Van Nuffel (2001), p. 873, referring to Article 20 (2) of the Statute of the ECJ and Article 103 ECJ Rules of Procedure.

[106]C-212/06, *Government of the French Community, and Walloon Government* v *Flemish Government*, O.J. 2006 C 178/18.

[107]C-212/06, *Government of the French Community, and Walloon Government* v *Flemish Government* [2008] ECR I-1683.

[108]Joined Cases C-428-434/06, *Unión General de Trabajadores de La Rioja (UGT-Rioja)* v *Juntas Generales del Territorio Histórico de Vizcaya and Others*, O.J. 2006 C 326/30.

General de Trabajadores de La Rioja (UGT-Rioja), who claimed that tax rules of the three Historical Territories infringed higher-ranking national law and constitute unlawful State aid for the purposes of Articles 87 and 88 EC [now Articles 107 and 108 TFEU]. The three Historical Territories of Biscay (Vizcaya), Álava (Araba) and Guipúzcoa (Gipuzkoa) are independent regional authorities and together form the Autonomous Community of the Basque Country. They have their own legislative powers in the field of tax law, under which they had lowered the corporation tax rate for companies established in their territory.[109] The ECJ had to interpret Article 87 (1) EC [now Article 107 (1) TFEU] "in order to verify whether legislation such as [those tax rules] adopted by the three Historical Territories within the limits of their areas of competence may be termed rules of general application within the meaning of the concept of State aid arising from that provision or whether those laws are selctive in nature".[110] As the boundaries of the Territories' areas of competence are laid down in the national constitution and other provisions, the ECJ considered it necessary to take those provisions into account as interpreted and enforced by national courts; "[i]t is not the review by the national court which is relevant for the purpose of verifying the existence of autonomy, but the criterion which that court uses when carrying out that review".[111] After some detailed elaboration on parameters determining an infra-State authority's institutional, procedural and economic autonomy, the ECJ left the assessment of such autonomy of the Historical Territories and the Autonomous Community of the Basque Country to the national court and held that

> the answer to the question referred must be that Article 87(1) EC [now Article 107 (1) TFEU] is to be interpreted as meaning that, for the purpose of assessing whether a measure is selective, account is to be taken of the institutional, procedural and economic autonomy enjoyed by the authority adopting that measure. It is for the national court, which alone has jurisdiction to identify the national law applicable and to interpret it, as well as to apply Community law to the cases before it, to determine whether the Historical Territories and the Autonomous Community of the Basque Country have such autonomy, which, if so, would have the result that the laws adopted within the limits of the areas of competence granted to those infra-State bodies by the Constitution and the other provisions of Spanish law are not of a selective nature within the meaning of the concept of State aid as referred to in Article 87(1) EC.[112]

Although it was left for the national courts in both cases to render a decision on the substance of the case, the ECJ elaborated on the impact of EU obligations on infra-national entities. The Court was, however, not in a position either to deal with Regions' position in the constitutional order of the EU or to define involved Regions' legislative and executive powers under EU law conclusively.

---

[109]See summary in Opinion of AG Kokott of 8 May 2008 in Joined Cases C-428-434/06, *Unión General de Trabajadores de La Rioja (UGT-Rioja)* v *Juntas Generales del Territorio Histórico de Vizcaya and Others* [2008] ECR I-6747, paras. 1–6.

[110]Joined Cases C-428-434/06, *Unión General de Trabajadores de La Rioja (UGT-Rioja)* v *Juntas Generales del Territorio Histórico de Vizcaya and Others* [2008] ECR I-6747, para. 78.

[111]Joined Cases C-428-434/06, *UGT-Rioja*, footnote 110, paras. 79 et seq.

[112]Joined Cases C-428-434/06, *UGT-Rioja*, footnote 110, para. 144.

C. Changes Through the Lisbon Treaty?

Since the Treaty of Lisbon entered into force, Article 230 EC has been substituted by Article 263 of the Treaty on the Functioning of the European Union (TFEU).[113] The role of the Committee of the Regions (CoR) in the context of annulment actions has been strengthened. The CoR – being one of the Union's Advisory Bodies[114] and consisting of "representatives of regional and local bodies who either hold a regional or local authority electoral mandate or are politically accountable to an elected assembly" (Article 300 (2) TFEU) – is entitled to bring annulment actions for the protection of its own prerogatives. The CoR would be affected in its prerogatives if the institutions did not comply with their obligation to consult the CoR under the Treaties; on its merits, this constitutes a "procedural requirement" within the meaning of Article 263 (2) TFEU.[115] The obligation would not be

[113]The wording of Article 263 of the TFEU is as follows:

"The Court of Justice of the European Union shall review the legality of legislative acts, of acts of the Council, of the Commission and of the European Central Bank, other than recommendations and opinions, and of acts of the European Parliament and of the European Council intended to produce legal effects *vis-à-vis* third parties. It shall also review the legality of acts of bodies, offices or agencies of the Union intended to produce legal effects *vis-à-vis* third parties.

It shall for this purpose have jurisdiction in actions brought by a Member State, the European Parliament, the Council or the Commission on grounds of lack of competence, infringement of an essential procedural requirement, infringement of the Treaties or of any rule of law relating to their application, or misuse of powers.

The Court shall have jurisdiction under the same conditions in actions brought by the Court of Auditors, by the European Central Bank and by the Committee of the Regions for the purpose of protecting their prerogatives.

Any natural or legal person may, under the conditions laid down in the first and second paragraphs, institute proceedings against an act addressed to that person or which is of direct and individual concern to them, and against a regulatory act which is of direct concern to them and does not entail implementing measures.

Acts setting up bodies, offices and agencies of the Union may lay down specific conditions and arrangements concerning actions brought by natural or legal persons against acts of these bodies, offices or agencies intended to produce legal effects in relation to them.

The proceedings provided for in this Article shall be instituted within two months of the publication of the measure, or of its notification to the plaintiff, or, in the absence thereof, of the day on which it came to the knowledge of the latter, as the case may be".

[114]Article 13 (4) TFEU.

[115]For a discussion with respect to the same situation under the Draft of the Constitution see J. Ziller, "The Committee of the Regions and the implementation and monitoring of the principles of subsidiarity and proportionality in the light of the Constitution of Europe", Chap. 9, para. 538; see also para. 557 for a list of mandatory consultation under the Draft Constitution. Those are now comprised in the Lisbon Treaty in the fields such as transport policy (Article 91 (1) TFEU), sea and air transport (Article 100 (2) TFEU), employment policy (Articles 148 (2), 149 (1) TFEU), social policy (Article 153 (2) TFEU), the European Social Fund (Article 164 TFEU), education, vocational training, youth and sport (Articles 165 (4), 166 (4) TFEU), culture (Article 167 (5) TFEU), public health (Article 168 (4), (5) TFEU), trans-European networks (Article 172 (1) TFEU), economic, social and territorial cohesion (Article 175 (2), (3) TFEU), Structural Funds, i.e. European Agricultural Guidance and Guarantee Fund, Guidance Section, European Social

infringed if opinions issued by the CoR were not accepted except where no opinion was requested at all, or insufficient time was given to the author of the opinion or for taking the content of the opinion into account.[116]

Individual Regions of the Member States are, however, not among the applicants listed in Article 263 (2) or (3) TFEU and will therefore continue to be considered as non-privileged applicants within the meaning of Article 263 (4) TFEU.[117] The wording of this paragraph has been slightly modified. According to the new provision, natural and legal persons can institute proceedings against (a) "an act addressed to that person", (b) an act of "direct and individual concern" to them, and (c) "a regulatory act which is of direct concern to them and does not entail implementing measures". The first two scenarios, here (a) and (b), were well known under the former Article 230 (4) EC. However, the last scenario, here (c), seems to introduce some change. The new provision seems to suggest that it suffices to demonstrate that a contested "regulatory act" is of direct concern in order to establish admissibility of an annulment action, without the necessity to show the act's individual concern to the applicant. It is emphasised, however, that this provision was drafted in the context of the Constitutional Treaty, which would have made the distinction between European laws, European framework laws, European regulations, European decisions, recommendations and opinions.[118] In this context, EU laws would have replaced "regulations", EU framework laws would have replaced "directives" (see Article 249 of the EC Treaty), EU regulations and decisions would have been non-legislative acts and binding at least to some extent, and recommendations and opinions would have had no binding force.[119] According to Craig and De Búrca, Article I-33 (1) CT defined the hierarchy of norms and classified "regulatory acts" as secondary norms, which had to be differentiated from EU laws, framework laws, decisions, and implementing acts; "the only way to avoid this conclusion would have been to read the phrase 'regulatory act' to mean something broader than the term European Reg. within Article I-33(1). This might have been possible, but it would have been difficult both textually and historically".[120]

The Treaty of Lisbon did not keep the classification of legislative and non-legislative measures as suggested by the Constitutional Treaty. Instead, the

---

Fund and European Regional Development Fund (Article 177 (1) TFEU), Cohesion Fund providing a financial contribution to projects in the fields of environment and trans-European networks in the area of transport infrastructure (Article 177 (2) TFEU), ERDF implementing regulations (Article 178 (1) TFEU), environmental policy (Article 192 (1), (2), (3) TFEU), energy policy (Article 194 (2) TFEU).

[116]For a discussion with respect to the same situation under the Draft of the Constitution see Ziller, "The Committee of the Regions and the implementation and monitoring of the principles of subsidiarity and proportionality in the light of the Constitution of Europe", Chap. 9, para. 539.

[117]See *supra* note 113.

[118]See Article I-33(1) of the Draft Treaty establishing a Constitution for Europe.

[119]*Ibid.*

[120]Craig and De Búrca (2008), p. 527 at note 70.

distinction between regulations, directives, decisions, etc., was retained under Article 288 TFEU [former Article 249 EC].[121] It remains to be seen how the Courts are going to interpret "regulatory act" in the context of annulment actions brought under the TFEU.[122] The Courts might come to the conclusion that it can only be interpreted as referring to regulations, which do not require further implementation. This would have the consequence that measures of general application of such sort could be challenged without the necessity to show individual concern. The applicant in *Regione autonoma Friuli-Venezia Giulia* v *Commission* had already claimed that account should be taken of the draft Treaty establishing a Constitution for Europe, which would also have waived the condition of applicants being individually concerned by the contested Community regulation.[123] The CFI did not take cognisance of this argument as the draft Treaty was not yet in force.[124]

The Treaty of Lisbon made the Charter of Fundamental Rights[125] legally binding on, *inter alia*, the EU institutions.[126] Craig and De Búrca questioned already in the context of the potential entry into force of the Constitutional Treaty whether this would have any impact on the scope of the access to judicial protection for natural and legal persons in the context of annulment actions.[127] They came to the conclusion that, given no explicit mentioning of standing rules and the Courts' approach on standing hitherto, it is unlikely that EU Courts would regard the right to good administration under Article 41 and the right to an effective remedy before a tribunal under Article 47 of the Charter necessitating a broader approach. Also, the memorandum stated in relation to Article 47 that there was no intent for this provision to make any change on standing rules other than those embodied in the revised provision on annulment actions itself. They added that "[t]here is however an uneasy tension between the Charter rights and the standing rules for direct actions. The Charter accords individual rights, yet the application of the standing rules means that a person who claims that his rights have been infringed by Community law would normally not be able to meet the requirements of individual concern.[128] There is something decidedly odd about the infringement of an individual right not counting as a matter of individual concern".[129]

While this aspect is covered in detail in a different chapter of this edited collection (see Chap. III for detailed discussion), it can be mentioned here that

[121]See Articles 288 et seq of the Treaty of Lisbon.

[122]Only Article 207 (6) TFEU (ex Article 133 EC) makes the distinction between legislative and regulatory provisions. However, this is in reference to provisions of the Member States, which are not in question in an annulment action before Community Courts.

[123]T-417/04, *Regione autonoma Friuli-Venezia Giulia*, footnote 12, para. 41.

[124]T-417/04, *Regione autonoma Friuli-Venezia Giulia*, footnote 12, para. 68.

[125]O.J. 2000, C 364/01.

[126]Article 6 (1) TEU.

[127]Craig and De Búrca (2008), p. 527 et seq.

[128]C-258/02 P, *Bactria* [2003] ECR I-15105, paras. 48–51.

[129]Craig and De Búrca (2008), p. 528.

the Treaty of Lisbon is accompanied by a new Protocol on the Application of the Principles of Subsidiarity and Proportionality, which is based on the Member States' wishing to "ensure that decisions are taken as closely as possible to the citizens of the Union", and resolved "to establish the conditions for the application of the principles of subsidiarity and proportionality, as laid down in Article 5 of the Treaty on the European Union, and to establish a system for monitoring the application of those principles". According to Article 8 (1) of the Protocol, the Court of Justice has jurisdiction for annulment actions on grounds of infringement of the principle of subsidiarity by a legislative act, brought "by Member States, or notified by them in accordance with their legal order on behalf of their national Parliament or a chamber thereof". According to Article 8 (2) of the Protocol, "the Committee of the Regions may also bring such actions against legislative acts for the adoption of which the Treaty [...] provides that it be consulted".[130] On the one hand, one could consider the principle of subsidiarity being one of the CoR's prerogatives in the interest of "decentralisation" (i.e. less EU action) as well as one of the ECB's and the Court of Auditor's prerogatives in the interest of "centralisation" (i.e. more EU action).[131] On the other hand, one could conclude that "*Protocol No 8 merely defines a specific case of an action for protection of prerogatives brought by the Committee of the Regions*. The fact that it has the possibility to bring an action for annulment to review compliance with the principle of *subsidiarity* therefore means that monitoring this *principle is a general prerogative of the CoR*".[132]

D. Critical Evaluation

There are a variety of regional and local entities within the Member States. Many have been granted certain legal status and competences by their national legal order before their joining the EU, which have been affected by the growing competences of the EU institutions.[133] Their interests are manifold, and it would be difficult for them to speak with one voice. Hence, despite the establishment of the Committee of the Regions as an advisory body to the European institutions, Regions and other autonomous communities have a continuous interest in defending their powers and interests at the EU level. This also becomes manifest in the context of the Regions' standing in direct actions before the EU Courts.

[130] See footnote 115.

[131] See Ziller (2006) published by the EC in 2006, see for full text of this study www.cor.europa.eu, under Opinions and Publications, Publications 2006.

[132] *Ibid.*, para. 532 [emphasis added].

[133] An indication of the powers enjoyed by the Regions within the national legal orders can be inferred from the areas in which the CoR now needs to be consulted by the Community institutions, see footnote 115.

The Courts' position, established in *Région Wallonne*, to consider Regions as non-privileged applicants only has been criticised by some. Van Nuffel claimed that the vague notion of "government authorities" used by the ECJ in this case indicates that not only "central government" but also other authorities authorised to represent a Member State can bring actions on behalf of the Member States.[134] What should be decisive for the admissibility of such actions is the conferral of the power to represent the Member State, independent of any specific interest of the authorised authorities.[135] Arnull also claimed that a legal person governed by public law should in some circumstances rather be equated with the Member State to whose law they are subject than being treated in the same way as a legal person governed by private law.[136] The reasons for this were that (a) Member States could also be represented by competent regional ministers rather than national ministers at relevant meetings of the Council (see Article 16 (2) TEU; former Article 203 (1) EC), (b) regional authorities were also responsible for the implementation and application of EU directives, and could be the addressees of related enforcement actions before national courts, and (c) Member States could be brought before the ECJ for their Regions' non-compliance with EU law.[137]

Over the last decade, several proposals have been made to strengthen the Regions' position before EU Courts. At the Inter-Governmental Conference in Nice in 2000, the Belgian Government suggested the insertion of a new paragraph – to follow Article 230 (2) EC – to give federal entities the right to bring an annulment action under the same conditions as Member States to counterbalance their obligation to implement directives and monitor compliance with Community law within their jurisdiction; however, this proposal did not find support from many Member States.[138] Subsequently, as part of the post-Nice debate on the future of Europe, a "Political Declaration of the Constitutional Regions Bavaria, Catalonia, North-Rhine Westphalia, Salzburg, Scotland, Flanders and Wallonia on the Strengthening of the Role of the Constitutional Regions in the European Union" was published, which demanded semi-privileged status for Regions, so that they could bring actions "when their prerogatives are harmed".[139]

Those suggestions were followed neither by the Member States (through a modification of the Treaty) nor the EU Courts. Instead, the Courts have confirmed their approach established in *Région Wallonne*. They reiterated the necessity for Regions to show their "direct and individual concern" by the contested EU measure in order to establish the admissibility of the annulment action.[140] As a consequence,

[134]Van Nuffel (2001), p. 880.

[135]Van Nuffel (2001), p. 880.

[136]Arnull (2001), p. 11.

[137]Arnull (2001), pp. 11, 12, with reference to relevant case-law; see also Van Nuffel (2001), p. 880 et seq. for a discussion of the meaning of Article 203 EC in this context.

[138]Burrows (2002), p. 45 et seq.

[139]Burrows (2002), p. 46.

[140]See footnote 7 for reference to case-law.

the Courts' interpretation of Article 263 (4) TFEU [former Article 230 (4) EC] with regard to the Region's standing has become crucial.

The analysis of case law delivered in the context of actions brought by Regions in their capacity as non-privileged applicants under Article 230 (4) EC [now Art. 263 (4) TFEU] has arguably shown inconsistencies in approaching the conditions of direct and individual concern. Where decisions were challenged, the Courts held actions in the context of State aid admissible relatively easily, while often rejecting those in the context of the cancellation or reduction of financial assistance under the Structural and Cohesion Funds as inadmissible. All cases concerned, at least *inter alia*, the financial interests of the Regions. A regional entity is not only in the context of State aid cases but also in the context of the cancellation of structural funding, under an obligation to adjust the granting or to recover aid. This has been recognised by the CFI in *Regione Siciliana*.[141] Subsequently, the ECJ overruled the CFI's decision by holding that the Region's responsibility to implement the ERDF project did not imply its own entitlement to assistance, and that nothing supported the conclusion that the Region was directly concerned in its capacity as the authority responsible for the implementation of the project.[142]

While it is true that Regions' financial interests are concerned both in State aid and Structural and Cohesion Fund assistance, there have probably been political reasons for the Courts to distinguish between those categories. First, the position that Regions have been entitled to defend in annulment actions in the context of State aid relates to their vested power to grant State aid as long as they act in compliance with the legal constraints imposed on them by the EU legal order, in particular the common market. The Courts' acknowledgement of the Regions' standing in this context can be seen as respect for "decentralised powers", i.e. the autonomy of sub-national entities. The Regions' interests claimed in the context of the cancellation of financial assistance granted by Structural and Cohesion Funds are of a different nature. The financial assistance previously received by or allocated to them "privileged" the Regions in question in the interest of EU objectives pursued by the Funds. Hence, Regions will always have an interest in defending this privilege, whether or not EU interests justify its continuation; the number of cases before the Courts could be high. Secondly, the financial privileges enjoyed by the Regions in the categories of State aid and Structural and Cohesion Funds have been constituted on the basis of different sources and in the light of different objectives. While the Regions and Member States grant State aid from their own budget in the interest of industries, the EU pays for the financial assistance granted under the Structural and Cohesion Funds in the interest of EU policies.

A different matter involves those cases in which Regions' actions were brought to challenge legislative measures of the EU in the interest of their prerogatives such as powers in the area of education, environmental policy and the principle of

[141]T-60/03, *Regione Siciliana*, footnote 11, para. 53.

[142]C-15/06, *Regione Siciliana*, footnote 11, para. 32; see also C-445 and 455/07 P, *Ente*, footnote 12, and discussion at footnote 43 et seq.

subsidiarity (see also Chap. III).[143] Measures of general application have been considered by the Courts to be of direct concern as long as they (a) directly affect the applicant's legal situation and (b) there is no discretion left with regard to their implementation. Individual concern was denied where Regions relied on their general socio-economic interests[144] but was acknowledged where the EU institutions had been under a duty specifically to take account of the negative effects that the regulations in question might have on the economy of the countries or territories concerned.[145] It is welcomed that the Court thereby recognised the prerogative of public authorities to defend their institutional rights granted by EU law.[146] This might be as far as it has got so far with the Courts' contribution to the process of "discovering the proper place for the regions in the form of EU government".[147]

It remains unclear to what extent the Courts should take cognisance of the national division and allocation of legislative and executive powers, which has so far been refrained from.[148] The respect for regional autonomy in the context of annulment actions not only with regard to direct but also individual concern would also mirror the Court's approach with respect to preliminary rulings, which had at their core the scope of rights and interests of Regions. In those cases, the ECJ, while interpreting the scope of EU law, took account of national provisions providing powers to regional entities, developing parameters for the national courts' assessment of the Regions' institutional, procedural and economic autonomy.[149]

Regions have often claimed the necessity to make actions admissible by referring to the need for effective judicial protection.[150] Instead of adapting their interpretation of the admissibility criteria to widen Regions' access to the EU judicature, the EU Courts have held that where the admissibility conditions of Article 230 (4) EC [now Article 263 (4) TFEU] are not met, effective judicial protection should be made available by the national legal systems in accordance

---

[143]See also Scott (1999).

[144]T-238/97, *Comunidad Autónoma de Cantabria*, footnote 7, para. 50; T-609/97, *Regione Puglia*, footnote 7, para. 22. C-142/00 P, *Commission* v *Nederlandse Antillen*, footnote 12, para. 69; Order of the President of the CFI of 7 July 2004 in T-37/04 R, *Região autónoma dos Açores (Portugal)* v *Council* [2004] ECR II-2153, para. 118; T-417/04, *Regione autonoma Friuli-Venezia Giulia*, footnote 12, para. 61. See discussion at footnote 77.

[145]Van Nuffel (2001), p. 888, with reference to T-32 and T-41/98, *Nederlandse Antillen*, footnote 7, paras. 50–57; T-310/97 R, *Nederlandse Antillen*, footnote 71, paras. 33–37.

[146]Van Nuffel (2001), p. 889.

[147]Dani (2004), p. 181.

[148]T-417/04, *Regione autonoma Friuli-Venezia Giulia*, footnote 12, paras. 62, 63. See for discussion of the current regime linking the admissibility of actions to restrictions made to their autonomous exercise of national powers and to rights or institutional interests guaranteed by Community law already Van Nuffel (2001), p. 891.

[149]Joined Cases C-428-434/06, *UGT-Rioja*, footnote 110, para. 144; see discussion above at Sect. B.II.

[150]See footnote 84.

with the principle of cooperation in good faith laid down by Article 10 EC [see now Article 4 (3) TEU] through access to national courts and thereby the prompting of national courts' reference to the ECJ for a preliminary ruling.[151] It is doubted that, where annulment actions are inadmissible, adequate judicial protection with regard to EU law clashing with regional powers can be provided through alternative routes at the national level. It would have gone beyond the scope of this chapter to analyse a representative number of Member States' legal systems with regard to both the Regions' rights (under national law) to compel their States to represent them before EU Courts, and the procedural rights of applicants before national courts. It is difficult to draw any conclusion from the few examples of cases, of which some have been introduced above (see Sect. B). It can be concluded, however, that the possibility for Regions – and other non-privileged applicants – to defend their interests in such an action can hardly be considered a substitute for their direct access to the EU judiciary as there is neither a right under EU law for applicants to request the referral of a question to the ECJ,[152] nor to compel States to bring direct legal action on behalf of Regions. It would require detailed analysis of the Member States' jurisprudence to assess whether the obligation for States under Article 4 (3) TFEU to provide effective judicial protection has been made enforceable for Regions, and which actual effect that had on Member States' bringing actions on behalf of Regions before the EU Courts.

Even with the entry into force of the Treaty of Lisbon, there are not many changes concerning the Regions' access to judicial protection before EU Courts. Although the Committee of the Regions is now a "semi-privileged" applicant, the Regions themselves still remain "non-privileged" applicants who need, in principle, to be directly and individually concerned by the contested EU measure. It should be added that the standing of the CoR will also not necessarily be of direct benefit for individual Regions with regard to their access to EU Courts. According to Article 300 (4) TFEU, the members of the CoR "shall not be bound by any mandatory instructions", "[t]hey shall be completely independent in the performance of their duties, in the Union's general interest". In other words, although the CoR might be able and willing to represent interests of *all* their members (agreed upon), it would not be in a position to "defend" specific interests of sub-national entities before the EU Courts. With regard to the Regions' standing as non-privileged applicants, it remains to be seen whether Courts will acknowledge "concern" of applicants without assessing the element of individual concern where "regulatory acts" are challenged, which could make it easier for applicants to bring admissible action challenging regulations that do not require further implementation.

---

[151]C-15/06 P, *Regione Siciliana*, footnote 11, para. 39; C-445 and 455/07 P, *Ente*, footnote 12, paras. 65 et seq.

[152]See in particular Opinion of AG Jacobs of 31 March 2002 in C-50/00 P, *UPA*, footnote 64, paras. 37 et seq.; see also Arnull (2001), p. 50.

Selected Bibliography

Arnull A (2001) Private applicants and the action for annulment since *Codorniu*. Common Market Law Rev 38(1):7–52

Burrows N (2002) *Nemo Me Impune Lacessit*: the Scottish right of access to the European courts. Eur Publ Law 8(1):45–68

Craig P (1994) Legality, standing and substantive review in community law. Oxf J Leg Stud 14 (4):507–537

Craig P, De Búrca G (2008) EU law – text, cases, and materials, 4th edn. Oxford University Press, Oxford

Dani M, Nomos, B. Baden (2004) Regions standing before the EU courts – towards a constitutional theory on "direct and individual" participation of the regions in the EU decision-making processes. In: Toniatti R, Palermo F, Dani M (eds) An ever more complex union

Gordon R (2007) EC law in judicial review. Oxford University Press, Oxford

Kurcz B (2007) How selectivity is selective? A few thoughts on regional selectivity. Camb Law J 66(2):313–324

Lindsay-Poulsen W (2008) Case comment – regional autonomy, geographic selectivity and fiscal aid: between "The Rock" and a hard place. Eur Compet Law Rev 29(1):43–49

Schweizer RJ, Brunner SC (1998) Die Mitwirkung der Bundesländer an EU-Vorhaben in der Bundesrepublik Deutschland und in Österreich – Ein Modell für die Mitwirkung der Kantone in der Aussenpolitik (Swiss Papers on European Integration). Stämpfli, Bern

Scott J (1999) Case comment on Case C-95/97 *Région Wallonne* v *Commission of the European Communities* [1997] ECR I1787 (ECJ) and Case T-70/97 [1997] ECR II1513 (CFI). Common Market Law Rev 36(1):227–233

Tridimas T, Poli S (2008) *Locus Standi* of individuals under Article 230 (4): the return of Euridice? In: Arnull A, Eeckhout P, Tridimas T (eds) Continuity and change in EU law – essays in honour of Sir Francis Jacobs. Oxford University Press, Oxford, pp 70–89

Van Nuffel P (2000) De rechtsbescherming van nationale overheden in het Europeesrecht. Kluwer, Deventer

Van Nuffel P (2001) What's in a member state? Central and decentralized authorities before the community courts. Common Market Law Rev 38(4):871–901

Ward A (2007) Judicial review and the rights of private parties in EU law, 2nd edn. Oxford University Press, Oxford

Ziller J (2006) Review by the Court of Justice of the application of the principles of subsidiarity and proportionality, Chap. 9, para. 529 et seq. In: Jeffery C, Ziller J (eds) The committee of the regions and the implementation and monitoring of the principles of subsidiarity and proportionality in the light of the Constitution of Europe. Study of the European University Institute, Florence

Chapter 3
The Protection of Member States' Regions Through the Subsidiarity Principle

Piet Van Nuffel

A. Introduction

Since its introduction in Art. 5 EC (current Art. 5 of the modified Treaty on European Union, hereinafter "TEU"), the principle of subsidiarity has been central to any discussion on the protection of Member States' competences against the ever-expanding action of the European Union (EU). From the outset, the subsidiarity principle has been considered as an instrument not only to safeguard the scope for decision-making at national level, but also to ensure that Member States' regional and local entities with autonomous powers are not unduly limited in the exercise of these powers through decisions adopted at EU level. The German *Länder* and other regions with constitutionally protected competences have indeed been amongst the advocates to have the subsidiarity principle recognised as a legally binding principle that can be judicially enforced. Even now, requests to have the application of the subsidiarity principle tightened mainly come from federal states, such as Belgium and Germany, as well as from the regional and local entities gathered within the Committee of the Regions, which presents itself as "custodian of the subsidiarity principle". [1]

All opinions expressed are personal to the author.

[1]Resolution of the Committee on the Regions of 11 March 1999 on the principle of subsidiarity, *OJ* 1999, C 198, p. 73 (point 1.1.4; see also point 1.1.3: "Since its first came into existence, the [Committee] has made defence of the application of the subsidiarity principle one of its primary objectives").

P.V. Nuffel (✉)
Institute for European Law, Faculteit Rechtsgeleerdheid, KU Leuven, Tiensestraat 41, 3000 Leuven, Belgium
and
Katholieke Universiteit Brussel (KUB), Brussel, Belgium
and
College of Europe, Natolin, Poland
and
Legal Service of the European Commission, Belgium
e-mail: Piet.vannuffel@law.kuleuven.be

C. Panara and A. De Becker (eds.), *The Role of the Regions in EU Governance*,
DOI 10.1007/978-3-642-11903-3_3, © Springer-Verlag Berlin Heidelberg 2011

It is by now generally accepted that the legality of all measures adopted by the Union in areas that do not fall within its exclusive competence depends on respect of the subsidiarity principle as expressed in Art. 5(3) TEU. Before the entry into force of the Lisbon Treaty, account had also to be taken of the guidelines for applying the principle of subsidiarity set forth by the European Council on 11 and 12 December 1992,[2] which were subsequently incorporated in a protocol annexed to the EC Treaty by the Treaty of Amsterdam (hereinafter the "Amsterdam Subsidiarity Protocol").[3] Having been turned into primary Union law, these guidelines acquired the same legal status as Art. 5 EC. In order to enhance the role of the subsidiarity principle within EU decision-making, Treaty amendments have been proposed in the Treaty establishing a Constitution for Europe (hereinafter the "Constitutional Treaty") and have eventually been adopted by the Lisbon Treaty, which entered into force on 1 December 2009. These amendments allow national parliaments to express their concerns on proposed measures being incompatible with the subsidiarity principle and also extend the possibility to have the Court of Justice review legislative measures on their compliance with the subsidiarity principle. To that effect, the Lisbon Treaty has introduced, on the one hand, a slightly modified definition of the principle of subsidiarity in Art. 5(3) TEU and, on the other, a new protocol on the application of the principles of subsidiarity and proportionality (hereinafter the "Lisbon Subsidiarity Protocol").[4] The present contribution analyses to what extent these amendments reinforce the protection that Member States, and their autonomous regions in particular, may expect from the subsidiarity principle.

B. Which EU Action Needs to Satisfy the Subsidiarity Test?

According to the Art. 5(3) TEU, wherever the Union does not possess exclusive competence, it may take action "only if and in so far as the objectives of the proposed action cannot be sufficiently achieved by the Member States, either at central level or at regional and local level, but can rather, by reason of the scale or effects of the proposed action, be better achieved at Union level". The principle does not define whether or not the Union is competent – a matter to be determined according to the principle of conferral of powers recalled in Art. 5(1) TEU. As laid down in the Treaty, the subsidiarity principle is no more than a limitation of the Union's possibility to exercise its competences. In order to assess to what extent

---

[2]Overall approach to the application by the Council of the subsidiarity principle and Art. 3b *[now Art. 5 of the EC Treaty]* (1992) 12 EC Bull. points I.15-I.22, adopted by the European Council held in Edinburgh on 11 and 12 December 1992.

[3]Protocol (No 30), annexed to the EC Treaty, on the application of the principles of subsidiarity and proportionality, *OJ* 1997 C 340, p. 105.

[4]Protocol (No 2), annexed to the Treaty on European Union and the Treaty on the Functioning of the European Union, on the application of the principles of subsidiarity and proportionality, *OJ* 2008 C 115, p. 206.

this "limitation" may constitute any protection for regional or local authorities, we need to examine what the subsidiarity principle exactly requires from Union institutions – and, first of all, in which circumstances.

According to Art. 5(3) TEU, the subsidiarity principle applies to the Union's action "[i]n areas which do not fall within its exclusive competence". This does not greatly restrict the scope of application of the subsidiarity principle as most of the Union powers are not exclusively attributed to the Union. The only areas that constitute exclusive Union powers are listed in Art. 3(1) of the Treaty on the Functioning of the European Union (hereinafter "TFEU"). They are: the customs union, the competition rules necessary for the functioning of the internal market, the protection of the biological resources of the sea and the common commercial policy. To these areas the monetary policy has to be added as regards those Member States that have accepted the euro.[5] Given the limited scope of the Union's exclusive powers, the bulk of Union harmonisation measures needs to satisfy the subsidiarity test. Moreover, the Treaties do not restrict the application of the subsidiarity principle to legislative measures, nor do they confine the principle to those instances where the Union introduces new measures. Therefore, the principle also needs to be respected where the Union modifies existing measures or where it implements such measures.

Until the entry into force of the Treaty of Lisbon, the subsidiarity principle also applied where the Union took action in the framework of Title V (Common Foreign and Security Policy or "CFSP") and Title VI (Police and Judicial Cooperation in Criminal Matters or "PJCC") of the EU Treaty. Indeed, according to Art. 2, second paragraph, EU, the objectives of the Union had to be achieved as provided for in that Treaty and in accordance with the conditions and the timetable set out therein "while respecting the principle of subsidiarity as defined in Art. 5 of the Treaty establishing the European Community". As far as the judicial enforcement of the principle was concerned, however, account had to be taken of the fact that the EU Treaty ruled out the competence of the Court of Justice to review the legality of CFSP measures and only provided for more limited judicial scrutiny of PJCC measures.[6] For example, direct actions against PJCC measures could only be brought by Member States or by the Commission whereas the possibility to have the legality of such measures reviewed through a preliminary reference emanating from a national judge only existed for Member States that expressly accepted the Court's competence in this respect. Admittedly, in so far as most CFSP and PJCC decisions were to be taken in the Council on the basis of a unanimity vote, a Member State could have other means to oppose a proposed measure than to invoke an infringement of the subsidiarity principle. Currently, with the entry into force of the Lisbon Treaty, which does away with the Union's current "pillar structure", the subsidiarity principle applies to all action *of the Union* in areas which do not fall within its exclusive competence.[7] However, in CFSP matters, the competence of the Court of Justice to review the

---

[5]On the exclusive competences of the EU see Lenaerts and Van Nuffel (2005), pp. 97–98.

[6]Arts. 35 and 46 EU, as applicable until the entry into force of the Treaty of Lisbon.

[7]Art. 5(3) TEU.

legality of Union action is still excluded. As far as PJCC matters are concerned, the introduction of majority voting may now raise the interest of Member States in having the fulfilment of the subsidiarity requirements assessed.

C. What Does It Need to Satisfy the Subsidiarity Test?

Having clarified the substantive scope of application of the subsidiarity principle, it needs to be shown what it means that the objectives of a proposed Union action cannot be sufficiently achieved by the Member States at their level of governance – the first limb of the subsidiary test expressed in Art. 5 TEU – and that these objectives can be better attained by the Union than by the Member States – the second limb of the subsidiary test. It should be noted that Art. 5 TEU allows for Union action not only "if" both conditions are met, but also "in so far as" they are met. The latter terms refer to yet another test, which is the proportionality requirement according to which all Union action should not go beyond what is necessary to achieve the proposed objectives. To the extent that the proportionality test requires the examination of whether the same objectives could not have been equally achieved with less burdensome measures, it may also be invoked by Member States and their regional entities to preserve their freedom of action against too intrusive Union action.[8] This explains the Amsterdam Subsidiarity Protocol which required Union institutions to leave as much scope for national decision as possible, to prefer directives to regulations and framework directives to detailed measures and to minimise the burden of Union measures for, *inter alia*, national governments and local authorities.[9] In practice, the opposition of national and regional authorities against a proposed Union measure on the basis that such a measure is not "necessary" often also relies on the alleged infringement of the principle of proportionality. Nonetheless, that principle should be distinguished from the subsidiarity principle as it presupposes the legitimacy of the Union action in question and only scrutinises its concrete intensity and scope.[10] The following therefore concentrates on the actual subsidiarity test.

I. The Ability of National and Regional Authorities to Achieve the Proposed Objectives

First of all, the subsidiarity test requires that the objectives of a proposed Union action cannot be sufficiently attained by the Member States. If the Member States

[8] Lenaerts and Van Nuffel (2005), pp. 112–113.

[9] Amsterdam Subsidiarity Protocol, points 6 and 7.

[10] Cf. ECJ, Case 491/01 *British American Tobacco (Investments) and Imperial Tobacco* [2002] ECR I-11453, par. 184–185, where that distinction has been somewhat blurred.

cannot attain the proposed objectives, there seems to be a clear need for the Union to act – that is why commentators have described the first limb of the subsidiarity test as the "necessity test".[11] This test requires the institutions involved in the decision-making to assess whether the Member States have the resources to attain the proposed objectives on their own. It should be clear that this is not a test of the political willingness of Member States to enact rules and/or reserve funds in view of the objectives to be achieved. Indeed, were this the case, then it would suffice for the Union to face one or more negative votes within the Council to be able to show that a proposed action stands the first limb of the subsidiarity test. Art. 5 TEU cannot be construed in such a way that, whenever a Union proposal is fiercely opposed by one or more Member States, the latter would lose the benefit of having the proposed action checked against the subsidiarity principle. The necessity test thus requires the assessment not of the Member States' willingness to promote the policy goals concerned, but of their capacity to do so. In this respect, useful criteria were to be found in the guidelines that the Amsterdam Subsidiarity Protocol gave in order to assess whether the conditions of Art. 5 EC were fulfilled, guidelines that referred, *inter alia*, to situations where "the issue under consideration has transnational aspects which cannot be satisfactorily regulated by action by Member States" or where "actions by Member States alone... would conflict with the requirements of the Treaty (such as .... avoid disguised restrictions on trade...)".[12] Remarkably, the Lisbon Subsidiarity Protocol does not incorporate the same guidelines, thus limiting itself more to the procedural aspects of the subsidiarity test than to the substantive conditions to be met.

The Lisbon Treaty slightly amended the definition of the necessity test so as to clarify that, in order to assess Member States' capacity to attain the proposed objectives, the Union should take into account all possible resources within the Member States, whether they exist at national, regional or local level. According to Art. 5(3) TEU, "the Union shall act only if and insofar as the objectives of the proposed action cannot be sufficiently achieved by the Member States, *either at central level or at regional and local level...*". This amendment meets the request that federal Member States and the Committee of the Regions had repeatedly put forward to have the Treaty reflect the political reality that in various Member States policy objectives can be attained, not only at central but also at regional or local level.[13] Even under the previous definition of the subsidiarity principle, however, it was clear that the capacity of the Member States to attain certain policy objectives must be considered while taking into account all possible action that can be taken

[11]Timmermans (2007), p. 224.

[12]Subsidiarity Protocol, point 5, second par.

[13]E.g. the proposals put forward in 1990 by the governments of the regional entities meeting as "Europe of the Regions" in Brussels on 24 and 25 May 1990 as well as the proposals presented by the German *Bundesrat* in 1990 and 1995 and by the Federal Republic of Germany during the 1996 Intergovernmental conference (all cited in Van Nuffel 2000, pp. 397–398); see also the opinions of the Committee of the Regions of 21 April 1995 (*OJ* 1996 C 100, p. 6 and 10), 20 November 1997 (*OJ* 1998, C 64, p. 98) and 11 March 1999 (*OJ* 1999, C 198, p. 73).

within the Member States at each level of governance and by any competent authority.[14]

II. The Added Value of Union Action to Achieve the Proposed Objectives

Article 5(3) TEU requires the Union to demonstrate not only that its action is "necessary" as the proposed objectives cannot be sufficiently attained by Member States but also that these objectives "can, by reason of the scale or effects of the proposed action, be better achieved at Union level" – the part of the test that some describe as the requirement to show the Union's action "added value".[15] It is clear that, where the Member States turn out to be incapable of achieving the objectives proposed by the Union legislator, an intervention by the Union itself would seem "better" than any action at Member State level. Accordingly, the EC Treaty text suggested that where the proposed objectives could not be sufficiently achieved by the Member States, they could "therefore" be better achieved by the Community.

However, pursuant to the Amsterdam Subsidiarity Protocol, the second limb of the subsidiarity test required an analysis of its own as Union action was justified only if "both aspects of the subsidiarity principle [were] met".[16] Thus, the guidelines developed in the Amsterdam Subsidiarity Protocol referred to situations where action at Member State level would not actually be unable to reach the proposed objectives, but where Union action would anyway be considered "better", namely where actions by the Member States alone or the lack of Union action would significantly damage Member States' interests or where action at Union level would produce clear benefits by reason of its scale or effects compared with action at the level of the Member States.[17] The requirement that both aspects of the subsidiarity test need to be met is no longer formulated in the Lisbon Subsidiarity Protocol, which has not taken over the illustrations provided by the previous Protocol. Nevertheless, the second limb of the subsidiarity test still seems to require the Union to come up with evidence that – notwithstanding the possible action at Member State level – an intervention by the Union would anyway have more benefits than action by the Member States. According to the Treaty text, regard should indeed be taken of the "scale" and the "effects" of the proposed action. In this connection, the Amsterdam Subsidiarity Protocol required the added value of the Union's action to be substantiated by qualitative or, wherever possible,

[14]See also point 5, first par., of the Amsterdam Subsidiarity Protocol ("... cannot be sufficiently achieved by Member States' action *in the framework of their national constitutional system...*").

[15]Timmermans (2007), p. 224.

[16]Amsterdam Subsidiarity Protocol, point 5, first par.

[17]*Ibid.*, point 5, second par.

quantitative indicators.[18] In some areas, such as the protection of the environment, one may indeed conceive the added value of Union regulation being calculated on the basis of a cost/benefit analysis. In the framework of such economic analysis, certain elements are liable to play in favour of Union-wide action, such as the possibility to rely on economies of scale and the facility to take into account spill-over effects of the proposed regulation in connected geographical or substantive areas. Whenever the Union's added value is being calculated by reference to the scope and effects of the proposed action, it may thus be rather difficult for Member States to come up with evidence that they would be "better" placed to do pursue the proposed objectives.

In practice, therefore, where Member States are unable to show that they can attain the proposed objectives, it will be rather obvious that action at Union level would be "better" than action taken at national level. It thus appears that, where Member States cannot sufficiently attain the proposed objectives, the Union is therefore better placed to do so. The fact that the Lisbon Treaty replaced in Art. 5 (3) of the TEU the terms "*and* can *therefore*...be better achieved at Union level" by "*but* can *rather*...be better achieved at Union level" will thus not have any real impact on the contents of the subsidiarity test. Indeed, if national and regional authorities can expect some protection from the subsidiarity test, then it would be under the first limb of the test.

D. What Protection Can National and Regional Authorities Expect from the Subsidiarity Principle?

Given the attention that the subsidiarity principle has attracted for almost two decades in both political circles and legal scholarship, it is quite surprising to see that this principle has so far played a rather moderate role in litigation. Still, there have been cases where litigants have challenged EU measures on the basis of an alleged violation of the principle of subsidiarity. It should therefore be examined to what extent these cases have resulted in any guidance for national and regional authorities wishing to exercise some influence on EU decision making. As the current case law on the subsidiarity principle is limited to EU action based on the former EC Treaty, the following paragraphs mainly refer to the "Community".

I. Legal Protection Through Judicial Enforcement

Only in a handful of cases have Member States directly challenged Community legislation by referring, *inter alia*, to alleged infringements of the subsidiarity

[18] *Ibid.*, point 4.

principle.[19] In some other cases, companies and other individuals have tried to establish such infringement as part of their campaign to have Community legislation or implementing decisions annulled or rendered invalid.[20] In none of these cases was the subsidiarity principle found to be infringed. So far, no such claims have been brought by regional or local authorities. This may be largely explained by the fact that those authorities do not themselves have the standing to challenge the legality of normative measures of a general nature and, moreover, are not affected by the implementation of these measures in the same way as private parties that operate in the field concerned, and that often contest before a national court the implementation given to these measures by national authorities in order to be in a position to question the validity of the measures through the preliminary ruling procedure.

1. Substantive Assessment of the Subsidiarity Test

Whatever the concrete reasons having inspired the subsidiarity arguments invoked before the Court of Justice, it is clear that the Court generally does not have to go into lengthy reasoning to dismiss those arguments. The general picture that can be drawn from the case law is the Court emphasising that the EU action in question aimed at eliminating differences between national legislation and/or laying down uniform rules in the field concerned and that such objectives could not be sufficiently achieved by the Member States alone.[21] Thus, in the first case in which the Court of Justice had to deal with a genuine subsidiarity concern – the action for

[19]ECJ, Case C-84/94 *United Kingdom* v *Council* [1996] ECR I-5755 (Working Time Directive); Case C-233/94, *Germany* v. *Parliament and Council* [1997] ECR I-2405 (Directive on deposit-guarantee schemes); Case C-376/98 *Germany* v *Parliament and Council* [2000] ECR I-8419 (Tobacco Advertising Directive; as the Court annulled for lack of legal basis, it did not go into the subsidiarity arguments); Case C-377/98 *Netherlands* v *Parliament and Council* [2001] ECR I-7079 (Directive on the legal protection of biotechnological inventions).

[20]For direct actions for annulment, see the cases mentioned in footnotes 24 and 29–33 and accompanying text. For actions before national courts in the context of which questions about the alleged invalidity of the Community act have been referred to the Court of Justice, see ECJ, Joined Cases C-36/97 and C-37/97 *Kellinghusen and Ketelsen* [1998] ECR I-6337, par. 35 (subsidiarity principle held not applicable in time to Regulations on support for agricultural producers adopted before the entry into force of the EU Treaty); C-74/99 *Imperial Tobacco a.o.* [2000] ECR I-8599 (no discussion of the applicant's arguments as the challenged Tobacco Advertising Directive was annulled by the judgment in case C-376/98, *Germany* v *Parliament and Council*); Case C-491/01 *British American Tobacco (Investments) and Imperial To*bacco [2002] ECR I-11453 (Directive on the manufacture, presentation and sale of tobacco products); Joined Cases C-154/04 and C-155/04 *Alliance for Natural Health a.o.* [2005] ECR I-6451 (Directive on food supplements).

[21]E.g. Case C-377/98 *Netherlands* v *Parliament and Council* [2001] ECR I-7079, par. 32; Case C-491/01 *British American Tobacco (Investments) and Imperial To*bacco [2002] ECR I-11453, par. 181–182; Case C-103/01 *Commission* v *Germany* [2003] ECR I-5369, par. 47; Joined Cases C-154/04 and C-155/04 *Alliance for Natural Health a.o.* [2005] ECR I-6451, par. 104–108.

annulment brought by the United Kingdom against the Working Time Directive – it made clear that where the Community legislator "has found that it is necessary to improve the existing level of protection as regards the health and safety of workers and to harmonise the conditions in this area while maintaining the improvements made, achievement of that objective through the imposition of minimum requirements necessarily presupposes Community-wide action".[22] Whereas such affirmation is often accompanied with a statement that, given the Community-wide scale of the matter, the objectives could also be achieved "better" or "best" at Community level,[23] the Court does not go into any detailed assessment of why the Community action is to be considered "better" than Member States' action.

A more specific reasoning is to be found in two cases regarding economic sanctions decided by the United Nations Security Council and which the EU Council of Ministers had taken on the basis of Arts. 60 and 301 EC (current Arts. 75 and 215 TFEU) to implement the CFSP decisions adopted to this effect. The Court of First Instance (hereinafter "CFI"; current General Court) found the necessity of the Community action proven irrespective of the Member States' capacity to implement those sanctions themselves.[24] The CFI recalled that Arts. 60 and 301 EC provided for action by the Community when that is "deemed necessary" in the form of a common position or a joint action adopted according to the provisions of the EU Treaty relating to the CFSP. The very fact that the EC Treaty thus conferred on the Union the power to determine whether action by the Community was necessary excluded for the CFI any right for individuals to challenge the lawfulness of the subsequent Community action in the light of the principle of subsidiarity enshrined in Art. 5 EC.[25] In any case, the CFI added the more "classic" consideration that, even if the principle of subsidiarity would find application in the case at hand, it was plain that the uniform implementation in the Member States of Security Council resolutions could be better achieved at Community than at national level.[26]

Where Member States or other parties believe the subsidiarity principle to be infringed, they often also disagree with the concrete manner in which the EU legislator combined and prioritised the relevant policy objectives. This is clear in several cases where parties have challenged the legality of harmonisation measures based on Art. 95 EC (current Art. 114 TFEU). Apart from the "subsidiarity argument", according to which Community action was not necessary to achieve the objectives in question, such litigants would typically also advance the claim that the Community legislator used the harmonisation of national law in a given field as a pretext to achieve other policy objectives, such as the protection of health. Such

[22]ECJ, Case C-84/94 *United Kingdom* v *Council* [1996] ECR I-5755, par. 47 (see also par. 55 and 81).

[23]See *Netherlands* v *Parliament and Council*, par. 32; *British American Tobacco (Investments) and Imperial To*bacco, par. 183; *Alliance for Natural Health a.o.*, par. 107.

[24]CFI, Case T-253/02 *Ayadi* v *Council* [2006] ECR II-2139, par. 108–113; Case T-362/04 *Minin* v *Commission* [2006] ECR II-2003, par. 89.

[25]*Ayadi* v *Council*, par. 110.

[26]*Ibid.*, par. 112; *Minin* v *Commission*, par. 89.

a claim then requires the Court to check whether Art. 95 EC (Art. 114 TFEU) constitutes the appropriate legal basis for a measure that allegedly focuses more on other policy objectives than the harmonisation of existing national law. As far as measures based on Art. 95 EC (Art. 114 TFEU) are concerned, however, the Court has made clear that, as long as such a measure genuinely aims at removing or preventing obstacles to trade, it is to be based on that legal basis even if other policy goals can be identified as decisive for the policy choices made.[27] On this basis, the Court then usually highlights the extent to which the measure in question also pursues objectives such as the removal or prevention of obstacles to trade or distortions of competition, which then allows it to confirm that, whatever other objectives pursued by the challenged measure, that measure has been adopted according to the correct legal basis. In those cases where the Court thus validates the priority-setting undertaken by the EU legislator, it can then easily dismiss the subsidiarity argument advanced against the measure concerned by merely recalling that this measure also aims at removing obstacles to trade or distortions of competition resulting from the existence of different national rules – one of the objectives that is difficult to achieve by action taken by the Member States.[28] Once the Court has confirmed the concrete way in which the EU legislator has prioritised the relevant policy objectives – that is to say, once it has determined that the legislator did not exceed the limits of the legal basis chosen – then the subsidiarity test cannot but assess the Member States' ability to attain the "objectives of the proposed action" by departing from the same understanding of these objectives.

In other cases, the Union Courts have been even more reluctant to dissociate the subsidiarity test – the check whether the Union could lawfully *exercise* its competence – from the preliminary assessment whether or not the Union actually *possessed* any competence to act. This happened in some competition cases where the then CFI considered that the fact that Arts. 81 and 82 EC (current Arts. 101 and 102 TFEU) are limited to infringements having an effect on trade between Member States already concretises the subsidiarity test. The CFI thus dismissed the subsidiarity argument brought against Commission decisions establishing such infringement by simply referring to the fact that the Commission rightly considered the infringements to have an effect on trade between Member States.[29] In an earlier judgment, the CFI found it nevertheless necessary to explain that the issue dealt

[27]Case C-376/98 *Germany* v *Parliament and Council* [2000] ECR I-8419, par. 88; Case 491/01 *British American Tobacco (Investments) and Imperial Tobacco* [2002] ECR I-11453, par. 62; Joined Cases C-154/04 and C-155/04 *Alliance for Natural Health a.o.* [2005] ECR I-6451, par. 30.

[28]See *British American Tobacco (Investments) and Imperial Tobacco*, par. 181–182; *Alliance for Natural Health a.o.*, par. 105–107.

[29]CFI, Case T-168/01 *GlaxoSmithKline Services* v *Commission* [2006] ECR II-2969, par. 201–203 (appeal dismissed: ECJ, Joined Cases C-501/06 P, C-513/06 P, C-515/06 P and C-519/06 P, *GlaxoSmithKline Services a.O.* v *Commission* [2009] not yet reported); Joined Cases T-259/02 to T-264/02 and T-271/02 *Raiffeisen Zentralbank Österreich a.o.* v *Commission* [2006] ECR II-5169, par. 165 (appeal dismissed: ECJ, Joined Cases C-125/07 P, C-133/07 P, C-135/07 P and C-137/07 P, *Erste Group Bank a.O.* v *Commission* [2009], not yet reported).

with in the contested decision had a wider Community importance and that the Commission decision would have the benefit of ensuring a coherent application of the competition rules to similar practices in other Member States.[30] In the near future, arguments based on the subsidiarity principle may be expected to be invoked more and more against Commission decisions implementing Arts. 101 and 102 TFEU, in particular where companies do not agree with the manner in which the Commission gives effect to the division of powers between national and Union competition authorities laid down in Regulation No 1/2003 and its implementing provisions.[31] Thus, the CFI already had to deal with claims of alleged violations of these provisions as well as of the subsidiarity principle with respect to a Commission decision that ordered an inspection in a case where, according to the company concerned, the national competition authority would have been better placed to intervene.[32] The CFI recalled that the subsidiarity principle does not call into question the powers conferred on the Community by the EC Treaty, including the Commission's power to apply the competition rules and in particular the right to carry out inspections to assess any suspected infringements. The CFI added that, anyway, the Commission decision in question only constituted a preliminary step that did not have the effect of relieving the national competition authority of its competence.[33] It remains to be seen whether for those Commission decisions that actually relieve national authorities of their competence – the initiation of formal proceedings – the General Court will be willing to subject the exercise by the Commission of its powers to a real test of "necessity" and/or "added value".

What is clear from this overview is that, contrary to what some commentators allege,[34] the Union Courts do not refuse to check EU measures against the requirements imposed by the subsidiarity principle. In most cases, the Court of Justice has taken up the challenge to give a concrete legal meaning to the constitutional principle laid down in the second paragraph of Art. 5 EC (current Art. 5(3) TEU). It is true that judicial review of EU legislation in the light of this principle generally comes down to a confirmation of the Union's assessment of the necessity to have the proposed objectives pursued at Union level. Nonetheless, this is not the result of a deliberate choice by the Court not to upset the Union's legislative process by the

[30]CFI, Case T-65/98 *Van den Bergh Foods* v *Commission* [2003] ECR II-4653, par. 197–198 (appeal dismissed: ECJ, Case C-552/03 *Unilever Bestfoods (Ireland)* v *Commission* [2006] ECR I-9091).

[31]Council Regulation (EC) No 1/2003 of 16 December 2002 on the implementation of the rules on competition laid down in Arts. 81 and 82 EC (current Arts. 101 and 102 TFEU), *OJ* 2003 L 1, p. 1; Commission's notice on cooperation within the network of competition authorities, *OJ* 2004 C 101, p. 43; Joint statement of the Council and the Commission of 10 December 2002 on the functioning of the network of competition authorities (declaration recorded in the minutes of the meeting of the Council concerning the adoption of Regulation No 1/2003, document No 15435/02 ADD 1).

[32]CFI, Case T-339/04 *France Télécom* v *Commission* [2007] ECR II-521.

[33]*Ibid.*, par. 89.

[34]E.g. Cooper (2006), p. 284 ("the ECJ has been consistently unwilling to review Community legislation for alleged violations of subsidiarity").

enforcement of the subsidiarity principle. It is nothing more than the normal outcome of a test that requires judges to assess whether the specific objectives of a Union-wide action proposed by the EU legislator could be equally achieved by action of the individual Member States. Given the fact that most EU legislation aims at achieving typical objectives that cannot be achieved in the same way by the Member States – such as eliminating differences between national legislation and other obstacles to cross-border activities and ensuring a uniform level of protection throughout the Member States – it is rather natural that, for most proposed EU actions, its "necessity" and "added value" can be established through a relatively brief reminder of the fact that such objectives cannot be sufficiently achieved by the Member States.[35] Likewise, for those measures that amend existing EU measures or implement EU legislation, it may be relatively easy to explain why action at Union level is necessary.

Admittedly, in some cases, the Union Courts could have been more specific or elaborate in dealing with subsidiarity arguments. More generally, one could submit that it would even have been possible for the Union judges to opt for a different kind of scrutiny that would have led them to highlight certain policy goals more than others, for example by attributing less importance to the objective of having uniform rules applied throughout the Member States than to the specific aim of having the highest level of protection in those Member States that can so afford. Such an approach would, however, have required the Court to depart from the proposed objectives as defined in the contested act, which would have opened the door to all kinds of criticism of the Court substituting its own policy preferences over those formulated by the Union legislator. The Union judges could also have given more emphasis to the second limb of the subsidiarity test by introducing various criteria against which Union action is to be considered less or more "desirable" than Member State action, for instance by requiring the Union to come forward with an in-depth cost/benefit analysis of alternative action at Member State level as compared to the action proposed by the Union. As mentioned above, it is, however, difficult to perceive how the second limb of the subsidiarity test could be constructed in such a way that "benefits" would lie more with Member State action than with Union action, unless the Court would have given to those policy goals that are to be pursued exclusively at national level more weight than to the "objectives of the proposed action" – which would again have led to easy criticism of the Court substituting its assessment for the one undertaken by the Union institutions.

2. Statement of Reasons with Respect to the Subsidiarity Test

The subsidiarity principle has often been connected with the duty to state reasons that Art. 296 TFEU imposes on the Union institutions. In some cases brought before the Court of Justice, Member States have submitted that the then Community

[35]For a detailed development, see Van Nuffel (2000), pp. 371–377 and 407–409. See also, more recently, Davies (2006), pp. 67–75.

legislator should at least have *explained* why the measure adopted fulfilled the subsidiarity requirements. Any obligation to include a specific subsidiarity reasoning in Union decisions would indeed have the advantage of rendering more visible the assessment undertaken by the Union institutions. In the action brought by the UK against the Working Time Directive, the Court, however, dismissed the argument that the Directive failed to explain the need for Community action. The Court referred, first, to the statement in the preamble to the Directive according to which harmonisation of national legislation on the organisation of working time was necessary. The Court also affirmed that the pursuit of such an objective necessarily presupposed Community-wide action.[36] Thereby, the Court thus explained itself the actual reason for action at Community level: indeed, its second affirmation featured neither in the preamble nor in the text of the Directive. Likewise, the Court considered the Directive on the deposit-guarantee scheme to be sufficiently reasoned by indicating certain parts of the preamble from which it could be deduced that the proposed objectives could not be achieved sufficiently by the Member States and could be achieved best at Community level – again without there being any express conclusion in this respect in that Directive.[37] In addition, the Court ruled that an express reference to the subsidiarity principle could not be required.[38] Along the same lines, the Court dismissed the argument brought forward by the Netherlands according to which the Directive on the legal protection of biotechnological inventions did not state sufficient reasons to establish that the subsidiarity principle had been taken into account. The Court found the Directive to be sufficiently reasoned as "[c]ompliance with the principle of subsidiarity is necessarily implicit in the fifth, sixth and seventh recitals of the preamble to the Directive, which state that, in the absence of action at Community level, the development of the laws and practices of the different Member States impedes the proper functioning of the internal market".[39] These three cases demonstrate a clear reluctance of the Court to perceive the obligation to state reasons as requiring the EU legislator to develop a specific subsidiarity reasoning.

In the light of the inherent limits for the Union judges to scrutinise EU measures against the substantive conditions of the subsidiarity test, one may regret that the Court has not gone so far as to require the EU legislator at least to explain in its decisions why it deems the subsidiarity test to be met. It is true that such requirement is not explicitly imposed by the Treaty provisions. The Amsterdam Subsidiarity Protocol did impose some requirements as to the reasons to be stated, but these applied only to legislative acts and, moreover, solely concerned the statement of reasons to be given in proposals and other documents tabled in the course of the negotiations. For any "proposed Community legislation", the Protocol required the reasons on which it is based to be stated "with a view to justifying its

---

[36]ECJ, Case C-84/94 *United Kingdom* v *Council* [1996] ECR I-5755, par. 81.

[37]Case C-233/94, *Germany* v. *Parliament and Council* [1997] ECR I-2405, par. 26–27.

[38]*Ibid.*, par. 28.

[39]Case C-377/98 *Netherlands* v *Parliament and Council* [2001] ECR I-7079, par. 33.

compliance with the principles of subsidiarity and proportionality".[40] The Commission was required to "justify the relevance of its proposals with regard to the principle of subsidiarity; whenever necessary, the explanatory memorandum accompanying a proposal will give details in this respect"[41] whereas the Council, within the context of the co-decision and co-operation procedures, was to inform the European Parliament of its position on the application of Art. 5 EC (current Art. 5 TEU) and of the reasons on the basis of which it would deem all or part of a Commission proposal to be inconsistent with that Treaty provision.[42] Whereas the Commission and the Council were thus required to give reasons as to the conformity with the subsidiarity principle of all measures proposed, no such obligation existed for the Council or, where the co-decision procedure applied, for the European Parliament as to the statement of reasons to be inserted in the final legislative text. This has not changed now that the Lisbon Subsidiarity Protocol has entered into force. Pursuant to that Protocol, all draft legislative acts are to be justified with regard to the subsidiarity principle, providing a detailed statement that allows to appraise compliance with the principle as well as qualitative and, wherever possible, quantitative indicators that substantiate the reasons for concluding that a Union objective can be better achieved at Union level.[43] There is thus no precise requirement for the subsidiarity reasoning to be inserted in a legislative text.

II. Political Pressure to Be Exercised Within the Decision-Making Process

The limited judicial scrutiny of the subsidiarity test does not prevent the subsidiarity principle from being discussed in day-to-day EU decision making. In accordance with the requirements flowing from the Amsterdam Subsidiarity Protocol (and now from the Lisbon Subsidiarity Protocol), the Commission systematically pays attention to the principle through explanatory paragraphs inserted in the memorandums that accompany its legislative proposals. Moreover, even without there being any clear legal requirement, the Union legislator usually refers in the preamble of legislative texts to the principles of subsidiarity and proportionality with a short explanation of the reason why it considered it necessary to take action at Union level.[44] The paragraphs in explanatory memorandums and legislative texts that are dedicated to the subsidiarity principle most frequently contain an

[40] Amsterdam Subsidiarity Protocol, point 4.

[41] *Ibid.*, point 9, second indent. The Commission has expressly accepted such obligation in point 15 of the Interinstitutional agreement concluded on 16 December 2003 between the European Parliament, the Council and the Commission on better law-making, *OJ* 2003, C 321, p. 1.

[42] Amsterdam Subsidiarity Protocol, point 12.

[43] Lisbon Subsidiarity Protocol, Art. 5.

[44] See Van Nuffel (2000), pp. 381–382 and 384–385.

explanation that remains at a rather abstract level. They normally explain the necessity of Union action by referring to the kind of objectives that have already been identified above as typical for most of the Union's legislative action, such as the need to tackle cross-border problems, to lay down uniform rules and/or to ensure an equal level of protection.

In itself, the fact that such explanation is made available may not have any significant political impact. Often, the political debate will turn around more sensitive issues than the objectives to be set for a given EU measure or the kind of subsidiarity reasoning to be included in the text of that measure. Nonetheless, the attention that the EU institutions and other political actors give to these elements may nourish the debate on the actual contents of the measure proposed. In this respect, it should not be neglected that the Amsterdam Subsidiarity Protocol explicitly foresaw that any discussion within the Council and the European Parliament on compliance with the subsidiarity principle was to be considered "as an integral part of the overall examination of Commission proposals". In negotiations on proposed EU measures, the political actors are moreover not supposed to clearly distinguish between arguments that are legally relevant for the application of the subsidiarity principle and other arguments on the basis of which a proposed action is being criticised. This political reality should not be ignored when analysing the role to be played by the subsidiarity principle in the course of the decision-making process.

In this respect, reference should be made to the requirements introduced by the Amsterdam Treaty – in a Protocol "on the role of the national parliaments in the European Union" (hereinafter Amsterdam Protocol on national parliaments) – for the Commission to make available its legislative proposals in good time so that the governments of the Member States may ensure that their national parliaments receive them as appropriate, and for the Council to provide for a period of at least 6 weeks between the moment that such a proposal is made available and the date when it is placed on the Council agenda.[45] These dual requirements allow national parliaments to timely reflect upon proposed legislation and to see whether they can live with such legislation being adopted at Union level. In federal states such as Belgium, where the federal government is under an obligation to inform the parliaments of the competent regions,[46] that procedure may also mobilise regional entities to formulate their opinion on the proposed Union action. It may well be that the arguments presented by the Commission in its proposals and explanatory memoranda as to the need for a Union action on the face of it already exclude

[45]Protocol (No 9), annexed to the EU Treaty and the Community Treaties, on the role of the national parliaments in the European Union, *OJ* 1997 C 340, p. 113, points 2–3. With the entry into force of the Lisbon Treaty, this Protocol has been replaced by the new Protocol (No. 1) on the role of the national parliaments annexed to the TEU, TFEU and the EAEC Treaty, *OJ* 2008, C 115, p. 203 (hereinafter referred to as the Lisbon Protocol on national parliaments). The Lisbon Protocol extended the six weeks period to eight weeks.

[46]See Art. 92 quater of the Special Law of 8th August 1980 on institutional reform. As far as other Member States are concerned, see Lenaerts and Van Nuffel (2005), pp. 525–530.

any real chance for national and regional authorities to claim that they would be able to attain the objectives themselves and/or that action at Union level has no added value. However, that should not stop national and regional authorities from examining the way in which the EU has formulated the objectives and elaborated the contents of any proposed action. The attention paid by national and regional authorities to the fulfilment of the subsidiarity principle may thus result in a broader reflection on behalf of these authorities on the opportunity of proposed Union action and, more generally, in a deeper involvement with EU decision-making.

E. The Impact of the Lisbon Amendments on the Protective Value of the Subsidiarity Principle

In light of this, one should view the amendments introduced by the Lisbon Treaty with respect to the subsidiarity principle. Apart from the aforementioned amendment to the definition of the principle in the sense that the Member States' capacity to act is to be assessed "either at central level or at regional and local level", the Lisbon Treaty mainly introduced changes as to the control that national parliaments may exercise over the application of the principle of subsidiarity. In the previous situation, the Community law eventually left it to every Member State to decide on the degree of involvement of the national parliament with the national governments' participation in EU decision-making. The Treaty of Lisbon has instead for the very first time directly empowered national parliaments.

I. Discussion of the Subsidiarity Principle in the Decision-Making Process

To start with, the Lisbon Treaty tightens the Protocol on the role of national parliaments in the sense that national parliaments not only receive Commission proposals and other draft legislative acts, but also each position taken by the European Parliament and the Council in the course of the legislative process.[47] Contrary to the previous situation, where it was ultimately up to each national government to ensure that its own parliament received such proposals "as appropriate", the Lisbon Treaty thus directly confers on each (chamber of the) national parliaments the right to be forwarded draft legislative acts.[48] In addition, the

[47]Art. 2 of the Lisbon Protocol on national parliaments.

[48]*Ibid.*, Arts. 2 and 8. See also the Lisbon Subsidiarity Protocol, Art. 4. National parliaments are also to receive the agendas for and the outcome of meetings of the Council, including the minutes of meetings where the Council is deliberating on draft legislative acts (Lisbon Protocol on national parliaments, Art. 5).

Commission specifically has to draw the national parliaments' attention where it proposes to base its action on the flexibility clause (Art. 352 TFEU).[49] The same goes for the initiative whereby the European Council makes use of the right to change the legislative procedure (substituting qualified majority for unanimity voting or the ordinary legislative procedure for a special legislative procedure).[50]

Secondly, the Lisbon Subsidiarity Protocol lays down a procedure allowing national parliaments to intervene in the Union's decision-making process if they find legislative proposals to be incompatible with the subsidiarity principle. This "early warning procedure" has been invented in the European Convention's Working group on the principle of subsidiarity[51] and featured in the Subsidiarity Protocol annexed to the Constitutional Treaty. Whereas that Protocol required national parliaments to take a position within 6 weeks of the date of transmission of a draft legislative act, the Lisbon Subsidiarity Protocol gives any national parliament (or any chamber of a national parliament) 8 weeks to issue a reasoned opinion stating why it considers that the draft in question does not comply with the subsidiarity principle. If the draft legislative act concerns a matter for which, under national law, competence exists with regional parliaments with legislative powers, the national parliament is to consult such regional parliaments "where appropriate".[52] The Commission, the European Parliament and the Council must take account of the reasoned opinions issued by national parliaments. The Commission is to review its draft where reasoned opinions on non-compliance with the subsidiarity principle represent at least one third of all the votes of the national parliaments (one quarter in the case of a Commission proposal or an initiative initiating from a group of Member States related to police cooperation or judicial cooperation in criminal matters). After having reviewed its draft legislative act, the Commission may decide to maintain, amend or withdraw it, while giving its reasons therefore.[53] To calculate the threshold of one quarter or one third of the allocated votes, every national parliament will have two votes, shared out on the basis of the national parliamentary system. In the case of a bicameral parliamentary system, each of the two chambers will have one vote.[54] This procedure has received the name "yellow card" after the football term for "warnings" issued by referees.

In the European Convention, some members had proposed to go further in the sense that a two-thirds majority of the parliaments would force the Commission to amend or even withdraw its proposal – there was, however, insufficient support to introduce a so-called "red card" procedure in the context of the Constitutional

[49]Previous Art. 308 EC.

[50]Art. 48(7) TEU. The same applies to the change in legislative procedure that the Council can decide in family law matters: Art. 81(3), third subpar., TFEU.

[51]Final Report of the Working Party on the Principle of Subsidiarity, CONV 286/02, p. 5–7.

[52]Lisbon Subsidiarity Protocol, Art. 6.

[53]*Ibid.*, Art. 7(1)-(2).

[54]Lisbon Subsidiarity Protocol, Art. 7(1). This seems to be the case even if these chambers are not equal under domestic laws, see Kiiver (2008), p. 80.

Treaty.[55] With respect to matters falling under the ordinary legislative procedure (the previous "co-decision procedure"), the Brussels European Council of June 2007 agreed, however, to introduce in the new Subsidiarity Protocol the possibility to have a legislative proposal being rejected, leaving the final decision to discard such proposal not to the national parliaments but to the Union legislator itself.[56] Under this so-called "orange card" procedure, the Commission has to review its draft proposal where in the course of the ordinary legislative procedure the reasoned opinions on the non-compliance with the subsidiarity principle represent at least a majority of the votes allocated to the national parliaments. The Commission can then maintain its proposal only if the alleged compliance with the subsidiarity principle is explained in a reasoned opinion. Moreover, in such a case, the Union legislator shall "not give further consideration" to the proposal where the Council (by a majority of 55% of the Member States) or the European Parliament (with a majority of the votes cast) considers that it is not compatible with the subsidiarity principle.[57] The possibility for the Council and the European Parliament to reject further consideration of a proposal only exists where the Commission "maintains" and not "amends" or "withdraws" its proposal. Of course, where the Commission decides to amend its proposal, that amended proposal will only pass this hurdle if the amendments actually meet the concerns expressed by national parliaments – if not, its proposal will have to be considered "maintained". The refusal by the Union legislator to further consider a proposal may appear more radical than it really is; where such majority would be found to vote against the proposal, its chances for being adopted would anyway have been rather reduced, irrespective of the prior criticism being formally voiced by national parliaments.[58] The interesting cases would therefore be the – more likely – instances where reasoned opinions would be issued by several, but not the majority, of the national parliaments.

Commentators have rightly stressed the practical difficulties that national parliaments may have to implement the early warning system. For national parliamentarians, the 8-week period may be very short to identify, amongst the various national and European preparatory acts submitted to them, those European documents that need attention from the angle of the subsidiarity principle, especially if they need to consult with experts in the national administration, with their political parties and, possibly, with their counterparts in other national parliaments.[59] Nonetheless, the national parliaments will not act on their own. Both the Conference of committees on European affairs of the Union's parliaments (COSAC) and the Committee of Regions have shown their eagerness to offer technical assistance through the construction of networks through which information and expertise can be shared.

[55]Cooper (2006), p. 289.

[56]Annex I (Draft IGC Mandate) of the Presidency Conclusions of the Brussels European Council of 21 and 22 June 2007, Doc. 11177/07, p. 17.

[57]Lisbon Subsidiarity Protocol, Art. 7(3).

[58]See also Kiiver (2008), p. 81.

[59]See Barber (2005), p. 204, Tans (2007), p. 443.

Without any doubt, the early warning procedure will encourage national parliaments to reflect and formulate opinions on the proposed Union acts. Even where only a limited number of national parliaments would issue an opinion raising doubts as to the compatibility of proposed action with the subsidiarity principle, the Union institutions would be under political pressure to respond to such doubts. The Commission would have to come up with convincing arguments to soothe any unrest that such negative opinions would cause with members of the Council and/or the European Parliament, who themselves will have to be able to explain whatever position they would take with respect to the concerns expressed. In practice, the introduction of such an early warning procedure may thus even lead to higher standards with respect to the statement of reasons as regards compliance with the subsidiarity principle than any formal requirement to have a specific subsidiarity reasoning included in the text of a finally adopted measure.

Admittedly, the very fact that certain national parliaments consider a proposal to be incompatible with the subsidiarity principle, does not necessarily mean that such a proposal, if adopted, would turn out to fail the subsidiarity test as laid down in the Treaty text. Given the difficulty for Member States to demonstrate their ability to achieve the objectives proposed at Union level, the Union legislator would thus not always be at great legal risk if it were to adopt a proposal in spite of negative opinions having been issued by one or more national parliaments. Moreover, as mentioned above, the doubts expressed by national parliaments may not be limited to the application of the subsidiarity principle but may also contain other concerns, connected or not.[60] Nevertheless, the success of such an early warning procedure is not necessarily to be found in the fact of whether or not it would be liable to facilitate judicial scrutiny of the fulfilment of the subsidiarity test, or even to prevent infringements of the subsidiarity principle to occur. The great advantage of the early warning procedure being available would indeed be that it would stimulate national parliaments to participate in the discussion of proposed Union legislation. Even where a national parliament would prefer not to issue a negative opinion, or would be unable to take a position with respect to proposed Union acts, the very presence of the early warning procedure would hold it responsible to at least reflect on proposed Union measures before their final adoption. As some commentator has put it, the existence of the possibility to complain about proposed Union acts would make it embarrassing for national parliamentarians if they face criticism with respect to Union acts and have not at least tried to make use of it.[61] If concrete results are to be expected from the introduction of the early warning procedure, they will thus be found in the democratic control exercised within the Member States on the position taken by the national government acting within the Council, rather than in the sphere of the legal protection of Member States' freedom

---

[60]The limitation to subsidiarity related concerns is indeed unenforceable, see Barber (2005), p. 203 (who also considers this limitation unnecessary and undesirable). Cf. Constantinesco (2005), p. 316 (who foresees the "risk" that this limitation will be circumvented to pursue "less honourable" objectives such as the defence of a specific national situation or production).

[61]Kiiver (2008), pp. 82–83.

of action vis-à-vis the Union legislator. The early warning procedure may not only put pressure on national governments but also alert other actors in the EU decision-making process. Indeed, even where the Commission should not be willing to meet all concerns expressed by national parliaments, such concerns might be taken up not only by some national governments but also by members of the European Parliament. From its side, the Committee of the Regions invited the national parliaments to contact it in order to develop "joint strategies" for the effective application of the subsidiarity protocol.[62] The Committee of the Regions announced its engagement in a subsidiarity assessment, through its mandatory or voluntary opinions, for which anyway the 8 weeks deadline does not apply.[63]

Finally, it needs to be stressed that, through the early warning procedure, Union law not only entitles national parliaments to formally issue an opinion on proposed Union legislation but also requires regional parliaments with legislative powers to be consulted by their national (federal) parliament. That does not mean, however, that whenever a parliamentary organ of a regional entity has not been consulted, it will be able to rely on the Lisbon Subsidiarity Protocol to legally contest this course of action. With respect to regional parliaments, the Lisbon Subsidiarity Protocol does not lay down a directly enforceable right. Indeed, apart from the fact that the existence of regional parliaments with "legislative powers" has to be determined pursuant to the constitutional law of the Member State concerned, the Protocol provides for the consultation of such regional parliaments "where appropriate" – which seems to leave some discretion to the national constitutional order to determine the cases in which the consultation of regional parliaments has to take place.[64]

In this respect, Belgium has gone further by putting the parliaments of its autonomous regions ("Regions" and "Communities") on the same level as the chambers of the federal parliament for the application of the Subsidiarity Protocol. In a declaration attached to the Lisbon Treaty, Belgium has made clear that, in accordance with its constitutional law, the parliamentary assemblies of its autonomous regions act, in terms of the competences exercised by the Union, as components of the "national parliamentary system".[65] As far as the Constitutional Treaty is concerned, Belgium had made a similar declaration, that was already implemented in the form of a cooperation agreement initialled by both chambers of the federal parliament and the parliaments of the regions.[66] The cooperation agreement

---

[62]Opinion of the Committee of the Regions of 16 November 2005 on guidelines for the application and monitoring of the subsidiarity and proportionality principles, point 2.22.

[63]*Ibid.*, points 3.9–3.12.

[64]The Committee of the Regions invites national parliaments however to "effectively and transparently" consult the regional parliaments with legislative powers, inviting all regional parliaments expressly to "liaise" with it: *ibid.*, points 2.22–2.23.

[65]Declaration (No 51) by the Kingdom of Belgium on national Parliaments *OJ* 2007 C 306, p. 267.

[66]Cooperation agreement initialled on 19 December 2005, to be consulted (in Dutch) as Doc. 628 of Parliamentary year 2005–2006 on the website of the Flemish Parliament: www.vlaamsparlement.be.

lays down rules with respect to the division of competences between the various entities and the allocation of the (maximum two) votes to be issued on behalf of the "national parliament". In those instances where either the federal state or the regions have exclusive powers, two votes would be given if a reasoned opinion would be issued by both chambers of the federal parliament (in matters of exclusive federal power) or by at least two regional parliaments with a different linguistic regime (in matters of exclusive regional powers). In matters of concurrent powers, two votes would be expressed where at least one federal chamber together with one regional parliament issue such opinion. In case of disagreement with respect to the competent entity, the advice of the Belgian Council of State would be sought and, if that would not settle the dispute, the issue would be discussed by the presidents of all parliamentary organs meeting together. A similar arrangement will have to be laid down to implement the Lisbon Subsidiarity Protocol, now the Treaty of Lisbon has entered into force.

In the Belgian understanding of the Lisbon Subsidiarity Protocol, the rights endowed to national parliaments can thus be exercised by competent regional parliaments. There is indeed no reason why it should not be up to the constitutional order of Member States with a federal structure to determine the internal organs that are mandated to represent the "national" point of view at the level of the Union. For instance, within the Council, a federal state such as Belgium often sends ministers of regional governments to act as a "representative of [the] Member State at ministerial level, who may commit the government of the Member State in question and cast its vote" in the sense of Art. 16 (2) TEU. Given the fact that, contrary to Art. 16 (2) TEU, the Lisbon Subsidiarity Protocol itself distinguishes between "national" and "regional" parliaments, it remains to be seen, however, whether the other Member States and the Union institutions will accept Member States to freely interpret the notion of "national parliament".[67] Still, it would be rather paradoxical if a text designed to give regional entities a say in the Union decision-making process would be interpreted as denying Member States the freedom to make this happen.

II. Judicial Review of Union Decisions Against the Subsidiarity Principle

The Lisbon Subsidiarity Protocol confirms that Member States may bring an action for annulment against a legislative act on grounds of infringement of the principle of subsidiarity, adding that such action may also be "notified by [Member States] in

[67]In another context, the Court of Justice has, for instance, been reluctant to recognise any freedom for Member States to have regional entities acting on behalf of the "Member State": ECJ (order of 21 March 1997), Case C-95/97 *Région Wallonne* v *Commission* [1997] ECR I-1787, par. 6–8. See Van Nuffel (2001), pp. 871–901.

accordance with their legal order on behalf of their national Parliament or a chamber thereof".[68] This right accompanies the right of national parliaments to express their opposition to a legislative proposal, but is not restricted to those cases where reasoned opinions have been issued, nor to parliaments who actually did so. It was the Constitutional Treaty that introduced this possibility for national parliaments to have actions brought before the Court of Justice, in terms that reveal a compromise between those who wished to confer national parliaments the right to request the annulment of Union legislative acts and those who preferred to leave it completely up to the Member States to decide whether national parliaments would be entitled to bring actions for annulment.

Even before the entry into force of the Treaty of Lisbon there was no rule proscribing the Member State to be represented before the Union Courts by its national government.[69] Consequently, a Member State could already arrange to have its national parliament appointing the "agent" representing the Member State.[70] Nevertheless, actions brought by Member States are generally introduced by the national government, who mandates an official to act as "agent" for the "Member State". By referring to rules to be enacted within the national legal order, the Lisbon Subsidiarity Protocol does not constitute a sufficient legal basis for national parliaments to bring action on behalf of their Member State on grounds of infringement of the subsidiarity principle. Nonetheless, one should not ignore the fact that the possibility to have actions for annulment notified "on behalf of" national parliaments has been introduced as a corollary of national parliaments' right to express their opinion on proposed legislation, independent from the stance taken by the national government within the Council. This corollary would not have any meaning if the national legal order would be completely free whether or not to provide for a possibility for the national parliament to bring action. The Protocol must thus be interpreted as requiring the Member States at least to provide for an internal procedure allowing the national parliament to have an action for non-compliance with the subsidiarity principle brought in those cases where the national government does not itself take such step. In response to this Protocol, for instance, the French Constitution allows for each chamber of the national parliament to bring an action before the Court of Justice for non-compliance with the subsidiarity principle, action that will be transmitted to the Court by the national government.[71] Likewise, in Germany, both the *Bundestag* and the *Bundesrat* are entitled to bring such action, which will be transmitted by the Federal Government.[72] The parliamentary chamber concerned will take care of the conduct of the

---

[68] Lisbon Subsidiarity Protocol, Art. 8.

[69] According to Art. 19 of the Statute of the Court of Justice, the Member States are to be represented by "an agent appointed for each case".

[70] So far, however, not to have regional governments acting for the Member State, see footnote 67.

[71] Art. 88(6) of the French Constitution.

[72] See Art. 1 of the constitutional revision act of 8th October 2008 (in *BGBl.*, I, p. 1926). This provision added a new paragraph 1a to Art. 23 of the *Grundgesetz*.

proceedings.[73] By requiring the *Bundestag* to bring such action at the request of one quarter of its members, the German system thereby intends to have even minority views represented. As far as Belgium is concerned, this matter needs to be regulated in a cooperation agreement implementing Art. 8 of the Protocol annexed to the Treaty of Lisbon. Pursuant to an earlier agreement, which would have implemented the corresponding provision of the Protocol on subsidiarity annexed to the Constitutional Treaty, an action would have been introduced if a competent parliamentary assembly had made the request.. However, under the same agreement, other parliamentary assemblies would have had the opportunity to initiate the aforementioned dispute settlement procedure.

Apart from the right to have actions for annulment brought on behalf of national parliaments, the Lisbon Subsidiarity Protocol foresees the right for the Committee of the Regions to bring such action on grounds of infringement of the subsidiarity principle against legislative acts where the TFEU provides that it be consulted.[74] Before the entry into force of the Treaty of Lisbon, the Committee did not have the right to bring an action for annulment against Union acts. The Lisbon Treaty also gives the Committee of the Regions standing to challenge Union acts to defend its prerogatives – for instance, where it has not been consulted even though the Treaty so requires. In those areas where the Committee is to be consulted, the Lisbon Subsidiarity Protocol thus also entitles the Committee to bring action against Union acts that it considers incompatible with the subsidiarity principle.

Finally, it should be noted that the negotiators of the Lisbon Treaty did not wish to respond to the long-standing request of various regions and of the Committee of the Regions to confer such regions standing to bring actions for annulment on behalf of the Member State. Even though this matter falls outside the scope of this contribution, it may be interesting to mention that the Committee of the Regions has announced its willingness to consider any requests stemming from its networking with regional and local authorities to itself bring action against EU legislative acts.[75] It remains to be seen, however, whether the opposition voiced by one or several regional or local entities would receive sufficient support amongst the members of the Committee to have action being brought by it. Anyway, such action would only be possible in matters where the Committee is to be consulted.

Interesting as these new perspectives for legal action may be in themselves, their practical significance may turn out to be rather limited in comparison to the influence that the early warning procedure will have. Admittedly, the fact that national parliaments may have their Member State bring action against Union legislative acts may lead to more cases being brought before the Court of Justice

[73]See § 12(4) of the Law on the Responsibility of the *Bundestag* and the *Bundesrat* for the European Integration (*Integrationsverantwortungsgesetz*, IntVG) of 22 September 2009.

[74]Lisbon Subsidiarity Protocol, Art. 8, second par.

[75]Opinion of the Committee of the Regions of 16 November 2005 on guidelines for the application and monitoring of the subsidiarity and proportionality principles, point 3.24.

on grounds of infringement of the subsidiarity principle. In the same way, the Committee of the Regions may have an obvious incentive to show the importance of its long-claimed right of standing[76] by confronting the Court with actions based on subsidiarity concerns. Nonetheless, as has been argued above, the subsidiarity test to be applied by the Court has its inherent limits which are mainly due to the fact that the Union is bound to pursue the kind of objectives that Member States can hardly achieve on their own. The fact that more actions would be brought on subsidiarity grounds before the Court should therefore not automatically result in the Court starting to annul Union legislation on the basis of violations of the subsidiarity principle. The introduction of such action on behalf of national parliaments – or even the threat of such actions being introduced – may, however, emphasise the need to consider the views expressed by national parliaments, not only directly – through their reasoned opinions, but also indirectly – through their influence on the position taken by a national government within the Council. The same goes for the threat of actions being introduced by the Committee of the Regions where its opinions would be ignored.

F. Guardians of Subsidiarity: To Be Found at National or Regional Level?

Even though the Lisbon amendments also extend the possibility to bring suit before the Court of Justice on grounds of non-compliance with the subsidiarity principle, the focus of the amendments is clearly on the possibility to have subsidiarity concerns duly considered in the course of the Union's decision-making process. The early warning procedure has the potential to increase the participation in the decision-making process of national and regional entities whose voice is currently not always heard. To a certain extent, this potential has already become reality as parliamentary organs of the Member States have not awaited the entry into force of the proposed amendments to participate in projects aimed at having proposed Union legislation checked for compliance with the subsidiarity principle. Even before the ratification of the Lisbon Treaty by all Member States, COSAC has conducted pilot projects with respect to some selected proposed legislative acts[77] and has installed the IPEX inter-parliamentary database.[78] The Committee of the Regions has gone even further with its Subsidiarity Monitoring Network that contains reports on compliance with the subsidiarity principle of various Community proposals.[79] Such reports bring together the contributions that parliamentary

---

[76]See, e.g. the Committee's resolution of 11 March 1999 on the principle of subsidiarity (*OJ* 1999, C 198, p. 73, at point 1.3.1).

[77]See http://www.cosac.eu/en/info/ (last visited on 15 June 2010).

[78]See http://ipex.eu/ (Interparliamentary EU Information Exchange, last visited on 15 June 2010).

[79]See http://subsidiarity.cor.europa.eu/ (last visited on 15 June 2010).

and governmental organs of regional and local entities may issue on the basis of a questionnaire prepared by the Committee of the Regions.

It is interesting to see how the entry into effect of the Lisbon early warning system has been anticipated by competing networks. Whereas COSAC relies on cooperation between parliamentary committees of "national" parliaments, the Committee of the Regions evidently focuses on regional and local consultative assemblies. It is no coincidence that COSAC and the Committee of the Regions invite national political entities through separate networks to exchange information and, eventually, coordinate their action. The co-existence of parallel "subsidiarity networks" demonstrates the differences in vision that still exist between those who perceive the subsidiarity principle exclusively as an instrument to protect the "national" Member States and "national" parliaments vis-à-vis the Union legislator and those who see the subsidiarity principle as a vehicle to propagate regional autonomy. The former vision used to be the only one recognised in Union legal documents. Where the Lisbon Treaty formally recognises the role to be played by "regional parliaments", its provisions are still phrased in terms prudent enough so as not to upset those Member States that are less inclined towards recognising the direct participation of regional entities at Union level. Whereas it is now clear that regional entities have a role to play in the subsidiary debate, that role is to be shared with all other actors that use subsidiarity arguments to ensure their opinions being heard. It would indeed be contrary to the idea itself of subsidiarity to reserve its protection to one specific level of governance.

Selected Bibliography

Barber NW (2005) Subsidiarity in the draft constitution. Eur Publ Law:197–205

Bribosia H (2005) Subsidiarité et répartition des compétences entre l'Union et ses États membres dans la Constitution européenne. Revue du droit de l'Union européenne:25–64

Constantinesco V (2005) Les competences et le principe de subsidiarité. Revue trimestrielle de droit européen:305–317

Cooper I (2006) The watchdogs of subsidiarity: national parliaments and the logic of arguing in the EU. J Common Mark Stud:281–304

Davies G (2006) Subsidiarity: the wrong idea, in the wrong place, at the wrong time. Eur Law Rev:63–84

Kiiver P (2008) The Treaty of Lisbon, the national parliaments and the principle of subsidiarity. Maastricht J Eur Comp Law:77–83

Lenaerts K, Van Nuffel P (2005) Constitutional law of the European Union. Sweet & Maxwell, London, pp 97–98

Sander F (2006) Subsidiarity infringements before the European Court of Justice: futile interference with politics or a substantial step towards EU federalism? Columbia J Eur Law:517–571

Tans O (2007) De oranje kaart: een nieuwe rol voor nationale parlementen? Sociaal-Economische Wetgeving:443

Timmermans CWA (2007) Is het subsidiariteitsbeginsel vatbaar voor rechterlijke controle? Sociaal-Economische Wetgeving:224–230

Van Nuffel P (2000) De rechtsbescherming van nationale overheden in het Europees recht. Kluwer, Deventer, pp 397–398

Van Nuffel (2001) What's in a Member State? Central and decentralised authorities before the Community Courts. Common Market Law Rev:871–901

Chapter 4
The Role and Function of Structural and Cohesion Funds and the Interaction of the EU Regional Policy with the Internal Market Policies

Christopher Bovis

A. Introduction

The European Regional policy should contribute to increasing growth, competitiveness and employment by incorporating the Union's priorities for sustainable development as defined at the Lisbon European Council and at the Göteborg European Council. Article 174 of the Treaty on the Functioning of the European Union (TFEU) provides that, in order to strengthen its economic and social cohesion, the EU is to aim at reducing disparities between the levels of development of the various regions and the adverse economic conditions of the least favoured regions or islands, including rural areas. Article 175 TFEU requires this action to be supported by the Structural Funds, the European Investment Bank (EIB) and the other existing Financial Instruments.

The Regional Policy of the European Union is one of the most important instruments in creating a genuine common market without disparities. The notion of *region* corresponds to the territorial division of Member States in accordance with their own administrative arrangements. Regions cover local authorities and municipalities, in as much as the latter belong, or exercise powers, within the relevant territory of a Member State. Regions thus cover sub-sections of Member States where the need for European intervention is needed in order to correct existing or persisting disparities.

Regions across Europe perform in distinctively variable manners, with productivity, employment and economic growth indicators reflecting systemic problems of structural adjustment. As early as the first transitional period of the European integration process in 1969, regional disparities posed a significant concern for subsequent enlargements and accession agreements. In this chapter, the role and function of the Structural Funds as special instruments to promote Regional Policy in the EU is examined, in conjunction with the ever-increasing interrelation of the EU Regional Policy with policies of the internal market such as procurement, state

C. Bovis
Law School, The University of Hull, Cottingham Road, Hull HU6 7RX, UK
e-mail: c.bovis@hull.ac.uk

C. Panara and A. De Becker (eds.), *The Role of the Regions in EU Governance*,
DOI 10.1007/978-3-642-11903-3_4,

aid and the financing of services of general interest in an attempt to create a level-playing field for regional economic growth.

The EU Regional Policy directs funding and investment at the regions of Europe, through the Member States governments, or designated Regional Development Agencies, which have the task of allocating, monitoring and assessing the impact of the funding. Although it might not look in alignment with the principle of subsidiarity, regions and other territorial authorities cannot directly access funds and benefit from the thrust of the EU Regional Policy. This is a shortcoming in governance terms that the Committee of the Regions needs to address in the future.

B. The Legal Basis of EU's Regional Policy and the EU Structural Funds

The Single European Act (SEA) has been the cornerstone for the establishment of Regional Policy in the European Union. Title V Part III of the Treaty created three separate priorities for Community Institutions; firstly, a better cohesion between economic and social policy; secondly, the harmonious development of economic activity in conjunction with regional adjustments, and thirdly, the harmonious development of economic activity with welfare and employment opportunities.

Article 174 TFEU second paragraph allows for the European Union to promote measures aiming at reducing disparities between the various regions and at combating the disadvantageous economic condition of the least-favoured regions. This emphasis is also evident in Articles 176–178 (first paragraph) TFEU and in the Declaration, annexed to the Final Act on the adoption of the Single European Act, concerning Article 130D (now article 177 TFEU). In the Declaration, particular emphasis is paid on the Integrated Mediterranean Programmes (IMPs).[1] The new Articles 174 first paragraph TFEU, 177 and 178 second paragraph TFEU provide for the ability to promote employment opportunities independently of the regional concerns of Member States (for example in the cases of richer regions experiencing major unemployment, adaptation of vocational training and long-tem unemployment, combating youth unemployment and long-term unemployment) and to achieve better adjustment of agricultural policy in comparison to the structural development in other sectors of the economies of the Member States.

Article 175 TFEU is the modern foundation of the EU's Structural Funds. It allows the European Union to support the achievement of regional policy objectives by the action it takes through the Structural Funds (the European Agricultural Guidance and Guarantee Fund, the European Social Fund and the European

[1]See Regulation 2088/85, O.J. 1985 L 197/1; see also see Decision 88/258, O.J. 1988 L 107/39 as an example of an IMP. Portugal and Spain did not come under the IMPs but other programmes were set up, see Regulation 2053/88 (O.J. 1988 L 185/21) setting up the Portuguese European Development and Investment Programme (PEDIP) for Portugal.

Regional Development Fund), the European Investment Bank (EIB) and the other existing financial instruments. Parts of these financial instruments also relate to aspects of economic and social cohesion different from regional aspects. Article 175 TFEU stipulates that the objectives mentioned therein are not merely guidelines for the economic policy of Member States but they reflect on a vision for the Regional Policy envisaged in the Title XVII of the Treaty, as an essential method of completing the internal market and maintaining its proper functioning.

The technical and substantive implementation of Article 175 TFEU (former 159 EC) is Regulation 2052/88[2] which has been the outcome of the comprehensive proposal submitted by the European Commission under Article 161 EC (current 177 TFEU). This Regulation was designed, in the words of former Article 130D EC, "to make such amendments to the existing operational and structural rules of the existing provision of structural financial support ... as are necessary to clarify and rationalise their tasks in order to contribute to the achievement of the objectives set out in Article 130A and Article 130C, to increase their efficiency and to coordinate their activities between themselves and with the operations of the existing financial instruments". Five priority objectives have been identified for this purpose:

- Promoting the development and structural adjustment of the regions whose development is lagging behind
- Converting the regions, frontier regions or parts of regions (including employment areas and urban communities) seriously affected by urban decline
- Combating long-term unemployment
- Facilitating the occupational integration of young people
- With a view to the reform of the common agricultural policy, (a) speeding up the adjustment of agricultural structure, and (b) promoting the development of rural areas

Regulation 2052/88, which was entered into force on 1 January 1989, divided the implementation of each of these priorities to the various Funds. The comitology for assisting the European Commission, which is responsible for implementing the Regulation and all amending instruments, varies:

- For the dispensation of financial instruments for the development and structural adjustment of EU regions whose development is lagging behind the rest of the EU and for the conversion of EU regions seriously affected by industrial decline, an Advisory Committee composed of representatives of the Member States has been set up.
- For the dispensation of financial instruments for the combating of long-term unemployment and the facilitation of the integration into working life of young people and of persons exposed to exclusion from the labour market, as well as the facilitation of the adaptation of workers to industrial changes and to changes

---

[2]See O.J. 1988 L 185/9. See O.J. 1988 L 374 and the International Agreement on Budgetary Discipline and Improvement of Budgetary Discipline (O.J. 1988 L 184/33, point 17).

in production systems, the speeding up of the adjustment of agricultural and fisheries structures in the framework of the reform of the Common Agricultural Policy and the administration of the European Social Fund, a Management Committee composed of representatives of the Member States being set up in accordance with Article 163 TFEU.
- Implementing Commission Decisions under Article 178 TFEU are adopted laying down provisions governing operations under each Structural Fund.

There has been a shortcoming in understanding the effect of the new Title V of the Treaty, as a result of the introduction of the Single European Act, when compared with the wording of Articles 175 and 177 TFEU. On the one hand, the latter Articles refer to existing funds and other existing financial instruments, including the European Investment Bank; on the other hand, Article 177 TFEU is the legal basis for a one-off rationalisation measure relating to the specified Structural Funds (the European Agricultural Guidance and Guarantee Fund, the European Social Fund and the European Regional Development Fund). In order to avoid the need to have recourse to Article 308 TFEU, Regulation 2052/88 included a review clause for the Council of Ministers to review the Regulation 5 years after its coming into force, acting in accordance with the procedure of Article 177 TFEU. This solution allowed the symbiotic co-existence of Structural Funds and various other existing financial instruments, and allowed for the future creation of new financial instruments relevant to regional development policies of the EU.

Whilst the European Agricultural Guidance and Guarantee Fund have found a specific legal basis in Article 40(3) TFEU and the European Social fund in Articles 162 and 165 TFEU, this was not the case with the European Regional Development Fund (ERDF). Even Article 176 TFEU (previously Art. 160 EC) did not provide for legal basis, merely containing a detailed description of what the ERDF (which was set up under Article 308 TFEU) is intended to do. This is "to help to redress the main regional imbalances in the Union through participation in the development and structural adjustment of regions whose development is lagging behind and in the conversion of declining industrial regions". This description indicates that the ERDF is not only concerned with the more economically backward regions (the southern parts of the Union, Ireland and the northern part of the United Kingdom) but also with areas elsewhere in the Union where industrial development is in decline (e.g. industrial or mining areas which became obsolete or are in structural recession). Because Article 176 TFEU does not afford a legal basis for a substantive action or policy of the European Union, any changing of the detailed description of the tasks of the ERDF and other rules relating to its working would have to take place either on the basis of Article 177 TFEU or on the basis of Article 308 TFEU. The co-ordination required by Regulation 2052/88 has been based on Article 178 TFEU.

Article 175 TFEU stipulates that the regional aspects of the European Union must be taken into account in the conduct and co-ordination of economic policies of Member States, the implementation of all parts of Union common policies and the implementation of the internal market. This infers to the complementarity of regional policy and the function of the Structural Funds with other policies and legal frameworks of the Union, including Article 39 TFEU (Common Agricultural Policy), Article 96 TFEU (Common Transport Policy), Article 107(3) TFEU (the possibility of exempting aid to regional development from the general prohibition) and 174 TFEU (the tasks of the European Investment Bank).

Article 23 TFEU contains a clear rule in relation to the establishment and function of the internal market. However, the inherent powers of European Institutions and the obligations conferred upon Member States by virtue of Article 23 TFEU could create problems in the implementation of the EU Common Commercial Policy and, in its execution, the danger of continued regional differentiation. Besides the primary legal bases already mentioned under the Treaty Articles, Regulation 2088/85[3] made provision for the Integrated Mediterranean Programmes (IMPs) on a temporary basis (until 1992) in order to place the southern regions of the Community of Ten to adjust to the new situation created by Spanish and Portuguese accession by improving their economic structures under optimal conditions. IMPs were partly financed by contributions of 2,500 million ECU from existing Funds, partly by an additional budgetary contribution of 1,600 million ECU (both from the Community budget) and partly in the form of an estimated 2,500 million EU as loans from the European Investment Bank or under the new Regulation. Regulation 2088/85 can be seen as a sort of (partial) precursor of the Regulation 2052/88.

The ERDF has been governed by Regulation 1787/84[4] which came into force on 1 January 1985. The task of the ERDF has been to contribute, in proportion to the degree of under-development of the areas concerned, to the realisation of national as well as specific Union development programmes. The ERDF is assisted by the Regional Policy Committee set up by Decision 75/185,[5] although the primary task of that Committee is to contribute to the co-ordination of national regional policy. Attempts have been made to replace project financing (under Articles 5–14 of Regulation 1787/84) by financing integrated national and Union programmes, which have to be submitted to the Commission by the Member States. For Union programmes, which as a rule involve more than one Member State, the initiative is taken by the Commission which must reach agreement with the Member States concerned. Besides the above-mentioned programme financing (contributions of up to 50–55% of the public financing of the project or set of projects), Regulation 1787/84 also provides in Articles 17–23 for special help for the development of small and medium-size undertakings in industry, in the crafts or services sector or in infrastructure; here, there are varying funding levels, depending on the size of the project, but the concept is again of funding a percentage of the contribution of a

[3]See O.J. 1985 L 197/1.

[4]See O.J. 1984 L 169/1, as amended by the Act of Spanish and Portuguese Accession, Reg. 3634/85 (O.J. 1985 L 350/6) and Reg. 3641/85 (O.J. 1985 L 350/40).

[5]See O.J. 1975 L 73/47, corrigendum in O.J. 1975 L 117/22, as amended by Dec. 79/137 (O.J. 1979 L 35/9).

public authority or equivalent body.[6] Feasibility or viability studies may also be part-financed under Article 24 of Regulation 1787/84.

The impact of the Single European Act was to crystallise the primary legal instruments in order to codify the appropriate measures for launching the European Regional Policy. Article 174 TFEU, together with Article 2 and the fifth recital to the preamble of the Treaty, placed emphasis on regional policy with a view to reducing disparities between various regions and the assistance of regions facing decline. Major and persisting socio-economic disparities between different regions of the European Union are attributed to a number of factors, including industrialisation, productivity, specialisation, inward investment and social cohesion. Often, different tiers of development and growth have emerged within Member States reflecting on a real threat to the economic and social cohesion of the European Union. In order to implement economic and social cohesion objectives envisaged in the Treaty, the European Commission has created the Structural Funds and, a decade after the introduction of the SEA, the Cohesion Fund as legal and financial instruments to promote regional and horizontal operations in the Member States. The Structural Funds and the Cohesion Fund provide the main method by which the EU encourages greater economic and social cohesion and uniformity of living standards across its area.

C. The General Principles of Structural Funds

The principles that underpin the function and operation of the Structural Funds have been harnessed over the years and formalised in four major themes:

I. The Principle of Programming

The principle of programming was introduced in 1988 and carried through subsequent reforms of the legal instruments and involves the preparation of multi-annual development plans by Member States. It is undertaken through a partnership-based decision-making process, in several stages, until the measures are taken over by the public or private bodies entrusted with carrying them out. Under the General Regulation on the Structural Funds, the programming period is

[6]Two most interesting ERDF projects are RESIDER programme (Reg. 328/88, O.J. 1988 L 33/1) and the RENAVAL programme (Reg. 2506/88, O.J. 1988 L 225/24) for the steel and ship building sectors respectively. As an example of the overlap between regional policy and high technology see Reg. 3300/86 (O.J. 1986 L 305/1) setting up the STAR programme and of the overlap with energy policy see Reg. 3301/86 (O.J. 1986 L 305/6) setting up the Valoren programme.

usually 7 years, although adjustments will be possible depending on the mid-term review.

Initial development plans are first submitted by the Member States. These plans are based on national and regional priorities and include a precise description of the current situation in the region (disparities, lagging behind development, overall development potential); a description of the most appropriate strategy for achieving the stated objectives; and indications as to the use and form of the contribution from the Funds. Member States submit full programming documents to the European Commission. Programming documents can take the form of either support frameworks which are translated into operational programmes; these are documents approved by the Commission in agreement with the Member State concerned, which contain both the Member State and the Funds' strategy and priorities for action, their specific objectives, the contribution from the Funds and the other financial resources; or single programming documents (SPDs) comprising a single document, approved by the Commission and combining the data contained in a support framework and operational programme (integrated regional programme containing the programme's priorities, a short description of the proposed measures and an indicative financing plan). The European Commission negotiates with the Member States on the basis of their programming documents and makes an indicative allocation from the Funds to each form of assistance for each Member State.

II. The Principle of Partnership

Utilisation of funding from the Structural Funds channeled to mitigate regional disparities presupposes a partnership approach by Member States to include the regional and local authorities, the economic and social partners and other competent bodies. The partnership approach complements the programming principle in as much as by involving the partners at all stages the approval of the development plan could be ascertained, prior to the submission of the full programming documents of the European Commission by Member States.

III. The Principle of Additionality

This principle requires Union assistance to be additional to national funding and not to replace it. Member States must maintain their own public expenditure at least at the level it was at in the preceding period and supplemented with funding matched by the Structural Funds. Additionality as a principle introduces an element of joint investment by Member States and the European Union, in regions where disparities threaten socio-economic cohesion. In doing so, the actions of Member States are immune from state aid regulation.

IV. The Principle of Authentication

In order to utilise their availability and draw down funding from the Structural Funds, Member States must appoint a managing authority for each programme. Its tasks cover the implementation, correct management and effectiveness of the programme (collection of statistical and financial data, preparation and transmission to the Commission of annual reports, organisation of the mid-term evaluation, etc.). Monitoring Committees are also set up, which fall under the responsibility of Member States. These Committees, chaired by a representative of the managing authority, ensure the efficiency and quality of the implementation of the structural measures.

There exist three types of authentication procedures, *ex ante*, mid-term and *ex post* with clear demarcations of responsibility for each one. The *ex ante* authentication is the responsibility of the competent authorities in the Member States, whereas the mid-term authentication must be carried out by the authority managing the programme in collaboration with the Commission; finally, the *ex post* authentication is the responsibility of the Commission, in collaboration with the Member State and the managing authority. All reports must be made available to the public.

V. The Principle of Probity

Member States and the Commission conclude a financial contract whereby the Commission undertakes to pay annual commitment appropriations from the Structural Funds on the basis of the adopted programming documents. Each Member State appoints a payment authority for each programme to act as intermediary between the final beneficiaries and the Commission. The payment authority, in collaboration with the managing authority, monitors the expenditure of the final beneficiaries and ensures that the Union rules relating to the application and use of Structural Funds are observed. The physical movement of funds (i.e. payment appropriations) from the European Union to Member States actually happens when the Commission reimburses the actual expenditure of the final beneficiaries, approved and certified by the payment authorities.

The increased decentralisation of programme management under the principle of authentication reflects the need for improved checking arrangements, which are the responsibility of Member States. The European Commission itself ensures the effectiveness of the arrangements set up by the managing and payment authorities. Detailed checks, such as on-the-spot checks and financial audits, must be made on 50% – as a minimum – of expenditure under each programme. When irregularities are found, Member States are responsible for making financial corrections by cancelling all or part of the financing of the operations concerned. In practice, this could create significant legal problems within the systems of Member States, as for example, contracts with relevant providers or contractors would have to be amended or cancelled, bringing into play contractual and non-contractual liability issues on both parties. The funds thus released by the Member States can be re-used; those recovered by the Commission are withdrawn and are not reusable. The most significant control mechanism for the function of the Structural and Cohesion Funds rests with the Member States themselves, in particular their obligations to observe and comply with European law. The European Commission *ab initio* requires a detailed set of procedures to monitor and evaluate the impact of the funding to the regions and insists on the utilisation of open and transparent procedures for the selection of the relevant private sector partner who will deliver the modalities of the regional aid programme in question. The European Commission might use compliance procedures under Art. 260 TFEU, if it is not satisfied that the regional aid programme has been dispensed or monitored correctly.

D. The Function of Structural and Cohesion Funds

The EU Regional Policy provides traction for the solidarity principles amongst the people of the European Union. It helps to achieve one of the fundamental objectives laid down in the Treaty: the strengthening of the EU's economic and social cohesion by reducing developmental disparities between its regions. It has a significant impact on the competitiveness of the regions and on the living conditions of their inhabitants, mainly by co-financing multiannual development programmes.

These programmes are supported by four Structural Funds: the *European Regional Development Fund* (ERDF) for infrastructure and investments, generating jobs and SMEs, the *European Social Fund* (ESF) for training, social integration and employment, the *European Agricultural Guidance and Guarantee Fund* (EAGGF) for rural development and aid to farms, and the *Financial Instrument for Fisheries Guidanc*e (FIFG) for the adaptation of the fisheries sector. In addition, the *Cohesion Fund* was introduced in 1994, in order to promote economic, social and territorial convergence in the European Union.

The Structural Funds absorb approximately one third of the EU budget. Their allocation for the 2000–2006 is EUR 195 billion for the EU 15, plus 15 billion for the new Member States between 2004 and 2006. The Cohesion Fund receives EUR 25.6 billion for the EU 25. Financial assistance from the Structural Funds has concentrated on seven Objectives, which have focused attention on the regions and groups in society most in need of assistance. These objectives are:

1. Objective 1: to promote the development and structural adjustment of regions whose development is lagging behind the rest of the EU
2. Objective 2: to convert regions seriously affected by industrial decline
3. Objective 3: to combat long-term unemployment and facilitate the integration into working life of young people and of persons exposed to exclusion from the labour market
4. Objective 4: to facilitate the adaptation of workers to industrial changes and to changes in production systems

5. Objective 5(a): speeding up the adjustment of agricultural and fisheries structures in the framework of the reform of the Common Agricultural Policy
6. Objective 5(b): facilitating the development and structural adjustment of rural areas
7. Objective 6: assisting the development of sparsely-populated regions (Sweden & Finland only)

For 2007–2013, the Commission proposes to concentrate its priorities in three areas, with a global budget of approx. EUR 336 billion. The Structural Funds will concentrate in the future on three priority areas: catch-up for regions lagging behind in development (Objective 1), socio-economic conversion of industrial, urban or rural zones or zones which are dependent on fisheries (Objective 2), and improved training and job opportunities (Objective 3), (Objective 1 region's programmes already include measures of this kind). Aid is also granted by four Initiatives which encourage cross-border, transnational and interregional cooperation throughout the EU (INTERREG III), the regeneration of cities and neighborhoods in crisis (URBAN II), equality in the labour market (EQUAL) and the development of rural areas (LEADER+). Finally, the Innovative actions support experimental regional programmes.

I. The European Regional Development Fund

The European Regional Development Fund (ERDF) contributes to the financial assistance of regions whose development is lagging behind and those undergoing economic conversion or experiencing structural difficulties. The European Regional Development Fund is currently the largest financial instrument of European Union's Regional Policy, which is intended to narrow the development disparities among regions and Member States. Since 1975, it has provided support for the creation of infrastructure and productive job-creating investment, mainly for businesses; ERDF resources are mainly used to co-finance the following priorities: productive investment leading to the creation or maintenance of jobs; infrastructure; and local development initiatives and the business activities of small and medium-sized enterprises. In practice, most regional development areas are covered, including transport, communication technologies, energy, the environment, research and innovation, social infrastructure, training, urban redevelopment and the conversion of industrial sites, rural development, the fishing industry, tourism and culture.

ERDF regional policy support measures have been concentrated on five strategic areas.

1. Objective 1 Measures: Development of the Least Favoured Regions

Objective 1 financial support from the Structural Funds is the main priority of the European Union's cohesion policy. In accordance with the Treaty, the Union works to "promote harmonious development" and aims particularly to "narrow the gap between the development levels of the various regions". More than 65% of the appropriations of the Structural Funds (EUR 135 billion) are allocated to helping areas lagging behind in their development ("Objective 1") where the gross domestic product (GDP) is below 75% of the Union average. The entire Objective 1 regions exhibit negative economic indicators and, in particular: low levels of investment; a higher than average unemployment rate; lack of services for businesses and individuals; and poor basic infrastructure.

More than 50 regions, representing 22% of the European population, have been covered by Objective 1 support measures in the period 2000–2006. The Structural Funds have supported the improvement of economic activities in these regions by providing the basic infrastructure they lack, whilst adapting and raising the level of trained human resources and encouraging investments in businesses.

2. Objective 2 Measures: Conversion of Regions Facing Difficulties

Objective 2 financial support from the Structural Funds aims to revitalise all areas or regions facing structural difficulties, whether industrial, rural, urban or regions dependent on fisheries. Although situated in regions whose development level is close to the Union average, such areas are faced with different types of socio-economic difficulties that are often the source of high unemployment. These include: the evolution of industrial or service sectors; a decline in traditional activities in rural areas; a crisis situation in urban areas; and difficulties affecting fisheries activity.

3. Interreg III: Measures of Interregional Cooperation

Interreg III is an initiative which aims to stimulate interregional cooperation in the EU, particularly during the period 2000–2006. It is financed under the European Regional Development Fund (ERDF). This phase of the Interreg initiative is designed to strengthen economic and social cohesion throughout the EU, by fostering the balanced development of the continent through cross-border, transnational and interregional cooperation. Special emphasis has been placed on integrating remote regions and those which share external borders with the candidate countries.

4. Urban II: Measures of Sustainable Development of Urban Areas

Urban II is an Initiative of the European Regional Development Fund (ERDF) for sustainable development in the troubled urban districts of the European Union for the period 2000–2006. As a follow-up to Urban I in 1994–1999, Urban II aims more precisely to promote the design and implementation of innovative models of development for the economic and social regeneration of troubled urban areas. It will also strengthen information and experience-sharing on sustainable urban development in the European Union.

5. Innovative Actions – Development of Innovative Strategies to Make Regions More Competitive

The innovative actions of the European Regional Development Fund (ERDF) were laboratories of ideas for regions to develop innovation policies. As the opportunities for experimentation were often limited under the main support of the Structural Funds, the innovative actions provided regional actors with the "risk space" needed to respond to the challenges set by the new economy. During the period 2002–2006, the programmes funded measures relating to one or more of the following three strategic themes: knowledge-based regional economies and technological innovation; e-EuropeRegio: the information society and regional development; and regional identity and sustainable development. Regional programmes for innovative actions will not be co-financed by the structural funds as distinct operational programmes for the period 2007–2013.

The Instrument for Structural Policies for Pre-accession (ISPA)[7] was developed by the European Commission to help the central and eastern European countries comply with Union environmental and transport standards. With an annual budget of EUR 1,040 million, ISPA's approach is similar to that of the Cohesion Fund.

The average GDP in the central and eastern European Countries (CEECs) is considerably lower than that of the Member States of EU 15. Out of 105 million people living in these countries, more than 98 million are in regions where per capita GDP is less than 75% of the projected average for the enlarged EU. CEECs have a substantial deficit to make up in all socio-economic sectors – industry, services, transport, the environment, agriculture, skills levels. Transport

[7]For the period 2000–2006, EUR 1,040 million a year (at 1999 prices) has been made available for this instrument. During its first 4 years of implementation (2000–2003), ISPA grant-aided over 300 large-scale infrastructure investments in the ten (at that time) candidate countries of Central and Eastern Europe (Bulgaria, Czech Republic, Estonia, Hungary, Latvia, Lithuania, Poland, Romania, Slovakia, Slovenia). Assistance amounted to EUR 7 billion for an investment value of over EUR 11.6 billion (current prices). After the EU enlargement in 2004, the remaining ISPA beneficiary countries were Bulgaria and Romania (until 2007), the other beneficiary countries having become eligible to the Cohesion Fund. Since 1 January 2005, Croatia benefits from ISPA as well.

infrastructure provision is well below average levels in the Union, in terms of both quantity and quality. In particular, a huge amount of work is needed to develop national networks and connect them to the trans-European networks.

As far as environmental law and policy compliance is concerned, the worst problems are water pollution, waste management and air pollution. Some 40% of the population in the applicant countries do not have running water and only 42% of liquid waste is treated, and then rarely to EU standards.

European Regions benefiting from Structural Funds – up to 2000. Source: Eurostat

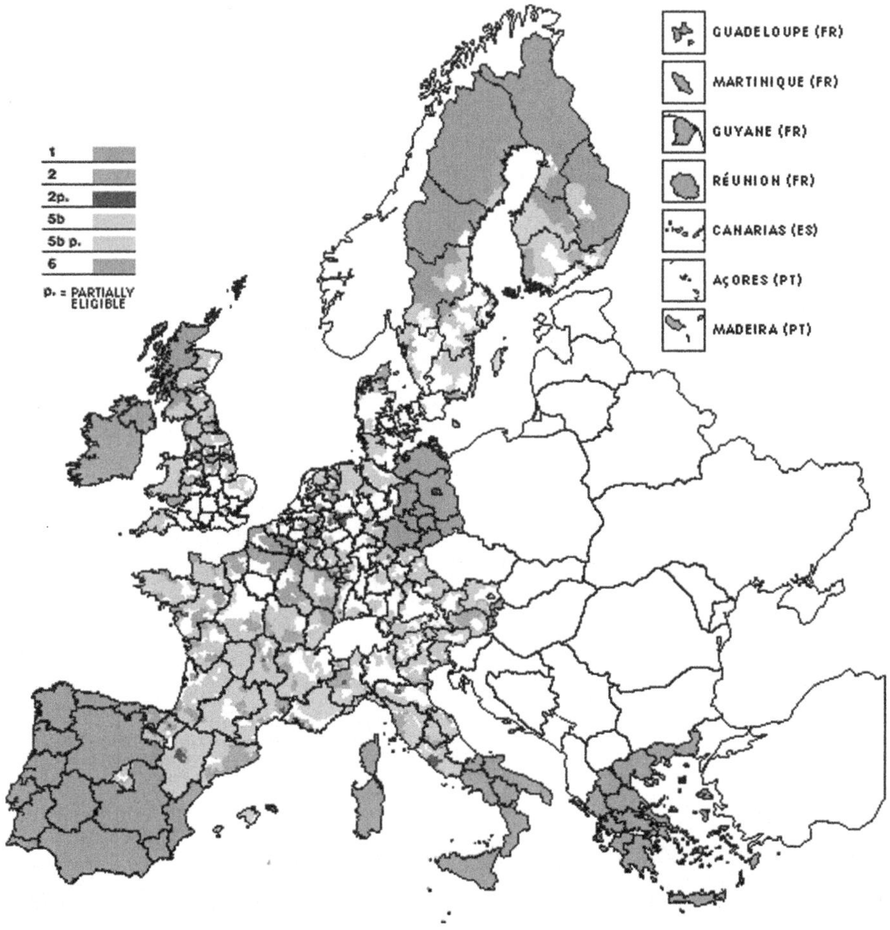

European Regions benefiting from Structural Funds – 2004–2006. Source: Eurostat

Regional policy in the enlarged Union
Structural Funds 2004-2006:areas eligible under Objectives 1 and 2

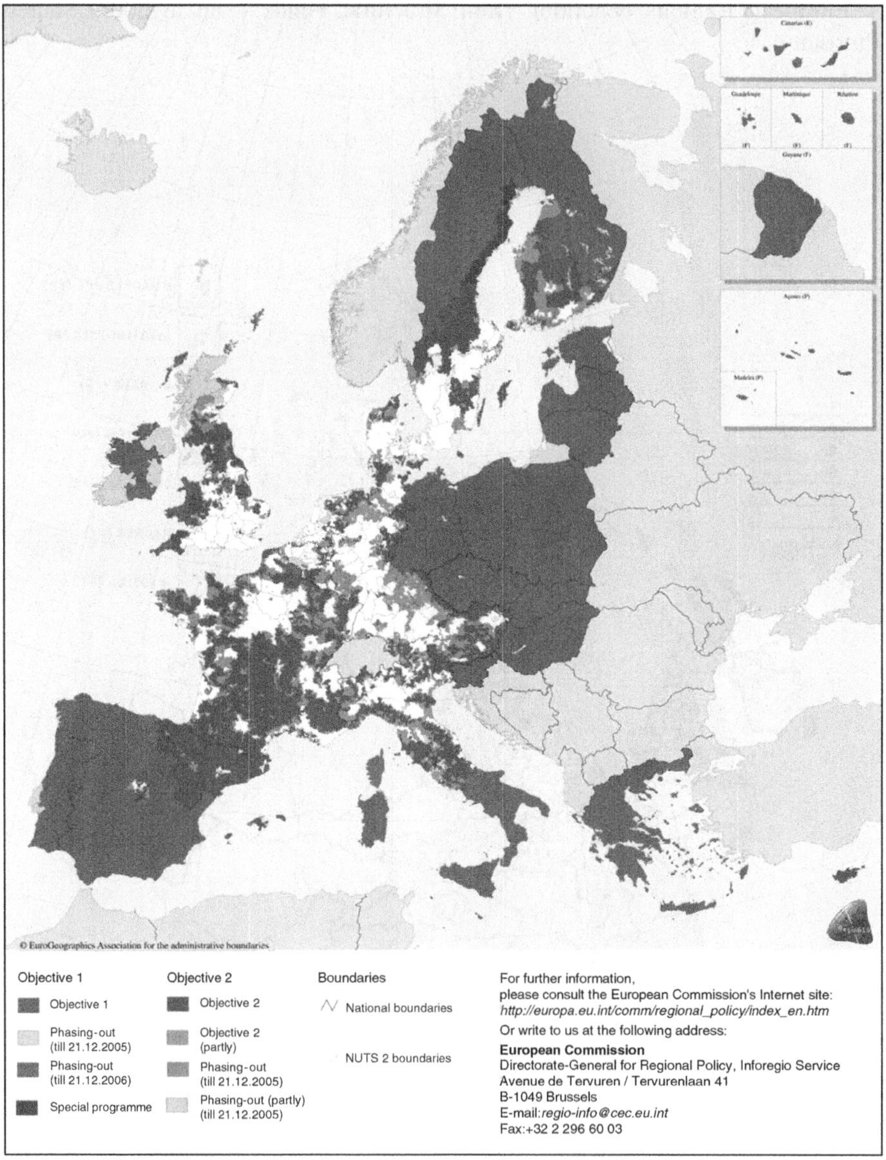

II. The European Social Fund

The European Social Fund provides assistance under the European Employment Strategy, to promote measures aiming at employment policies. The European Social Fund (ESF), which was set up in 1958, contributes to the integration into working life of the unemployed and disadvantaged sections of the population, mainly by funding training measures. The European Social Fund aims to prevent and combat unemployment, as well as developing human resources and promoting integration into the labour market. The main fields of applications of European Social Fund include: occupational integration of the long-term unemployed; occupational integration of young unemployed persons; occupational integration of persons excluded from the labour market; promoting equal opportunities for all in accessing the labour market, through the EQUAL Initiative; specific actions to improve women's access to the labour market; improving education and training systems; and promoting a skilled workforce and boosting human potential in the field of research and development.

ESF Contributions per Member State – 2000–2009. Source Eurostat

	ESF co-funding breakdown			Total (€)
	EU (€)	National (€)	Private[a] (€)	
Austria	524,412,560	549,921,560	110,000,000	1,184,334,120
Belgium	1,073,217,594	1,155,010,157	91,656,855	2,319,884,606
Bulgaria	1,185,459,863	209,198,799	0	1,394,658,662
Cyprus	119,769,154	29,942,289	0	149,711,443
Czech Republic	3,774,521,428	661,259,283	0	4,435,780,711
Denmark	254,788,619	169,989,437	84,799,182	509,577,238
Estonia	391,517,329	51,514,377	18,775,822	461,807,528
Finland	618,564,064	801,836,655	0	1,420,400,719
France	5,394,547,990	3,692,289,165	1,188,416,953	10,275,254,108
Germany	9,380,654,763	4,786,130,114	1,499,483,428	15,666,268,305
Greece	4,363,800,403	1,362,266,800	0	5,726,067,203
Hungary	3,629,088,551	640,427,395	0	4,269,515,946
Ireland	375,362,370	981,757,963	3,000,000	1,360,120,333
Italy	6,938,007,896	8,382,975,181	0	15,320,983,077
Latvia	550,653,717	85,691,846	20,612,487	656,958,050
Lithuania	1,028,306,727	105,884,641	75,822,521	1,210,013,889
Luxembourg	25,243,666	25,243,666	0	50,487,332
Malta	112,000,000	19,764,705	0	131,764,705
Netherlands	830,002,737	467,973,207	407,350,315	1,705,326,259
Poland	9,707,176,000	1,713,031,059	0	11,420,207,059
Portugal	6,512,387,865	2,697,500,732	0	9,209,888,597
Romania	3,684,147,618	651,225,177	0	4,335,372,795
Slovakia	1,499,603,156	264,635,856	0	1,764,239,012
Slovenia	755,699,370	133,358,718	0	889,058,088
Spain	8,057,328,822	3,243,162,467	125,323,084	11,425,814,373
Sweden	691,551,158	691,551,158	0	1,383,102,316
United Kingdom	4,474,917,728	4,134,516,286	215,162,274	8,824,596,288
	75,952,731,148	37,708,058,693	3,840,402,921	117,501,192,762

[a]Private expenditure: any eligible expenditure contributing to the financing of operations whose origin is not the public budget, for example own expenditure from private bodies benefiting from ESF support

The EQUAL Initiative supersedes two previous human resources initiatives ADAPT and EMPLOYMENT. The EQUAL budget for 2000–2006 has been EUR 2,847 million. The main aim of EQUAL is to promote new ways of tackling all forms of exclusion, discrimination and inequality in relation to the labour market. Although eligible areas include all EU Members, in order to ensure optimum cost effectiveness, funding has been concentrated on a limited number of large-scale projects run by several partners. The EQUAL Initiative priorities cover three large strands:

- Strand A: tackling discrimination and inequalities linked to the labour market. Projects run under this strand of the initiative must reflect the priorities agreed between the Member States and the Commission under the European Employment Strategy. These are carried out by public and private partners and associations through transnational cooperation.
- Strand B: networking projects at national level to enable information exchanges and the dissemination of best practice.
- Strand C: joint work by the Commission and Member States to learn the lessons of good practice and take into account in policy development the priorities to be implemented through the EQUAL initiative.

The Commission has set out an indicative financial allocation per Member State for each priority strand taking into account factors including the level of employment and training inequality in access to the labour market, the level of poverty and the number of asylum seekers.

ESF contributions to member states from EQUAL programme. Source: Eurostat

Indicative financial allocation per Member State	EQUAL € m
BE	70
DK	28
D	484
EL	98
E	485
F	301
IRL	32
I	371
L	4
NL	196
A	96
P	107
FIN	68
S	81
UK	376
Networks	50
EUR15	2,874

III. *The European Agricultural Guidance and Guarantee Fund*

The European Agricultural Guidance and Guarantee Fund (EAGGF), set up by Regulation 25/1962 on the financing of the common agricultural policy[8] consumes a large part of the general budget of the European Union. The EAGGF is composed of two sections, the Guidance section and the Guarantee section. Within the framework of European economic and social cohesion policy, the EAGGF supports rural development and the improvement of agricultural structures. The main fields of application of EAGGF include: investment in agricultural holdings (modernization, reduction in production costs, product quality, the environment, etc.); aid for the setting up of young farmers and vocational training; aid for early retirement; compensation for less-favoured areas; agri-environmental measures; processing and marketing of agricultural products; development and optimal utilisation of forests; and development of rural areas through the provision of services, support for the local economy, encouragement for tourism and craft activities. In Objective 1 regions, these measures are financed by the EAGGF-Guidance section, with the exception of compensatory allowances, aid for early retirement, agri-environmental measures, and measures for the development of forests, which are financed by the EAGGF-Guarantee section. Outside Objective 1 areas, all measures are financed by the EAGGF-Guarantee section.

The European Agricultural Guidance and Guarantee Fund Guidance Section provides financial assistance for the development and the structural adjustment of rural areas whose development is lagging behind by improving the efficiency of their structures for producing, processing and marketing agricultural and forest products. The Fund's Guarantee Section finances, in particular, expenditure on the agricultural market organisations, the rural development measures that accompany market support and rural measures outside of Objective 1 regions, certain veterinary expenditure and information measures relating to the CAP. The Guidance Section finances all other rural development expenditure which is not financed by the EAGGF Guarantee Section.

The Fund is administered by the Commission and the Member States, cooperating within the EAGGF Committee. The Fund Committee consists of representatives of the Member States and of the Commission. The financial resources required to cover EAGGF expenditure are made available to the Member States by the Commission by means of advances on the provision for expenditure incurred. In effect, the Commission reimburses expenditure incurred (pre-financed) by the Member States. In addition, working capital can be made available to the Member States for the implementation of rural development programmes. At the end of the financial year, the Member States forward to the Commission their annual statement of expenditure in addition to an attestation regarding the completeness, accuracy and veracity of the accounts transmitted. The Commission clears the accounts of the paying agencies before May. Its decision covers the completeness, accuracy and veracity of the accounts submitted. This clearance of accounts decision does not

[8] Amended by Regulation 728/70 and subsequently superseded by Council Regulation 1258/1999 of 17 May 1999 on the financing of the common agricultural policy [O.J. L 160 26 June 1999].

prejudice the adoption of subsequent (*ad hoc*) decisions excluding expenditure from Union financing if it has not been incurred in compliance with Union rules. The amounts concerned (financial corrections) are recovered from the Member States.

IV. The Financial Instrument for Fisheries Guidance

Finally, the Financial Instrument for Fisheries Guidance[9] supports restructuring in the fisheries sector. Financial support is also given through the European Investment Bank and the Cohesion Fund.[10] The FIFG aims to contribute to achieving a sustainable balance between fishery resources and their exploitation. It also seeks to strengthen the competitiveness of the sector and the development of areas dependent upon it. The fields of application of FIFG include: adjustment of the fishing effort; fleet modernisation; aquaculture development; protection of marine areas; fishing port facilities; and processing and marketing of fishery products and product promotion.

V. The Cohesion Fund

With a view to facilitating economic, social and territorial convergence, the European Union set up a Cohesion Fund in 1994. The Cohesion Fund is intended for countries whose per capita GDP is below 90% of the Union average. The purpose of the Cohesion Fund is to grant financing to environment and transport infrastructure projects. However, aid under the Cohesion Fund is subject to certain conditions. If the public deficit of a beneficiary Member State exceeds 3% of national GDP (EMU convergence criteria), no new projects under the Cohesion Funds could be approved until the deficit has been brought under control.

For the period 2007–2013, the EU Budget has allocated to Regional Policy appropriations amounting to circa EUR 348 billion, comprising EUR 278 billion for the Structural Funds and EUR 70 billion for the Cohesion Fund. This represents 35% of the Community budget and is the second largest budget item, after the Common Agricultural Policy (CAP) appropriations.

The Structural Funds, as well as the Cohesion Fund will be utilised by the European Commission and Member States as financial instruments involving co-financing regional policy objectives between 2007 and 2013. The rates of co-financing may be reduced in accordance with the "polluter pays" principle or where a project generates income. A precondition for all projects receiving European funding under the

[9]The FIFG was not a Structural Fund, but it financed structural actions in the fisheries sector. It became a Structural Fund in the 2000–2006 programme period.

[10]The Cohesion Fund initially was only applicable to Greece, Spain, Ireland and Portugal under the provisions of the Maastricht Treaty, but cannot be used to finance projects that receive support from the ERDF, the ESF or the guidance section of the EAGGF.

Structural Funds and the Cohesion Fund is their compliance with EU competition legislation, particularly with regard to public procurement.

Between 2000 and 2007, Cohesion Fund the biggest beneficiaries include Spain, Portugal, Greece, Poland, Austria, Lithuania, Latvia and Cyprus.

E. The EU Regional Policy and the Structural Funds in the Twenty-First Century

Economic, social and territorial disparities at both regional and national level have increased in the enlarged European Union. The Funds providing assistance under the cohesion policy include the European Regional Development Fund (ERDF), the European Social Fund (ESF) and the Cohesion Fund. The rules applicable to each Fund are to be specified in implementing regulations adopted under Articles 148, 161 and 162 of the Treaty. The Cohesion Fund should be integrated into the programming of structural assistance in the interest of greater coherence in the intervention of the various Funds. The outermost regions should benefit from specific measures and additional funding to offset the handicaps resulting from the factors referred to in Article 299(2) of the Treaty.

To increase the outcomes of the EU Regional Policy, the intervention of the Structural Funds and of the Cohesion Fund should be concentrated on objectives seeking the convergence of the Member States and the regions, regional competitiveness and employment and European territorial cooperation. Within those three objectives, both economic and social characteristics and territorial characteristics of Member States should be taken into account. Objective criteria for designating eligible regions and areas have been established, where the identification of the priority regions and areas at Union level is based on the common system of classification of the regions established by on the establishment of a common classification of territorial units for statistics (NUTS).[11]

Financial assistance to the European regions through the Structural Funds and the Cohesion Fund should be dispensed having consideration to the principles of subsidiarity and proportionality. However, under Article 317 TFEU, in the context of shared management, the conditions allowing the Commission to exercise its responsibilities for implementation of the general budget of the European Union should be specified and the responsibilities of cooperation by the Member States clarified. The application of these conditions should satisfy the European Commission that Member States are using the Funds in a legal and regular manner and in accordance with the principle of sound financial management.[12] To that extent,

---

[11]See Regulation (EC) No 1059/2003 of the European Parliament and the Council of 26 May 2003.

[12]The Commission should establish the indicative annual breakdown of available commitment appropriations using an objective and transparent method, taking into account the Commission's proposal, the conclusions of the European Council of 15 and 16 December 2005 and the Inter-

contributions from the Structural Funds should not replace public expenditure by Member States, in order to ensure a genuine economic impact. Verification of the principle of additionality should concentrate on the regions under the Convergence objective because of the extent of the financial resources allocated to them and may result in a financial correction if additionality is not observed.

For the period 2007–2013, three new objectives should be pursued by the Structural Funds and the Cohesion Fund:

Firstly, the "convergence" objective with the view to accelerating the convergence of the least developed EU Member States and regions by improving growth and employment conditions. This objective is financed by the ERDF, the ESF and the Cohesion Fund. It represents 81.5% of the total resources allocated. The co-financing ceilings for public expenditure amount to 75% for the ERDF and the ESF and 85% for the Cohesion Fund. The Convergence objective is to cover the Member States and regions whose development is lagging behind. The regions targeted by the Convergence objective are those whose per capita gross domestic product (GDP) measured in purchasing power parities is less than 75% of the Union average. The regions suffering from the statistical effect linked to the reduction in the Union average following the enlargement of the European Union are to benefit for that reason from substantial transitional aid in order to complete their convergence process. This aid is to end in 2013 and is not to be followed by a further transitional period. The Member States targeted by the Convergence objective whose per capita gross national income (GNI) is less than 90% of the Union average are to benefit under the Cohesion Fund. Financial concentration on the Convergence objective should be increased because of the greater disparities within the enlarged European Union, the effort in favour of the Regional competitiveness and employment objective to improve competitiveness and employment in the rest of the Union should be maintained and the resources for European territorial cooperation objective should be increased in view of its particular value added.

Secondly, the "regional competitiveness and employment" objective to anticipate economic and social change, promote innovation, entrepreneurship, environmental protection and the development of labour markets which include regions not covered by the Convergence objective. It is financed by the ERDF and the ESF and accounts for 16% of the total allocated resources. Measures under this objective can receive co-financing of up to 50% of public expenditure. The Regional competitiveness and employment objective is to cover the territory of the Union beyond the Convergence objective. The regions eligible are those under Objective 1 in the 2000–2006 programming period which no longer satisfy the regional eligibility criteria of the Convergence objective and which therefore benefit from a transitional aid, as well as all the other regions of the Union.

---

institutional Agreement of 17 May 2006 between the European Parliament, the Council and the Commission on budgetary discipline and sound financial management (O.J. C 139, 14 June 2006, p. 1) with a view to achieving a significant concentration on the regions whose development is lagging behind, including those receiving transitional support because of the statistical effect.

Thirdly, the "European territorial cooperation" objective to strengthen cooperation at cross-border, transnational and interregional levels in the fields of urban, rural and coastal development, and foster the development of economic relations and networking between small and medium-sized enterprises (SMEs). This objective is financed by the ERDF and represents 2.5% of the total allocated resources. Measures under the Territorial Cooperation objective can receive co-financing of up to 75% of public expenditure. The European territorial cooperation objective is to cover regions having land or sea frontiers, the areas for transnational cooperation being defined with regard to actions promoting integrated territorial development and support for interregional cooperation and exchange of experience.

Three per cent of the Structural Funds appropriations allocated to Member States under the Convergence and Regional competitiveness and employment objectives may be placed in a national reserve for rewarding performance. The annual appropriations allocated to a Member State under the Funds should be limited to a ceiling fixed with regard to its capacity for absorption and should be indexed on a flat-rate basis for use in programming. With a view to improving complementarities and simplifying execution, the assistance of the Cohesion Fund and the ERDF should be jointly programmed in the case of operational programmes on transport and the environment and should have a national geographical coverage. Within the operational programmes co-financed by the ERDF under the Convergence and the Regional competitiveness and employment objectives, Member States, regions and managing authorities may organise sub-delegation to urban authorities in respect of priorities concerning the regeneration of towns and cities.

Programming should ensure coordination of the Funds between themselves and with the other existing financial instruments, the EIB and the European Investment Fund (EIF). Such coordination should also cover the preparation of complex financial schemes and public–private partnerships. Member States must ensure that improved access to finance and innovative financial engineering are available primarily to micro-, small and medium-sized enterprises and for investing in public–private partnerships and other projects included in an integrated plan for sustainable urban development. Member States may decide to set up a holding fund through the award of public contracts pursuant to public procurement law, including any derogation in national law compatible with EU law. In other cases, where Member States are satisfied that public procurement law is not applicable, the definition of tasks of the European Investment Fund (EIF) and the European Investment Bank (EIB) justifies that Member States award them a grant that is a direct financial contribution from operational programmes by way of donation. Under the same conditions, national law may provide for the possibility of awarding a grant to other financial institutions without a call for proposal. It is appropriate to define what expenditure in a Member State can be assimilated to public expenditure for the purpose of calculating the total national public contribution to an operational programme. For this purpose, Member States are referred to the definition and operational functions of "bodies governed by public law" as defined in the public procurement directives, since such bodies comprise several types of public or private body established for the specific purpose of meeting needs in the general interest not having an industrial or commercial character and which are controlled by the State, or regional and local authorities. The EU Regional Policy interacts with public procurement,[13] which represents not only the procedural framework of the contractual interface between public and private sectors[14] but it also reflects on the nature of activities of the state and its organs in pursuit of public interest.[15] In the epicenter of the debate regarding the relation between regional policy and public services within the internal market, public procurement has emerged as an essential component of understanding the complementarity of the objectives of the European Institutions and of the Member States. The existence of public procurement, as a system, verifies conceptual links, creates compatibility safeguards, and authenticates established principles applicable in state aid jurisprudence. Three per cent of the Structural Funds appropriations allocated to Member States under the Convergence and Regional competitiveness and employment objectives may be placed in a national reserve for rewarding performance.

In accordance with the principles of subsidiarity and proportionality, Member States should have the primary responsibility for the implementation and control of the interventions. The obligations on the Member States as regards management and control systems, the certification of expenditure, and the prevention, detection and correction of irregularities and infringements of EU law should be specified to guarantee the efficient and correct implementation of operational programmes. In particular, concerning management and control, it is necessary to establish the procedures by which Member States give the assurance that the systems are in place and function satisfactorily. The extent and intensity of Union controls should be proportionate to the extent of the Union's contribution. Where a Member State is the main provider of the financing for a programme, it is appropriate that there should be an option for that Member State to organise certain elements of the control arrangements according to national rules. In these same circumstances, it is necessary to establish that the Commission differentiates the means by which Member States should fulfill the functions of certification of expenditures and of verification of the management and control system and to establish the conditions

[13]See Bovis (2005), pp. 290–310. Also Communication from the European Commission to the Council, the European Parliament, the Economic and Social Committee, and the Committee of the Regions, "Working together to maintain momentum" 2001 Review of the Internal Market Strategy, Brussels, 11 April 2001, COM (2001) 198 final. Also, European Commission, Commission Communication, Public procurement in the European Union, Brussels, March 11, 1998, COM (98) 143. See Commission Interpretative Communication on the Community law applicable to public procurement and the possibilities for integrating social considerations into public procurement, COM (2001) 566, 15 October 2001. Also, Commission Interpretative Communication on the Community law applicable to public procurement and the possibilities for integrating environmental considerations into public procurement, COM (2001) 274, 4 July 2001.

[14]See Directive 2004/18, O.J. L 134, 30 April 2004 on the coordination of procedures for the award of public works contracts, public supply contracts and public service contracts and Directive 2004/17, O.J. L 134, 30 April 2004 coordinating the procurement procedures of entities operating in the water, energy, transport and postal services sector.

[15]See Bovis (2003a).

under which the Commission is entitled to limit its own audit and rely on the assurances provided by national bodies. In addition to the suspension of payments where a serious deficiency is detected in the management and control systems, there are measures allowing the European Commission to interrupt payments where there is evidence of significant deficiencies in the operation of these systems.

F. The EU Regional Policy and the Internal Market Policies

During the past two decades, public procurement developed a correlation with regional policy and state aid regulation, in the sense of preferential purchasing favouring indigenous undertakings. Specifically allowed by the public procurement regime, but phased out since the completion of the internal market (1992), preferential procurement sought to accommodate liberalisation principles with secondary Community policies such as regional development, social cohesion and industrial policies.[16]

The frequently exposed nature of public procurement as the most significant non-tariff barrier for the functioning of the common market[17] and the presentation of the arguments in favour of an integrated public market across the European Union[18] have contributed to the debate that public purchasing is indissolubly linked with national policies and priorities.[19] In the history of European economic integration, public procurement has been an important part of the Member States' industrial policies. It has been utilised as a policy tool[20] in order to support indigenous suppliers and contractors and preserve national industries and the related workforce. The legislation on public procurement in the early days clearly allowed for "preference schemes" in less favoured regions of the common market which were experiencing industrial decline. Such schemes required the application of award criteria based on considerations other than the lowest price or the most economically advantageous offer, subject to their compatibility with EU Law in as much as they did not run contrary to the principle of free movement of goods and to competition law considerations with respect to state aid. Since the completion of the internal market (1992), they have been abolished, as they have been deemed capable of contravening directly or indirectly the basic principle of non-discrimination on grounds of nationality.

---

[16]See Bovis (2002).

[17]See European Commission, White Paper for the Completion of the Internal Market, (COM) 85 310 fin., 1985. Also Commission of the European Communities (1988). Also the report by Cecchinni (1988).

[18]See European Commission, Special Sectoral Report no 1, Public Procurement, Brussels, November 1997.

[19]See European Commission, *Public Procurement: Regional and Social Aspects* (*COM(89) 400.*

[20]See Articles 29(4) and 29(a) of the EC Public Works Directive 71/305; also Article 26 of EC Public Supplies Directive 77/62.

There has been a great deal of controversy over the issue of the compatibility of preferential procurement with EU law. The justification of preference schemes to promote regional development policies have revealed the interaction of public procurement with state aid.[21] Preferential procurement reflects protectionism, and as such is regarded as a non-tariff barrier. However, protectionist public procurement, when strategically exercised, has resulted in the evolution of vital industries for the state in question.[22] Preferential public procurement can be seen through a multi-dimensional prism. First, it appears in the form of an exercise which aims at preserving some domestic sectors or industries at the expense of the principles of the European integration process. Impact assessment studies undertaken by the European Commission showed that the operation of preference schemes had a minimal effect on the economies of the regions where they had been applied, both in terms of the volume of procurement contracts as well as in terms of real economic growth attributed to the operation of such schemes.[23] Thus, in such format, preferential public procurement perpetuates the sub-optimal allocation of resources and represents a welfare loss for the economy of the relevant state. On the other hand, preferential purchasing in the format of strategic investment to the sustainability of selected industries might represent a viable instrument of industrial policy, to the extent that the infant industry, when specialised and internationalised, would be in a position to counterbalance any welfare losses during its protected period. In the above format, preferential public procurement, as an integral part of industrial policy could possibly result in welfare gains.[24]

Preference schemes have been indissolubly linked with regional development policies, but their interpretation by the European Court of Justice has always been restrictive.[25] Although the utilisation of public procurement as a tool of regional development policy in the form of state aid may breach directly or indirectly primary Treaty provisions on free movement of goods, the right of establishment, and the freedom to provide services, it is far from clear whether the European Commission or the Court could accept the legitimate use of public procurement as a means of state aid. Prior notification to the European Commission of the measures or policies intended to be used as state aid does not, apparently, legitimise such measures or absolve them from the well-established framework of the four freedoms. The parallel applicability of rules relating to state aid and the free movement

[21]See, Fernadez-Martin and Stehmann (1991).

[22]See Bovis (1998a).

[23]European Commission, *Public Procurement: Regional and Social Aspects* (*COM(89) 400*).

[24]See Commission of the European Communities (1992).

[25]See Case 84/86, *Commission v. Hellenic Republic*, not reported; Case C-21/88, *Dupont de Nemours Italiana S.p.A v. Unita Sanitaria Locale No.2 di Carrara*, judgment of March 20, 1990, [1990] ECR 889; Case C-21/88, *Dupont de Nemours Italiana S.p.A v. Unita Sanitaria Locale No.2 di Carrara*, judgment of March 20, 1990, [1990] ECR 889; Case C-351/88, *Lavatori Bruneau Slr. v. Unita Sanitaria Locale RM/24 di Monterotondo*, judgment of 11 July 1991; Case C-360/89, *Commission v. Italy*, [1992] ECR I 3401; Case C- 362/90, *Commission v. Italy*, judgment of March 31, 1992.

of goods, in the sense that national measures conceived as state aids must not violate the principle of free movement of goods, renders the thrust of regional policies through state aid practically ineffective. It appears that the Court has experimented with the question of the compatibility between state aid and free movement of goods in a number of cases where, initially, it was held that the two regimes are mutually exclusive, to the extent that the principle of free movement of goods could not apply to measures relating to state aid.[26] The acid test for such mutual exclusivity was the prior notification of such measures to the European Commission. However, the Court departed from such a position when it applied free movement of goods provisions to a number of cases concerning state aid, which had not been notified to the Commission.[27] Surprisingly, the Court also brought notified state aid measures under the remit of the provision of free movement of goods and reconsidered the whole framework of the mutual exclusivity of state aid and free movement of goods.[28]

The Court's jurisprudence on state aid has also revealed the catalytic position of regional policy consideration in the process of determining whether subsidies or state financing of public services represent state aids. The significance of the subject is epitomised in the attempts of the European Council[29] to provide for a policy framework of greater predictability and increased legal certainty in the application of the state aid rules to the funding of services of general interest. Along the above lines, public procurement rules have served as a yardstick to determine the nature of an undertaking in its contractual interface when delivering public services. The regulation of the award of public contracts has created a separate type of markets within the common market, often described as public markets. The funding of services of general interest by the state may materialise through different formats, such as the payment of remuneration for services under a public contract, the payment of annual subsidies, preferential fiscal treatment or lower social contributions. The most common format is the existence of a contractual relationship between the state and the undertaking charged to deliver public services. The above relationship should, under normal circumstances, pass through the remit of public procurement framework, not only as an indication of market competitiveness but mainly as a demonstration of the nature of the deliverable services as services of "general interest having non-industrial or commercial character".

---

[26]See case C-74/76, *Ianelli & Volpi Spa v. Ditta Paola Meroni*, [1977] 2 CMLR 688.

[27]See case C-18/84, *Commission v. France*, 1985, ECR 1339; case 103/84, *Commission v. Italy*, 1986, ECR 1759; also, case C-244/81, *Commission v. Ireland*, 1982, ECR 4005.

[28]See Bovis (1998b); Fernadez-Martin and Stehmann (1991)

[29]See the Conclusions of the European Council of 14 and 15 December 2001, paragraph 26; Conclusions of the Internal Market, Consumer Affairs and Tourism Council meeting of 26 November 2001 on services of general interest; Commission Report to the Laeken European Council on Services of General Interest of 17 October 2001, COM (2001) 598; Communication from the Commission on the application of the State aid rules to public service broadcasting, O.J. 2001 C 320, p. 5; see also the two general Commission Communications on Services of General Interest of 1996 and 2000 in O.J. 1996 C 281, p. 3 and O.J. 2001 C 17, p. 4.

There are three approaches under which the European judiciary and the Commission have examined the financing of public services: *the state aid approach, the compensation approach, and the quid pro quo approach*. The above approaches reflect not only conceptual and procedural differences in the application of state aid control measures within the common market but also raise imperative and multifaceted questions relevant to the state funding of services of general interest.

The State aid approach[30] examines state funding granted to an undertaking for the performance of obligations of general interest. It thus, regards the relevant funding as state aid within the meaning of Article 107(1) TFEU[31] which may, however, be justified under Article 106(2) TFEU,[32] provided that the conditions of that derogation are fulfilled and, in particular, if the funding complies with the principle of proportionality. The state aid approach provides for the most clear and legally certain procedural and conceptual framework to regulate state aid, since it positions the European Commission in the center of that framework.

The compensation approach[33] reflects upon a "compensation" being intended to cover an appropriate remuneration for the services provided or the costs of providing those services. Under that approach, State funding of services of general interest amounts to State aid within the meaning of Article 107(1) TFEU, only if and to the extent that the economic advantage which it provides exceeds such an appropriate remuneration or such additional costs. European jurisprudence considers that state aid exists only if, and to the extent that, the remuneration paid, when the state and its organs procure goods or services, exceeds the market price.

The *quid pro quo* approach distinguishes between two categories of state funding; in cases where there is a direct and manifest link between the state financing and clearly defined public service obligations, any sums paid by the State would not constitute state aid within the meaning of the Treaty. On the other hand, where there is no such link or the public service obligations were not clearly defined, the sums paid by the public authorities would constitute state aid.

[30]See Case C-387/92 [1994] ECR I-877; Case T-106/95 *FFSA and Others* v *Commission* [1997] ECR II-229; Case C-174/97 P [1998] ECR I-1303; Case T-46/97 [2000] ECR II-2125.

[31]Article 107(1) TFEU defines State aid as "any aid granted by a Member State or through State resources in any form whatsoever which distorts or threatens to distort competition by favoring certain undertakings or the production of certain goods . . ., in so far as it affects trade between Member States".

[32]Article 106(2) TFEU stipulates that. . . "Undertakings entrusted with the operation of services of general economic interest . . . shall be subject to the rules contained in this Treaty, in particular to the rules on competition, insofar as the application of such rules does not obstruct the performance, in law or in fact, of the particular tasks assigned to them. The development of trade must not be affected to such an extent as would be contrary to the interests of the Community".

[33]See Case 240/83 [1985] ECR 531; Case C-53/00, judgment of 22 November 2001; Case C-280/00, judgment of 24 July 2003.

G. Conclusions

European Law provides for specific financial instruments to promote Regional Policy as a means of state intervention in regions of the European Union that need assistance towards economic restructuring. The function of the Structural Funds has been instrumental in smoothing the ever-increasing disparities between regions that are diametrically different from each other, although they belong to Member States of the European Union that purports to have created a common market.

Over the past decades, the strategic funding and investment of the regions of Europe has made a significant contribution to the completion of the internal market in 1992 and the introduction of the EU Monetary Union and the single currency before the end of the millennium.

In addition, the symbiotic relation of the EU Regional Policy with policies of the internal market, namely public procurement and state aid regulation, reveals the flexibility embedded in the applicable regimes. In addition to the flexibility conferred to pubic authorities, Member States have a wide margin of discretion to introduce public policy considerations in dispersing public services. State aid, as regional development considerations, or as part of a national of EU wide industrial policy, is inherently a part of this symbiotic policy approach. This finding removes the often misunderstood justification of the pursuit of the EU Regional Policy as an economic exercise and places it in the heart of an ordo-liberal interpretation of the European integration process. On the other hand, the conceptual interrelation of Regional Policy considerations with the financing of services of general interest reveals the policy and jurisprudence links between public procurement and state aid regulation.

Selected Bibliography

Bachtler J, Turok I (eds) (1997) Coherence of EU regional policy: contrasting perspectives on the structural funds. European Studies Association, Kingsley Publishers, London

Bovis CH (1998a) The liberalisation of public procurement in the European Union and its effects on the common market. Ashgate-Dartmouth, Aldershot

Bovis CH (1998b) Public procurement as an instrument of industrial policy in the European Union, Chap. 7. In: Lawton T (ed) Industrial policy and competitiveness in Europe. McMillan Publishers, Kansas City

Bovis CH (2003, September) La notion et les attributions d'organisme de droit public comme pouvoirs adjudicateurs dans le régime des marchés publics. Contrats Publics

Bovis CH (2002) Recent case law relating to public procurement: a beacon for the integration of public markets. Common Market Law Rev 39:1025–1056

Bovis CH (2005) Public procurement and the internal market of the 21st century: economic exercise versus policy choice. In: P. Nebia and T. Tridimas (eds), EU law for the 21st century: rethinking the new legal order, Hart Publishing, Oxford, pp 290–310

Bovis CH (2006) Public procurement: case law and regulation. OUP, Oxford

Cecchinni P (1988) The European challenge: 1992. Wildwood House, Aldershot

Commission of the European Communities (1992) Statistical performance for keeping watch over public procurement. Commission of the European Communities, Brussels

Cremona M (ed) (2003) The enlargement of the European Union. OUP, Oxford
Commission of the European Communities (1988) The cost of non-Europe, basic findings, vol. 5, Part. A: the cost of non-Europe in public sector procurement. Official Publications of the European Communities, Luxembourg
European regional Policy (2007), The basic essentials, Office for official publications of the European Communities, Brussels
Fernadez-Martin JM, Stehmann O (1991) Product market integration versus regional cohesion in the community. Eur Law Rev 16:216–243
Funck B, Pizzati L (eds) (2003) European integration, regional policy, and growth. The World Bank, Washington
Jones RA (2001) The politics and economics of the European Union. Edward Elgar, Cheltenham
O'Brennan J (2006) The eastern enlargement of the European Union. Routledge, Abingdon
Vanhove N (1999) Regional policy: a European approach. Ashgate, Aldershot
Wosniak-Boyle JR (2006) Conditional leadership: the European Commission and regional policy. Lexington, Lanham

Chapter 5
The Committee of the Regions and the Challenge of European Governance

Silvia Ricci

A. Premise

Since its establishment in 1994, the Committee of the Regions (hereinafter referred to as CoR) was vested with two main political roles: to involve local and regional authorities in the European decision-making process and to make good the EU democratic deficit. This is in accordance with the needs that have emerged during the progressive widening of the Union's role and the consequent greater impact of EU law on local and regional policies in Member States.

The CoR's activity is inspired by three principles, subsidiarity, proximity and partnership, each of which appears to offer an adequate response (or currently, perhaps, the sole conceivable answer) to the needs mentioned above. The EU also relies on these principles to promote a more tangible sense of belonging among European citizens.

Given that the CoR shares its responsibility with the other institutions, in the following analysis we will focus our attention on the elements which best highlight the rules governing the nature, role and functions of the Committee, and the coherence of its activities. This is analysed in relation to the fundamental principles on which the work of the Committee is based and the reform of Union governance. [1] The issues resulting from the Treaty of Lisbon (hereinafter referred to as ToL) will also be examined.

The following analysis adopts the concept of Governance as defined in the 2001 White Paper: "rules, processes and behaviour that affect the way in which powers are exercised at the European level". This is a wide and generic definition which embodies a number of principles: "openness, participation, accountability, effectiveness and coherence". From the Commission's perspective, the European

[1] See *European Governance – A white Paper*, COM (2001) 428 of 25 July 2001, available at http://europa.eu/documents/comm/white_papers/index_en.htm (last checked on 15 June 2010).

S. Ricci
Facoltà di Giurisprudenza, Università degli Studi di Perugia, Via A. Pascoli, 33, 06123 Perugia, Italy
e-mail: si.ricci@libero.it

C. Panara and A. De Becker (eds.), *The Role of the Regions in EU Governance*,
DOI 10.1007/978-3-642-11903-3_5, © Springer-Verlag Berlin Heidelberg 2011

governance includes "multilevel governance": the 2001 White Paper also represents an attempt to confirm and foster the role of regional and local authorities in the EU institutional equilibrium.

B. Role and Legal Nature of the Committee

As mentioned above, the CoR came into being in 1994, with the Maastricht Treaty, as a consultative assembly of a political nature aimed at the representation of regional and local interests. On the one hand, the CoR would have had to ensure the participation of regional and local levels of government in the EU decision-making process, given the growing involvement of those levels in the implementation and application of EU Law. On the other hand, the CoR would have had to allow citizens to become more involved in the EU and in its decisions through regional and local authorities, since these levels of government are closer to the people.

The CoR came into being during a period of great transformation in the European Community; a period in which the European Union and European citizenship were established, and in which the principles of subsidiarity, proximity to the citizens and transparency were affirmed as the cornerstone of the Union. The CoR has the aim of expanding democratic guarantees in the exercise of Union powers, beyond the representation of the "European citizens" in the European Parliament.

Therefore, the Maastricht Treaty, in providing for the CoR, introduced a new Community body endowed with autonomy, taking the place of the Consultative council of local and regional authorities, an advisory body to the Commission.[2]

The CoR does not have the status of a Union institution. Nevertheless, the Committee is involved in the decision-making process of the Union and contributes to the inter-institutional equilibrium within the EU. The Committee performs an advisory function for the benefit of the EU institutions responsible for legislation: the Commission, the Council, and the European Parliament. The CoR is allowed to intervene in the overall legislative activity of the EU, even if its intervention may have a different weight depending on the subject of the decision and the manner in which the CoR participates in the decision-making process.

The practical impact of the CoR can be appreciated by clarifying the nature of the CoR and the extent of its advisory functions provided for by Art. 307 of the Treaty on the Functioning of the European Union (TFEU) (ex 265 EC).

According to Art. 307, § 1, TFEU, the CoR is an advisory body to the European Parliament, the Council and the Commission in their adoption of legislation "where

[2]See N. PARISI, *Art. 263 EC*, in Pocar (2001), p. 893. The 42 members of the Council were appointed by the Commission: see Commission Decision of 24 June 1988, No. 487, Art. 3, § 2, in O.J.C.E., L 247, of 6 September 1988, pp. 23–25.

the Treaties so provide". In particular, there are subject matters (e.g. Economic and Social Cohesion or Environment; for a list of all the subject matters, see § 5 below), in which "consultation" of the CoR is mandatory. In such cases, the Commission and the Council are bound to request the opinion of the Committee. In the absence of such a request, the legislative act may be regarded as illegal on the grounds of the infringement of an essential procedural requirement. However, the Commission and the Council may come to the conclusion of the decision-making process without actually examining the opinion of the CoR. This may happen if they set a deadline within which the Committee will have to issue its opinion.[3] The rationale for this provision is that, in its absence, the Committee would have the power to endlessly delay the adoption of an act. In any case, it seems reasonable that the Committee does not lose the power to submit its opinion following the expiry of the time limit, where the Committee considers this opinion as useful in order to reach a decision. It must be underlined that the CoR's opinions are never binding on the institutions.[4] Even in those situations in which the opinion of the CoR is "mandatory" (i.e. it must be requested), this opinion is nonetheless non-binding and the institutions can depart from it.

The ToL gave the Committee the power to bring an action before the Court of Justice for the purpose of protecting its prerogatives (Art. 263, § 3, TFEU; ex 230 EC). This means that the advisory tasks of the CoR are judicially enforceable in case of mandatory opinions. The new version of the Rules of Procedure regulates actions that the CoR can bring in the case of a failure to carry out obligatory consultation of the Committee.[5]

Apart from those cases in which the opinion is "mandatory" by express provision of the Treaty, the CoR is entitled to issue an opinion on its own initiative (Art. 307, § 4, TFEU[6]), or on discretionary request coming from an institution. In fact, according to Art. 307, § 1, TFEU, the CoR "shall be consulted by the European Parliament, the Council or by the Commission where the Treaties so provide and in all other cases, in particular those which concern cross-border cooperation", but only if "one of these institutions considers it appropriate".

Finally, the Committee has to be informed about every request for an opinion which the institutions submit to the Economic and Social Committee, to assess if any issue of "specific regional interest" is involved that might require an opinion of the CoR (Art. 307, § 3, TFEU).

[3]According to Art. 307, § 2, TFEU, the time limit "may not be less than one month from the date on which the President receives notification to this effect", and "Upon expiry of the time limit, the absence of an opinion shall not prevent further action".

[4]N. PARISI, *Art. 265 EC*, in Pocar (2001), pp. 901–902.

[5]Art. 54 of the Rules of Procedure. The latest version of the Rules of Procedure of the CoR was adopted in 2010 (following the entry into force of the ToL): see *Rules of Procedure – Committee of the Regions*, in O.J.E.U., L 6 of 9 January 2010, pp. 14–31.

[6]Art. 307, § 4, TFEU, provides: "[The Committee] may issue an opinion on its own initiative in cases in which it considers such action appropriate".

C. Composition

The Committee of the Regions currently consists of 344 members and 344 alternate members. Its members must be "representatives of regional and local bodies who either hold a regional or local authority electoral mandate or are politically accountable to an elected assembly" (Art. 300, § 3, TFEU). They are appointed for 5 years (Art. 305, § 3, TFEU, ex 263 EC). The regional or local electoral mandate/accountability requirement was originally introduced by the Treaty of Nice in order to affirm and strengthen the democratic role of the Committee as a body representing the citizens. This rule limits the discretionary power of the Member States to influence the composition of the Committee.[7]

Neither the Treaties nor the Rules of Procedure of the Committee establish sufficient criteria to provide an equilibrium among regional and local authorities. The composition of the CoR does not take into account the difference between authorities with or without legislative power, or between regional and local authorities. Before the ToL, it was the EC Treaty that established the actual number of members of the CoR for each Member State.[8] Currently the composition of the Committee and the allocation of the representatives between the Member States (Art. 305, § 2, TFEU) is left to a unanimous decision by the Council upon a proposal from the Commission (in actuality, this is an agreement between the Member States).

The rationale for the existence of the Committee lies with the growing regional and local decentralisation of the Member States of the EU. The introduction of the CoR reflects the acknowledgment by the EU of the relevance of regional and local levels of government. It also reflects the obvious inadequacy of the original Community institutional setting which responded exclusively to the needs of national sovereignty and did not consider sub-state entities. From this point of view, the CoR may provide a significant opportunity for the EU to overcome its "Landesblindheit" (regional blindness).[9]

The large number of Committee members reflects the multitude of regional and local authorities in Europe and also the differences in their status in the Member States. This allegedly heterogeneous and plethoric composition may be seen as an

[7]Before the Treaty of Nice, legal scholarship was very critical of the previous text of Art. 263 EC extending the discretionary power of the Member States to the designation of "representatives of local and regional bodies", thus leaving unresolved the question regarding the necessity for an electoral mandate or for political accountability. See, e.g. Huici Sancho (2003), pp. 160–164.

[8]This is the allocation under former Art. 263, § 3, EC: Austria 12, Belgium 12, Bulgaria 12, Cyprus 6, Czech Republic 12, Denmark 9, Estonia 7, Finland 9, France 24, Germany 24, Greece 12, Hungary 12, Ireland 9, Italy 24, Luxembourg 6, Lithuania 9, Malta 5, Netherlands 12, Lettonia 7, Poland 21, Portugal 12, Romania 15, Slovakia 9, Slovenia 7, Spain 21; Sweden 12, United Kingdom 24.

[9]This is the view of Domenichelli (2007), p. 8. On the concept of "regional blindness" see Ipsen (1966), p. 248 ff.

advantage or a disadvantage depending on the activities the CoR performs. For instance, when adopting an opinion, it may be an obstacle to the achievement of a majority. At the same time, it allows the emergence of the interests of different sub-national levels of government.[10]

Art. 305, § 3, TFEU, regulates the procedure for the appointment of the CoR's members and provides that the members of the Committee and an equal number of alternate members shall be appointed by the Council in accordance with the proposals of each Member State. This ensures that the national procedures of selection are respected. In practice, each State proposes two lists of candidates, members and alternate members, and the Council does not make a real choice, but merely provides ratification for national decisions. In addition the Council approves the appointment of Committee members *by qualified majority* rather than unanimously as was the case in the past until the Treaty of Nice. It has been argued that the Council has substantially lost its power of appointment to the advantage of the growing autonomy of the Member States in this field. However, an intervention by the Council would be useful in order to ensure the general equilibrium of the Committee's composition (e.g. to ensure the proportion of local and regional bodies represented, or compliance with the principle of equal opportunities between men and women).[11]

The autonomy of the Member States in appointing the Committee members seems to be adherent to the principles of proximity and democracy. There appear to be two main reasons why this is the case. First, it would be contradictory to give the Council the task of democratic control given that the Council consists of representatives of the Executives of the Member States. Second, the discretion of the Member States when choosing the Committee members is limited by the provision (Art. 300, § 3, TFEU) according to which the Committee members must hold an electoral mandate at regional or local level or be politically accountable to an elected assembly.

As regards the independence of Committee members, Art. 300, § 4, TFEU, makes the following provision: "The members of the Committee of the Regions shall not be bound by any mandatory instructions. They shall be completely independent in the performance of their duties, in the Union's general interest". Such "independence" differs from the similar provision defining the status of the EU Commissioners according to Art. 245 TFEU (ex 213 EC). The Committee members have a democratic mandate and the fact that they are not bound by any mandatory instruction is a further recognition of the political nature of this body.

In conclusion, the rules governing the composition of the CoR seem to ensure respect for the principles of proximity and subsidiarity. This is a starting point in the effort to overcome the democratic deficit within the EU.

[10]See Domenichelli (2007), p. 21, for a summary of the opinions in the literature on this issue.
[11]Huici Sancho (2003), pp. 154–155.

D. Organisation

The Committee has full autonomy in relation to its internal organisation. Art. 306 TFEU (ex 264 EC) provides only for the CoR's President (called "chairman"), allowing the CoR to organise itself freely. Moreover, following the Amsterdam Treaty the Committee now has the right to pass its own Rules of Procedure without any external intervention by the Council.

According to the Rules of Procedure, the constituent bodies of the CoR are the Plenary Assembly, the President, the Bureau, and the commissions. We should also note that the national delegations and the political groups originally emerged in the functioning praxis of the Committee and are now provided for by the Rules of Procedure. The internal organisation of the CoR thus resembles that of a parliamentary assembly, suggesting the idea of a chamber of representatives of the local and regional interests. This is in addition to the representation of the people in the European Parliament. As in many other assemblies, the President, who is appointed for two and half years, takes a pre-eminent institutional role. He directs the work of the Committee and is the Committee's representative.

The Plenary Assembly (PA) is primarily a deliberative body, whose main tasks are the adoption of opinions, reports and resolutions. The PA also approves the draft estimates of expenditure and revenue of the Committee and the CoR's political programme. The PA is responsible for: the election of the President of the Committee, the first Vice-President and the remaining members of the Bureau, the setting up of the various commissions of the CoR, the adoption and amendment of the Rules of Procedure, and also for bringing cases before the ECJ upon a proposal by the President of the Committee[12] (see § 2 and § 7.7 on the right of the CoR to bring a direct action for annulment before the ECJ).

The activity of the PA in relation to the adoption of its main acts (opinions, reports, and resolutions) is supported by the commissions. They are internal bodies aimed at organising the work of the Committee according to the principle of specialisation. Indeed each CoR commission is vested with a particular field of action.[13] The commissions debate the EU policies and draw up the draft versions of the opinions, reports and resolutions, before the final discussion and vote take place in the plenum.[14] Each CoR member must belong to at least one commission

[12]Art. 13 of the Rules of Procedure.

[13]The CoR commissions are: COTER-Commission for Territorial Cohesion; ECOS-Commission for Economic and Social Policy; DEVE-Commission for Sustainable Development; EDUC-Commission for Culture, Education and Research; CONST-Commission for Constitutional Affairs, European Governance and the Area of Freedom, Security and Justice; RELEX-Commission for External Relations and Decentralised Cooperation. There is also the Committee for Administrative and Financial Affairs and an ad hoc Temporary Commission on the European Budget Review.

[14]Art. 47 of the Rules of Procedure. Art. 26 of the Rules of Procedure provides for "Simplified procedures" for the approval of opinions and reports. It establishes that draft opinions or reports can be submitted to the Plenary Assembly for approval without change if adopted unanimously by a lead commission. In this case a debate can still take place in the Plenary Assembly. The lead

(but to no more than two) and the composition of the commissions must proportionally reflect the national (but not necessarily the political) composition of the Committee.[15]

The element of nationality, in addition to featuring in the composition of the Assembly and the commissions, is also important for another reason. The previously consolidated provision for national delegations (which were considered as an almost "natural" element of the internal organisation of the Committee) gives each national delegation a particular role.[16] The national delegations offer an important opportunity in strengthening the subsidiarity principle. In fact, they can become an internal forum that may foster the punctual representation of the different regional and local authorities of a Member State. They may also assist in the resolution of potential conflicts of interest among local and regional bodies of a Member State on a subject dealt with by the CoR and so promote collaboration between the different levels of government.

All Committee members are entitled to express their political orientation. This explains the presence of political groups within the Committee and is consistent with the principle of democracy. The political groups[17] are freely constituted by the members and alternates of the CoR, which "may form" groups according to the conditions laid down in the Rules of Procedure. These establish criteria to guarantee the proportion between the number of members of each group and the number of Member States represented in the same group (cf. Art. 9, § 2, of the Rules of Procedure).

The provisions of the Rules of Procedure regarding national delegations and political groups have put an end to a rather heated debate about their existence. This debate originally arose from the fear of a possible alteration of the role of the Committee and of an overlap with the representative role of the European Parliament.[18] The Rules of Procedure contain a remnant of this debate where they prescribe that "National delegations and political groups shall help in a balanced way with the organisation of the Committee's work" (Art. 7 of the Rules of Procedure). As a consequence, delegations and groups have to contribute to ensure an adequate representation of regional and local interests within the Committee.

commission can propose that the approval of an opinion by the Plenary Assembly takes place without preliminary debate. This is only possible if the lead commission is of the view that the Plenary Assembly would not raise any objections.

[15]Art. 45, § 2, of the Rules of Procedure. Art. 45, § 3, confirms the proportionality of the commissions when it stipulates that "Exceptions [to the belonging of each Committee member to at least one commission but no more than two] may be made by the Bureau for members belonging to national delegations which have fewer members than the number of commissions".

[16]Art. 8 of the Rules of Procedure provides that "The members and alternates from each member State shall form a national delegation".

[17]There are four political groups: European People's Party (EPP), Party of European Socialists (PES), Alliance of Liberals and Democrats for Europe (ALDE), Union for Europe of the Nations – European Alliance (UEN-EA).

[18]On this debate, see Huici Sancho (2003), p. 180 ff.

All the aforementioned bodies are involved in the work of the Bureau. The Bureau is composed of the President, one first Vice-president, one Vice-president per Member State, the chairs of the political groups, and 27 members divided among the national delegations.[19]

The duties of the Bureau are fundamental for the functioning of the plenum and of the Committee in general. The Bureau establishes its policy programme and submits this to the Plenary Assembly. It then monitors its implementation and, at the end of its term, submits a report on the implementation of the programme to the Plenary Assembly. It also organises and coordinates the work of the Assembly and adopts the commissions' working programme. The Bureau is also responsible for financial, organisational and administrative matters concerning members and alternates, and in general for the internal organisation of the Committee. In particular, the Committee is assisted by a Secretariat-General with executive tasks and the Bureau is responsible for the organisation of the Secretariat-General "in such a way that it can ensure the efficient functioning of the Committee and its constituent bodies" (see Art. 66, § 3, of the Rules of Procedure).[20]

Finally, in the organisation of the CoR, the principle of partnership between different Regions is recognised, where the Rules of Procedure provide that "Members and alternates may form interregional groups".[21] However, the role and function of such groups are not further specified in the Rules of Procedure but in a Committee decision (CdR of 13 February 2007, No. 23). The interregional groups are composed of at least ten members of the CoR belonging to at least four national delegations or belonging to a group of Regions working on the basis of an international agreement promoting trans-border cooperation. Each group is approved by a decision of the Bureau. Since then the Bureau has approved eight groups: "Saar-Lor-Lux", "Wine", "Regions with Legislative Power", "Baltic Sea Regions", "Mediterranean", "Danube", "North Sea" and "Crisis in the car industry". Some groups are set up in order to coordinate the different Regions in the development of the European policies (e.g. the group "Saar-Lor-Lux" or the group "Baltic Sea Regions", or also the group "Mediterranean"). Some groups are set up in order to achieve specific goals. An important example of the latter is the group "Regions with Legislative Power". The aim of this group is to take the initiative in

[19] See Art. 28 of the Rules of Procedure.

[20] Moreover the Bureau may (Art. 36 of the Rules of Procedure):

(a) "Set up working groups of Bureau members or of Committee members to advise it in specific areas" and "invite other members of the Committee, by virtue of their expertise or mandate, and persons not belonging to the Committee, to attend its meetings".
(b) Engage the Secretary General and the officials and other servants listed in Rules 69.
(c) Submit the draft estimates of expenditure and revenue to the Plenary Assembly in accordance with Rule 72.
(d) Authorize meetings away from the usual place of work.
(e) Draw up provisions for the membership and working methods of working groups and of joint committees with applicant countries.

[21] Art. 10 of the Rules of Procedure.

order to promote better EU legislation and European multilevel governance, with specific attention to the monitoring of the implementation of the subsidiarity principle. Some groups have more of a circumscribed impact, e.g. the group "Wine" which promotes the monitoring of wine policy in the interest of wine-producing regions, or the group "Crisis in the car Industry" (set up in April 2009). The interregional groups do not replace the political groups. The latter bring the CoR members together and coordinate their actions in accordance to their political orientation. One may argue that they are a direct expression of the principle of democracy. Instead the interregional groups bring the CoR members together and coordinate their activities on the basis of their territorial belonging. This is an expression of the principles of subsidiarity and proximity.

E. Tasks

It is appropriate, after describing its composition and organisation, to analyse the tasks of the CoR. The non-binding force of the CoR's opinions, together with its right to intervene in every subject matter it considers appropriate, urges us to focus our attention on the praxis rather than the rules. We must do so in order to evaluate the effectiveness of the role played by the CoR in the inter-institutional equilibrium within the European Union.

The Treaty on the Functioning of the EU requires an opinion of the Committee in relation to the following policies: Transport (Art. 91, § 1); Employment (Art. 148, § 2, and 149, § 1); Social policy (Art. 153, § 2); Education, Vocational training, Youth and Sport (Art. 165, § 4, and 166, § 4); Culture (Art. 167, § 5); Public health (Art. 168, § 4); Trans-European networks (Art. 172); Economic, social and territorial cohesion (Art. 175, § 3, 177, § 1, and 178, § 1); Environment (Art. 192, §§ 1, 2, and 3). All the aforementioned subjects were within the sphere of competence of the CoR before the entry into force of the ToL. The ToL increased the number and the range of policies in which the opinion of the CoR is required. To the areas detailed, the ToL added the following: Sea and air transport (Art. 100, §2, TFEU; within the framework of the Transport policy); a number of measures aimed at protecting public health (Art. 168, § 5, TFEU; within the framework of the Public health policy); extension of the ordinary legislative procedure to some areas of environmental protection (Art. 192, § 2, TFEU; within the framework of the Environment policy); and Energy policy (Art. 194, § 2. TFEU). In these fields, the Union acts in the exercise of shared competences; therefore, according to Art. 5 of the Treaty on European Union (TEU; ex Art. 5 EC), the subsidiarity principle plays a decisive role.

In addition to the specified fields, the CoR has a residual area of intervention. It is entitled to submit an opinion in any other area on its own initiative or on the basis of a discretionary request from an EU institution. This may happen whenever local and regional interests are involved. In this area (which potentially includes all Union policies), the CoR's intervention may take forms other than providing an opinion and it may consist of the adoption of resolutions and in the drafting of reports.[22] More specifically, resolutions are adopted only on issues of "topical interest" (Art. 43, § 1, Rules of Procedure). For example, the CoR adopted a resolution on the financial crisis (CdR 379/2008) and another on the climate change (CdR 179/2008).

The field of intervention of the CoR is therefore potentially unlimited. This fact represents both great opportunity and great risk. On the one hand, the CoR can intervene in every Union policy of significant impact on regional and local interests, allowing the CoR to make the most of its role as a representative of local and regional authorities. On the other hand, its potentially unlimited field of intervention may represent the CoR's weakness, if the Committee fails to take action or to achieve tangible results in the interest of regional and local authorities.

In relation to the role of the CoR in the context of multilevel governance, it must be highlighted that the 2001 White Paper's main objective is to strengthen the relationship between the Commission and the sub-state entities. The rationale is to overcome part of the democratic deficit of the EU through stronger involvement of the regional and local authorities in the EU decision-making process. Primarily, this goal is pursued via the introduction of direct communication between the Commission and the regional and local authorities. This is essentially the consultation of these authorities before the formulation of legislative proposals and policies by the Commission. Direct channels of communication are more specifically: the consultation of the associations of regional and local authorities by the Commission, the promotion of the "structured dialogue", and the experimentation of tripartite contracts.[23] The White Paper's (that is the Commission's) preference for a "direct" approach did not emerge suddenly; in fact, regional and local authorities (and their associations) have developed several forms of direct communication with the EU institutions over time.[24] With its role of institutional consultation and its representative nature, the CoR rather constitutes a means of "indirect communication" completing the model of multilevel governance designed by the 2001White Paper.

The existence of direct channels between EU institutions and local and regional levels of government operate in parallel to the intervention of the CoR. This situation urges the Committee to extend its field of intervention beyond institutional consultation and to re-think its overall role in order to prevent a deprivation of its authority. The following analysis of the activities of the CoR will show that the CoR is fully aware of the risk of its exclusion from the EU decision-making process.

[23]The tripartite contracts are binding agreements among the Union, a State and a local or regional authority for the achievement of specific goals, especially in the field of the environment or of social and economic cohesion (see Communication of the Commission COM (2002) 709 of 11 December 2002). The use of tripartite contracts has not proven very successful so far.

[24]There are various organisations of regional and local authorities: general, such as the Council of European Municipalities and Regions or the Assembly of European Regions, or sector-based, such as the Conference of European Regions with Legislative Power, or the Conference of European Regional Legislative Assemblies. For an overview see Domenichelli (2007), p. 31 ff. In addition it must be highlighted that there are the regional liaison offices in Brussels.

F. Political Priorities

The CoR's activities are based on its "political priorities".[25] Therefore, before analysing the activities of the CoR, it is appropriate to introduce this concept. The political priorities are adopted by means of a Resolution of the Plenary Assembly and cover a period of 3 years. They consist of a list of fields of intervention, each followed by specific goals. This list of priorities is notified to the Commission, the European Parliament, the Council and every President of the Union in the period concerned. These general criteria of orientation are the basis for the definition of the agenda of the commissions, of the Bureau and of any other internal organisational body of the CoR.[26]

The transparency of this operation may contribute to ensuring that the actions of the CoR have a more effective impact by focusing the attention of the institutions on the CoR's priorities and by compelling the members of the Committee to share some general goals. In addition the CoR may also take into account some "further topics which may be considered relevant to its priorities following the EU and EU presidencies agenda".[27]

G. Activities

I. Cooperation with Associations of Local and Regional Authorities

According to the indications of the 2001 White Paper on European Governance, a key role of the CoR is to improve collaboration with some of the major European associations of local and regional authorities. To that end, since 2003, the CoR has

---

[25]See the document Committee of the Regions (2010).

[26]The political priorities for the period 2008–2010, are the following: "• Implementing the Lisbon agenda's goals for growth and jobs through the involvement of RLAs and making their voice heard by the European Council; • facing the challenge of climate change and diversification and sustainable use of energy resources; • participating in the inter-institutional exercise for the EU budgetary review stressing the need for reorganising the CAP – making it possible to maintain sustainable agriculture and food autonomy, and shaping the economic, social and territorial cohesion policy beyond 2013 – emphasising its leverage effect; • improving the quality of life of citizens, including facilitating cross-border cooperation for civil protection and access to better quality health services; • giving the necessary platform to RLAs to promote solidarity, intercultural and interfaith dialogue, as well as promoting all forms of regional culture and traditions; • taking part in the European debate towards a common policy on immigration and asylum and in particular exchanging the best practices on integration; • proposing a modern single market with a strategy to promote the quality of social services; • assisting and cooperating with RLAs of candidate and pre-candidate countries on their journey towards the EU": see Committee of the Regions (2010), p. 6.

[27]See Committee of the Regions (2010), p. 6.

adopted "Action plans". The "Action plans" are agreements between the CoR and single associations defining areas of collaboration with the CoR.[28]

II. Debate Europe

This activity started following the Commission's *Plan D for Democracy, Dialogue and Debate* (2005) and the Commission's *White Paper on a European communication policy* (2006). These were both adopted in the context of the reflection period, opened by the institutions after the failure of the ratification of the Treaty establishing a Constitution for Europe. The CoR has been vested with the important role of promoting EU proximity to European citizens, involving the local and regional authorities in the framework of a renewed model of communication based on Decentralisation (a fourth "D" in addition to Democracy, Dialogue and Debate). Indeed, the CoR, often in partnership with the Commission, has organised many communication events[29] in municipalities or in regional or other local authorities' sites in the Member States.

III. Lisbon Strategy

In 2006, after the launch of the Lisbon Strategy for Growth and Jobs, the CoR created the Lisbon Monitoring Platform (LMP), the purpose of which is to assess the contribution of local and regional authorities to the Lisbon Strategy. The involvement of the CoR aims to ensure that local employment and development policies are taken into consideration at national and EU level. The instruments of the European cohesion policy are strictly linked to the objectives of the Lisbon Strategy. Both in the political priorities of the CoR and in its activities there many elements which reflect the aims of the Lisbon Strategy.

For the achievement of the Lisbon Strategy's goals, the CoR created a network for local and regional levels of government by promoting thematic workshops and by creating a "virtual community" through the use of a website (http://lisbon.cor.europa.eu). This network monitors the opinions of more than 100 local and regional

---

[28]The report for 2007, available from the web site of the CoR http://cor.europa.eu (last checked on 15 June 2010), p. 1, lists the areas of cooperation as follows: "Involvement of association expertise in selected task forces set up by the CoR in order to support the work of the rapporteurs, cooperation in the dialogue between the European Commission and the Associations, participation in joint conferences, cooperation in Subsidiarity monitoring, cooperation on Regional Policy, Territorial Cooperation and the Lisbon Strategy, joint activities in Communication".

[29]For a list, see the web site of the CoR http://cor.europa.eu/pages/EventTemplate.aspx?view=folder&id=1bc1444b-9a12-4411-a559-aea8aaf1a3a1&sm=1bc1444b-9a12-4411-a559-aea8aaf1a3a1. Last checked on 15 June 2010.

members about the impact of the Lisbon strategy on their employment and development policies. It also allows the collection and exchange of experiences and best practices in that domain.

IV. Multilevel Governance

"Multilevel governance" is an initiative of the CoR laid down in the CoR's political programme for 2008–2010. The objective of the Committee is to take on a leading role in researching and promoting models of European governance by involving the local and regional authorities at an early stage of the EU decision making. This is expected to bring about improved proximity between citizens and European institutions.

In June 2009, the CoR published the *White Paper on Multilevel Governance.*[30] The strategic goals of the *White Paper* are twofold: to promote participation in the EU decision-making process and to strengthen the effectiveness of Union action. "Multilevel governance" is defined as "coordinated action by the European Union, the Member States and local and regional authorities, based on partnership and aimed at drawing up and implementing EU policies" .[31] In this document, the CoR outlines its role as a political player representing regional and local authorities. The most important objective of multilevel governance is not the preservation of the existing distribution of competences between the different levels of government. Instead, it is the creation of a system of European governance characterised by the participation of all levels of government in the definition and implementation of Union policies. Multilevel governance emphasises the interaction between the competences whereas the principle of subsidiarity is concerned with their rational allocation.[32]

In the CoR *White Paper*, the theme of participation of local and regional authorities in the European governance is complemented by the proposal of "responsibility being shared between the different tiers of government".[33] The CoR envisages a profound transformation in the way EU policies should be formulated. According to the CoR, local and regional authorities should be involved in the definition of the political priorities at EU level. This is the only way to improve the definition of these political priorities and is ultimately the best way to enhance the efficiency and effectiveness of EU action. This is why the *White*

[30]Committee of the Regions (2009).

[31]*White Paper on Multilevel Governance*, p. 1.

[32]*White Paper on Multilevel Governance*, p. 7.

[33]*White Paper on Multilevel Governance*, p. 1.

Paper devotes a great deal of attention to this problem.[34] To this purpose, old and new proposals have been submitted by the CoR; from monitoring subsidiarity to implementing territorial cohesion, from evaluating the territorial impact of EU policies to establishing "European territorial pacts". The *White Paper* recommends the adoption of policies by the Union in line with the practical experience gained by local and regional authorities.[35] If put into practice, the *White Paper*'s recommendations would enhance the proximity of the Union to its citizens and promote better governance.

V. Structured Dialogue

The idea of Structured Dialogue is founded on a Commission communication adopted in 2003 following the White Paper on European Governance and the Commission's consequent initiatives to promote a culture of consultation and dialogue.[36] This Communication lays down "the frameworks, goals and modalities governing this dialogue with associations of regional and local authorities". From this act, Structured Dialogue emerges as a particular consultation method complementary to the institutional EU decision-making process. The purpose of the Structured Dialogue is to produce a systematic and immediate collaboration between the Commission and the associations of regional and local authorities. This is "to give the parties in question the opportunity to express their views" face to face at an early stage of the definition of the EU policies, before the decision-making process starts with the presentation of a legislative proposal.

The Communication gives the CoR the task of identifying (according to the established criteria) which associations of regional and local authorities the Commission should consult. This is to avoid the failure of the consultation process due to inappropriate and/or excessive participation. It is then within the responsibility of the Commission to organise dialogue meetings with the associations admitted. The Commission has the right to consult other associations in addition to those selected by the Committee.

This new task of the CoR led to the development of stronger ties between the Committee and regional and local authorities. However, the Committee's role appears a fairly formal rather than an active one. In fact, it is limited to putting the Commission and the regional and local authorities in contact with each other.

---

[34]*White Paper on Multilevel Governance*, pp. 18–34.

[35]*White Paper on Multilevel Governance*, p. 18.

[36]Commission's Communication "Dialogue with associations of regional and local authorities on the formulation on European policy", COM(2003) 811, 19 December 2003.

VI. The European Grouping of Territorial Cooperation

In accordance with Art. 175 TFEU (ex 159 EC), the CoR has actively promoted and supported the EU initiative to establish "European groupings of territorial cooperation" (hereinafter referred to as EGTCs). This is the final result of the efforts of the CoR to find a tool capable of improving regional cooperation. As such it is based on the longstanding experience of the Committee with supporting activities.[37]

EC Regulation No. 1082/2006 of the European Parliament and the Council of 5 July 2006 lays down the rules for the establishment of an EGTC. An EGTC may be composed of regional and local authorities, central governments, bodies governed by public law and associations from at least two Member States; its objective is "to facilitate and promote cross-border, transnational and/or interregional cooperation ... with the exclusive aim of strengthening economic and social cohesion". Its role is primarily linked to "the implementation of territorial cooperation programmes or projects co-financed by the Community through the European Regional Development Fund, the European Social Fund and/or the Cohesion Fund", but it may also carry out "other specific actions of territorial cooperation between its members in pursuit of the objective" mentioned above "with or without a financial contribution from the Community" (thus, for example, also for European Resources and Development programmes). Moreover, an EGTC is vested with legal personality, which is acquired after the registration and/or publication of its statute (Art. 1 of EC Regulation No. 1082/2006).

According to Art. 5, § 1, of the Regulation, the members of an EGTC shall inform the CoR of the agreement and of the registration and/or the publication of the statute. The CoR has a special consultative role in the matter of territorial cooperation as per Art. 175 TFEU. The Committee monitors the implementation of the Regulation and the practical experiences of EGTCs established in the Member States.[38]

VII. The Committee and the Principle of Subsidiarity

The CoR is actively involved in the implementation of the principle of subsidiarity with the aim of establishing a real "subsidiarity culture" in Europe. With the entry into force of the Treaty of Lisbon, the CoR consolidated its role as "subsidiarity watchdog". In addition to its consultative role in the EU legislative process, the CoR has now the right to challenge an EU legislative act on grounds of an

[37]For more information about the supporting activities of the CoR, see the website http://www.cor.europa.eu (last checked on 15 June 2010).

[38]For further information on the creation of EGTCs see the web page http://www.cor.europa.eu/egtc (last checked on 15 June 2010).

infringement of the principle of subsidiarity (Art. 8 § 2 of the *Protocol on the Application of the Principles of Subsidiarity and Proportionality* annexed to the Treaty of Lisbon, hereafter Subsidiarity Protocol). This only applies to those EU legislative acts for whose adoption the consultation of the Committee is mandatory.

Yet the CoR does not seem to have a great deal of confidence in the effectiveness of judicial control. This is because the CoR regards subsidiarity as a political principle and as such judicially unenforceable. As Barber suggests, the view of the CoR is that "to make use of subsidiarity ... runs against the spirit of the Court" as "the broad ethos of the Court is to favour action at the Community [now the Union: Ed.] level over action at the Member State level".[39]

But such self-restraint could be abandoned by the ECJ now that the ToL is in force. The CoR's power to react to an infringement of the principle of subsidiarity could encourage the ECJ to develop judicial control. In addition, the "early warning procedure" (Arts. 6–7 of the Subsidiarity Protocol) could also persuade the ECJ to depart from its traditional "light touch" approach.[40]

At the same time, the CoR's right to bring an action for infringement of the subsidiarity principle adds new life to the consultative role of the CoR. The CoR stated that "adding in CoR's opinions a specific reference to subsidiarity and proportionality would, where possible, strengthen the possibilities of success of eventual legal action before the Court of Justice".[41] The close link between the participation of the CoR in the legislative process and the action for infringement of the subsidiarity principle is further highlighted by the Rules of Procedure (Art. 53 § 1): "The President of the Committee or the commission responsible for drawing up the draft opinion may propose bringing an action before the Court of Justice". The Plenary Assembly has the final decision on whether or not to bring an action for infringement of subsidiarity.[42]

When performing its consultative role, the CoR has the duty to express its point of view on the compliance of a legislative proposal with the principle of subsidiarity.[43] The CoR's opinions help the law-making institutions to produce legislation which is respectful of this principle. For this purpose the CoR has "vested the

[39]See Barber (2005, p. 199).

[40]On the "early warning procedure" see the thorough analysis by Piet Van Nuffel in Chap. III of this book.

[41]See http://www.cor.europa.eu, under "Subsidiarity Monitoring for COR rapporteurs" (last checked on 15 June 2010).

[42]If the Plenary Assembly is not able to convene in time to decide whether or not to bring a case, this decision is taken by the Bureau and it requires confirmation by the Plenary Assembly. If the Assembly does not confirm the decision of the Bureau, the application for judicial review will be withdrawn (cf. Art. 53 of the Rules of Procedure).

[43]Art. 51, § 2, of the Rules of Procedure states: "Committee opinions shall contain an explicit reference to the application of the subsidiarity and proportionality principles". At § 3 the same article states that: "The opinions and reports shall also, wherever possible, address the expected impact on administration and regional and local finances".

Bureau with the power to check that legislation proposed by the Commission in areas where consultation of the CoR is mandatory is compatible with the principles of subsidiarity and proportionality".[44] It has also prepared the "Subsidiarity Grid", a sort of pro forma providing guidance on how to analyse the Commission's proposals and made this available to its rapporteurs (whose task is to draw up draft opinions and reports on behalf of a commission: see Art. 56 of the Rules of Procedure). One of the sections of the "Grid" requires the rapporteurs to examine whether the proposals have taken the regional and local interests sufficiently into account and requires them to assess the extent and depth of the consultations made by the Commission.[45]

The CoR pursues the objective to "focus its action on the pre-legislative phase and act in advance, mainly through early consultation".[46] In relation to this, the CoR promotes contacts between the regional and local authorities and the Commission when legislative proposals are being drafted.

In 2005 the CoR created an interactive website called "Subsidiarity Monitoring Network" (SMN) "in order to facilitate the exchange of information between local and regional authorities of the European Union as regards the various policy documents and proposals of the European Commission".[47] The SMN is a sort of public forum available to regional and local authorities which gives them an opportunity for continuing consultation prior to the adoption of any EU act potentially affecting them. The project was launched in two trial phases in 2005 and 2006[48] and has been operative since 2007. The SMN confirms the existence of a "procedural" facet of the principle of subsidiarity characterised by early consultation of all the levels of government concerned. The same "philosophy" is the basis of the "early warning procedure". It is submitted that the principle of subsidiarity would be best implemented through "procedures" which ensure consultation and, if this is the case, agreements between the different levels of government. Agreements would be of particular importance when the application of the principle leads to the attribution of a competence to the Union. These agreements would ensure that the

[44] See CoR's Opinion of 16 November 2005, *Guidelines for the application and monitoring of the subsidiarity and proportionality principle*, CdR 220-2004_fin_ac_en_doc, of 16 November 2005, par. 3.13, p. 9, available at http://www.cor.europa.eu (last checked on 15 June 2010).

[45] See "Subsidiarity & Proportionality Assessment Grid", Section 5, available at http://www.cor.europa.eu (last checked on 15 June 2010).

[46] See the CoR's Opinion on *Guidelines for the application and monitoring of the subsidiarity and proportionality principles*, footnote 39, at p. 3.

[47] See the document CoR's Annual Activity Report 2007 (p. 7) available at http://www.cor.europa.eu (last checked on 15 June 2010); the SMN took off on the basis of two of the CoR's opinions: Opinion on *Better lawmaking 2004*, CdR 121-2005_fin_ac_en_doc, of 12 October 2005, and the CoR's Opinion on *Guidelines for the application and monitoring of the subsidiarity and proportionality principles*, footnote 39.

[48] See the Report on the first test of the SMN, Executive summary, CdR 5-2006_fin_ac_en_doc, and the Report on the second test of the SMN, CdR 2-2007_fin_ac_en_doc, in www.cor.europa.eu.

attribution of a competence to the Union is "accepted" by the other levels of government and is not "imposed" on them.[49]

The Subsidiarity Protocol confirms the importance of direct consultation at an early stage of the decision-making process by affirming that "Before proposing legislative acts, the Commission shall consult widely".[50] Moreover the new definition of the subsidiarity principle in the Treaty on the European Union is complemented by the stipulation that: "National Parliaments ensure compliance with the principle of subsidiarity in accordance with the procedure set out in that Protocol [that is, the Subsidiarity Protocol]".[51] This is the foundation of the "early warning" procedure regulated by the Subsidiarity Protocol. Art. 6 of the Protocol allows any national parliament to send a reasoned opinion on draft legislative proposals within 8 weeks from the transmission date of the draft "stating why it considers that the draft in question does not comply with the principle of subsidiarity". Those regional parliaments with legislative powers may be consulted on the initiative of the national parliament. If the quorum of at least one third of all the votes allocated to national parliaments (two votes for each parliament) is achieved, this procedure obliges the Commission to reconsider the draft legislative act. However, the Commission is not obliged to withdraw the proposal and it would still have the option to amend it or to maintain it in its current form.[52]

H. Impact Analysis of the Action of the Committee

In order to foster the achievement of its goals, the CoR monitors its activity by drafting reports aimed at the assessment of its political influence. These documents show in detail each activity or initiative taken by the Committee, outlining their themes, objectives and results. The reports offer an account of the impact that the opinions of the CoR have had in the decision-making process. They provide details on whether the EU institutions acknowledged the issues raised by the Committee.[53] For example, they state that members of the Commission have pledged to follow the opinion of the CoR on a given matter. They detail official documents of the European Parliament reacting to the CoR's opinion or highlight the total lack of

[49]Consultation and agreements are required in Italy in order to allow the exercise of competences of the Regions by the State on the basis of the principle of subsidiarity. This "procedural" solution to the application of the principle of subsidiarity was for the first time envisaged by the Italian Constitutional Court in the Ruling No. 303 of 1 October 2003.

[50]Art. 2 of the Subsidiarity Protocol.

[51]Art. 5, § 3, subparagraph 2, TEU.

[52]Art. 7, § 2, of the Subsidiarity Protocol.

[53]See the Assessment of political influence of the CoR and the various *Impact Assessment Report(s)* in http://www.cor.europa.eu (last checked on 15 June 2010).

reaction by an institution.[54] Overall, there seems to be a reasonable degree of consistency between the reports on the activity of the CoR and its stated political priorities. The reports clearly demonstrate the engagement of the CoR in performing its consultative role at a very early stage in the decision-making process.

Furthermore, the CoR may adopt opinions on matters of general interest on which the Commission has yet to decide its own position ("outlook opinions"). In these specific cases, it is not easy to assess the immediate impact of the consultative action of the CoR. Theoretically, the outlook opinions provide a good opportunity for the CoR to influence the EU decision-making process.[55]

I. Final Remarks: The Role of the Committee in the European Governance

The 2001 *White Paper on the European Governance* acknowledged the relevance of the regional and local authorities by promoting the development of direct channels of communication between them and the Commission. In fact these direct channels were developed prior the 2001 *White Paper*.

The 2001 White Paper highlighted that the sole institutional tasks of the CoR are not sufficient in offering regional and local governments the opportunity to express their point of view in the EU decision-making process. The advisory tasks of the CoR should be the final stage in a wider consultation process directly involving regional and local bodies and EU institutions. It is submitted that the effectiveness of the opinions of the CoR may be fostered by this process of direct consultation. The CoR should therefore find a new role as promoter of a "multilevel network" in the context of the European governance.

The Committee's desire to play a role in the European governance can be seen in several initiatives linked to the 2001 White Paper (namely, the activity "Multilevel Governance", started in 2008, and "Structured Dialogue", expressly mentioned in

[54]E.g. see, *Review of the CoR Political impact*, 2008, available at http://www.cor.europa.eu, p. 2 (last checked on 15 June 2010).

[55]See Domenichelli (2007), pp. 136–137. The topics of the outlook opinions in the last reviews of political impact of the CoR are: *Multilingualism*, Outlook Opinion, CdR 6-2008_fin_ac_en_doc; *Education and Awareness-Raising Promoting Sustainable Development*, Outlook Opinion, CdR 127-2007_fin_ac_en_doc; *Common Agricultural policy Health Check,* Outllook opinion, CdR 197-2007_fin_ac_en_doc; *Future of the single market and stocktaking of European Society*, Outlook Opinion, CdR 339-2006_fin_ac_en_doc; *Success Factor for Local and Regional Restructuring Strategies,* Outlook Opinion, CdR 340-2006_fin_ac_en_doc; *The situation of Migrant women in the European Union*, Outlook Opinion, CdR 396-2006_fin_ac_en_doc; *The Contribution of Local and Regional Authorities to the European Union's Sustainable Development Strategy*, CdR 85-2007_fin_ac_en_doc, all available at http://www.cor.europa.eu under "Opinions and Resolutions" (last checked on 15 June 2010).

the Commission's White Paper). This desire also materialises as a recurring objective to establish "networks" between regional and local authorities ("horizontal network") and/or with the EU institutions ("vertical network") in almost all the Committee's activities. It is apparent that the Committee is departing from its traditional image as a "chamber of the regions" with an advisory role in the decision-making process.

The CoR favours the involvement of regional and local authorities in the EU decision-making process at an early stage. This should happen in the phase of the elaboration of Union draft acts through the promotion of direct consultation by the Commission with these authorities. This form of involvement is important in order to ensure respect for the subsidiarity principle by the lawmaking EU institutions and in order to compel these institutions to achieve an acceptable equilibrium between the powers of the EU, the Member States and the sub-state entities.

The CoR is an epiphany of participatory democracy. All the activities which form the real core of the CoR's action pursue the goal to provide the decision of the institutions with the broadest possible degree of inclusion and legitimacy. This is the case of the promotion of communication and collaboration between the sub-state authorities among themselves ("horizontal cooperation") and with the EU institutions ("vertical cooperation"). The consultative tasks of the CoR have the same objective.[56] It is true that there are elements of representative democracy in both the composition and the organisation of the CoR: for example, the presence of political groups within the Committee and the requirement of an electoral mandate for membership of the CoR.

The development of forms of communication and collaboration between sub-state entities and EU institutions is not sufficient for the creation of a fully democratic Union.[57] More specifically the proximity of the EU to its citizens is still far from having been achieved if one is measuring it by the allegiance of the citizens to the Union and/or by their comprehension of and participation in its decisions. This is despite the effort by the ToL to strengthen the CoR's ability to promote the principle of proximity.

In the *White Paper on Multilevel Governance* the CoR appears to suggest an adjustment of European governance through the proposal of "shared responsibility". The involvement of local and regional autonomies is expected to bring about a more effective democratic participation of EU citizens in the life of the Union. However the CoR is merely an "indirect" channel for the establishment of Union–citizens proximity. It would be an excellent result if future action of the CoR contributes to making Union policies more respondent to the needs of sub-national communities. But it is doubtful whether this result alone would be sufficient to "convey" the Union to its citizens in a way that ensures that Union political decisions are perceived by the citizens as "their own".

---

[56]On the possible development of participatory democracy after the entry into force of the ToL see Cuesta Lopez (2010), p. 123 ff.

[57]On the difference between European governance and democracy see Tsakatika (2007), p. 867 ff.

Selected Bibliography

Barber NW (2005) Subsidiarity in the draft constitution. Eur Publ Law:197–205
Blanke HJ (2002) Der Ausschuss der Regionen. Normative Ausgestaltung, Politische Rolle und verwaltungsorganisatorische Infrastuktur. Europäisches Zentrum für Föderalismus, Tübingen
Calonge Velasquez A, Sanz Rubiales I (2000) El comité del las regiones: anàlisi de una futura instituciòn? Granada, Comares
Committee of the Regions (2009) White Paper on Multilevel Governance, 17–18 June 2009. http://www.cor.europa.eu. Accessed 15 Jun 2010
Committee of the Regions (2010) Political Priorities for the Period 2008–2010. http://www.cor.europa.eu. Accessed 15 Jan 2010
Cuesta Lopez V (2010) The Lisbon treaty's provisions on democratic principles: a legal framework for participatory democracy. Eur Publ Law:123
Domenichelli L (2007) Le Regioni nella Costituzione Europea. Elogio delle virtù nascoste della consultazione. Giuffré, Milano
Ipsen HP (1966) Als Bundesstaat in der Gemeinschaft. In: Caemmerer EV et al (eds) Probleme des europäischen Rechts. FS Hallstein, Frankfurt, p 248
Moreno Vasquez M (2001) Comité de las regiones y Union Europea: su incidencia en las Comunidades Autonomas. Tirant lo Blanch, Valencia
Pankiewicz AW (2001) Realtà regionali ed Unione Europea: il comitato delle regioni. Giuffrè, Milano
Pocar F (ed) (2001) Commentario breve ai Trattati dell'Unione Europea. CEDAM, Padova, p 893
Sancho LH (2003) El Comité de Las Regiones: su función en el proceso de intergración europea. Universitat de Barcelona, Barcelona
Staub BP (2004) Il ruolo del comitato delle Regioni alla luce del nuovo Trattato Costituzionale Europeo. Parlamenti Regionali:134
Tsakatika M (2007) Governance vs. Politics: the European Union's constitutive 'democratic deficit'. J Eur Public Pol:867
Warleigh A (1999) The committee of the regions: institutionalising multi-level governance? Kogan Page, London
Ziller and Jeffery (2006): Le Comité des régions dans la mise en oeuvre et le contrôle des principes de subsidiarité et de proportionnalité à la lumière de la Constitution pour l'Europe, European university Institute, Florence

Part II
National Patterns

Chapter 6
Germany: A Cooperative Solution to the Challenge of the European Integration

Carlo Panara

A. Introduction

The Federal Republic of Germany was the only federal state among the founding Members of the European Communities. The solutions to the problems raised through the participation of the German federate entities, the *Länder*, in European law- and policy-making and their role in the implementation of Community law have thus found in Germany an original "workshop".

This chapter focuses on the current German position as implemented by the 1992 constitutional amendment, which introduced the "*Europa-Artikel*" ("Article on Europe") at Art. 23 of the *Grundgesetz* (the German constitution, named "Basic Law", hereinafter referred to as BL). [1] The chapter will also summarily look at the earlier evolution of the participation of the *Länder* in European law- and policy-making.

The current system pivots on Art. 23 BL, which has been recently amended by the 2006 *Föderalismusreform* (the reform of German federalism), [2] and on the

---

This chapter builds on, revises, and updates my article *The German* Länder *in the Process of European Integration between* Föderalismusreform *and Reform Treaty* which has been published on the journal *European Public Law*, Vol. 14 (2008), No. 4, pp. 585–614. I express my gratitude to the editor of the journal, Prof. Patrick J. Birkinshaw. I am also grateful to Prof. Dr. Rudolf Hrbek, Dr. Diana Zacharias, Dr. Jürgen Bast, and Dr. Eike Michael Frenzel for their valuable help and advice. I accept all responsibility for any remaining mistakes.

[1]Constitutional revision act of 21 December 1992 (in *Bundesgesetzblatt*, hereinafter *BGBl.*, 1992, I, p. 2086). Art. 23 of the Basic Law has been completely rewritten by the constitutional amendment. Previously, this article listed the *Länder* in whose region the Basic Law was in force and it contained a provision regarding the reunification of Germany. Therefore, this norm lost its significance after 1990.

[2]See the constitutional revision act of 11 September 2006 (in *BGBl.*, I, 2006, p. 2098). On the 2006 reform see Starck (2007), Hrbek (2007), p. 225 ff., Kluth (2007), Meyer (2008), Gunlicks (2008), p. 111 ff., Burkhart (2009), p. 341 ff.

C. Panara
School of Law, Liverpool John Moores University, John Foster Building, 98 Mount Pleasant, L3 5UZ Liverpool, UK
e-mail: c.panara@ljmu.ac.uk

C. Panara and A. De Becker (eds.), *The Role of the Regions in EU Governance*,
DOI 10.1007/978-3-642-11903-3_6, © Springer-Verlag Berlin Heidelberg 2011

Gesetz über die Zusammenarbeit von Bund und Ländern in Angelegenheiten der Europäischen Union of 12 March 1993 (Act on the Cooperation of the Federation and the *Länder* in Matters Related to the EU, hereinafter referred to as EUZBLG).[3] Major legislative innovations have been introduced in September 2009, in order to align the system with the requirements set in the ruling of the Federal Constitutional Court of 30 June 2009 (henceforth the "Lisbon ruling"[4]). In this ruling, the Court found the Treaty of Lisbon (hereinafter ToL) to be compliant with the BL and it therefore allowed its ratification, provided that the national legislative bodies (the *Bundestag* and the *Bundesrat*) are given sufficient participation rights in the law-making and treaty amendment procedures of the EU. For this purpose, four pieces of legislation ("*Begleitgesetze*", laws accompanying the ratification of the ToL) were passed in September 2009 and, following their passage, the instrument of ratification of the ToL was signed by Federal President Horst Köhler and deposited. For the scope of this paper, the most important amongst the "*Begleitgesetze*" is the Law Extending and Strengthening the Rights of the *Bundestag* and the *Bundesrat* in Matters Related to the EU (*Gesetz über die Ausweitung und Stärkung der Rechte des Bundestages und des Bundesrates in Angelegenheiten der Europäischen Union*), which, at Art. 1, contains the Law on the Responsibility of the *Bundestag* and the *Bundesrat* for the European Integration, *Integrationsverantwortungsgesetz* (in acronym, IntVG).[5]

The objective of this paper is to examine whether the current constitutional and legislative arrangements provide an adequate solution to problems associated with the *Länder* involvement in European matters. When evaluating the system, one must be aware that there is not only a need to safeguard the rights of the *Länder* but also a need to prevent their rights of participation from becoming an excessive constraint on the Federal Government, capable of precluding it from conducting negotiations in the Council in an effective way.

---

[3]Published in *BGBl.*, 1993, I, p. 313. The act was later amended in 2006 and 2009.

[4]The English text is available at http://www.bverfg.de/entscheidungen/es20090630_2bve000208en.html (last checked on 15 June 2010).

[5]The Law Extending and Strengthening the Rights of the *Bundestag* and the *Bundesrat* in Matters Related to the EU was published in *BGBl.*, 2009, I, p. 3022. The other pieces of legislation referred to in the text as "*Begleitgesetze*" are: the Law Amending the Act on the Cooperation of the Federal Government and the *Bundestag* in Matters Related to the EU (*Gesetz zur Änderung des Gesetzes über die Zusammenarbeit von Bundesregierung und Deutschem Bundestag in Angelegenheiten der Europäischen Union*; in *BGBl.*, 2009, I, p. 3026); the Law Amending the Act on the Cooperation of the Federation and the *Länder* in Matters Related to the EU (*Gesetz zur Änderung des Gesetzes über die Zusammenarbeit von Bund und Ländern in Angelegenheiten der Europäischen Union*; in *BGBl.*, 2009, I, p. 3031); the Law Implementing the Constitutional Amendments for the Ratification of the ToL (*Gesetz zur Umsetzung der Grundgesetzänderungen für die Ratifizierung des Vertrags von Lissabon*; in *BGBl.*, 2009, I, p. 3822).

B. The German Federal System

"The Federal Republic of Germany is a democratic and social federal state". Art. 20 (1) of the BL expresses the "principle of federal state" ("*Bundesstaatsprinzip*"). The German Republic is formed by 16 *Länder* listed in the Preamble to the BL: Baden-Württemberg, Bavaria, Berlin, Brandenburg, Bremen, Hamburg, Hessen, Lower Saxony, Mecklenburg-Western Pomerania, North Rhine-Westphalia, Rhineland-Palatinate, Saarland, Saxony, Saxony-Anhalt, Schleswig-Holstein and Thuringia.

The basic principle of the distribution of competences between the Federation and the *Länder* is established at Art. 30 BL, according to which "Except as otherwise provided or permitted by this Basic Law, the exercise of state powers and the discharge of state functions is a matter for the *Länder*". From this provision, which is typical in federal constitutions,[6] derives that, as a matter of principle, all powers not expressly conferred to the Federation by the BL will be left with the federate entities: the "residuary powers", in other words, rest in the hands of the *Länder*.

The general rule of Art. 30 BL is echoed first of all by Art. 70(1) BL, regarding legislation, according to which "The *Länder* shall have the right to legislate insofar as this Basic Law does not confer the legislative power on the Federation". Despite the provision of the general competence of the *Länder*, the matters of competence of the Federation listed in the BL are so many and wide-ranging, that in actual fact most legislation ends up being within the responsibility of the Federation.[7] It is sufficient to think that, just to limit ourselves to a few examples, the critical sectors of civil law, criminal law and court organisation and procedure are all within the sphere of competence of the Federation and are therefore regulated by federal laws, like other important matters, such as public welfare, economic matters and social security. For this reason, legal scholarship maintains that the German pattern of federalism is quite "centralised" as far as legislation is concerned.[8] The main areas of "exclusive" legislative competence of the *Länder* are school education, culture, broadcasting (radio/TV), press law, building regulation and police law.

In the field of administration, the rule of Art. 30 is mirrored by Art. 83 BL, which states that "The *Länder* shall execute federal laws in their own right insofar as this Basic Law does not otherwise provide or permit". The exceptions provided for by the BL to this rule are the execution of federal laws by the *Länder* "on federal

[6]See for instance the X Amendment to the US Constitution, Art. 3 of the Swiss Constitution, Art. 15(1) of the Austrian Constitution, and Art. 35 of the Belgian Constitution.

[7]See in particular Art. 73 and Art. 74 of the BL.

[8]The seminal work in this regard is Hesse (1962). In this regard it is worth noting that the Federal Constitutional Court has strongly contributed to such a "centralised" outcome through its case law on implied federal powers, through its broad construction of federal titles of competence, and especially through its extremely "light touch" approach regarding the requirements set out at Art. 72(2) BL for federal legislative intervention in the fields of concurrent legislation (*konkurrierende Gesetzgebung*).

commission" (Art. 85 BL) and the execution of federal laws directly by the Federation (Art. 86 BL). When the *Länder* execute federal laws, the BL grants the Federation relevant powers of control ("*Bundesaufsicht*"). Notwithstanding these exceptions, the *Länder* are actually most prevalent in the administrative area; such prevalence, combined with the predominance of the Federation in the legislative field, sketches out the characteristic of German federalism as "executive federalism" ("*Exekutivföderalismus*").

As to the judiciary, Art. 92 BL states that "The judicial power shall be vested in the judges; it shall be exercised by the Federal Constitutional Court, by the federal courts provided for in this Basic Law, and by the courts of the *Länder*". Here, there is no division of matters of competence between Federation and *Länder*, but a division of roles according to which the *Länder* do establish their own courts in every sector, with the supreme judicial instance always being a federal court. Furthermore, every *Land* has a Constitutional Court ruling: on the conformity of the statutes passed by that *Land* with the respective constitution, on conflicts between constitutional bodies within the *Land*, and on constitutional complaints filed by Municipalities and Associations of Municipalities.

The national law-making bodies are the *Bundestag* and the *Bundesrat*. The *Bundestag* is the national parliament. The *Bundesrat* (Federal Council) is a federal chamber where the *Länder* are represented and through which they participate in federal legislation, administration and in matters of the European Union.[9] The weakening of the powers of the *Länder* may be a consequence of the transfer of their competences to the EU. It may also be a consequence of the transfer of federal powers in areas for which the BL provides an absolute veto power of the *Bundesrat*; that is, a veto that cannot be overturned by a subsequent vote in the *Bundestag*.[10]

The important role of the *Bundesrat* at the federal level, coupled with the execution of federal laws by the *Länder*, makes the Federal Republic a paradigmatic example of "cooperative federalism" ("*kooperativer Föderalismus*"). This contributes to a situation of mutual influence and conditioning between the levels of government known as "political tangle" ("*Politikverflechtung*").[11] Indeed the main objective of the 2006 *Föderalismusreform* has been to unravel such "political tangle". On the one hand, this goal has been pursued by means of a more clear-cut distribution of competences between Federation and *Länder*, and on the other, through the reduction of the power of the *Bundesrat* to veto federal legislation.

---

[9]See Arts. 50–53 BL.

[10]Müller-Graff (2005), p. 108.

[11]The concept of "political tangle" ("*Politikverflechtung*") has been elaborated in the seminal work by Scharpf et al. (1976).

C. The Transfer of Powers to the European Union[12]

Until 1992, the transfer of powers to the Communities was carried out according to Art. 24(1) BL ("The Federation may by law transfer sovereign powers to international organisations"). The 1992 constitutional amendment introduced at Art. 23(1) BL an hoc provision on the transfer of powers to the Union.[13]

German participation in the European integration process (including the transfer of powers to the supranational level) is conditional upon the Union being committed to: democratic, social and federal principles, the rule of law ("*Rechtsstaatsprinzip*"), the principle of subsidiarity and a level of protection of fundamental rights essentially comparable to that provided for by the BL.[14] This commitment is called the "*Struktursicherungsklausel*" (clause preserving the constitutional structure of the BL). It can be traced back to the case law of the Federal Constitutional Court initiated by the 22 October 1986 *Solange II* case.[15]

A federal act is required to transfer powers to the Union, this must obtain the consent of the *Bundestag* and the *Bundesrat*.[16] It is, therefore ,impossible to transfer any power to the Union without the approval by the *Länder*, meaning the majority of their votes in the *Bundesrat*.[17] The act performs a twofold function: that of a "*Vetragsgesetz*", a law dealing with the ratification and incorporation of the treaty, as well as that of an "*Übertragungsgesetz*", a law for the transfer of competences.

Changes in treaty foundations of the Union and comparable regulations that amend or supplement the BL need to be approved by a qualified majority of two-thirds of votes in both the *Bundestag* and the *Bundesrat*.[18] The procedure for such

---

[12]With the aim of specifying the powers to be transferred, the Basic Law uses, both in Art. 23 and in Art. 24, the expression "*Hoheitsrechte*", which is translated into English as "sovereign powers". This expression refers to the exercise of public power in all branches of state activity: legislative, executive, and judicial.

[13]See footnote 2. It shall be remembered, though, that – with the agreement of the Federation – delegates of the *Länder* participated in the intergovernmental conference (IGC) leading to the 1992 Treaty of Maastricht. For more details, see Gunlicks (2003), p. 366.

[14]Art. 23(1), first subparagraph, BL.

[15]In that decision, the Court declared that it would not control the conformity of Community acts with the fundamental rights of the Basic Law as long as the European Community, and in particular the Court of Justice, could guarantee a general standard of fundamental rights protection comparable to that envisaged by the Basic Law. The unabridged text of this historic case can be read in *BVerfGE*, Vol. 73, p. 339 et seq.

[16]See Art. 23(1), second subparagraph, BL.

[17]Each *Land* has a number of allocated votes depending of the size of their respective populations. The number of votes varies from a minimum of three to a maximum of six.

[18]Art. 23(1), third subparagraph, BL. The expression "comparable regulations" ("*vergleichbare Regelungen*") refers to what the German legal scholarship calls the "*Evolutivklauseln*" ("clauses allowing for evolution") contained in the European Treaties. These clauses authorise integrations of the EU primary law through unanimous Council decisions, followed by the members states' acceptance according to their constitutional laws. The main examples of "*Evolutivklauseln*" prior to the entry into force of the Treaty of Lisbon were Arts. 190(4) EC (election of European

approval must comply with the limits on constitutional revision established by Art. 79(3) BL. These are: organisation of the federal state into *Länder*, the principle of *Länder* participation in legislation, human dignity, respect for human rights and fundamental rights, principles of the democratic and social state, popular sovereignty, the principle of constitutional rigidity and that of legality.

The violation of these limits determines the constitutional unlawfulness of the incorporation act. It has been argued that this would also affect the international treaty transferring powers to the Union. Art. 46 of the 1969 Vienna Convention on the Law of Treaties stipulates that the invalidity of an international treaty can be invoked by a state when there is a "manifest violation of a provision of its internal law regarding competence to conclude treaties".[19]

Rojahn and *Streinz* argue that all laws transferring powers to the European Union should be approved by a two-thirds majority.[20] They believe that this is because an act that entrusts powers to the Union *ex novo*, or that simply strengthens the powers already transferred, would always end up affecting the BL.

Conversely, other scholars distinguish whether a transfer of powers to the supranational level is of such importance that it requires a two-thirds majority.[21] It is worth noting that the ratification acts dealing with the Treaties of Maastricht, Amsterdam, Nice, the Constitutional Treaty, and, lastly, the Lisbon Treaty, have been passed by two-thirds majority votes in both the *Bundestag* and the *Bundesrat*.

If there is no transfer of "sovereign powers", there is no requirement for a two-thirds majority. This was the case with Europol and Eurojust[22] and with the European Union enlargement treaties. In addition, it is doubtful whether the Common Foreign and Security Policy (owing to its intergovernmental features) implies a real transfer of "sovereign powers" to the Union.[23]

An expansion of the Union sphere of intervention can be achieved by using the "flexibility clause" pursuant to Art. 352 of the Treaty on the Functioning of the European Union (TFEU, ex 308 EC). This article states (at paragraph 1) that "If action by the Union should prove necessary within the framework of the policies defined in the Treaties to attain one of the objectives set out in the Treaties and the Treaties have not provided the necessary powers, the Council, acting unanimously

---

Parliament), 269(2) EC (system of own resources of the EC), 22 EC (new contents relating to citizenship), 42 EU (provision regulating the transfer of the PJCC under the Community aegis). The issue of the "*Evolutivklauseln*" contained in the Treaties after the amendments of the Treaty of Lisbon has been tackled through the recent IntVG (see the next section of this paper).

[19]See Hobe (2001), p. 35 (Rn. 55).

[20]See Rojahn (2001), p. 153 (Rn. 43) and spec. pp. 154–155 (Rn. 47), Streinz (2007), p. 912 (Rn. 65).

[21]See Pernice (2006), p. 482 (Rn. 90), Hobe (2001), pp. 32–33 (Rn. 49), Scholz (1996), pp. 100–101 (Rn. 84), Jarass (2007), p. 547 (Rn. 23), Zuleeg (2001), p. 44 (Rn. 48).

[22]Europol was established by a convention between the member states of 26th July 1995, while Eurojust was established by a Council decision of 28 February 2002 on the basis of the provisions included in the Nice Treaty.

[23]Pernice (2006), p. 478 (Rn. 82).

on a proposal from the Commission and after obtaining the consent of the European Parliament, shall adopt the appropriate measures".

The Law on the Responsibility of the *Bundestag* and the *Bundesrat* for European Integration (*Integrationsverantwortungsgesetz, IntVG*) establishes that approval of the proposed measure (as well as abstention), requires the passage of a law in accordance with Art. 23(1) BL. Without this law, the German representative in the Council must vote against the adoption of the measure.[24]

Furthermore, an extension of the powers of the European Union can take place through the "*Kompetenzerweiterungsklauseln*" (lit. clauses on the extension of the competence). The IntVG establishes that the approval of the extension (or abstention) requires a law passed in accordance with Art. 23(1) BL. Without this law, the German representative in the Council must vote against the extension. This procedure applies to the following; "dynamic blanket empowerment" (Art. 83(1), subparagraph 3, TFEU), expansion of the European Public Prosecutor's powers (Art. 86(4) TFEU) and amendments to the statute of the European Investment Bank (Art. 308(3) TFEU).[25]

D. The Role of the *Länder* Vis-à-Vis Further Amendments to the Treaties

The ToL contains a number of provisions which make it possible to adopt a simplified revision of the Treaties or other adjustments via the "bridging clauses". The Lisbon ruling clarified that a transfer of sovereign powers from the national level to the European Union could be compliant with the BL only if the democratically representative bodies are involved in the decision. The rationale for all the modifications introduced by the IntVG is to expand the involvement of the *Länder* and of the *Bundestag* in the transfer of powers to the European Union and also to make clear all situations in which the procedure of Art. 23(1) BL is required.

The ToL introduced a simplified revision procedure in Art. 48(6) of the Treaty on European Union (TEU). According to this procedure, the European Council is entitled to pass, by unanimity, amendments to provisions contained in Part Three of the TFEU. This applies to the internal policies and action of the Union. Such "simplified" amendments can only enter into force after their approval by all the Member States and in conformance with their respective constitutional requirements. In Germany, the requirement set by the IntVG is a law passed in accordance with Art. 23(1) BL.[26]

According to § 3 of the IntVG, Art. 23(1), BL shall also apply to other simplified amendments of the treaties; specifically to a number of measures which can be

[24]See § 8 IntVG.

[25]See § 7 IntVG.

[26]See § 2 IntVG.

unanimously adopted by the Council or the European Council and which have an impact on the basic structure of the European Union. Within this category is the decision of the Council on the accession of the Union to the European Convention on Human Rights and the decision of the European Council to establish a common defence policy.[27] In this last case, there are two prerequisites: a decision by the *Bundestag* and a statute passed in accordance with Art. 23(1) BL.[28] There is no doubt that the decision to establish a common defence policy would have an impact on the BL and would require a qualified majority of two-thirds in both the *Bundestag* and the *Bundesrat*.

The IntVG devotes § 4 to the "*Brückenklauseln*" ("bridging clauses") of Art. 48 (7) TEU and Art. 81(3) TFEU. These provisions allow for changes in the procedure of Union decision-making. Art. 48(7) lays down a "bridging clause" with general application. Its first paragraph allows a shift from unanimity to qualified majority voting in the Council and deprives the Member States of their veto power (this is not available for decisions with defence or military implications). Its second paragraph allows a shift from a "special legislative procedure" to the "ordinary legislative procedure" (the former co-decision procedure). Art. 81(3) TFEU gives the Council the power to unanimously determine (after consulting the European Parliament) aspects of family law with cross-border implications. These may become the subject of acts adopted pursuant to the "ordinary legislative procedure" (instead of a "special legislative procedure"). The German approval of the proposed procedural change (as well as their abstention) requires the passage of a law in accordance with Art. 23(1) BL. Without this law, the German representative in the European Council or in the Council must vote against the procedural change.

The IntVG contains two paragraphs (§ 5 and § 6) which relate to the "special bridging clauses". As their scope is sufficiently defined, no law under Art. 23(1) BL is necessary for their approval by Germany. These clauses only normally require the sanction ("*Beschluss*") by the *Bundestag*. However, if the BL requires the consent of the *Bundesrat* to pass a law in a specific area, or it is an area belonging to the legislative competence of the *Länder*, approval by the *Bundesrat* is also necessary.[29]

---

[27]See Art. 218(8), subparagraph 2 (sentence 2), TFEU, and Art. 42(2), subparagraph 1 (sentence 2), TFEU, respectively. § 3 of the IntVG also applies to the passage of: provisions relating to the system of own resources of the EU (Art. 311(3) TFEU); provisions adding further EU citizenship rights or strengthening those already provided (Art. 25(2) TFEU); uniform rules for the election of the European Parliament (Art. 223(1), subparagraph 2, TFEU); provisions conferring on the ECJ the jurisdiction on disputes relating to the European intellectual property rights (Art. 262 TFEU).

[28]See § 3(3) of the IntVG.

[29]§ 5 of the IntVG is devoted to the approval of "special bridging clauses" in the European Council. In such cases the European Council is entitled to authorise, *by unanimity*, the shift from unanimity to qualified majority voting in the Council. In this way, the Council may be allowed to decide by qualified majority in areas of the CFSP other than those listed in Art. 31(2) TEU (cf. Art. 31(3) TEU). Furthermore, it may be allowed to pass the multi-annual financial framework regulation of Art. 312(1) TFEU by qualified majority instead of by unanimity (cf. Art. 312(2), subparagraph 2, TFEU). Instead, § 6 of the IntVG applies to the approval of "special bridging clauses" in

E. The Participation of the *Länder* in the EU Law-Making Phase: Indirect Participation

It is possible to distinguish between two forms of intervention by the *Länder* in the Union legislative process; their direct and indirect participation. In the first, the *Länder* are present within Union institutions and can influence decisions directly. By contrast, in the second case, such entities are entitled to participate in procedures which take place within the Member State. These are aimed at determining the position of the national Government within the Council and, as such, they contribute only indirectly to the decisions of the latter.

As late as 1992, the BL did not contain any provision on direct or indirect *Länder* participation in the Community law-making phase. The incorporation statute of the Treaties of Rome of 1957 granted a mere right of information to the *Bundesrat* about any development in the Council. From 1979, there has been an agreement in place between the Federation and the *Länder* which created a special cooperation procedure. This had to be put into action where a Community draft act related to a matter falling within the exclusive competence of the *Länder* or touched upon their vital interests. In such cases, the *Länder* had the right to adopt a common position that the Federal Government had to uphold within the Council. The exception to this was the right to depart from the common position on overriding grounds of foreign or European policy.

In 1986, the system of *Länder* participation in European policy was improved by the law transposing the Single European Act (SEA) and by an agreement with the Federal Government. For the first time, the new system made the *Bundesrat* the central body of the cooperation between the Federation and *Länder* in matters of European policy. The *Bundesrat* was given the right to express its opinion on all Community draft acts affecting exclusive *Länder* competences or vital *Länder*'s interests. The Federal Government had to take the opinion of the *Bundesrat* into account in Council negotiations and could only deviate from it on overriding grounds of foreign or European policy.

This participation system was far from satisfactory. There was no provision on how to overcome a disagreement between the Federal Government and the *Bundesrat* and the standing of the *Länder* in Council negotiations was judged as still too limited. This led to the 1992 constitutional amendment, which is how the

---

the Council. According to these clauses, the Council can decide, *by unanimity*, to make the "ordinary legislative procedure" (instead of a "special procedure") applicable to specific issues in the area of social policy (cf. Art. 153(2), subparagraph 4, TFEU) and in the area of environment (cf. Art. 192(2), subparagraph 2, TFEU). § 6 also applies to the Council decision, taken *by unanimity*, to allow the adoption of measures by qualified majority instead of by unanimity, or by using the "ordinary legislative procedure" instead of a "special procedure", in the context of enhanced cooperation (Art. 333(1) and (2) TFEU).

Länder obtained constitutional recognition and further enhancement of their participation rights.[30]

Since the 1992 amendment, the BL allows indirect *Länder* participation in Union law-making and policy-making as a rule and direct participation as an exception. Art. 23(2), first subparagraph, BL states that the *Länder* should cooperate on matters relating to the European Union through the *Bundesrat*. Furthermore, Art. 23(2), second subparagraph, BL stipulates that the Federal Government should inform the *Bundesrat* in an exhaustive and timely way about all draft Union acts in which the *Länder* may have an interest.

The *Bundesrat* has to be involved in European Union-related decisions in two specific cases. The first is when the agenda of the Council deals with topics on which the *Bundesrat* has the right to intervene. The second is when the matter dealt with by the Council falls within the competence of the *Länder*.[31]

According to Art. 23(3) BL, the involvement of the *Bundesrat* (and the *Bundestag*) is consistent with the acknowledgement that the European integration is not merely a question of foreign policy but is also an important matter of national law and national policy.[32] This explains why the issue of the participation rights of the *Länder* was settled via constitutional rules and was not left to agreements between Federation and *Länder* or to sub-constitutional legislation.

The weight the *Bundesrat* carries varies according to the particular circumstances. One possible scenario is when the interests of the *Länder* are affected by an EU proposal falling within the exclusive competence of the Federation,[33] or in another area in which the Federation has legislative power.[34] In this case, the position of the *Bundesrat* does not have a binding character and must be only taken into account ("*berücksichtigt*") by the Federal Government. Consequently, the Federal Government may depart from that position if it considers it appropriate.

When the *Länder*'s legislative powers, the structure of their authorities, or their administrative procedures form the focus ("*Schwerpunkt*") of a draft Union act, the position of the *Bundesrat* acquires a quasi-binding (if not a fully binding) value. The BL states that when this occurs, the Federal Government must give the position of the *Bundesrat* "the greatest possible respect" ("*maßgeblich zu berücksichtigen*") .[35] It is controversial whether or not this expression means that the position of the *Bundesrat* is binding. Attaching binding character to the position of the *Bundesrat* could have serious shortcomings. The Federal Government would have its hands tied when conducting negotiations at the Union level and could not act with the

---

[30]On the historical evolution of the participation rights of the *Länder* see Suszycka-Jasch and Jasch (2009), p. 1231 ff.

[31]Art. 23(4) BL.

[32]See Streinz (2007), p. 918 (Rn. 91).

[33]Within this framework, we should include the issues listed in Art. 73 BL, the conduct of relations with foreign States (Art. 32(1) BL), the administration by the *Länder* on behalf of the Federation (Art. 85 BL), as well as the Federation's own administration (art. 86 BL).

[34]Art. 23(5), first subparagraph, BL.

[35]Art. 23(5), second subparagraph, BL.

required flexibility. Therefore, it seems preferable to embrace the thesis that the Federal Government would have to do what it could to conform with the views of the *Bundesrat*, except when this proves to be in the best interests of the Federal Republic.[36]

It is worth noting that the debate on the binding or non-binding character of the *Bundesrat*'s positions has a rather academic character. Just 37 out of the total 900 positions adopted by the *Bundesrat* from 1998 to 2003 have been regarded as being due "the greatest possible respect" (amounting to 4%). In 20 out of these 37 cases, the Federal Government initially took a different view to that of the *Bundesrat*, but an agreement was ultimately reached, or as an opinion suggests, the Government yielded to the *Länder*'s requests.[37] In practice, it has always been possible to find political solutions capable of preventing a full clash between the *Bundesrat* and the national government.[38]

No doubts remain about the non-binding character of the *Bundesrat*'s position when increases in expenditures or reduced federal revenues could result from the approval of an EU draft act. In such events, the Federal Government has the last say.[39]

Art. 23(4) BL does not set any limits on the cooperation of the *Bundesrat* on issues concerning the European Union, but § 11 of the EUZBLG does exclude Common Foreign and Security Policy from that cooperation (with the exceptions now provided for by the IntVG; see section 4).

A major innovation has been introduced by § 9 of the IntVG. The rights of the *Bundestag* and of the *Bundesrat* are regulated in relation to the "emergency brake procedure" ("*Notbremsemechanismus*"). This procedure applies where the TFEU entitles the single Member State representative in the Council to request that an issue is referred from the Council to the European Council for further discussion before a decision is made. In order to safeguard the rights of the democratically legitimised bodies at national level, § 9 IntVG establishes that in such situations the *Bundestag* can oblige the German representative in the Council to file the request. The *Bundesrat* has the same power when the focus of an EU proposed action falls within an area for which the BL requires the consent of the *Bundesrat* to pass a law, or it falls within an area belonging to the legislative competence of the *Länder*.

---

[36]The Federation actually remains responsible for the nation as a whole: Art. 23(5), second subparagraph, BL.

[37]Huber (2007), p. 214. The above statistical data are reported in Meyer (2008), p. 368.

[38]A conflict resolution mechanism is provided by § 5(2) of the EUZBLG. It establishes that, in the case of an insurmountable disagreement with the Federal Government, the *Bundesrat* can confirm its initial position with a two-thirds majority. The position would become "decisive" ("*maßgebend*") and in this context is probably intended as synonymous with "binding". The conflict resolution mechanism of § 5(2) EUZBLG has found no application so far. There has only been one occasion, involving Directive 96/61/CE of 24 September 1996 on integrated pollution prevention and control, when the conflict was so difficult to overcome that the *Bundesrat* was close to confirming its position by two-thirds majority. On that occasion, an agreement was ultimately found.

[39]See Art. 23(5), final subparagraph, BL, and § 5(2), sixth subparagraph, of the EUZBLG.

The "emergency brake procedure" and, as a result, the regime of § 9 IntVG, applies to draft legislative acts in the field of social security and to draft directives in the field of the Judicial Cooperation in Criminal Matters.[40]

F. The Direct Participation of the *Länder* at EU Level

Besides indirect participation of the *Länder*, Art. 23(6), BL provides for their direct participation in Union decision-making. Such participation relies on Art. 16(2) TEU (ex 203 EC), which allows for the representation of a Member State in the Council by a representative, even of a sub-state entity, "at ministerial level", "who may commit the government of the Member State in question and cast its vote".

Art. 23(6) BL establishes that, when an EU draft act focuses on a matter falling under the exclusive legislative competence of the *Länder* in the areas of school education, culture or broadcasting (radio/TV), then the exercise of the rights of Germany as a member of the European Union are conferred to a representative of the *Länder* appointed by the *Bundesrat*.[41] However, the *Länder* representative must act "with the participation of and in coordination with" the Federal Government since, ultimately, the responsibility for the nation as a whole still falls under the duties of the Federation.[42] It should be underlined that this provision is the result of a major amendment introduced by the 2006 constitutional reform of the federal system. Prior to 2006, the direct participation mechanism of the *Länder* provided for by Art. 23(6) BL, instead of being limited only to the above-mentioned three sectors, embraced all fields of exclusive legislative competence of the *Länder*.

But why did the 2006 constitutional reform decide to restrict the direct *Länder* participation to school education, culture and broadcasting (radio/TV)? It happened because the wide-ranging sphere of application of the previous rule had very often led to disputes opposing the *Bundesrat* and the Federal Government. Such disputes were in relation to whether a matter of exclusive competence of the *Länder* formed the focus of a given act. They were typically extra-judicially settled by granting the representative of the *Länder* the right to issue statements during the Council

---

[40]See, respectively, Art. 48(2)(first sentence), TFEU, on the one hand, as well as Art. 82(3), first subparagraph (first sentence), TFEU, and Art. 83(3), first subparagraph (first sentence), TFEU, on the other.

[41]Art. 23(6), subparagraph 1, BL. It should be noted that there is no formal rotation system among the *Länder*. The *Länder* have nominated the following representatives in the Council: Minister Ute Erdsiek-Rave (Schleswig-Holstein), in the field of school education, and Minister Wolfgang Heubisch (Bavaria), in the field of culture. In both cases a deputy will be nominated internally, if necessary. In the field of radio/TV, the *Länder* have nominated three representatives: Minister Siegfried Schneider (Bavaria), Prime Minister Kurt Beck (Rhineland-Palatinate), and Prime Minister Peter Harry Carstensen (Schleswig-Holstein); all three are nominated and they will decide internally who will attend the respective meetings in the Council. This system seems to be working well and without tensions amongst the *Länder*.

[42]Art. 23(6), subparagraph 2, BL.

meetings at which the drafts were discussed.[43] For that reason, the direct *Länder* participation has been limited to three "sensitive" areas, which are traditionally of great importance to the *Länder* from a political point of view. This limitation is also consistent with organisational requirements, since these are sectors that are within the competence of the Council in its "Education, Young people and Culture" formation. Its tasks include stimulating artistic and literary creativity in the field of media.

Although the sphere of application of their rights of direct participation is theoretically more limited than in the past, the *Länder* have received a benefit. The transfer of the exercise of the rights of Germany as a member state to a representative of the *Länder* is now compulsory. Previously, this provision took the form of a "*Sollvorschrift*" (literally "shall-provision") whereby in principle the Federation had to transfer the exercise of Germany's rights to a representative of the *Länder*. The Federation could withhold such rights if this was in the best interests of the German state.[44]

In legal terms, a "*Sollvorschrift*" is much stronger than "should" or "may". It is rather equivalent to "shall, if possible". Hence, the difference between the old and the new version is not substantial. In addition, it is hard to imagine which fields could qualify as being "legislative powers exclusive to the *Länder*" other than those listed in the new Art. 23(6) BL. One could argue that the general police power rests exclusively with the *Länder*. But there are so many special police powers of the Federation that this view would not be convincing. Similar considerations apply to the area of building regulation. Accordingly, the trade-off between less discretion on the part of the Federation and an arguably narrower definition of the relevant fields on the part of the *Länder* does indeed exist, but the "turn-over" is not high.

Limited exceptions to the obligation to transfer powers to the representative of the *Länder* are still expressly provided for by law. First of all, when the German Federal Republic holds the Council presidency, chairing Council meetings will always and in any way be the domain of the Federal Government.[45] Secondly, the *Länder* may exceptionally abstain from direct participation in the Council when the

[43]Müller-Graff (2007), p. 717.

[44]The pre-reform text contained the following: "*Wenn im Schwerpunkt ausschließliche Gesetzgebungsbefugnisse der Länder betroffen sind, soll die Wahrnehmung der Rechte ... vomBund auf einen vom Bundesrat benannten Vertreter der Länder übertragen warden*", while the text in force now contains: "*Wenn im Schwerpunkt ausschließliche Gesetzgebungsbefugnisse der Länder ... betroffen sind, wird die Wahrnehmung der Rechte ... vom Bund auf einen vom Bundesrat benannten Vertreter der Länder übertragen*". The passive present indicative form of the verb "*übertragen*", which has replaced the previous modal verb "*sollen*", emphasises the binding character of the transfer to the *Länder*'s representative of the exercise of the rights pertaining to Germany as a Member State.

[45]See § 6(3), first subparagraph, of the EUZBLG. But § 6(3), second subparagraph, of the EUZBLG specifies that, where the Council deals with draft acts affecting the *Länder*'s exclusive legislative competences with respect to school education, culture or broadcasting, the Federal Government must keep the *Länder*'s representative informed and consider his opinion, even when dealing with the exercise of rights pertaining to it in its role of holding the Council presidency.

Council's agenda includes "Part A" items; i.e. draft legislation which has been agreed within the Committee of the Permanent Representatives (Coreper) and which can therefore be put immediately to the vote without the need for preliminary discussion.[46] In such a case, the participation rights of the *Länder* would not be very meaningful, as their representative would be sitting in the Council without being able to influence the content of a draft. This explains why the *Länder* are involved prior to the Council meeting and the German position within the Coreperis agreed at this time.

These exceptions to the direct participation of the *Länder* are justified because they are grounded on the rules and procedures followed by the Union. If exceptions are not rooted in Union law, they must be based on sound foundations since the constitutional rights of the *Länder* are at stake. Clearly, it would be unlawful to exclude the *Länder* representative from Council meetings simply for administrative or political convenience.[47]

The representative of the *Länder* has the right to sit in the Council on behalf of Germany and has responsibility for conducting negotiations within Commission and Council advisory bodies.[48] Whilst the representative is called "*Vertreter der Länder*" in Art. 23(6) BL, he or she is actually required to represent the whole Federal Republic of Germany at the Union level. Art. 16(2) TEU requires the representative to be in office as Minister of a *Land* but does not presuppose membership of the *Bundesrat*.[49] Furthermore, he or she must act "with the participation of and in coordination with" the Federal Government.[50] "Participation" implies that the representatives of the Federal Government are involved in all meetings and formal external contacts in which the *Länder* representative takes part.[51] "Coordination" is more difficult to construe. Legal scholars generally accept that it means less than a proper "agreement", but more than simple "respect for the other's point of view".[52] It is arguable that the representative of the *Länder* should pay the greatest possible respect to the position of the Federal Government.

When Union draft acts lie outside the "sensitive" areas mentioned in Art. 23(6) BL, but involve a sector falling under the *Länder*'s exclusive legislative competence (police law, building regulation, etc.), the *Länder* will still have the

[46]See § 6(4) of the EUZBLG.

[47]In this direction, see Rojahn (2001), p. 169 (Rn. 74) and Streinz (2007), p. 971 (Rn. 116). On the contrary, the affirmative thesis was upheld by the Federal Government during the preliminary works for the 1992 constitutional amendment.

[48]See § 6(2), first subparagraph, of the EUZBLG.

[49]The status of Minister is determined on the basis of each *Land*'s constitutional rules. On this point see Streinz (2007), p. 923 (Rn. 115).

[50]Art. 23(6), second subparagraph, BL.

[51]Rojahn (2001), p. 169 (Rn. 75), Streinz (2007), p. 923 (Rn. 117).

[52]See the report made by the *Gemeinsame Verfassungskommission* of the *Bundestag* and by the *Bundesrat* on the constitutional law draft which gave rise to the 1992 constitutional amendment (*Drucksache des Bundestages*, 12/6000, p. 24; 12/3896, p. 20). On this point see Scholz (1996), pp. 139–140 (Rn. 138), Streinz (2007), p. 923 (Rn. 117).

opportunity to make their point of view known within the European Union. The *Bundesrat* then has the power to appoint a *Länder* representative who has the right to release statements in coordination with the Federal Government during the Council sessions.[53] The Federal Government must act in coordination with the *Länder* representative when conducting negotiations within the Commission and Council advisory bodies, as well as at the Council meetings.[54] It important to note that the position taken by the *Bundesrat* "shall be given the greatest possible respect" by the Federal Government in areas which fall under the *Länder*'s exclusive competence.

If an EU draft act deals with an issue falling outside the *Länder*'s exclusive competence, the Federal Government has to consult with the *Länder* during negotiations within the Commission and the Council advisory bodies.[55] *Länder* spokespersons are entitled to issue statements within these bodies with the consent of the federal representative.[56]

G. Representation Offices of the *Länder* in Brussels and the *Länderbeobachter*

An important form of *Länder* participation in European issues is the right to establish their own representation offices ("*Landesvertretungen*") in Brussels.[57] These offices have no diplomatic status, as this would be incompatible with the Federation's foreign policy monopoly, provided for by Art. 32(1) BL. Since the 1980s, offices have been established by the *Länder*. Their purpose is to enable the *Länder* to take part in the political process within the European Union in an informal way, that is to establish informal contacts with the European Union, to gather and send information and above all to lobby the political institutions in the interest of the individual *Länder*.[58]

The legitimacy of these offices lies in Art. 32(3) BL ("Insofar as the *Länder* have the power to legislate, they may conclude treaties with foreign states with the consent of the Federal Government"). This provision allows the *Länder* to conclude treaties regarding issues that the Basic Law assigns to their legislative competence. By so doing, it envisages the possibility for the *Länder* to establish contacts with third states and international organisations with the aim of safeguarding their interests.

---

[53]See § 6(2), fifth subparagraph, of the EUZBLG.

[54]See § 6(2), second subparagraph, of the EUZBLG.

[55]See § 6(1), first subparagraph, of the EUZBLG.

[56]See § 6(1), second subparagraph, of the EUZBLG.

[57]See § 8 of the EUZBLG.

[58]On the *Länder*'s offices in Brussels see Fastenrath (1990), p. 125 ff., Jeffery (1997), p. 183 ff., Burgsmüller (2003).

Since 1959, the *Länder* have had a common observer (called "*Länderbeobachter*") in Brussels. He is appointed by the Conference of the Ministers (of the *Länder*) responsible for the EU (*Europaministerkonferenz*, EMK in acronym) and works closely with the Permanent Representation of the Federal Republic of Germany in the EU. The observer is enabled to attend the EU advisory and institutional bodies' meetings, but he is not allowed to participate in discussions or to vote. The observer's task is to pass all useful information to the *Länder*.[59]

H. The German *Länder* in the Committee of the Regions

The Committee of the Regions is currently made up of 344 members and 344 alternate members appointed for a 4-year period by the Council on the proposal of the Member States.[60] The members of the Committee must be representatives of regional and local bodies, who either hold a regional or local authority electoral mandate, or are politically accountable to an elected assembly.[61] Overall, Germany has been allocated 24 members in the Committee. Each of the 16 *Länder* has the right to one representative. Three representatives are guaranteed for Municipalities and Associations of Municipalities and a system of rotation among the different *Länder* is in place for the remaining five seats.[62]

I. Defence of the *Länder* Competences on the Judicial Level

A crucial issue is the judicial defence of the *Länder*'s competences against possible invasions by EU institutions. What is to be done if the EU, going beyond the limits of its own sphere of competence, adopts a measure in a sector that the Basic Law assigns to the *Länder*?

As to the direct challenge of EU acts before the Court of Justice, Art. 263 TFEU (ex 230 EC) only recognises the institutions listed in it and Member States as having the status of a privileged applicant. In contrast, sub-state bodies do not have the status of a privileged applicant and as per their *locus standi* they are on the same

---

[59]The work of the *Länderbeobachter* is regulated in detail by the Erfurt Agreement of 24 October 1996 between the *Länder* (*Abkommen über den Beobachter der Länder bei der Europäischen Union*). The text of this agreement is available at http://www.laenderbeobachter.de/ (last checked on 15 June 2010).

[60]Art. 305(1) TFEU (ex 263 EC) establishes that the number of members of the Committee shall not exceed 350.

[61]Art. 300(3) TFEU.

[62]See § 14(2) of the EUZBLG.

level as natural persons and private legal persons.[63] This means that the *Länder* can only impugn the decisions addressed to them, as well as regulations or decisions intended for other entities but which concern them "directly and individually".[64] As usually acknowledged, these prerequisites represent an almost insurmountable obstacle to conferring the capacity to impugn EU acts on individuals, as well as on the *Länder*, which are on the same level from this point of view. As a matter of fact, only the Federation is legitimised to appeal to EU courts in order to obtain the annulment of a regulation or of a directive exceeding the limits of EU competences.[65]

Which viable alternatives remain for the *Länder*? The answer is to be found in the EUZBLG. When it comes to European legislation which affects issues falling under their legislative competence, the *Länder* can oblige the Federal Government, on request of the *Bundesrat*, to make use of the remedies offered by EU law.[66] This means that the (majority of the) *Länder* can compel the Federal Government to challenge an EU measure on their behalf. Once a challenge has been made, they can contribute to determining the Federal Government's conduct in the proceedings, which must be agreed upon with the *Bundesrat*.[67]

At this point, it is appropriate to highlight a contradiction between Art. 23(6) BL and § 7 of the EUZBLG. The first envisages the *Länder*'s direct participation within the EU when their exclusive competences in the areas of school education, culture and broadcasting are involved; this should mean, at least in those cases, that the *Länder* representative appointed by the *Bundesrat* should have the right to act as the representative of the Federal Republic of Germany before the EU courts. However, § 7 of the EUZBLG confers judicial representation without exception to the Federal Government, whose conduct in the proceedings should in all cases be agreed upon with the *Bundesrat*.

In October 2008, a constitutional amendment was passed. According to this, the *Bundestag* and, which is more important for our purposes, the *Bundesrat*, are entitled to initiate a direct claim for judicial review before the ECJ against EU legislation. This can be done if it is believed that there has been an infringement on the principle of subsidiarity.[68] This provision implements what is provided for in

---

[63]This is the established case law of the ECJ. Note the landmark decision of 21 March 1997 in Case C-95/97, *Région Wallonne* v. *Commission*, in ECR, 1997, at I-1787.

[64]According to Art. 263 TFEU, any natural or legal person may also institute proceedings against a regulatory act which is of "direct concern" to them and does not entail implementing measures.

[65]However the Court of First Instance has considered an appeal filed by the *Land* Saxony as admissible. The challenge was against a Commission's decision addressed to the German Federal Republic on the restitution of a subsidy granted by that *Land* to Volkswagen: see the decision of 15 December 1999, in Joint cases T-132/96 and T-143/96, *Freistaat Sachsen and Others* v. *Commission*, in ECR, 1999, at II-3663.

[66]See § 7(1), first subparagraph, of the EUZBLG.

[67]See § 7(3) of the EUZBLG.

[68]See Art. 1 of the constitutional revision act of 8th October 2008 (in *BGBl.*, I, p. 1926). This provision added a new paragraph 1a to Art. 23 BL.

the Protocol on Subsidiarity and Proportionality annexed to the ToL. That is that any national Parliament, or any chamber thereof, will be entitled to make the respective Member State notify on their behalf a direct action for annulment against EU legislative acts on grounds of an infringement on the principle of subsidiarity.[69]

But can the *Länder* rely on any judicial protection at the national level against EU measures which are affected by incompetence? By means of the "Maastricht ruling" of 12 October 1993, the Federal Constitutional Court stated that acts of the EU institutions have no legal effect nationally if adopted *ultra vires*.[70] However, according to some legal scholars, this does not mean that all domestic courts (and all administrative authorities) have the right to disregard the application of the EU secondary law. On the contrary, in this respect, there should be an obligation to refer the matter to the Federal Constitutional Court; therefore, the latter would be the only judicial body being legitimised to decide on non-application.[71] On 30 June 2009 in the "Lisbon ruling", the Federal Constitutional Court reaffirmed that it is competent to carry out an *ultra vires* review ("*Ultravireskontrolle*") on EU acts. The Court pointed out that this type of review may result in legal instruments of the EU being declared inapplicable in Germany. This may occur if they transgress the confines of the EU competences, or are incompliant with the principle of subsidiarity. On this occasion, the Court also clarified that the review power is incumbent on the Federal Constitutional Court alone.[72] But from the standpoint of the EU, such a solution is unacceptable. Under EU law, the Federal Constitutional Court must refer to the ECJ in all issues concerning the validity of EU acts. Under no circumstances should a domestic court be allowed – even if it were a constitutional court – not to apply an EU act on its own initiative. This is even though it seems to the domestic court that the invalidity of an act is manifest.

Finally, it should be emphasised that the *Länder*'s constitutional participation rights are judicially safeguarded. With the aim of protecting such rights, the *Bundesrat* can bring a case against the Federal Government (see Art. 93(1), No. 1, BL), while the *Länder* can bring a case against the Federation before the Federal Constitutional

[69]See Art. 8(1) of the Protocol. In judicial proceedings initiated on request of the *Bundesrat* or of the *Bundestag* under Art. 23(1a) BL/Art. 8(1) of the Lisbon Protocol on Subsidiarity, the *Bundesrat* or the *Bundestag*, respectively, become responsible for the conduct of the proceedings (§ 12(4) of the IntVG). In addition § 13(7) of the IntVG establishes the obligation for the Federal Government to inform the *Bundesrat* and the *Bundestag* at the earliest opportunity of the passage of any new piece of legislation by the EU. Contextually the Federal Government has to make it known whether it regards the EU act as consistent with the principles of subsidiarity and proportionality.

[70]*BVerfGE*, Vol. 89, p. 188.

[71]M. Herdegen, Europarecht, München, Beck, 2007, 9th ed., p. 214 ff. (Rn. 26 ff.).

[72]In the same ruling, the Court pointed out that it also had the competence to carry out an "identity review" ("*Identitätskontrolle*"): that is, that it had the right to declare EU legislation infringing on the "inviolable core content of the constitutional identity of the Basic Law" ("*unantastbare Kerngehalt der Verfassungsidentität des Grundgesetzes*") non-applicable in Germany, pursuant to Art. 23(1), last sentence, and Art. 79(3) BL.

Court (see Art. 93(1), No. 3, BL).[73] On the basis of the constitutional regulations prior to the 1992 constitutional amendment, specifically the principle of federal loyalty ("*Bundestreue*"), the Federal Constitutional Court declared the Federal Government's behaviour as illegitimate for not respecting the participation rights of the *Bundesrat* in accordance with the adoption of directive 89/522/EEC regulating television.[74] However, this declaration of illegitimacy has not resulted, nor could it result, in the invalidity of the aforementioned directive. This situation could limit the effectiveness of the constitutional provisions regulating the participation rights of the *Länder*. The Lisbon ruling failed to address this particular question.

J. The Fulfilment of EU Obligations in the Domestic Sphere

The fact that the Federal Republic of Germany is a member of the EU does not alter the distribution of competences outlined by the BL. On the other hand, European integration affects the substance of the competences because, in cases where a competence has been passed on to the supra-national level, fundamental political decisions regarding a specific sector are taken between Brussels and Strasbourg instead of at the national level. European measures require implementation and execution at the national level. As far as the German Federal Republic is concerned, this is dealt with by the Federation or the *Länder* in compliance with the BL's distribution of competences. The failure or inertia of the *Länder* in implementing the EU law would also be an infringement of the principle of federal loyalty. In practice, if such an event occurs, there is no way for the Federation to step in and act instead of the *Land*. The intervention of the federal power would be only possible under Art. 37 BL, in order to coerce the *Länder* to comply (this mechanism is called "*Bundeszwang*", federal execution).[75] Although Germany, also due to the federal structure of the state, is not always able to implement the European measures promptly, Art. 37 has not so far received any application. The application of this article would be too time-consuming and extremely costly in political terms.[76]

It is also worth mentioning the repeal of the power to enact framework legislation (*Rahmengesetzgebung*) by the 2006 *Föderalismusreform*, provided for by the previous Art. 75 BL. This framework legislation was characterised by the following: in sectors that were subject to it, the Federation was competent to lay down a general legislative framework, whilst the *Länder* were competent to issue

[73] On this point see Streinz (2007), p. 924 (Rn. 120).

[74] *BVerfGE*, Vol. 92, p. 203 ff.

[75] Art. 37 stipulates: "(1) If a *Land* fails to comply with its obligations under this Basic Law or other federal laws, the Federal Government, with the consent of the *Bundesrat*, may take the necessary steps to compel the *Land* to comply with its duties. (2) For the purpose of implementing such coercive measures, the Federal Government or its representative shall have the right to issue instructions to all the *Länder* and their authorities".

[76] See Huber (2007), p. 217.

additional regulations to implement the federal framework law. First of all, the *Rahmengesetzgebung* was repealed owing to its excessive complexity (where did the Federation's competence end and where did the *Länder*'s begin?), but also because it was a possible source of delays and non-compliance when implementing EU secondary law.

The *Länder* are not members of the EU, nor are they endowed with full international personality. So, in the case of a violation of a European obligation, only the Federation will bear responsibility before the European institutions. But at the domestic level, who bears the costs which derive from the responsibility for a breach of international obligations? The BL did not provide an answer to this question until 2006. The new Art. 104a(6), first subparagraph, of the BL, added by the 2006 constitutional amendment, filled this gap providing that expenses deriving from Germany's violation of "supranational" or "international" obligations must be at the last borne by the responsible authorities, which can be the Federation, the *Länder*, or a single *Land*.[77] One cannot exclude that situations could arise where both the Federation and the *Länder* are collectively responsible for an infringement; under these circumstances, costs must be allocated in proportion to the quota of responsibility of each government level.[78] If the Commission initiates an infringement procedure under Art. 258 TFEU (ex 226 EC) against the Federal Republic of Germany on the grounds of the missed or faulty implementation of an EU obligation by one or more *Länder*, the Federal Government will need to agree its defence plan with the *Bundesrat* in infringement proceedings before the ECJ.[79] This is because it would be in breach of the constitutional rights of the *Länder* to hold them responsible without giving them any right of defence.

A special regulation has been introduced by the 2006 *Föderalismusreform* at Art. 109(5) BL for the violation of the parameters set by the "European Stability and Growth Pact". Under such circumstances, the Federation will carry 65% and the *Länder* 35% of the overall burden of the sanctions applied by the EU to the

[77]An infringement can result from legislative, administrative or jurisdictional State acts. This is established by § I(1) of the law on the division between the Federation and the *Länder* of costs resulting from the infringement of supra-national and international obligations (*Lastentragungsgesetz*, acronym LastG) contained in Art. 15 of the law accompanying the 2006 federalism reform (*Föderalismusreform-Begleitgesetz*): in *BGBl.*, I, 2006, p. 2098. It should also be emphasized that, for the first time, the Basic Law utilizes the adjective "supranational", coined by legal scholars to refer to the EU phenomenon; see Hellermann (2007), p. 155 (Rn. 336).

[78]§ I(2) LastG. Please note § 3 LastG concerning the division between the *Länder* of a sanction (lump sum or penalty payment) issued by the ECJ on the Federal Republic of Germany under Art. 260 TFEU (ex 228 EC). In such a case each responsible *Land* will pay in accordance with the "*Königsteiner Schlüssel*" (a ratio established for the first time in the Königsteiner Agreement of 30 and 31 May 1949), i.e. two thirds according to the tax revenue and one third according to the population of each *Land*. A further special rule applies where the infringement of a European obligation stems from a judicial decision. In such a case, § 4 LastG establishes that the allocation of the economic burden depends on the belonging of the responsible court to the Federation or to a *Land*. However, where a federal court simply confirms the ruling of a *Land* court, the burden is equally divided between the Federation and the *Land*.

[79]§ 7(3) of the EUZBLG.

Federal Republic under Art. 126(11) TFEU (ex 104 EC). This 65%/35% "vertical" division of liability between the *Bund* and the *Länder* will always apply. This is without taking into consideration the responsibility of each government level in causing the violation of the above parameters. It would probably have been more adequate if the proportion was not rigid and that there was the possibility to take into account to what extent each level of government has contributed to the exceeding of the deficit level. As to the "horizontal" division of liability between the *Länder*, the 35% falling on the *Länder* is split as follows: 35% (i.e. 12.25% of the whole sum) is carried by all the *Länder* in proportion to their number of inhabitants, while 65% (i.e. 22.75% of the whole sum) is only paid by the *Länder* responsible for the exceeding public expenses in proportion to their level of responsibility. This is an incentive for the German federate entities to avoid deficits.[80]

K. Concluding Remarks

A loss of the *Länder*'s individual powers seems to be inevitably connected with the European integration process. Also, the participation rights of the *Länder* are provided for by the BL as the rights of a "level of governance" and not as the rights of the single *Länd*. For example, the "*Länder* representative" in the Council does not represent his own *Land* but the whole Federal Republic.

As far as the transfer of powers to the EU is concerned, the participation right granted to the *Länder* is only indirect and collective as it is exercised through the constitutional body representing them at the federal level – the *Bundesrat*. The single *Land* must be subject to the decision of the majority of the *Länder*.[81] On the other hand, under the circumstances, this is the only possible form of participation, as only states and not sub-national entities are and can ever be members of the EU.

The transfer of powers of regulation to the EU does not affect the distribution of competences within the German Federal Republic in respect of the implementation and enforcement of EU acts. Therefore, the Federation and the *Länder* will implement and enforce European measures in compliance with the domestic distribution

[80]At the same time, some problems posed by the new constitutional law should not be underestimated. On the one hand, the problematic nature of this responsibility imposed on all the *Länder* including those whose budgets are in order. On the other hand, the practical difficulty of enforcing such responsibility against those *Länder* whose financial situation is in trouble. On Art. 109(5) BL see Classen (2007), p. 114 ff. (Rn. 246 ff.).

[81]It should be stressed that only the Federation is authorised to transfer such powers, while the *Länder* are not authorised, neither according to Art. 23(1), nor according to Art. 24(1) BL, to transfer their sovereign powers to the Union. See Rojahn (2001), p. 152 (Rn. 41). According to Art. 24(1a) the *Länder* can transfer their sovereign powers to transfrontier institutions in neighbouring regions.

of legislative and administrative powers established by the BL. At the domestic level, they will carry the financial responsibility in the event of their non-compliance with European obligations.

The *Länder*'s participation rights in the EU legislative process are designed to make up for the loss of powers they have suffered, but they are also intended to fulfil a fundamental democratic function; indeed, within the framework of the federal and regional states, in addition to a horizontal separation of powers (legislative, executive, judiciary), there is a vertical separation between central government and regional governments. An excessive weakening of the *Länder* would undermine this vertical separation and, as a consequence, it would jeopardise the democratic structure created by the BL. The Lisbon ruling further stressed the risk of a loss of democracy when it spoke out about the necessity of reinforcing the participation rights of the democratically legitimised constitutional bodies (*Bundestag* and *Bundesrat*) in the EU law- and policy-making.

The *Länder*'s participation rights in the making phase of EU law, both those pertaining to indirect participation (through the *Bundesrat*) and those pertaining to direct participation, even though they fulfil the aforementioned fundamental and inalienable functions, also present disadvantages. In practice, the process of determining the position to be taken within the Council has proved to be very complex, and the German contractual position might turn out to be too rigid.[82] This is partly an inevitable price to be paid for the *Länder*'s involvement in decisions regarding European issues. But together with the rights of the sub-state entities, one should not neglect the rights of the Federal Republic as a whole; therefore, interpretations geared to denying the binding character of the positions taken by the *Bundesrat* seem to be reasonable. A different solution may prevent the Federal Government from negotiating and carrying out its tasks effectively within the Council.

In the past, the BL has proved not to be very effective in securing the direct participation of the *Länder* in Council meetings. Once again it must be stressed that until 2006 the constitutional provision on direct participation was a "*Sollvorschrift*" (shall-provision) in the outlined sense. Before the 2006 constitutional amendment, the *Länder* did not often take advantage of this opportunity. The 2006 reform addressed the issue by reducing the discretion of the Federal Government when handing over the representation power to the *Länder*. At the same time, the reform restricted direct participation to the three areas which are of specific importance to the *Länder* (school education, culture, and broadcasting). In the long run, this change is expected to increase regional participation in the Council.

The most important characteristic of the system devised by Germany is that it requires a cooperative approach from the two government levels involved (the Federation and the *Länder*). The "coordination" and the achievement of the necessary "agreements" is only possible if reciprocal vetoes are overcome. Recently, such cooperative character of the German system has been further significantly

---

[82] Huber (2007), p. 215, reports that the Federal Republic of Germany is the Member State that more often finds itself in minority within the Council.

increased by the Lisbon ruling and the laws accompanying the ratification of the ToL ("*Begleitgesetze*"). Therefore, the efficient functioning of the system substantially depends on the good will of the levels of government involved. As highlighted by the Federal Constitutional Court, they must behave in ways inspired by the principle of federal loyalty.

Selected Bibliography

Burgsmüller Ch (2003) Die deutschen Länderbüros in Brüssel – verfassungswidrige Nebenauβenpolitik oder zeitgemäβe Ausprägung des Föderalismus? Shaker, Aachen
Burkhart S (2009) Reforming Federalism in Germany: incremental changes instead of the big deal. Publius 39(2):341
Classen CD (2007) Verbesserung der Europatauglichkeit. In: Starck Ch (ed) Föderalismusreform., p 114
Fastenrath U (1990) Länderbüros in Brüssel: Zur Kompetenzverteilung für informales Handeln im auswärtigen Bereich. In: Die Öffentliche Verwaltung., p 125
Gunlicks A (2003) The Länder and German Federalism. Manchester University Press, Manchester and NY
Gunlicks A (2008) German Federalism Reform: Part One. German Law J 8(1):111
Hesse K (1962) Der unitarische Bundesstaat. C.F. Müller, Karlsruhe
Hobe S (2001) Art. 23 BL. In: Friauf KH, Höfling W (eds) Berliner Kommentar zum Grundgesetz. Erich Schmidt, Berlin
Hrbek R (2007) The reform of German federalism: Part I. Eur Constitut Law Rev 3(2):225
Huber PM (2007) Die Europatauglichkeit des Art. 23 GG. In: Merten D (ed) Die Zukunft des Föderalismus in Deutschland und Europa. Duncker u. Humblot, Berlin, p 209 ff
Jarass HD (2007) Art. 23 BL. In: Jarass HD, Pieroth B (eds) Grundgesetz für die Bundesrepublik Deutschland, 9th edn. Beck, München, p 547 ff
Jeffery C (1997) Regional information offices in Brussels and multi-level governance in the EU: a UK-German comparison. In: Jeffery C (ed) The regional dimension of the European Union. Towards a third level in Europe? Frank Cass, London and Portland, p 183
Kluth W (ed) (2007) Foederalismusreformgesetz. Einführung und Kommentierung. Nomos, Baden-Baden
Meyer H (2008) Die Foederalismusreform 2006. Konzeption, Kommentar, Kritik. Duncker u Humblot, Berlin
Müller-Graff P-Ch (2005) The German Länder: Involvement in EC/EU Law and Policy Making. In: Weatherill S, Bernitz U (eds) The role of regions and sub-national actors in Europe. Hart, Oxford and Portland, p 103 ff
Müller-Graff P-Ch (2007) Die Europatauglichkeit der grundgesetzlichen Föderalismusreform. In: Pitschas R (ed) Wege gelebter Verfassung in Recht und Politik. Festschrift für Rupert Scholz zum 70. Geburtstag. Duncker u. Humblot, Berlin, p 705 ff
Pernice I (2006) Art. 23 BL. In: Dreier H (ed) Grundgesetz. Kommentar, vol II, 2nd edn. Mohr Siebeck, Tübingen, p 415 ff
Rojahn O (2001) Art. 23 BL. In: von Münch I, von Münch I, Kunig Ph (eds) Grundgesetz-Kommentar, vol II. C. H. Beck, München, p 121 ff
Scharpf FW, Reissert B, Schnabel F (1976) Politikverflechtung: Theorie und Empirie des kooperativen Foederalismus in der Bundesrepublik. Scriptor, Kronberg
Scholz R (1996) Art. 23 BL. In: Maunz T, Dürig G (eds) Grundgesetz. Kommentar, vol III. C. H. Beck, München
Starck Ch (ed) (2007) Föderalismusreform. Einführung. C. H. Beck, München

Streinz R (2007) Art. 23 BL. In: Sachs M (ed) Grundgesetz. Kommentar, 4th edn. C. H. Beck, München, p 895

Suszycka-Jasch M, Jasch H-Ch (2009) The participation of the German Länder in formulating German EU-Policy. German Law J 10(9):1215

Zuleeg M (2001) Art. 23 BL. In: Denninger E et al (eds) Kommentar zum Grundgesetz für die Bundesrepublik Deutschland, 3rd edn. Luchterhand, Neuwied, p 44

Chapter 7
State and Regions Vis-a-Vis European Integration: The "Long (and Slow) March" of the Italian Regional State

Stefano Villamena

A. Introduction

I. The Italian Regional State

The Italian constitutional structure comprises the central State and a complex system of regional and local authorities.[1] Since its entry into force on 1 January 1948,[2] the Italian Constitution established a regional State, divided into Regions endowed with political,[3] legislative,[4] administrative,[5] and financial [6] autonomy. Fifteen Regions (out of 20) are directly governed by constitutional provisions. These Regions are usually called "Regions with ordinary autonomy" or "ordinary Regions" (*Regioni ad autonomia ordinaria, Regioni ordinarie*).

In addition to these 15 Regions, there are 5 other Regions (Sicily, Sardinia, Friuli-Venezia Giulia, Trentino-Alto Adige, and Valle d'Aosta), all of which are endowed with a peculiar degree of autonomy, that is to say, with powers which are

---

[1]Art. 114(1) of the Italian Constitution (amended in 2001) states that "The Republic consists of Municipalities, Provinces, Metropolitan Cities, Regions, and the State".

[2]The Italian Constitution was approved by the Constituent Assembly on 22 December 1947, it was published on the Official Journal of the Italian Republic (*Gazzetta Ufficiale*, hereinafter G.U.) on 27 December 1947, and it entered into force on 1 January 1948.

[3]Power to freely establish their own political direction – even a political direction different from that of the central state.

[4]Power to pass legislation on the matters enunciated by the Constitution (see the original version of Art, 117 of the Constitution).

[5]Power to enact administrative measures in the same matters where the Regions were entitled to pass legislation (see the original version of Art. 118 of the Constitution).

[6]Attribution to the Regions of the financial resources which are required in order to concretely allow them to exercise their legislative and administrative competences (see the original version of Art. 119 of the Constitution).

S. Villamena
Facoltà di Giurisprudenza, Università degli Studi di Macerata, Piazza Strambi, 1, 62100 Macerata, Italy
e-mail: stefano.villamena@unimc.it

C. Panara and A. De Becker (eds.), *The Role of the Regions in EU Governance*,
DOI 10.1007/978-3-642-11903-3_7, © Springer-Verlag Berlin Heidelberg 2011

wider than those of the ordinary Regions, especially in the legislative and financial fields.[7] The Regions in this second group are usually referred to as "Regions with special autonomy", "special Regions", or "Regions with different autonomy" (*Regioni ad autonomia speciale*, *Regioni speciali*, or *Regioni ad autonomia differenziata*). The powers of these Regions are not provided for by the Constitution, but by individual Statutes (*statuto* means the constitution of a given organization or institution: for instance, the 1848 *Statuto albertino* was the name of the first Italian constitution). In fact, sometimes the special Regions are referred to as *Regioni a statuto speciale* ("Regions with a special Statute"). Furthermore, there are two Autonomous Provinces, Trento and Bolzano, which are part of the special Region Trentino-Alto Adige, and which are themselves endowed with powers and competences very similar to those of the special Regions.[8]

All Regions – irrespective of whether they are ordinary or special – have a Statute called *Statuto regionale*, which is the *statuto* of that Region. However, in the case of Regions with special autonomy, the Statute is adopted with a special procedure which is more complex than that used for the enactment of the Statutes of the Regions enjoying ordinary autonomy. Until 2001, the Statutes of the Regions with ordinary autonomy were approved through an act of the national Parliament; since the 2001 constitutional reform, they are not approved by any national body. The Statutes of the special Regions, instead, are approved and amended through constitutional statutes passed by the national Parliament following the procedure described at Art. 138 of the Constitution.[9]

The Italian Constitution, moreover, recognizes the autonomy of Provinces and Municipalities[10] (these are local authorities, which in Italian are called *enti locali*). These authorities are territorially smaller than the Regions. Apart from that, the most significant difference between the Provinces and Municipalities, on the one hand, and the Regions (and the two Autonomous Provinces of Trento and Bolzano), on the other, is that only the Regions and the two aforementioned Autonomous Provinces have legislative powers. Local authorities only have the power to create subordinate legislation ("regulations", *regolamenti*) and, like the Regions, have political, administrative and financial autonomy. In addition, the Provinces and

---

[7]See Art. 116(1) of the Constitution.

[8]See the constitutional statute No. 5 of 26 February 1948 approving the special Statute of the Region Trentino-Alto Adige (published on G.U. 13 March 1948, No. 62). Arts. 11 and 12 of that Statute provide for wide-ranging legislative powers of the Provinces of Trento and Bolzano.

[9]Article 138 Constitution "Procedure for Constitutional Amendment: (1) Law amending the Constitution and other Constitutional acts are adopted by each of the two Chambers twice within no less than three months and need the approval of a majority of the members of each Chamber in the second voting. (2) Such laws are afterwards submitted to popular referendum when, within three months of their publication, a request is made by one fifth of the members of either chamber, by 500,000 electors, or by five regional councils. The law submitted to referendum is not promulgated if it does not receive the majority of valid votes. (3) No referendum may be held if the law has been approved by each chamber in the second vote with a majority of two thirds of its members".

[10]Art. 114 mentions also Metropolitan Cities but to date no Metropolitan City is in existence.

Municipalities, and their autonomy, find their definitions and limits in national, ordinary (non-constitutional) statutes,[11] whereas the autonomy of the Regions is defined and finds its limits in the Constitution.

In 2001, the Parliament passed a constitutional reform which significantly strengthened the powers of both the Regions and the local authorities.[12] Until that constitutional reform, the Constitution (Art. 117) gave the Regions the power to pass legislation only in a few enunciated matters and, in these sectors, the legislation issued by the Regions had to comply with basic principles expressly established by special State statutes (so-called "framework acts", *leggi quadro* or *leggi cornice*) or to be derived from the entire State legislation regulating a given sector. This type of legislative competence of the Regions was called "shared" or also "concurrent" legislation (*legislazione ripartita* or *legislazione concorrente*). All non-enunciated legislative powers belonged to the central State.

The 2001 constitutional amendment (see the new Art. 117) overturned this criterion and established the right of the Regions to enact legislation in all fields not enumerated by the Constitution. Therefore, the Italian State – like the federation in some important federal States such as the USA, Austria, or Germany[13] – retains exclusive legislative power only in the areas expressly enumerated by the Constitution (see Art. 117(2) of the Italian Constitution).

As before the 2001 constitutional amendment, Art. 117 contains a list of matters where the legislative power is still shared by the State and the Regions. In those areas, the State sets basic principles and the Regions implement those principles through detailed legal provisions (so-called "normativa di dettaglio").

II. Constitutional Reform and "Regional EU Power"

The relationship between the State and the Regions in making and implementing EU law has undergone profound changes since the foundation of the European Communities in 1957 up until the present.[14] The most important changes were enacted via the constitutional reform passed in 2001,[15] even if there are those who

[11]The most important act regulating local authorities is an act of delegated legislation issued by the National Government in 2000 with the aim to consolidate the complex legislation existing on local authorities: this is the legislative decree No. 267 of 18 August 2000 "Testo unico delle leggi sull'ordinamento degli enti locali" (published in G.U. 28 September 2000, No. 227).

[12]See Constitutional Law No. 3, of 18 October 2001, "Modification to Title V of Part II of the Constitution" (published in G.U. 24 October 2001, No. 248), available at http://www.senato.it/parlam/leggi/01003lc.htm (last time checked on 15 June 2010).

[13]On the Federal Republic of Germany see Panara (2008a).

[14]See Caretti (1979); but also Pinelli (1999), pp. 635–641; finally, Villamena (2004), pp. 14–18.

[15]Constitutional Law No. 3, of 18 October 2001, cit. and comments D'Atena (2002a), pp. 913–939; D'Atena (2002b), pp. 373–379; Caretti (2003), pp. 555–574; Chieffi (2004), pp. 87–114; finally Di Salvatore (2007), pp. 641–672.

say that the reforms were not particularly innovative.[16] It was through this reform that a constitutional basis was established for "regional EU power" (the relationship between the State and the Regions in making and implementing EU-law).

In order to examine the current legal framework, other than the aforementioned constitutional reform, we have to analyse the subsequent ordinary legislation implementing it. Indeed, the ample reference in the new constitutional provisions to the implementation required by the national Parliament has led to two Acts of Parliament being passed: the "La Loggia" Act[17] and the "Buttiglione" Act[18] (both Acts are named after the proposing Minister). They are of great importance in relation to the present discussion. These two Acts regulate regional participation in the EU law-making process (so-called *rising* phase – *fase ascendente*) and in the implementation of EU law (so-called *falling* phase – *fase discendente*). However, in order to more adequately guarantee regional power in EU affairs, the constitutional reform should have indicated in greater detail exactly what this power consists of and bound the resultant national legislation in a *tighter* and *more cogent* way.

Further, we certainly cannot forget that the main limitation regarding the Regions' participation rights is – compared for instance with Germany – the lack of a House of the national Parliament which represents regional interests.[19] The *Conferenza Stato-Regioni*[20] ("State–Regions Conference") is a body which is provided for by the Italian legal system; it is the only tool which seeks to *connect* the State and the Regions. However, this body is inadequate in protecting the interests of the Regions because it has a somewhat modest *weight* and, moreover, it is also *unbalanced* in that it is biased in favour of the State (and, particularly, of the Government).

Any study which deals with the relationship between the State and the Regions within the Italian legal system, should take into account the aforementioned distinction between Regions with *ordinary* autonomy and Regions with *special* autonomy (as well as Autonomous Provinces Trento and Bolzano). However, for

---

[16]See especially Costanzo (2010); see also Pinelli (2004), pp. 57–61.

[17]Law No. 131, of 5 June 2003, "Provisions for the Adjustment of the Republic to the Constitutional Law, 18 October 2001, No. 3", available at http://www.senato.it.

[18]Law No. 11, of 4 February 2005, "General Rules on the Participation of the EU Regulatory process and Procedures of Implementation of Community obligations", available at http://www.senato.it (last checked on 15 June 2010).

[19]See Di Salvatore (2008).

[20]According to Art. 12, paragraph 2, Act No. 400 of 23 August 1988, "Disciplina dell'attività di Governo e Ordinamento della Presidenza del Consiglio dei Ministri" (published in Supplemento Ordinario, G.U. No. 214 of 12 September 1988): "The State-Regions Conference is composed of the President of the Council of Ministers (and chaired), the Presidents of the Regions and the Presidents of the Autonomous Provinces of Trento and Bolzano)". See, also, Legislative Decree No. 281 of 28 August 1997 on definition of the powers of the State-Regions Conference. According Italian Constitutional Court (sentence No. 116 of 1994, available at http://www.giurcost.org, last checked on 15 June 2010) State-Regions Conference "is the privileged forum for the discussion and negotiation of policy between the State and the Regions". See especially Marini (2003), p. 163.

the purposes of the present discussion, the two types of regions are analysed together in a unitary format for two reasons. Firstly, there is a need to maintain an expositive coherence in carrying out the investigation and to avoid the excessive complications which would result from frequent reference to many legal sources. Secondly, and substantially, if we look closely indeed, whenever we are dealing with making and/or enforcing EU law, there are not any really important distinctions between Regions *with* ordinary autonomy and Regions (and Provinces) with special autonomy. Indeed, the fundamental aim of the entire national (constitutional and sub-constitutional) regulation is that of avoiding the non-fulfilment of EU obligations, regardless of the character of the Region in question.

In the Italian Constitution, the most important references to the EU framework are contained in Art. 117. This is not only concerned with the State–Regions relationship *in the context* of EU law, but rather, more generally, it is concerned with the distribution of legislative competences – as well as relating limitations – within the national legal system.

The role of the Italian Regions in EU law varies in connection with the degree of autonomy recognised by the Constitution on a particular matter: if it is within its competence, a Region will only be able to exercise a certain prerogative.[21] For example, social security (*previdenza sociale* [22]) is exclusively the domain of the central State which explains why the Regions would find it difficult to influence the political decisions of the central State at national as well as at EU level. Or, conversely, consider "land-use regulation and planning" (*governo del territorio*[23]), which is a shared competence of the State and the Regions.[24] Here, the Regions may exercise their powers in making and implementing EU law, although, as will be shown below, there is little scope for such intervention.

As mentioned earlier (see Sect. A.I. above), with the constitutional reform of 2001, three different criteria for the distribution of legislative competences between the State and the Regions have been introduced into the Italian Constitution.

In accordance with Art. 117 of the Italian Constitution, the first criterion is based on a *list* of matters that are the exclusive competence of the State (that is, attributed to the national Parliament[25]). The second criterion, the so-called *shared* or legislative competence, in accordance with Art. 117 of the Constitution, is based upon a list of matters that are the competence of both national and regional legislative bodies.[26] On these subjects, the national Parliament has the right to establish the

---

[21]See Vesperini (2008), pp. 1427–1452.

[22]See Art. 117, paragraph 2, lit. *o*), Constitution.

[23]See Chiti (2003), pp. 91–107.

[24]See Art. 117, paragraph 3, Constitution.

[25]See Art. 117, paragraph 2, Constitution: "The State has exclusive legislative power in the following matters: (...)".

[26]See Art. 117, paragraph 3, Constitution: "The following matters are subject to the shared competence of both the State and Regions (...)".

basic principles,[27] whereas the regional Councils (which are the regional legislative bodies – in a sense they can be described as regional parliaments in that they consist of representatives elected by the people) – implement the State legislation by means of *detailed rules*. Finally, the third criterion, as provided for in Art. 117(4) of the Constitution,[28] states that matters not included in any of the two aforementioned lists fall within the sphere of the Regions and the national Parliament does not have any right to intervene. Indeed, as stated verbatim in the aforementioned provision: "The Regions have legislative power with respect to any matter not expressly reserved to State Law" (so-called "residuary" or "exclusive" regional powers).

Art. 117 of the Constitution makes several references to the EU. First and foremost, the State has exclusive competence vis-à-vis relations of the State with the EU.[29] Matters which concern the international or EU relations of the Regions are the shared competence of the State and the Regions. But these two allocations of competence do not exhaust the points of contact between the Regions and the EU in Art. 117. Indeed, the *lists* of subject areas included in the quoted article also concern: "protection of competition",[30] "protection of the environment",[31] "harbours and civil airports",[32] and "health protection".[33] These are all matters which are directly influenced by EU law, in the sense that corresponding European legal norms exist and are contained in the EU Treaty or in EU secondary law.[34] Among these matters, some are reserved for the exclusively for the central State, others for the shared competence of the State and the Regions, and yet others are the exclusive competence of the Regions. An example of the latter is "public contracts", notwithstanding that it also relates to "protection of competition", which is the exclusive competence of the State. It is axiomatic that whenever the State or the Regions regulate one of these *areas* by law, they have to consider, in order to avoid an infringement of EU law, the legislation issued by the EU institutions on the same area.

By the same token, a Region has participation rights in the EU law-making process when EU measures relate to a matter of its competence. This is the so-called *fase ascendente* of EU law (literally meaning "*rising* phase") will be discussed in the Sects. B.I and B.II. The enforcement and implementation of EU law by the Regions, the so-called *fase discendente* of EU law (literally meaning "*falling* phase") will be approached in Sect. D.

It is also appropriate to mention that the principle provided by Art. 117, paragraph 1 of the 2001 constitutional reform: "Legislative power belongs to the

[27]See Art. 117, paragraph 3, Constitution (last period): "In matters of concurrent legislation, the Regions have legislative power except for basic principles which are reserved to State law".

[28]See Art. 117, paragraph 4, Constitution.

[29]See Art. 117, paragraph 2, lit. *a*), Constitution.

[30]See Art. 117, paragraph 2, lit. *e*), Constitution.

[31]See Art. 117, paragraph 2, lit. *s*), Constitution.

[32]See Art. 117, paragraph 3, Constitution.

[33]See Art. 117, paragraph 3, Constitution.

[34]See, for example, Abbondante (2006), pp. 109–146.

State and the Regions in accordance with the Constitution and within the limits set by European Union law and International Obligations". It has been maintained by leading scholars that this principle does not add very much to the existing legal framework. Indeed, the Italian Constitutional Court has in the past decided that EU law prevails over the domestic law inclusive of the Constitution.[35] This was made possible through a broad construction of Art. 11 of the Constitution.[36] This provision, even though it does not directly concern European integration, has traditionally formed the *constitutional basis* for Italian participation in the European integration process, as it is the vindicating foundation of direct applicability and direct effect of EU law within the Italian legal system.[37]

The only limit, still in force today, to the prevalence of EU law over Italian domestic law is that of the inviolability of the "fundamental principles of the constitutional system" (*principi fondamentali dell'ordinamento costituzionale*) and of the "inalienable rights of the human person" (*diritti inalienabili della persona umana*), which the same Constitutional Court upheld.[38] It is for this reason that the prevailing opinion as to the relationship between EU law and domestic law is that the 2001 constitutional amendment was limited to the codification of the already existing *acquis*.

It has nevertheless to be remembered that the Constitutional Court with its ruling No. 406 of 3 November 2005,[39] declared (for the first time) the unconstitutionality of a statute, a regional one, owing to the violation of EU law (that is, owing to the violation of the "limits set by European Union law", *vincoli derivanti dall'ordinamento comunitario*, referred to by Art. 117, paragraph 1, of the Italian Constitution). Therefore, the Court now will judge on the validity of national statutes according to whether they comply with EU obligations. It is the first time, indeed, that a statute has been declared void by the Constitutional Court because it is in breach of EU law.[40] The topic is of great interest, but, in keeping with the ambit of this work, at this juncture of our discussion, we need to analyse the relationship between State and Regions in making and implementing EU law.

---

[35]See D'Atena (2002c). See also Panara (2006), pp. 796–799.

[36]See Art. 11 Constitution ("Repudiation of War"): "Italy repudiates war as an instrument offending the liberty of the peoples and as a means for settling international disputes", and especially "it agrees to limitations of sovereignty where they are necessary to allow for a legal system of peace and justice between Nations, provided the principle of reciprocity is guaranteed; it promotes and encourages international organizations furthering such ends".

[37]See Cassese (1975), pp. 565–591; but also Bartole (2004), p. 276.

[38]This is the "controlimiti" doctrine elaborated by the Italian Constitutional Court. See the decisions on the case *Frontini* No. 183 of 27 December 1973 and above all on the case *Granital* No. 170 of 8 June 1984 (point 7 of the reasoning), available at http://www.giurcost.org (last checked on 15 June 2010). In the literature see Sorrentino (2002), p. 1355. See also Tizzano (2007), pp. 734–744, and Panara (2008b), pp. 158–159.

[39]Available at http://www.giurcost.org (last checked on 15 June 2010).

[40]See Napoli (2010); Celotto (2010); and finally Calvano (2006).

B. Regional Participation

According to the Italian leading legal scholar Antonio D'Atena, regional participation in the formulation of the *Italian position* for the making of EU law may be defined as the "rising phase" (*fase ascendente*) of EU-law.[41]

The involvement of the Regions at any point preceding the creation of EU legislation is important, especially in terms of the democracy of EU law.[42] As noted above, indeed, EU legislation influences matters which at the national level may be assigned to the Regions. If the Regions are not involved in the EU law-making process, one of the risks would be the debasing of the political worth of the regional legislators.[43] The second appreciable result of regional participation is that it acts like a sort of *cooling chamber* (*camera di raffreddamento*) *combining* different positions, resolving – or at least trying to resolve – potential conflicts between State and Regions right at the very start, as well as those between Regions and the European Union. Last but not least, such participation results in a greater inclination of the Regions to *more closely observe* (*stretta osservanza*) EU legislation throughout the process of its national implementation and enforcement.

The Italian Regions equipped with legislative power, play a major role in the implementation of EU law at the domestic level (see Sect. D below). However, notwithstanding this, they do not significantly influence the EU law-making process, they effectively *execute* decisions taken by others (the central Government).

The law-making process has both *internal* and *external* phases.

In the *external* phase, Regions' representatives participate, in the meetings organised at the EU level, with the aim of explaining and *protecting* their own interests.

In the same way, and with the same purpose, the Regions also take part internally by way of the meetings organised at the national level, and in this substantiates what we have defined above internal phase (see Sect. B.I below).

The constitutional basis of the law making process (both *internal* and *external*) can be traced back to the *new* Art. 117(5) of the Constitution, which provides for the participation of the Regions in the making of EU law.[44] This constitutional provision is further detailed by two "ordinary" (sub-constitutional) national parliamentary statutes. The first one, dealing with the *external* participation of the Regions, is known as the "La Loggia" Act (Act No. 131 of 5 June 2003, published in G.U. No.

---

[41]See D'Atena (1981), p. 110.

[42]See Ridola (2002), pp. 75–91.

[43]See Paladin (1996), pp. 1031–1040.

[44]See Art. 117, paragraph 5: "Regarding the matters that lie within their field of competence, the Regions and the Autonomous Provinces of Trento and Bolzano participate in any decisions about the formation of community law. The Regions and Autonomous Provinces also provide for the implementation and execution of international obligations and of the acts of the European Union in observance of procedures set by State law (. . .)". See, also, Mastroianni (2006), pp. 423–442. See Tufarelli and Rollè (2005), p. 139.

132 of 10 June 2003). The second one, dealing with *internal* participation, is known as the "Buttiglione" Act (Act No. 11 of 4 February 2005, published in G.U. No. 37 of 15 February 2005).

I. Internal Participation

Participation of the Regions in the EU law-making process is useful in order to achieve a "unitary position" that can be presented in the various EU bodies and organs. Even before the 2001 constitutional reform, Italian law provided for the obligation of the Government to communicate EU legislative proposals to the Regions so that they could make "observations".[45]

The first significant intervention regarding this area is that of the so-called "Fabbri" Act[46] (so-named after the proponent), which established certain information duties in favour of the Regions in relation to EU matters.[47] However, various circumstances contributed to the overall very poor performance of this instrument. In particular, there was no deadline setting a time by which EU draft acts should have been communicated to the Regions, with the inevitable risk of making eventual observations of the Regions late and useless.[48]

There were numerous attempts to alleviate this *deficiency*. In particular, the State–Regions Conference was introduced, but had little impact.[49]

Ultimately, in order to implement the new version of Art. 117, paragraph 5, of the Constitution, as amended in 2001, the so-called "Buttiglione" Act was passed.[50] This Act repealed the earlier so-called "La Pergola" Act[51] and – together with the aforementioned "La Loggia" Act – it completed the legal framework relating to the law-making process.

In order to improve regional participation in making EU law at the *internal* level (so-called *internal* rising phase), the "Buttiglione" Act provides for a number of *communication mechanisms*, aimed at making the *point of view* of the Regions known to the Government. It is important to note that the *protagonist* of EU law-making process within the context of the Italian legal order is certainly the national Government (the Council of Ministers); other organs and bodies, especially

[45]See strozzi (1988), p. 354

[46]Statute No. 183, of 16 April 1987 ("Coordination of policies related to membership of the European Communities and the adaptation of the internal Community legislation").

[47]See Arts. 9 and 10, Statute No. 183, of 16 April 1987, cited.

[48]See Tesauro (1989), pp. 11–26.

[49]See Bifulco (1997), pp. 101–141.

[50]See Bientinesi (2007), pp. 967–998; Mastroianni (2006), pp. 423–442; Cannizzaro (2005), pp. 153–156; finally Contaldi (2005), pp. 515–527.

[51]Statute No. 86 of 9 March 1989 "General rules on the participation of the Community regulatory process and procedures of implementation of Community obligations". See Tizzano (1997), pp. 795–809; and critics of Strozzi (1992), pp. 111–123.

national Parliament and Regions, perform a secondary role.[52] However, a significant result of the "Buttiglione" Act is that the content of the rules stipulating the participation of the Parliament and of the Regions is almost identical. This demonstrates that the national Government is privileged to the detriment of the powers of intervention of organs of great importance (national Parliament, Regional Executives and Regional Councils). It goes without saying that this situation compounds the participation problem which can be seen at the EU level by adding problems at the national level, perhaps termed an 'Italian democratic deficit'.

It does not escape our attention that the national Parliament could recuperate some of the power lost by virtue of the so-called *legge comunitaria*, which is a special statute passed by the Parliament every year in order to conform the Italian State to all EU directives and regulations issued the year before (see further Sect. D below). However, the *legge comunitaria* concerns the implementation of EU law, whereas the real issue is the formation of such a law. Moreover, we must remember that the bill of *legge comunitaria* is drafted by the Government and that such a bill rarely undergoes significant alteration by the national Parliament. This is compounded because of the rather brief period of time which is permitted for discussion.

In relation to those activities which are directed towards the making of EU law, Arts. 3 and 5 of the "Buttiglione" Act provide for a substantially analogous system of rules for the Parliament and the Regions which is resolved in the possibility of expressing "observations" – or at most – a "reservation of examination by the Parliament" (*riserva di esame parlamentare*). In accordance with Art. 3 of the "Buttiglione" Act, the Government must submit EU legislative proposals to the two Houses of the Italian Parliament (*Camera dei Deputati* and *Senato della Repubblica*) in order for the Parliament to be able to formulate its "observations" (Art. 3, paragraph 7).

In addition, during the EU Council of Ministers, the National Government may set a "reservation of examination by the Parliament" regarding a EU legislative proposal, in order to allow the Parliament to express its position on it. However, this is a *weak* constraint because the effects of an eventual negative outcome are not clarified. Furthermore, whenever such a parliamentary pronouncement is not adopted within a brief period of time, the national Government may proceed even in the absence of observations or a statement of reservation.[53] It is doubtful that this mechanism measures up to EU law. According to a Protocol annexed to the Treaty of Lisbon, EU legislative proposals must be forwarded to national Parliaments at least eight weeks prior to being adopted.[54] At the end of eight weeks, the EU

[52]See Baroncelli (2008), pp. 151–179.

[53]See Art. 4, paragraph 3, "Buttiglione" Act: "On expiry of the period of 20 days of Communication, the Government may proceed even without parliamentary pronouncement [..]".

[54]See Art. 4 Protocol (No. 1) on the "Role of National Parliaments in the European Union", adopted on 9 May 2008, available at http://www.issirfa.cnr.it/4719,46.html?PHPSESSID=5b909da245614997b17af9df2bc9d867 (last checked on 15 June 2010), which provides for a period of eight weeks instead of six weeks (see Art. 4). See also Salmoni (2005), pp. 16–19.

Council of Ministers may make a decision. Moreover, in the generality of cases, the EU Council of Ministers shall decide by qualified majority voting, so that non-participation of one State shall certainly not impede the functioning of the Council. Therefore, the reservation of examination by the Parliament only has the effect of blocking the activity of the Italian Government, without placing constraints on the EU Council of Ministers.

At the national level, such reservations of examination by the Parliament produce effects only in the relationship between the Parliament and the Government, and not between the State and the Regions. In the Italian constitutional setting, in fact, only the Parliament is equipped with real powers to control the work of the Government and may invoke political liability of the latter through a vote of confidence.[55]

A system similar to that provided for in Art. 3 of the "Buttiglione" Act also operates in favour of the Regions (see Art. 5 of the "Buttiglione" Act).[56] Here too – so that, within a brief period,[57] the Regions may transmit "observations" – Art. 5 provides that the Government must inform the Regions of EU legislative proposals which fall within the subject areas of the regional legislative competence. By the same token as for the Parliament, but this time upon request of the State–Regions Conference, the "Buttiglione" Act provides for the possibility of raising a "reservation of examination" before the EU Council of Ministers (and this, obviously, in the case of Union legislative proposals relating to matters attributed to regional legislative competence). Such a "reservation", also for organisational reasons, given the high number of Regional Councils, is placed before the State–Regions Conference, the only body able to represent the Italian Regions in a unitary way.[58] However, as previously seen, the regional "reservation of examination" is *weak*, because of the fact that the Government may decide to proceed in its absence.[59] Therefore, in a case where a Union legislative proposal concerns a matter within the regional legislative competence, the Government, upon the request of the Regions, is obliged to convene the State–Regions Conference in order to try to reach an "agreement" as to which position to adopt.[60] This agreement, too, has to be reached within a short period of time, upon the expiry of which the Government may proceed anyway, just as it may proceed when there is lack of agreement in cases

[55]See Art. 94 Italian Constitution, paragraphs 1 and 5: "Government has to enjoy the confidence of both Houses. [. . .]. The request for a vote of no-confidence requires the signatures of at least one-tenth of the members of either House and is not debated until three days after it has been filed".

[56]See Carbone and Ivaldi (2005), pp. 701–743.

[57]See Art. 5, paragraph 3, "Buttiglione" Act, cit.: "For the position of the Italian Regions (...) within twenty days from the date of receipt of documents (...) may submit comments to the President of the Council of Ministers or the Minister for Community Policies".

[58]See Spadacini (2007), pp. 353–430.

[59]See Art. 5, paragraph 5, "Buttiglione" Act, cit.: "On expiry of the period of twenty days (...), the Government may proceed even without the delivery of the Conference".

[60]See Art. 3, Legislative Decree No. 281 of 28 August 1997, "Definition and extension of the powers of the State–Regions Conference".

of "unexpected and motivated urgent need" (*casi di urgenza motivata sopravvenuta*).[61] Mastroianni has pointed out that there is a direct correlation between a "reservation of examination" and the procedure for reaching an "agreement".[62] The right to ask the Government to raise a "reservation of examination" (parliamentary or regional) before the EU Council of Ministers may in fact have the consequence of slowing down the EU procedure while an agreement is reached at the national level.

By way of summary, even in the internal phase, we have to point out that the participatory tools available to both the Parliament and the Regions are relatively unimportant compared to the power of the Government. Therefore, D'Atena's longstanding criticisms are confirmed in that the Conference-based system ends up being a *weak* tool, whereby the "agreements" are really "camouflaged opinions" (*pareri camuffati*) which in no way contribute to, or reinforce, the regional position.[63]

Internal regional participation in the EU law-making process is, finally, enriched by the introduction of a new body: the *Comitato Interministeriale per gli Affari Comunitari Europei* (Interministerial Committee for EC/EU Affairs, hereinafter referred to as CIACE"), which is convened and chaired by the Prime Minister, or the Minister for European Affairs.[64] Within a framework for the general strengthening of the principle of "loyal collaboration" (*leale collaborazione*) between the levels of governance,[65] the CIACE reinforces the coordination and the link between the national Government and the Regions in the EU law-making process. As established by Art. 2 of the "Buttiglione" Act, the negotiating position of Italy in the EU law-making process is agreed by the Government and the Regions within the CIACE. In light of the various functions of this body, the Regions may request to be allowed to participate in the meetings of the CIACE in order to express their *point of view*.[66]

There is, however, in relation to the CIACE, a problem in that there is a risk of encroachment and overlapping with the powers of the State–Regions Conference.[67] Looking at this issue more closely, though, we can see an important and substantial difference between the CIACE and the State–Regions Conference: this is the fact that the activity undertaken in the State-Regions Conference finds expression in formal acts, such as, especially, the aforementioned "observations" and "agreements". The State–Regions cooperation within the CIACE does not take place in

[61]See Art. 5, paragraph 4, "Buttiglione" Act, cit.

[62]See Mastroianni (2006), pp. 423–442.

[63]See D'Atena (1988), p. 343; but also D'Atena (1991), pp. 3908–3909. To this criticism, besides, it is to add that concerning the costs of the information system.

[64]See Art. 2, paragraph 1, "Buttiglione" Act, cit.: "Participating Foreign Minister, one for Regional Affairs (now 'for Regional Affairs and Local Autonomy') and Ministers with responsibility for matters that are the subject of the topics covered in individual CIACE meetings".

[65]See Anzon (1986), pp. 1039–1042.

[66]See Art. 2, paragraph 2, "Buttiglione" Act, cit.

[67]See Parodi and Puoti (2006).

the form of "observations" and "agreements", nor does it lead to the adoption of any other formal act. The CIACE is instead limited to the functions of *link, reflection, study and discussion* between those organs and bodies involved in the making of EU law. To conclude, the role and activities of the CIACE, are distinct from the typical acts of the State–Regions Conference.[68] Rather, it could be said that there is a *functional connection* between the two bodies and one could argue that the CIACE carries out a "subservient" role (that is, an auxiliary rôle) to the State–Regions Conference. In sum the CIACE defines the position of the Government, which – in cases where the matter is of regional competence – will then confront the Regions in the State–Regions Conference.

The overall impression is that the "Buttiglione" Act offers a truly *statist* point of view (*lettura statalista*) – that is, in favour of the *central State* and not of the *Regions* – of the constitutional reform of 2001, since it recognises that Regions only have consultative powers with respect to decisions taken by the national Government.[69]

II. External Participation

It will be recalled that even in the absence of a specific legislative provision, some Italian Regions have traditionally held "direct contacts" with the EU institutions (especially with regard to economic and cultural issues).

These "contacts" were later covered by the *legge comunitaria* 1994 (Act No. 52 of 6 February 1996), which provides the option for the Regions (and Autonomous Provinces) to set up special liaison offices (*uffici di collegamento*) in Brussels. According to Art. 58, paragraph 4, of the cited act, the specific purpose of these offices is to "maintain relations with the EU institutions on matters within their competence". The cited act does not specify the duties of those offices. In this regard, however, it can be said that their main function is to promote – especially through information and documentation – EU initiatives in favour of interests sponsored by the Regions. In essence, the liaison offices have the task of "lobbying" with the EU institutions to protect the interests of one or more Regions. Also in the same cited act, an additional direct link is expected (*collegamento diretto*) between Regions and EU. Indeed, in paragraph 2 of Art. 58, we find that among the "experts" from the Permanent Representation of the Italian Ministry of Foreign Affairs to the European Union, there shall be four regional officers (or officers of the Autonomous Provinces) designated by the Conference of Presidents of Regions and Autonomous Provinces (*Conferenza dei Presidenti delle Regioni e delle Province Autonome*).[70]

---

[68] See "Buttiglione" Act, cit. and also Decree of President of the Council of Ministers (of 9 January 2006) "Regulations for the Interministerial Committee for European Affairs Committees (CIACE) working".

[69] See Cannizzaro (2005), pp. 153–156.

[70] See Rivello (1995), p. 265.

Article 5 of the "La Loggia" Act, relating to "enforcement of Art. 117, paragraph 5, of the Constitution", provides for the participation of the Italian Regions in the Union institutions. This is, more specifically, about participation in the meetings of the EU Council of Ministers, as well as working groups and committees of the Council and of the Commission. Therefore, in light of this provision, "participation rights" of the Regions in the external phase of EU law-making are recognised. The true and actual weight of such participation is restricted by the *indivisibility* of the Italian delegation before EU bodies. This is due to the need to guarantee the unitary position (*posizione unitaria*) of the Italian Republic by way of the Chief representative designated by the Government.[71] This unitary position is a response to the national interest as referred to by Art. 5 of the Italian Constitution.[72] It seems evident that the duty of guaranteeing the unitary position noticeably reduces the degree to which regional participation may be influential.

Indeed, such limitation was at the core of a State–Regions litigation settled by the Constitutional Court with its ruling No. 239 of 19 July 2004.[73] The Regions challenged the constitutionality of Art. 5 of the "La Loggia" Act, because it endows the Regions with participation rights which in practice are ineffective.[74] Moreover, according to the claimants – that is: the Sardinia Region, which is a Region with special autonomy, and the Autonomous Province of Bolzano – Art. 5 was in breach of the new Art. 117, paragraph 3, of the Constitution, which assigns "international relations and relations of the Regions with the European Union" to the shared legislative competence of the State and the Regions (see also above). Indeed, according to the claimant Regions, the new constitutional system would have allowed for the national legislator to exclusively adopt a general legal framework, reserving detailed regulation for the regional legislature. The Constitutional Court, however, made it clear – justifying the constitutional legitimacy of the "La Loggia" Act – that the system contained in Art. 5 is the expression of a *further* and *exclusive* legislative power of the State, which can be traced back to the fifth paragraph of Art. 117 Italian Constitution.[75]

Art. 5 of the "La Loggia" Act – after declaring that the Regions (and the Autonomous Provinces) have a right of *direct* participation in the EU decision-

---

[71]See Cannizzaro (2003), pp. 3–11; but also Diverio (2005), pp. 1153–1165.

[72]See Art. 5 Italian Constitution: "The Republic, one and indivisible, recognizes and promotes local autonomy (. . .)"; and also Parodi (2003), p. 41.

[73]Available at http://www.cortecostituzionale.it (last checked on 15 June 2010); see Cerulli Irelli and Luciani (2007), pp. 859–891; Violini (2005), pp. 226–236; finally Diverio (2005), pp. 1153–1165.

[74]See point 1, "Part in law", case No. 239 of 19 July 2004, available at http://www.giurcost.org (last checked on 15 June 2010).

[75]Indeed, according to the paragraph 5 of Art. 117, "Regarding the matters that lie within their field of competence, the Regions and the Autonomous Provinces of Trento and Bolzano participate in any decisions about the formation of Community Law. The Regions and Autonomous Provinces also provide for the implementation and execution of international obligations and of the acts of the European Union in observance of procedures set by State act".

making process and that, in matters of exclusive legislative competence of the Regions, a President of a Region (or of an Autonomous Province) can be the head of the Italian delegation to the Council – also establishes that it shall be for the State–Regions Conference to set up the "methods" (*modalità*) of regional participation in the EU institutions.[76] Almost three years after the approval of the "La Loggia" Act, the State-Regions Conference defined the methods of participation of the Regions in the activities of the EU bodies in Brussels in the "General Cooperation Agreement" of 16 March 2006.[77] Regarding the composition of the Government delegation that takes part in the activities of the Council, the 2006 Agreement establishes, at Art. 2, that the regional representation within the Government delegation is constituted by a Region President[78] (designated by the Regions with ordinary autonomy) and a President of a Region with special autonomy or of an Autonomous Province (designated by the five Regions and the two Provinces concerned). Furthermore, Art. 4 of the Agreement sets out criteria for the choice of the head of the Italian delegation to the Council. It establishes that, in matters of exclusive legislative competence of the Regions, a central Government representative will normally be the head of delegation; however, the Government and the Regions may agree within the State-Regions Conference to adopt "a different solution". This statement implicitly paves the way to the appointment of a President of a Region (or of an Autonomous Province) as head of the Italian delegation. However, this will be possible *only if* an agreement will be reached within the State-Regions Conference.

The aforementioned provisions need to be compared with Art. 16, paragraph 2, TEU (ex Art. 203 EC). Indeed, according to this article: *The Council shall consist of a representative of each Member State at ministerial level, who may commit the government of the Member State in question and cast its vote.* Therefore the State representatives in the Council must be of "ministerial level" and the Presidents of the Regions acting as head of the Italian delegation must be considered as being of "ministerial level" even at the price of a juridical misrepresentation. In fact the Italian constitutional law does not confer ministerial status to the Presidents of the Regions or of the Autonomous Provinces. In practice, it was never the case that a regional representative was appointed head of the Italian delegation to the Council. It must be highlighted, however, that the presence of Region delegates in the EU Council does not suitably guarantee Regional *interests*, since the duty to ensure the "unitary position" of the State remains paramount, which as we have already stated previously, is bound up with the need for Italy to speak with a *single voice* in the international arena.[79]

---

[76]See Posillipo (2006), pp. 155–199.

[77]The text of the agreement is available at http://notes1.regione.vda.it/dbweb/rapist/rapist.nsf/(apri)/2D27EC66FBD9A44CC12572E5003A0051/$file/accordo%2016marzo2006.pdf?OpenElement (last checked on 15 June 2010).

[78]See Art. 121 ("Regional Organs"), paragraph 4, Constitution: "The President of the Regional Cabinet represents the Region".

[79]See Ruggeri (2005).

Finally, it is necessary to say something on the selection of Italian members of the Committee of the Regions. Italy has 24 members.[80] The selection of the members is regulated by the recent Act No. 88 of 7 July 2009 (*legge comunitaria 2008*).[81] This Act, at Art. 6, provides that the Italian members of the Committee are not only the representatives of the Regions and of the Autonomous Provinces of Trento and Bolzano, which, as noted above, have legislative powers, but also of the other authorities that constitute the Italian Republic, including all other Provinces (i.e. other than Trento and Bolzano) and Municipalities. The appointment of the Italian members of the Committee is proposed to the EU Council by the Italian President of the Council of Ministers (i.e. the Italian Prime Minister) with the agreement of the Unified Conference State–Regions and State–Cities and Local Autonomies (a Conference where regional and local authorities are represented vis-à-vis the central government). More specifically: the Regions and the Autonomous Provinces of Trento and Bolzano have the right to be represented by 14 Committee members, the other Provinces by 3 members, and, finally, the Municipalities by 7 members. It is possible to observe that the composition of the Italian delegation to the Committee does not seem to particularly favour the representation of the Regions. In fact there are 20 Regions in Italy (plus 2 Autonomous Provinces) and some Regions do not have their own representative in the Committee.[82]

C. The Procedure Before the European Court of Justice

We have to remember that the "La Loggia" Act establishes a new power in favour of the Regions which is substantiated by the right to bring a direct claim for judicial review before the European Court of Justice.

Traditionally, the Regions can directly challenge EU measures before the European Court of Justice as simple "legal persons". Differently from Member States, Regions are not privileged applicants. Unless they are the direct addressee of a decision, they will have to prove their standing, that is to say, that they have been "directly and individually" affected by the European measure.[83]

All this taken into consideration, the "La Loggia" Act states that the Italian Government *must* bring a claim for judicial review if the relative request comes from the State-Regions Conference and is supported by an absolute majority of the Regions' and Autonomous Provinces' votes.[84] This provision is of great interest in

---

[80]See the recent Protocol No. 36, published in the Official Journal of the European Union of 9 May 2008, C 115/322).

[81]Published in G.U. No. 161 of 14 July 2009. The matter was previously regulated by a sub-legislative act: Decree of the President of the Council of Ministers of 19 December 2006 (published in G.U. No. 302 of 30 December 2006).

[82]See D'Atena (2000), pp. 555–562.

[83]See Adinolfi (2002) , pp. 309–328; Cartabia (2001), pp. 238–241.

[84]See art. 5, paragraph 2, "La Loggia" Act., cit.

that it partly compensates for the limitations which result from the EU Treaty regarding the Regions' ability to directly access the Union courts. The provision would seem to resolve the problems which regional bodies face in attempting to challenge Union action, which result from the European Court of Justice's traditional standpoint regarding this issue.[85]

This limitation, was confirmed recently in the case of the Sicily Region, which had tried (unsuccessfully) to gain *direct* access to the Union courts.[86] In detail, the controversy centred on the inadmissibility of a claim that a EU measure interrupted funding from the European Regional Development Fund (ERDF). On this occasion, the European Court of Justice confirmed, once again, that: "[...] an action by a local or regional entity cannot be treated in the same way as an action by a Member State, the term Member State within the meaning of the second paragraph of Art. 230 EC [current Art. 263 TFEU] referring only to government authorities of the Member States. That term cannot include the governments of regions or other local authorities within Member States without undermining the institutional balance provided for by the Treaty".[87]

This provision of the "La Loggia" Act,[88] is causing a sort of salvage operation of the power of the Italian Regions via *domestic channels*. In other words, in the event of Union *encroachment*, the Regions could attempt to compensate for the little weight they enjoy at EU level, through the legal device just mentioned. Considering that the EU Treaty does not contemplate the division of the competences within the Member States, it is *indifferent* to the fact that there exist Regions with and Regions without legislative powers (and this, obviously, disadvantages the former ones): so much so that Hans Peter Ipsen was used to speak of *Landes-Blindheit*, that is of an EU *blindness* with reference to the internal structure (federal or regional) of the Member States.[89]

D. The Implementation of EU Law

The State and the Regions are under the duty to implement EU law in a timely manner. The specific aim of the whole State (and constitutional) regulation is that of avoiding *infringements* brought about by breaches of EU law.

There is no doubt that in matters of regional competence[90] implementation of EU law is the responsibility of the Regions.[91] In this regard, we need to remember

[85]See Villamena (2006), pp. 25–27.

[86]See the ruling of the ECJ C-417/04 [2006], *Regione Siciliana v. Commission*, in: ECR I-3881.

[87]See point 21 of the aforementioned case.

[88]See art. 5, paragraph 2, "La Loggia" Act, cit.

[89]See Ipsen (1966), pp. 248–265; and also D'Atena (1998), pp. 1401–1425.

[90]See Furlan (2005), pp. 125–151.

[91]See Odone (2007), pp. 327–352.

an essential point, which is represented by the structure of Italy as a regional State. Indeed, if there were no Regions in the Italian context, the central State would be the sole body having to deal with the timely and punctual fulfilment of obligations deriving from EU law. However, with Italy being a regional State, quite the opposite applies. Sharing responsibility with regional authorities for the implementation of EU law results in a complex system which risks *confusion* in the correct implementation of EU obligations. In addition, the State is the sole body responsible to the European institutions for all breaches of EU law, including those which are exclusively attributable to inertia or bad implementation by the Regions.[92]

Attention to this profile came into being especially with the passing of the 1989 "La Pergola" Act,[93] through which the annual *legge comunitaria* mechanism was introduced.[94] Since the enactment of the "La Pergola" Act, the old issue of delays in implementing EU legislation has largely been overcome.[95] According to recent studies, the infringements of EU law that are attributable to sub-state entities are, in a large number of cases, the result of positive action which leads to *violations* of EU law. Fewer cases of infringement are caused by *omitted* implementation of EU law by the Regions.[96] A final and interesting factor which arises from the aforementioned studies is that the Italian Regions, especially because of normative complexity, are responsible for the infringement of EU obligations to a large degree in those matters relating to the "internal market" (and, above all, with public procurement)[97] and the "environment".

The Italian authorities have tried to tackle this issue. This has led, for example, to the very recent introduction of a particularly *strong* tool against regional breaches of EU law, which consists of the "right of redress"[98] ("diritto di rivalsa") for *damages* sustained by the State. The right of redress serves, in particular, to keep the attention of the Regions *alive* regarding the implementation of EU obligations in those areas of their competence and carries with it the payment by the Regions of a sum of money for "financial damages" resulting from judgments of the European Court of Justice[99]: in practice the "right of redress" is a deterrent tool which confers relief for the loss suffered by the State. An initial criticism of this normative system

[92]See Manfredi (2000), pp. 843–848; and Parodi and Puoti (2006).

[93]See Tizzano (1999), pp. 303–310.

[94]See Caretti (1991), pp. 331–350; and De Rose (1994), pp. 81–90.

[95]See Bientinesi (2005), pp. 849–910.

[96]See Parodi and Puoti (2006).

[97]See De Maio (2006), pp. 147–182.

[98]See Art. 16 *bis*, "Buttiglione" Act, cit.; and see also Sterpa (2010). Art. 16 *bis* has been added to the "Buttiglione" Act by Art. 6, paragraph 1, of the Act No. 34 of 25 February 2008 (*legge comunitaria 2007*), in G.U. No. 56, Supplemento ordinario, of 6 March 2008.

[99]See Art. 16 *bis*, paragraph 4, "Buttiglione" Act, cit. Paragraph 5 of the same Act establishes that the State has a similar "right of redress" against the Regions (and other public bodies) responsible for a violation of the European Convention on Human Rights (ECHR). On this point see Spadea (2009), pp. 263–271.

is that the "right of redress" seems to be classified not as an *obligation* but as a *right*. To guarantee the effectiveness of the tool, the legislature should have considered an obligatory action. Having provided a "right" in favour of the State, however, seems to have allowed for a certain amount of discretion in the proposition of the action. This may result in decreasing the effectiveness of this new tool.

All this considered, we have to remember the main tool for implementing EU obligations: the aforementioned *legge comunitaria*.

This is a statute enacted every year by the national Parliament in order to update the national legal system with the EU legislation of that year, with the aim of preventing infringements of EU obligations.[100] This statute has two principal purposes: the first is *informative* in nature, the other *operational*. As to the former, the *legge comunitaria, looking into the past*, considers whether Italian law is fully compliant with EU law.[101] To this end, the national Government is given the task to report to the Parliament on existing infringement actions against the Italian State for non-fulfilment of EU law and on the outcome of cases decided by the European Court of Justice against Italy. As to the latter, the *operational* purpose, in order to ensure conformity with EU law, the *legge comunitaria* itself, *looking at the future*, identifies the future actions that provide for implementation of EU law. This increasingly comes about by way of acts of the Government, through the mechanism of legislative delegation (Art. 76 of the Constitution[102]) or via Government regulations.[103] In other words, the Government is entitled to implement the EU directives in *all* areas (including the areas falling within the sphere of legislative competence of the Regions). This is an *ex ante* substitution power exercisable by the Government via delegated legislation. However, the substitution norms issued by the State are characterised by the "pliability" (*cedevolezza*). This means that, if the State substitutes its norms for those of the Regions, then at a later stage the Regions may repeal such norms by means of their own statutes and regain control over the areas of their competence.

Several other points are noteworthy vis-à-vis State-Regions relations regarding the approval of the *legge comunitaria*.

The first is that by means of a *legge comunitaria* the "basic principles"[104] (in matters of shared legislative competence) for exercising regional legislative competences are established (see also Sect. A.II above).[105] Secondly, on the basis of the *legge comunitaria* the national Government may adopt legislative provisions

---

[100] See Art. 8, paragraph 4, "Buttiglione" Act, cit.: "by January 31 of each year the bill should be presented to the Parliament".

[101] See Art. 8, paragraph 5, lit. *a*), "Buttiglione" Act, cit.

[102] Which states: "Legislative power may not be delegated to the Government unless Parliament specifies principles and criteria of guidance, and only for limited time and well-specified subjects".

[103] See Art. 9, paragraph 1, lit. *c*) and lit. *d*), "Buttiglione" Act, cit.

[104] See last period Art. 117, paragraph 3, Constitution cit., states: "In matters of concurrent legislation, the Regions have legislative power except for basic principles which are reserved to State law" (see above, Art. 117, paragraph 3, Constitution, last period).

[105] See Art. 9, paragraph 1, lit. *f*), "Buttiglione" Act, cit.

(legislative decrees) providing for *criminal penalties* for the event of a violation of EU provisions implemented by the Regions.[106] This is justified by the fact that the Regions do not have legislative power as regards "criminal law" ("ordinamento penale"). Indeed, the matter[107] belongs to the exclusive competence of the State (Parliament). Finally, the written introduction by the Government to the Bill of the *legge comunitaria* should provide a list of all the acts by means of which the Regions have implemented EU laws in their areas of competence.[108]

This regional implementation of EU law, clearly in matters of shared or exclusively regional competence (see Sect. A.II above), may also occur by means of the not much used *leggi comunitarie regionali* (lit. regional Community acts).[109] The regional Community act is a compact mechanism, that is, an annual regional statute, which imposes clear and tight deadlines for the implementation of EU obligations by the Region, so as to avoid the risk of delays in implementation and, therefore, of fines.

E. The Substitution Power

In the part of the *legge comunitaria* of the State which we have called *informative*, the events are provided for where the substitution power shall be exercised.[110] This power represents the main tool of the central State against the inertia or *violations committed by the Regions* in implementing EU law. In this regard, we have first of all to consider the two hypotheses of *substitution* regulated by Art. 117, paragraph 5, and Art. 120, paragraph 2, of the Constitution.[111] Both provisions have been rewritten by the aforementioned 2001 constitutional reform.

Art. 117, paragraph 5, establishes the methods of exercising the substitution power; a "regional breach of EU law", will be rectified by means of a State act. Art. 120, paragraph 2, establishes instead a series of specific hypotheses where the exercise of the substitution power is possible; among those hypotheses there is the "violation of international rules or treaties or of Community Law". Other cases, in which the national Government may exercise its substitution power for the Regions, are: "whenever there is a serious danger for public safety and security, and whenever such substitution is required in order to safeguard the legal or economic unity of the Nation, and particularly in order to safeguard the basic standards of

[106] See Art. 9, paragraph 1, lit. *g*), "Buttiglione" Act, cit.

[107] In accordance with Art. 117, paragraph 2, lit. *l*), of the Constitution. See Romano (2008), pp. 538–558.

[108] See Art. 8, paragraph 5, lit. *e*), "Buttiglione" Act, cit.

[109] See Art. 8, paragraph 5, lit. *e*), "Buttiglione" Act, cit. See Vipiana (2007), pp. 449–480 and Villamena (2007), pp. 259–288.

[110] See Art. 9, paragraph 1, lit. *h*), "Buttiglione" Act, cit.

[111] See Fontana (2005); and Villamena (2002), p. 231.

welfare relating to civil and social rights, irrespective of the boundaries of the local authorities".

The existence of two constitutional provisions dealing with the same matter creates a certain amount of confusion.[112]

The "La Loggia" Act does not dedicate a great deal of attention to this issue; on the contrary, it is concerned mainly with the *external* law-making process (see Sect. B.II above). The "La Loggia" Act exclusively regulates the regime of the State substitution power in the particular situations provided for in Art. 120 of the Constitution. This system (Art. 8) is not very detailed because it establishes only that, in the situations envisaged by Art. 120 – that is, in every case and not just the ones relating to EU matters – the national Government, after having assigned a proper timescale to allow the Regions to act, and in the absence of their activity, adopts the necessary measures.[113]

It is interesting to note that the "La Loggia" Act also requires consideration of the principle of proportionality.[114] The State measure ("due" and/or "necessary") by means of which the substitution is carried out, must respect the limit of the "mildest possible means" towards the Region undergoing the substitution. The above outlined normative framework makes implicit but clear reference to the constitutional (and administrative) case law, according to which an evaluation of the proportionality of the measure adopted shall be carried out on a *case by case* basis depending on the particular circumstances of each case. Such a measure, as it has been recently noted, should be adopted with the participation of the relevant regional body, which is competent in the matters regarding which the substitution takes place.[115]

The "Buttiglione" Act deals with substitution in more detail. This is not surprising, since this Act, in contrast to the "La Loggia", is entirely devoted to adopting legal measures in order to comply with "Community obligations" (in addition to the system of participation in the EU legislative process).

The "Buttiglione" Act contains a number of legal provisions which regulate substitution power.[116] The fundamental provision is Art. 16 *bis*, paragraph 2, according to which "The State exercises the necessary substitution powers against those sub-state entities that are responsible for violation of obligations deriving from EU law or that do not provide timely implementation of the rulings of the European Court of Justice, according to the principles and procedures established by Art. 8 of the Act No. 131, 5 June 2003 [so-called 'La Loggia' Act], and by Art. 11, paragraph 8, of the present act". Art. 11, paragraph 8, of the "Buttiglione"

---

[112]See Rescigno (2002), pp. 729–752; and Caranta (2002), pp. 828–833.

[113]It is interesting to recall that, in this case, the President of the of the Region concerned has the right to take part in the meeting of the Council of Ministers deciding on the measure.

[114]See Art. 8, paragraph 5, "La Loggia" Act, cit.

[115]See Villamena (2008), p. 127.

[116]See above all Art. 9, paragraph 1, lit. *h*), of the "Buttiglione" Act and Art. 13, paragraph 2, of the same act.

Act contains a rather controversial method of substitution. In the title of this article, reference is made to the implementation of EU law "by means of regulations [subordinate legislation issued by bodies within the executive branch]", but, if we look at paragraph 8, we notice that the terminology used by the legislator is much wider in scope. It is affirmed that – so as to remedy possible inactivity of the Regions in implementing EU law – State substitution powers may be exercised by means of a "normative act". Therefore, the substitution power may be exercised by means of a mere regulation (ministerial decree) or by means of legislation. In fact, the category of "normative act" includes not only subordinate legislation but also those in a hierarchical position higher than mere sub-legislative measures. However, the main legal problem with this article remains that of the admissibility of State (sub-legislative) regulations for those matters that the Constitution attributes to regional legislative competence in accordance with Art. 117.[117]

Such an issue can be resolved by resorting to primary legislation for the substitution. Otherwise, it may be resolved by means of another tool that to a certain extent overcomes the problems with the hierarchy of legal sources in the relationship between statutes and regulations. The substitution norms issued by the State are characterised by an explicit *safety-valve rule* consisting in the "pliability" (*cedevolezza*) of the State rules. As previously noted, if the State substitutes its norms for those of the Regions, at a later stage the Regions may repeal such norms by means of their own legislation.[118] In this way, by exercising the legislative competence which they had not exercised before, the Regions, or better, those Regions that had not fulfilled all their duties, may *regain control* of their sphere of legislative competence: for example, in the case provided for by Art. 11, paragraph 8, of the "Buttiglione" Act, it is established that "State normative acts" *shall cease to be effective* in that Region from the date of the entry into force of the regional statute which implements EU law. It is obvious that the *substitution system* determines a *multivariate* situation. In certain Regions which have not implemented EU law, there may be State substitution norms in place. In others, State norms will not find application, given that these Regions implemented (rightly and within the deadline) EU law through their own norms.

To date, the only example of the exercise of the State substitution power (apart from the *ex ante* substitution taking normally place on the basis of the *leggi comunitarie*, normally through legislative decrees of the Government "authorized" by a *legge comunitaria*: see Sect. D above), is the suspension in 2006 of the

---

[117]See Salerno (2000), p. 307, and Guzzetta (1999), pp. 3746–3752; finally, Di Cosimo (2003), pp. 268–275.

[118]The Regions do not properly "repeal" the State law. In actual fact they "derogate" from it. Should the Region repeal its own statute without replacing it with a new one, then the State law previously in force would be brought back into effect and fill the gap (this phenomenon is known as the "*reviviscenza*", i.e. "reviviscence", of the State law).

application of a statute of the Liguria Region by a Government decree law.[119] This was in order to prevent an infringement of EU law due to the non-execution of a decision of the European Court of Justice.[120]

F. Conclusions

The *suit* tailored by recent national legislation in favour of the Regions indeed appears to be very *tight* for regional autonomy.

For the reasons detailed above, the complexity of the Italian regional system is likely to have resulted in a fear that an approach excessively in favour of regional participation may increase the risk of infringements of EU obligations. Our analysis fully confirms the that the Member States are the *Masters* of EU law[121] both in relation to *external* and the domestic issue.[122] Yet we also envisage that a stronger or weaker national approach in favour of the Regions in EU matters probably depends on the State–Regions balance of powers within each legal system.

This standpoint is further confirmed by the Treaty of Lisbon. This Treaty introduces into the Protocol on the application of the principles of subsidiarity and proportionality[123] a very interesting mechanism for the protection of sub-state entities. In particular, Art. 8 of the Protocol, states that the European Court of Justice decides on complaints regarding the violation of the principle of subsidiarity, even when such claims are filed by a national Parliament or a House thereof.

This innovation is of great importance for the Member States of the European Union that have a House of the Regions. In contrast, in the case of Italy, this innovation does not imply any advantage for the Regions, because none of the two Houses of the national Parliament represents them.

---

[119]See the Decree Law No. 297 of 27 December 2006 (in G.U. No. 299 of 27 December 2006) suspending the regional statute No. 36 of 31 October 2006. The Decree Law has been confirmed by the Act of the Parliament No. 15 of 23 February 2007 (in G.U. No. 46 of 24 February 2007). After about 2 months of suspension, the Liguria Region repealed its statute of 31 October 2006 by means of regional statute No. 4 of 2 February 2007.

[120]See Calini (2006); Diverio (2007), pp. 61–67; finally Arconzo (2007), pp. 618–621. The Government had previously made another attempt at exercising its substitution power on the basis of Art. 8 of the "La Loggia" Act through the Decree Law No. 251 of 16 August 2006 in order to ensure the implementation of the Directive 79/409/EEC on the protection of wild birds. However this Decree Law, lost effect given that the Parliament did not confirm it within the term of 60 days provided for by Art. 77 of the Constitution.

[121]See Ferrara (2004); and Mangiameli (2010).

[122]See Segni (2007), pp. 371–376; but also Savino (2007), pp. 433–471.

[123]Available at http://www.issirfa.cnr.it/4719,46.html?PHPSESSID=5b909da245614997b17af9df2bc9d867 (last checked on 15 June 2010).

Selected Bibliography

Abbondante F (2006) L'ambiente fra diritto comunitario e diritto interno dopo la riforma del Titolo V della Costituzione italiana. Rassegna di diritto pubblico Europeo:109–146

Adinolfi A (2002) La legittimazione delle Regioni ad impugnare atti comunitari. Rivista di diritto internazionale:309–328

Anzon A (1986) Principio cooperativo e strumenti di accordo tra le competenze statali e regionali. Giurisprudenza costituzionale:1039–1042

Arconzo G (2007) Sospensione con decreto-legge di leggi regionali: quando i casi di scuola diventano realtà. Quaderni costituzionali:618–621

Baroncelli S (ed) (2008) Il ruolo del Governo nella formazione e applicazione del diritto dell'Unione Europea. Giappichelli, Torino, pp 151–179

Bartole S (2004) Interpretazioni e trasformazioni della Costituzione repubblicana. Il Mulino, Bologna, p 276

Bientinesi F (2005) L'evoluzione della legge comunitaria nella prassi applicativa e nelle riforme istituzionali. Rassegna parlamentare:849–910

Bientinesi F (2007) La partecipazione delle Regioni e delle Province autonome ai processi normativi comunitari, alla luce della legge 4 febbraio 2005, n. 11. Rassegna parlamentare:967–998

Bifulco R (1997) Forme di Stato composto e partecipazione dei livelli regionali alla formazione della volontà statale sulle questioni comunitarie. Diritto dell'Unione Europea:101–141

Calini CB (2006) Un nuovo intervento sostitutivo dello Stato sulle Regioni per violazione della normativa comunitaria: il D.L. 27 dicembre 2006, n. 297 e l'"esecuzione" dell'ordinanza del 19 dicembre 2006 del Presidente della Corte di giustizia dell'Unione Europea. http://www.giustamm.it. Accessed 15 Jun 2010

Calvano R (2006) La Corte costituzionale e il nuovo orizzonte della tutela multilivello dei diritti fondamentali alla luce della riflessione di S. Panunzio. http://www.associazionedeicostituzionalisti.it. Accessed 15 Jun 2010

Cannizzaro E (2003) Convenzione Europea e Titolo V della Costituzione italiana: spunti critici. Il Diritto dell'Unione Europea:3–11

Cannizzaro E (2005) La riforma della 'legge La Pergola' e le competenze di Stato e Regioni nei processi di formazione e di attuazione di norme dell'Unione Europea. Rivista di diritto internazionale:153–156

Caranta R (2002) Inadempimento delle Regioni agli obblighi comunitari e poteri sostitutivi dello Stato. Urbanistica e appalti:828–833

Carbone SM, Ivaldi P (2005) La partecipazione delle Regioni agli affari comunitari e il loro potere estero. Quaderni regionali:701–743

Caretti P (1979) Ordinamento comunitario e autonomia regionale. Giuffrè, Milano

Caretti P (1991) La nuova disciplina della partecipazione dell'Italia al processo normativo comunitario e delle procedure di esecuzione degli obblighi comunitari, dettata dalla legge n. 86 del 1989 alla prova: la prima legge comunitaria. Rivista italiana di diritto pubblico comunitario:331–350

Caretti P (2003) Potere estero e ruolo 'comunitario' delle Regioni nel nuovo Titolo V della Costituzione. Le Regioni:555–574

Cartabia M (2001) Le Regioni come soggetti dell'ordinamento comunitario? Segni da decifrare nella giurisprudenza della Corte di giustizia. Quaderni costituzionali:238–241

Cassese A (1975) Articolo 11. In: Branca G, Pizzorusso A (eds) Commentario della Costituzione. Zanichelli, Bologna-Roma, pp 565–591

Celotto A (2010) La Corte costituzionale finalmente applica il primo comma dell'art. 117 Cost. http://www.giustamm.it. Accessed 15 Jun 2010

Cerulli Irelli V, Luciani F (2007) Diritto comunitario e diritto interno, tra Stato e Regioni. Rivista italiana di diritto pubblico comunitario:859–891

Chieffi L (2004) La nuova dimensione costituzionale del rapporto tra Regioni e Unione Europea. Democrazia e Diritto:87–114

Chiti MP (2003) Il ruolo della Comunità Europea nel governo del territorio. Rivista giuridica dell'edilizia:91–107

Contaldi G (2005) La disciplina della partecipazione italiana ai processi normativi comunitari alla luce della riforma della legge 'La Pergola'. Diritto dell'Unione Europea:515–527

Costanzo P (2010) La Costituzione italiana di fronte al processo costituzionale Europeo. http://www.giurcost.org. Accessed 15 Jun 2010

D'Atena A (1981) Le Regioni italiane e la Comunità economica Europea. Giuffrè, Milano, p 110

D'Atena A (1988) "Regioni", *Enciclopedia del diritto,* XXXIX. Giuffrè, Milano, p 343

D'Atena A (1991) Sulle pretese differenze tra intese 'deboli' e pareri, nei rapporti tra Stato e Regioni. Giurisprudenza costituzionale:3908–3909

D'Atena A (1998) Il doppio intreccio federale. Le Regioni:1401–1425

D'Atena A (2002b) Le Regioni e l'Europa. Quaderni Regionali:373–379

D'Atena A (2000) Il difficile cammino Europeo delle regioni italiane. Le Regioni:555–562

D'Atena A (2002a) La nuova disciplina costituzionale dei rapporti internazionali e con l'Unione Europea. Rassegna parlamentare:913–939

D'Atena A (2002c) Il nuovo Titolo V della parte II della Costituzione – Primi problemi della sua attuazione. La nuova disciplina costituzionale dei rapporti internazionali e con l'Unione Europea. http://www.associazionedeicostituzionalisti.it. Accessed 15 Jun 2010

D'Atena A (ed) (2003) L'Europa delle autonomie. Le Regioni e l'Unione Europea. Giuffrè, Milan

De Maio G (2006) Fonti regionali e direttive comunitarie in materia di appalti pubblici. Rassegna di diritto pubblico Europeo:147–182

De Rose C (1994) La legge comunitaria annuale dall'inizio al 1993: un omnibus spesso in ritardo ma che ci avvicina all'Europa. Il Consiglio di Stato:81–90

Di Cosimo G (2003) La proteiforme cedevolezza: il caso dei regolamenti di delegificazione nelle materie concorrenti. Le Regioni:268–275

Di Salvatore E (2007) Le relazioni delle Regioni italiane con l'Unione Europea: fondamento costituzionale, normativa statale e disciplina statutaria. Rassegna Parlamentare:641–672

Di Salvatore E (2008) L'identità costituzionale dell'Unione Europea e degli Stati membri: il decentramento politico-istituzionale nel processo di integrazione. Giappichelli, Torino

Diverio D (2005) La partecipazione delle regioni italiane ai lavori della commissione nel procedimento normativo comunitario. Rivista italiana di diritto pubblico comunitario:1153–1165

Diverio D (2007) Le Regioni tra l'incudine e il martello del potere sostitutivo e del diritto di rivalsa in tema di infrazioni comunitarie. Diritto pubblico comparato ed Europeo:61–67

Ferrara G (2004) La costituzione Europea: un'ambizione frustrate. http://www.costituzionalismo.it. Accessed 15 Jun 2010

Fontana G (2005) I poteri sostitutivi nella Repubblica delle autonomie. http://www.issirfa.cnr.it. Accessed 15 Jun 2010

Furlan F (2005) Recenti sviluppi in materia di attuazione della normativa comunitaria da parte delle Regioni. Rivista italiana di diritto pubblico comunitario:125–151

Guzzetta G (1999) Regolamenti statali a carattere suppletivo e competenze regionali: dalla 'decostituzionalizzazione' alla 'delegificazione' dell'autonomia territoriale in nome del diritto comunitario. Giurisprudenza costituzionale:3746–3752

Ipsen HP (1966) Als Bundesstaat in der Gemeinschaft. In: von Caemmerer E, Hallstein W (eds) Probleme des Europaeischen Rechts. Klostermann, Frankfurt a.M, pp 248–265

Manfredi G (2000) Inadempimenti nell'attuazione della valutazione di impatto ambientale e diretta applicabilità delle direttive comunitarie. Urbanistica e appalti:843–848

Mangiameli S (2010) Governo tra Unione Europea e autonomie territoriali. http://www.associazionedeicostituzionalisti.it. Accessed 15 Jun 2010

Marini FS (2003) La partecipazione regionale alle decisioni statali dirette alla formazione del diritto dell'Unione Europea. In: D'Atena A (ed) L'Europa delle autonomie. Le Regioni e l'Unione Europea. Giuffrè, Milano, p 163

Mastroianni R (2006) Il contributo delle Regioni italiane all'elaborazione del diritto dell'Unione Europea. Il Diritto dell'Unione Europea:423–442

Napoli C (2010) La Corte dinanzi ai "vincoli derivanti dall'ordinamento comunitario": tra applicazione dell'art. 117, primo comma e rispetto dei poteri interpretativi della Corte di Giustizia. http://www.forumcostituzionale.it/site/. Accessed 15 Jun 2010

Odone C (2007) Regioni e diritto comunitario: il quadro delle norme di procedura e l'attuazione regionale delle direttive CE. Istituzioni del federalism:327–352

Paladin L (1996) Il deficit democratico nell'ordinamento comunitario. Le Regioni:1031–1040

Panara C (2006) I vincoli derivanti dall'ordinamento comunitario cinque anni dopo: quid novi? Quaderni costituzionali:796–799

Panara C (2008a) Il federalismo tedesco della legge fondamentale dalla cooperazione alla competizione. Aracne, Roma

Panara C (2008b) Offene Staatlichkeit: Italien. In: von Bogdandy A et al (eds) Ius Publicum Europaeum, vol II, C. F. Müller, Heidelberg, pp 158–159

Parodi G (2003) Interessi unitari e integrazione comunitaria negli ordinamenti decentrati. La "razionalizzazione" degli strumenti di garanzia del principio unitario. In: Rolla G (ed) La definizione del principio unitario negli ordinamenti decentrati. Giappichelli, Torino, p 41

Parodi G, Puoti ME (2006) L'attuazione del diritto comunitario nelle materie di competenza regionale dopo la legge n. 11 del 2005. http://www.issirfa.cnr.it. Accessed 15 Jun 2010

Pinelli C (1999) The Italian regions in the perspective of European integration. Rivista italiana diritto pubblico comunitario:635–641

Pinelli C (2004) I limiti generali alla potestà legislativa statale e regionale e i rapporti con l'ordinamento internazionale e ordinamento comunitario. Il Foro Italiano:57–61

Posillipo M (2006) La Conferenza Stato-Regioni nei processi decisionali comunitari. Rassegna di diritto pubblico Europeo:155–199

Rescigno GU (2002) Attuazione regionale delle direttive comunitarie e potere sostitutivo dello Stato. Le Regioni:729–752

Ridola P (2002) Il principio democratico fra Stati nazionali e Unione Europea. Nomos:75–91

Rivello R (1995) Il ruolo delle Regioni nel diritto comunitario e nel diritto internazionale: considerazioni sulla normativa vigente e sui progetti di revisione costituzionale. Diritto commerciale e degli scambi internazionali:265

Romano M (2008) Complessità delle fonti e sistema penale. Leggi regionali, ordinamento comunitario, Corte costituzionale. Rivista italiana di diritto e procedura penale:538–558

Ruggeri A (2005) Integrazione Europea e ruolo delle autonomie territoriali (lineamenti di un "modello" e delle sue possibili realizzazioni). http://www.federalismi.it. Accessed 15 Jun 2010

Salerno GM (2000) Riserva di legge e principio di legalità nel processo di integrazione Europea. In: Modugno F (ed) Trasformazioni della funzione legislative. Giuffrè, Milano, p 307

Salmoni F (2005) Il Trattato che adotta una Costituzione per l'Europa. Il ruolo dei Parlamenti nazionali nell'Unione Europea. Foro italiano:16–19

Savino M (2007) Regioni e Unione Europea: il mancato 'aggiramento' dello Stato. Le Regioni:433–471

Segni L (2007) La Regione soggetto fantasma dell'ordinamento comunitario? Giornale di diritto amministrativo:371–376

Sorrentino F (2002) Nuovi profili costituzionali dei rapporti tra diritto interno e diritto internazionale e comunitario. Diritto pubblico comparato ed Europeo:1355

Spadacini L (2007) Integrazione Europea e ordinamenti regionali: la debolezza dei Consigli. Istituzioni del federalism:353–430

Spadea G (2009) L'esecuzione delle sentenze della Corte Europea dei diritti dell'uomo in Italia. Rivista italiana di diritto pubblico comunitario:263–271

Sterpa A (2010) L'attuazione della riforma. (Estratto dal "Quinto Rapporto sullo stato del regionalismo in Italia" – 2008). http://www.issirfa.cnr.it. Accessed 15 Jun 2010

Strozzi G (1988) Recenti sviluppi nella disciplina dei rapporti tra Stato e Regioni in materia internazionale. Rivista di diritto internazionale:354

Strozzi G (1992) Partecipazione delle Regioni all'elaborazione delle politiche comunitarie e loro competenza all'attuazione degli atti comunitari alla luce della legge n. 86 del 1989. Rivista italiana di diritto pubblico comunitario:111–123
Tesauro G (1989) Partecipazione delle Regioni alla formazione delle decisioni comunitarie. Rivista di diritto internazionale privato e processuale:11–26
Tizzano A (1997) L'integrazione Europea dalla Costituente alla Commissione bicameral. Il diritto dell'Unione Europea:795–809
Tizzano A (1999) I meccanismi della 'legge La Pergola': una radiografia dei problemi di funzionamento. Foro italiano:303–310
Tizzano A (2007) Ancora sui rapporti tra Corti Europee: principi comunitari e c.d. controlimiti costituzionali. Il Diritto dell'Unione Europea:734–744
Tufarelli F, Rollè N (2005) La partecipazione alla fase ascendente (e discendente) della normativa comunitaria. In: De Benedetto M (ed) Istituzioni, politica e amministrazione. Otto Paesi Europei a confront. Giappichelli, Torino, p 139
Vesperini G (2008) Il diritto Europeo e la ripartizione nazionale delle competenze tra lo Stato e le Regioni. Rivista italiana di diritto pubblico comunitario:1427–1452
Villamena S (2002) Il potere sostitutivo statale e le influenze sul "governo del territorio. In: Ferrari E (ed) La disciplina pubblica dell'attività edilizia e la sua codificazione. Giuffrè, Milano, p 231
Villamena S (2004) Il ruolo delle Regioni nella elaborazione ed attuazione del diritto comunitario: profili evolutivi. Quaderni del Consiglio regionale Marche:14–18
Villamena S (2006) Il contesto Europeo. In: Pföstl E (ed) Il processo di integrazione Europea e lo sviluppo di nuove forme di regionalismo in Italia: il caso della Regione Lazio. Istituto di Studi Politici S. Pio V, Roma, pp 25–27
Villamena S (2007) L'ordinamento comunitario nei nuovi statuti regionali. In: Di Cosimo G (ed) Statuti atto II. Le regioni e la nuova stagione statutaria. EUM, Macerata, pp 259–288
Villamena S (2008) Contributo in tema di proporzionalità amministrativa. Giuffrè, Milano, p 127
Violini L (2005) Legge 'La Loggia' e partecipazione delle Regioni ai processi decisionali comunitari: la Corte (a buon diritto) assolve le scelte legislative, benché incompiute. Le Regioni:226–236
Vipiana P (2007) Le leggi comunitarie regionali: un innovativo strumento per l'attuazione delle direttive comunitarie da parte delle regioni. Quaderni regionali:449–480

Chapter 8
The Spanish Autonomous Communities in the EU: "The Evolution from the Competitive Regionalism to a Cooperative System"

Alicia Chicharro Lázaro

A. Competitive Regionalism in the Spanish Autonomic State

I. The Autonomic State in the Spanish Constitution

The Autonomic State (*Estado Autonómico*) designed by the Spanish Constitution of 1978, is a complicated system of intergovernmental relations which emphasises the institutional autonomy of the sub-national level of government from the central State. The distribution of competences is made sector by sector (sectoral distribution). The 1978 Constitution incorporates a list of the sectors in which the Autonomous Communities can assume competences (Art. 148) and a list of exclusive competences of the central State (Art. 149).

The sectoral distribution of competences in the Spanish Autonomic State is very different from the functional distribution of powers in German cooperative federalism. This is the reason why some authors refer to the Spanish system as *competitive regionalism.*[1]

In some areas of exclusive State competence, the State can only dictate framework legislation. Additionally Art. 148.2 states that after 5 years from the entry into force of the Constitution, the Autonomous Communities may, by amendment of their Autonomic Statutes, progressively enlarge their powers within the framework laid down in Art. 149 (exclusive competences of the central State).

As a result, the majority of competences are now shared or concurrent. But this does not mean that central government and Autonomous Communities must take joint action. Rather, the Autonomous Communities must build upon the framework legislation (*legislación básica*) adopted by the central State.[2] This framework

[1]See Börzel (2002), pp. 93–102.

[2]Framework legislation can be passed in some sectors such as Health, Social Security, Environment, Media, Contract Obligations, Mining and Energy Industry, Mountains and Forest Resources.

A. Chicharro Lázaro
Dpto. de Derecho Público, Universidad Pública de Navarra, Campus de Arrosadía, E – 31006 Pamplona (Navarra), Spain
e-mail: alicia.chicharro@unavarra.es

C. Panara and A. De Becker (eds.), *The Role of the Regions in EU Governance*,
DOI 10.1007/978-3-642-11903-3_8,

legislation is the exclusive competence of the central government; so the Autonomous Communities do not participate at all in its law-making process. However, the Autonomous Communities implement the framework legislation and the central State cannot intervene in such implementation.

In the Spanish system, there is no mechanism for coordinating the exercise of shared competences. As a consequence, when the central government creates framework legislation containing norms which are considered to be too detailed, the Autonomous Communities may bring an action before the Spanish Constitutional Court, where the competence conflict will be considered. The number of competence conflicts increased after the accession of Spain to the European Community. This situation pushed the two levels of government to find forms of intergovernmental cooperation between the central State and regional administrations.

Another characteristic of the Spanish system is the asymmetric nature of the Autonomic State designed by the 1978 Constitution. In the first few years after the Constitution was passed, the Autonomous Communities did not have the potential to assume the same number of competences and the procedure for obtaining them varied; either Art. 151 (fast track procedure or full autonomy) or Art. 143 (slow track procedure or no full autonomy). Ultimately, the attempt by the central State to harmonise the level of autonomy among the Autonomous Communities has further reduced the number and nature of competences assumed by the autonomous entities.[3]

All in all, it can be said that the Spanish Autonomic State is oriented toward the American model of dual federalism, which emphasises the separation of central State and regional powers. In order to secure the cultural pluralism of Spain, the constitutional design does not provide for any form of intergovernmental cooperation among the Autonomous Communities, or between them and the central State. This bilateralism causes many problems, the solutions to which require multilateral coordination and consensus-seeking.[4]

Given the necessity of this kind of mechanism, successive Spanish governments have presented different proposals for alternative mechanisms of intergovernmental coordination. This chapter will focus on these methods.

The regionalisation process in Spain and its integration in the European Community have been developing in parallel. However, in the early years of Spain's accession, the regional entities claiming autonomy did not take into account the fact that the construction of the Union was absorbing State and sub-State competences.[5] The Autonomous Communities quickly realised that all their devolved competences were threatened by the transfer of powers from the Member States to the

---

[3]Some differences in terms of competences are still kept for those Autonomous Communities (Basque Country and Navarra), which have particular historical prerogatives in taxation and financial sectors.

[4]The Spanish system used to solve problems by means of bilateral bargaining; bilateral agreements or informal *ad hoc* meetings were the major instruments of "cooperation" between central State and the Autonomous Communities.

[5]Portelli (1993), pp. 15–20.

Community. Soon, the development of European law and the increase of the competences transferred to the Community, led to a movement driven by autonomic entities which demanded more participation in Community decision-making. This arose particularly when Community legislation involved matters of competence devolved to the regional level.

The Maastricht Treaty, and to a lesser extent the Amsterdam and Nice Treaties, have widened the EU's objectives and competences. This has brought about potential conflicts with the rights of regional and local entities in Member States having complex internal organisation. This means a greater risk of interference with the regional and local competences.

II. The Spanish Autonomic State and Accession to the European Communities

The Spanish Constitution of 1978 established a regime of public liberties very similar to those in European countries with a long democratic tradition. It meant the end of the centralised State of the Franco's regime, allowing the implementation of what would be known as the *Autonomic State* (Estado Autonomico).

The Autonomic State was established in the 1978 Constitution as a process that would be developed incrementally over time. Unlike Germany, in Spain the progressive devolution of competences took place from the State to the regional level. The formal norm for receiving these powers was the Statute of Autonomy (*Estatuto de Autonomía*).

Each Autonomous Community[6] has a Statute of Autonomy of its own. It has to be passed by Parliament through an organic law (*Pey orgánica*), a norm that requires a qualified majority for its adoption.

The Statutes set out the institutional system of Autonomous Communities. They have executive and legislative powers but do not have a judiciary. Judicial matters are the exclusive competence of the central State. The newborn Autonomous Communities acquire the competences put at their disposition by the Constitution. Finally, the Constitutional Court has the power to rule over the conflicts of competences that might arise between the Autonomous Communities or between them and the State.

Art. 93 of the Constitution led to Spain's eventual accession to the European Communities. It allows for the signing of international treaties by which competences established in the Constitution can be transferred to international organisations. This allowance has to be done through an organic law, which requires a qualified majority for its adoption.

[6]In Spain, there are 17 Autonomous Communities (Comunidades Autónomas): Andalucía, Aragón, Asturias, Canarias, Cantabria, Castilla-La Mancha, Castilla-León, Cataluña, Extremadura, Galicia, Islas Baleares, La Rioja, Madrid, Murcia, Navarra, País Vasco and Valencia and there are also two further autonomous cities: Ceuta and Melilla.

With reference to Art. 93, it can be said that the distribution of competences between the Autonomous Communities and the State, set up in Title VIII of the Constitution, was provisional. If Spain joined the Community (which was likely to occur), the initial distribution of competences set in that Title would be altered to the benefit of the European level, at the expense of the State and Autonomous Communities' powers.

On the basis of Art. 93, Spain joined the European Communities in 1986 at the same time that its internal decentralisation was being implemented.[7] Spain's accession to the Community was a decision that needed not only its own national will, but also the agreement of all the Member States.[8] From there on, the distribution of competences set in Title VIII of the Constitution took account of Spanish participation in the European Community and of the interpretation of the Constitutive Treaties undertaken by the European Court of Justice.

The complex architecture in the Spanish Constitution tries to balance unity and diversity. This balance is achieved by harmonising decentralisation (Autonomous Communities) and integration (EU).

From the European perspective, the nature of the holder of the competences now transferred is irrelevant; the EU assumes all the powers set out in the Treaties and will use its competences according to EU law. The European Court of Justice has asserted this principle in its case law.[9]

III. Restatement of the Internal Share of Competences After Accession to the European Communities

In Spain, the transfer of competences to the European Community was a decision taken by the central State without the direct participation of the Autonomous Communities. This occurred because the transfer is based on Art. 93 of the Constitution. Art. 93 allows the Parliament to authorise the Government to conclude

[7]Ley Orgánica 10/1985, de 2 de agosto, por la que se autoriza la adhesión de España a las Comunidades Europeas.

[8]Treaty on the accession of Spain and Portugal to the ECC and the EAEC (12 June 1985).

[9]The German Federal Republic brought a direct action for annulment before the Court of Justice against Art. 9 of Council Directive 92/59/EEC of 29 June 1992, on General Product Safety. Germany submitted that powers conferred upon the Commission by Art. 9 exceeded those which, in a federal state such as Germany, are enjoyed by the Federation (the *Bund*) in relation to the *Länder*. The ECJ stated that: "...it must be borne in mind that the rules governing the relationship between the Community and its Member States are not the same as those which link the *Bund* with the *Länder*. Furthermore, the measures taken for the implementation of Art. 100a of the Treaty are addressed to Member States and not to their constituent entities. Nor do the powers conferred on the Commission by Art. 9 of the directive have any bearing upon the division of powers within the Federal Republic of Germany"; ECJ, C-359/92, Federal Republic of Germany *v*. Council [1994] ECR 3681.

international treaties through which competences established in the Constitution can be transferred to international organisations.

It would be rather naive to think that the only competences affected by the process of European integration would be the ones belonging to the central governments of Member States. It is quite clear that an organisation such as the European Community (now the European Union) has an effect upon a very wide range of competences and also upon the division of powers between central government and regional authorities.

This phenomenon, which also occurred in other Member States having complex institutional structures, has a special characteristic in Spain: the decentralisation process to construct the Autonomic State and the integration process took place almost in parallel. Some Autonomous Communities had just started to enjoy their recently acquired competences but saw them limited due to the accession of Spain to the European Communities.[10]

The Constitution is the State's supreme rule. Consequently, its principles are binding on all the organisations which are part of it. The Autonomic Statutes have to be interpreted subject to the constitutional terms, because they are subordinate to the Spanish Constitution. This means that Art. 93 allows the transfer of competences to the EU, which may belong either to the State or to the Autonomous Communities.[11] The assignment of a shared or exclusive competence of the State or of the Autonomous Communities[12] to the EU meant that the domestic authority could no longer carry it out. This reduced the powers of the Autonomous Communities, despite the fact that the scheme established by the Constitution had not been amended.

Powers which belonged to the Autonomous Communities relating to agriculture, fisheries, industry, economic planning, transport, health, social welfare, environment, taxes, competition law and consumer protection were significantly diminished after Spanish accession to the Community.

The Constitutional Court held that in the implementation of EU measures, the internal distribution of competences had to be respected. This decision of the Constitutional Court arose despite contrary arguments which were based on the international overtone of the matter, as it affected the implementation of international decisions.[13] Due to the need for legislative efficiency, the implementation of EU law has to be done by the Autonomous Communities when it relates to matters of their competence. This is the case even though the Member State is the only body responsible for the application of EU law before the European institutions.

---

[10]Only 5 years went by from the early Autonomy Statutes to the *Ley Orgánica* on the accession of Spain to the ECC and the EAEC.

[11]Mangas Martín (1987), pp. 224–227.

[12]See Arts. 148 and 149 of the Spanish Constitution.

[13]The Spanish Constitutional Court wanted to avoid Arts. 93 and 149.1.3 of Spanish Constitution being turned into the legal basis by which the central state would gain exclusive competence in the field of European Law implementation.

However, when EU decisions had to be made, the shift of powers to the EU meant that the central State recovered those powers previously transferred to the Autonomous Communities. In addition, the central executive power acquired some legislative power which originally belonged to the Autonomous Communities.[14] This was known as "*ejercicio en común de la soberanía*" (exercise in common of sovereign powers). This phenomenon, characteristic of the accession to the EU, created the need for a reconsideration of the constitutional scheme. The central State's interests, as well as these of the Autonomous Communities, needed to be respected in the EU decision-making process.

The solution to this problem was difficult: the Autonomous Communities not only wanted more competences devolved from the central State, they also demanded more powers to protect them from the consequences of the State's decisions in the EU. Due to the influence of German cooperative federalism,[15] both the central State and the Autonomous Communities found the answer to this problem in the establishment of cooperation and participation procedures in areas where regional and EU competences overlap.[16]

B. Internal Participation

I. Main Characteristics

As previously stated, Spain's accession to the European Communities eroded the Autonomous Communities' powers. Therefore, a participation mechanism needed to be created which would strive to allow a return to the situation prior to the accession.

Every Member State has to adjust its internal functioning to the requirements of the EU. This has also occurred in Spain. Due to its territorial organisation, it was urgent to find a way that allowed the Autonomous Communities to have effective

[14]The same happens with the central Parliament's powers, giving rise to a hard criticism of the Union's "democratic deficit".

[15]Börzel (2002), pp. 178–188. This author emphasizes the advantage of German federalism over competitive Spanish regionalism.

[16]In the Case 252/1988 – one of the first cases about the conflict of competence arisen from the Spanish power conferring to the Community – the Spanish Constitutional Court advocated this solution. In the original text of the Constitutional Court: "tanto de la interpretación sistemática de la Constitución como de la supremacía de ésta sobre los Estatutos se deriva la necesidad de colaboración entre la Administración Central y las Administraciones Autonómicas, colaboración que puede exigir en muchos casos, en relación, sobre todo, con nuestra incorporación a la Comunidad Económica Europea, formas de articulación (por ejemplo, realización por la Administración Autonómica de tareas de competencia estatal, con sumisión en consecuencia, y sólo en cuanto a ellas, a instrucciones y supervisiones de la Administración Central) que sólo una interpretación inadecuada de los preceptos constitucionales y estatutarios puede obstaculizar".

participation in decisions relating to EU matters that also concern their competences.

Following the entry into force of the Treaty of Maastricht, Member States' regions began to participate in the EU law-making process through the Committee of the Regions. However, since the Committee only has a consultative role on the EU level, some reform was required on the national level. More specifically, the Regions needed to be permitted to contribute to the development of the position of the respective Member State in the Council.

There are two stages of the EU law-making process:

- The ascending stage, intervening in the configuration of the Spanish position that will be manifested in the Council.
- The descending stage, the implementation of EU law, which will be done according to the internal distribution of powers.

There would be a further difficulty in the Spanish situation; when the Autonomous Communities began to govern themselves, they did it through the systems established in the Spanish Constitution. This led to important differences between the competences of the individual Autonomous Communities, because not all the Communities assumed the same powers.[17] A solution to this was provided by the *Ley Orgánica* 9/1992, which gave all the autonomous entities the same level of competences.

The Spanish Government has adhered to the following two ideas:

- The Autonomous Communities' participation has to abide by the cooperation principle between the central government and the Autonomous Communities. This is an articulation of the constitutional loyalty principle and has to be the result of the gathering of all the positions.
- Within the EU, the common will is created by the Member States; as they defend most of their own interests and positions in the Council, they surrender some of them in order to permit growth and development in the EU.

Before the Maastricht Treaty, the Council was made up of representatives of the Member States. They were chosen in accordance with requirements set in their respective domestic laws.[18] The Council, answering the questions from Members of the European Parliament,[19] made clear that Council ministers had to be members of a national government, and that it was the task of each national government to choose their representatives in each of the Council's sessions. This was independent of the distribution of internal power between national governments and regions.

---

[17]As previously stated, the Spanish Constitution established two different procedures to obtain autonomy: on the one hand, Art. 151 (fast track procedure or full autonomy) and, on the other, Art. 143 (slow track procedure or no full autonomy).

[18]Art. 98.1 of the Spanish Constitution stipulates that: "The Government shall consist of the President, Vice-Presidents, when appropriate, Ministers and other members as may be created by law".

[19]OJ C 125, 21 May 1990, pp. 53–54 and OJ C 233, 17 September 1990, p. 46.

However, since the entry into force of the Maastricht Treaty, it is specified that the Council shall be composed of a representative from each Member State who is endowed with ministerial rank ("at ministerial level" in Art. 16.2 of the Treaty on the European Union; ex Art. 203 EC). This representative has the power to commit the government of that Member State and to cast its vote (Art. 16.2 cit.).

Hereafter, it is necessary to question whether the members of the governments of the Spanish Autonomous Communities possess a ministerial rank. If they do, does this give them the power to commit the central government? Both questions do not depend on EU law, but on Spanish law. It is important to emphasise that, according to the Treaty on the European Union, the Spanish representative in the Council will represent Spain and not the Autonomous Communities (or a specific Community).

II. Autonomous Communities' Intervention in the EU Decision-Making Procedure

1. The Creation of the CARCE as a Body of Cooperation Between the State and the Autonomous Communities

After the first and only attempt at establishing power sharing through law was declared unconstitutional,[20] the development of the Autonomic State arose through political cooperation. It became necessary to create an institutional collaboration/cooperation principle between the State and the Autonomous Communities.[21] At first, the State offered the Autonomous Communities a general framework covenant (*convenio-marco*), which included an agreement that was expected to cover the whole system.[22] This was ruled out in favour of more pragmatic solutions.

The first step in the Autonomous Communities' participation in European affairs came with the creation of the *Conferencia de Asuntos relacionados con las Comunidades Europeas* (CARCE) in 1988. It is the most original body in the system of cooperation in Spanish government. It acts as an institution of cooperation between the State and the Autonomous Communities, allowing the participation of the Communities in matters of their competence when they are affected by EU action. In particular, CARCE has to guarantee the effective participation of the autonomic entities in the formulation of Spain's position on European matters and in the implementation of EU law.[23]

[20]Spanish Constitutional Court Case (STC), 76/1983, de 5 de agosto, that declared unconstitutional the *Proyecto de Ley Orgánica de Armonización del Proceso Autonómico*.

[21]STC 18/1982, de 4 de mayo, from which the "inter-territorial cooperation principle" begins to gain an increasing worth in the development of the State designed in the 1978 Spanish Constitution.

[22]Resulting in 1985 and April 1986 Draft Agreements.

[23]This Sectoral Conference was set up in 1988 and its first meeting took place in March 1989. Its experience has shown that it is the best possible forum to jointly resolve problems related to the

In 1997, the *Ley* 2/1997 of 13 March was passed. This meant that all the provisions relating to the composition and functions of CARCE acquired legal rank. On 5 June 1997, CARCE approved its Rules of Order (*Reglamento Interno*).

The State is represented by the Public Administration Minister who chairs the meetings, the Secretary of State for Foreign and EU Affairs and the Secretary of State for the territorial administrations. Every Community is represented by a Counselor (*Consejero*), who is a member of the regional government responsible for the respective matter, and by a member of the Government Council of Ceuta and Melilla (two Spanish autonomic cities situated in North Africa). The subjects that CARCE will consider are prepared by second rank officials. This has led the Autonomous Communities to appoint a coordinator for this task.

The CARCE works either through a plenary meeting, or through a coordinator's commission, or, finally, through working groups. Agreements within CARCE are reached through the adoption of a final position that requires unanimity by all CARCE members participating in a plenary meeting. If this is not possible, then the positive vote of the central government and the majority of the Autonomous Communities (including autonomic cities) is required. The negative vote of four or more Communities may veto the agreement. The resulting agreement will only bind those Autonomous Communities which have voted in its favor or those which eventually adhere to it.

Art. 3 of *Ley* 2/1997 sets out the functions of CARCE as follows:

The Conference, as a body of cooperation, consultation and deliberation between the State and the Autonomous Communities [...], will have the following competences:

1. To inform the Autonomous Communities and discuss with them the development of the European construction process.
2. The establishment of mechanisms that will make effective the Autonomous Communities participation in the formation of the State's will in European affairs.
3. To process and settle, respecting the cooperation principle, those matters of general relevance or institutional content related with the EU as the following:
   (a) Technical proceedings that ensure the reception of general information from the EU to the Autonomous Communities
   (b) Regulatory technique for integrating the directives into national law, as well as for applying, developing or executing rules and decisions
   (c) Ways of participation in the internal proceedings for the accomplishment of obligations assumed with EU authorities
   (d) Problems caused by the application of EU law, because it imply the material or temporal application of various EU policies

Autonomous Communities' participation in EU matters. At the 29 October 1992 meeting, this Sectoral Conference was institutionalized (Acuerdo de institucionalización de 29 de octubre de 1992, completado por el Acuerdo de 14 de junio de 1994).

(e) Questions regarding the Autonomous Communities participation in EU related matters that lack of a Sectoral Conference or a similar body
4. The promotion and monitoring of the Autonomous Communities participation procedure, through the correspondent Sectoral Conference or equivalent body, in those EU policies or actions that affect those competences.
5. Guarantee that the proceedings and ways that the Autonomous Communities have for participating in the Sectoral Conferences, in matters ruled in 3°A) and 4°, are respected and carefully applied.
6. Deal, when considered necessary, with any other question involving the Autonomous Communities participation in matters related to the EU.

When CARCE initiated its activity, it recognised that the central government has exclusive power over foreign affairs. However, it also stated that European integration must not alter the power sharing framework between the central level and the Autonomous Communities, hence protecting constitutional loyalty[24] and the general interests of Spain as a whole.[25]

2. CARCE Agreement for Autonomic Participation in EU Matters Through Sectoral Conferences

In 1994, CARCE adopted the *Agreement of internal participation between the Autonomous Communities in EU affairs through Sectoral Conferences*[26] (*Conferencias Sectoriales*). It was through these bodies that the Autonomous Communities started

[24]The principle of constitutional loyalty implies that each level – central State or Autonomous Communities or Local Authorities – should exercise its own powers and competence taking into account the powers and competence other levels'.

[25]The general interest of Spain as a whole is an indeterminate concept which means that the achieved "common position" cannot be the mere addition of each individual position. Nor does it mean that the Government is bound by the autonomic common position. This is because flexibility in the search for agreements is required in the European decision-making process.

[26]Sectoral Conferences are co-operation bodies between the central State and Autonomous Communities Governments. They include State representatives, the subject-matter competent Minister and the Autonomous Communities Government representatives (*Consejeros*) in order to exchange points of view and reach agreements, if it is possible to do so. One example of this kind of Conferences is precisely the *Conferencia para Asuntos relacionados con las Comunidades Europeas* (*CARCE*), which has a more horizontal composition because it may deal with many different matters. Other Sectoral Conferences, which could have some involvement with European matters are these: *Conferencias Sectoriales de Agricultura y Desarrollo Rural, de Pesca, de Asuntos Sociales, de Asuntos Laborales, de Educación, de Medio Ambiente, de Industria y Energía, de Ciencia y Tecnología, de Infraestructura y Ordenación del Territorio, de Cultura, de Consumo, de Turismo, de Telecomunicaciones y Sociedad de la Información, el Consejo de Política de Seguridad, el Consejo de Política Fiscal y Financiera, la Conferencia Nacional de Transportes y el Consejo Interterritorial del Sistema Nacional de Salud.*

to play a role in the formation of the national will before the EU (what Spanish scholars call "*fase ascendente*", the "ascending stage"). Prior to the development of these Conferences, the Autonomous Communities had only participated in the implementation of EU law (which is what Spanish scholars indicate as "*fase descendente*", the "descending stage").

The Agreement established the framework procedure of cooperation.[27] Every Sectoral Conference has a field of competence. The Sectoral Conference will, upon receipt, send each Commission's legislative proposal to the Autonomous Communities without delay. The Autonomous Communities will have a period of time for expressing their opinion. The duration of this period is determined in accordance with the Council timetable. The Commission's proposal will be included in the Sectoral Conference's agenda. This will allow the debate over it between the central State and the Autonomous Communities. Once the proposal is passed over to the Council for approval, the autonomic representative will be informed about its status. Upon receipt of the proposal, every Sectoral Conference will have the opportunity to convene a meeting prior to the Council, in order to debate and if necessary take a stance on the measure concerned.

In Spain, regional authorities (the Autonomous Communities) have the right to express common positions in matters which fall within their sphere of competence. There are two possible scenarios depending on the type of competence of the Autonomous Communities. If an EU draft act falls within an area of exclusive autonomic competence, the common position of the Autonomous Communities "will be taken into account [by the national government] in a decisive way" ("*será tenida en cuenta de forma determinante*").[28]

If an EU proposal falls within an area of nonexclusive autonomic competence (that is an area where the legislative power is shared by the State and the Autonomous Communities), the Autonomous Communities need to reach a common position, and this position needs to be then negotiated with the national government.[29]

In both scenarios, the government will normally uphold the regional position (or the position agreed with the regional authorities). However, the government can *exceptionally* sacrifice their position if this proves to be necessary during the negotiation process in the Council.

This process is still a method of indirect participation, resulting from the autonomic role over internal affairs. In contrast, direct participation would envisage the

[27]The participation of the Autonomous Communities in European matters turned to the cooperation principle. Following the German example, this principle came to orchestrate the mechanism and skills in which the participation procedures become a reality. Starting from the respect of the autonomy of each level, the cooperation principle is in pursuit of understanding among all the parties. In Spain, the cooperation relationships have their institutional body in the Sectoral Conferences.

[28]Art. I § 3 (point 1.2) of CARCE Agreement of 30 November 1994.

[29]Art. I § 3 (point 1.3) of CARCE Agreement of 30 November 1994.

incorporation of a representative of the Autonomous Communities into the Spanish delegation to the European Council. It took a further 10 years for this to happen.[30]

3. The Creation of an Office for Autonomic Affairs

In 1996, the Office for Autonomic Affairs (*Consejería de Asuntos Autonómicos*), within the core of the Spanish Representation in the EU Council (*REPER*), was created. It developed a system of relations between the Autonomous Communities' Offices in Brussels and the central body, which represents Spain before the European institutions.

The work done by the Office is very positive. It has allowed the formalisation of collaborative relations and has also given the Autonomous Communities access to a body which is essential in the system of the Member State participation in the European decision-making process. This has been brought about through the direct participation of the Office's staff in the working groups and other preparatory stages within the Council. On 9 December 2004, the CARCE adopted an Agreement by which every job in the Office would be done by civil servants proposed by the Autonomous Communities. The intention was to guarantee a greater involvement and autonomic presence in the Office. At the same time, the Agreement provided that the Autonomous Communities' participation in the Council's workgroups should be done in the following ways:

1. Through the Office for Autonomic Affairs, whose members are incorporated into the workgroups preparing the following Councils: Employment, Social Policy, Health and Consumer Affairs; Agriculture and Fisheries; Environment; Education, Youth and Culture).
2. Through the direct representation of the Autonomous Communities in the Council's workgroups. This should be done through the incorporation of an autonomic expert into the Spanish delegation at the relevant workgroup.

Likewise, in 1997, CARCE adopted its first agreement concerning the Autonomous Communities' participation in comitology committees within the EU. This agreement allows for an autonomic representative, to be part of the Spanish delegation to the auxiliary committees of the Commission.[31]

4. The Spanish Senate's Reform: An Opportunity for Autonomic Participation in EU Affairs?

The Autonomous Communities' participation in the Senate is not truly complete, even if the Senate is theoretically the institution of territorial representation. Art. 69

[30]CARCE, *Acuerdo sobre el sistema de representación autonómica en las formaciones del Consejo de la Unión Europea*, 9 de diciembre de 2004.

[31]Especially in areas such as agriculture, transport, commercial policy or regional policy.

of the Spanish Constitution establishes its composition, basing it on provinces (four senators per province) instead of creating its basis in the Autonomous Communities (one senator each and one more for every million inhabitants). In fact, the Senate is a body with very few powers and low activity, because the Spanish bicameral system favours the Congress. An example of this is the weakness in the Senate's ability to veto a law. In the case of a veto, the Congress may pass a law by absolute majority or if it waits for 2 months, by simple majority. There is little comparison with the powers of the German *Bundesrat*.[32]

Due to its composition and weak decision-making powers, the Senate does not constitute a real chamber of territorial representation, nor does it provide a means for integrating regional interests into national policy-making.

The Senate's reform has given root to a profound theoretical and political debate. Some argue that the Senate should become a chamber of real territorial representation, following the lead of the 1978 Constitution.[33] This reform would protect the Autonomous Communities' interests: not only it would give them a decisive role in the decision-making process that could affect their own powers, but it would also allow them to control the State's internal and EU related decisions that could affect them.

In the absence of a constitutional reform, the Senate's Rules of Procedure (*Reglamento Interno del Senado*) were modified in 1994. These were based on a 1989 agreement, by which current senators pledged to boost territorial powers and through which the General Commission for the Autonomous Communities was created. This Commission received powers which favoured the Autonomous Communities' participation in EU affairs. These powers were: to receive information about the processes of a regulation's adaptation and of EU bodies actions with regional or autonomic relevance; to acknowledge the quantity and distribution of EU funds intended to redress regional economic imbalances in Spain; to implement self-financed investment projects; and to report to the Government on the role played by the Spanish delegation in every EU forum with regional participation.[34]

Parejo Alonso argues that this last power is undoubtedly the only mechanism which establishes a permanent participation of the Senate in EU matters. Nevertheless, the same author adds that this device should not be overestimated. It is still being formed, since it does not have all the powers which would be necessary for guaranteeing that the Autonomous Communities' opinions are taken seriously by the central State.[35]

In conclusion, the Senate does not provide a real forum for the participation of the Autonomous Communities in national and EU affairs. The General

[32]The German *Länder* have the *Bundesrat* to make their position known to the Federal Government, whilst in Spain the channels are the Sectoral Conferences, not the Senate.

[33]The Spanish Senate was established before the 1978 Constitution (prior to the creation of the Autonomic State). This explains the lack of coherence with the objectives of a proper chamber of territorial representation.

[34]Art. 56 Lit. q of the Senate's Rules of Procedure.

[35]Parejo Alonso (1994), p. 101.

Commission for Autonomous Communities appears to be a patchwork structure which cannot replace constitutional reform. The Senate needs to obtain the powers of a proper territorial chamber in the "ascending" and "descending" stages of the EU law-making process in all areas falling within the sphere of competence of the Autonomous Communities.

5. Autonomic Participation in Some European Council Formations

Along with the aforementioned Office for Autonomic Affairs agreement, CARCE reached another accord on 9 December 2004,[36] which finally allowed the Autonomous Communities to participate in four of the EU Council formations: Employment, Social Policy, Health and Consumer Affairs; Agriculture and Fisheries; Environment; and Education, Youth and Culture. These formations were chosen because they are the only ones which involve Autonomous Communities' powers. Some other decentralised Member States had developed this kind of participation in the formations that were chosen.

The autonomic representation system runs as follows. A representative, with Autonomic Government Officer rank (*Consejero*) or member of the same Office, is incorporated into the Spanish delegation. He will represent all Autonomous Communities in matters involving their powers. The plenary session of the relevant Sectoral Conference will choose the autonomic representative. This Conference has to ensure the stability in the representation (each Autonomous Community has to cover a semester at least) and at the same time the succession of the representatives of different autonomic entities.

In each of the Sectoral Conferences concerned, the Autonomous Communities may decide those matters in which direct representation will be needed. This decision will be taken in light of the Council's formation and of the matters included in the council agenda. The Sectoral Conferences used to take this decision at the beginning of every EU Council's six months presidency. The practice may have to change in light of the modifications introduced by the Treaty of Lisbon.

The chosen autonomic representative will develop a common position among the affected Autonomous Communities. This common position will reflect the conclusions reached by the Autonomous Communities which have manifested their opinion.[37] The autonomic representative is responsible for reaching a compromise with the central government. He will allow any Autonomous Community to consult all the papers in relation to it, and he will periodically inform them about any negotiations carried out.

The autonomic representative is a member of the Spanish delegation with full rights. He can make statements when matters concerning the Autonomous Communities are raised and there is a common autonomic position. If this occurs, the head

[36]CARCE, *Acuerdo sobre el sistema de representación autonómica en las formaciones del Consejo de la Unión Europea*, footnote 29.

[37]CARCE, Acuerdo de institucionalización, footnote 23, 4th paragraph.

of delegation will give him the floor if he thinks it is in accordance with Spanish interests.

This agreement was applied as a trial during 2005 and 2006. In the 48th CARCE meeting held in December 2006, the elaboration of a support document (or Good Practice Guide) was agreed. This document offered solutions to various practical issues, including elements that would make the Agreement's implementation easier and also making the Autonomous Communities' participation in the Council more effective. The main goal was to improve the 2004 Agreement and to prevent conflicting interpretations of its provisions by the parties involved (that is Autonomous Communities and central Government). The Guide specifies the criteria used for the designation of the autonomic representative who will be part of the national delegation to the Council of Ministers of the EU.

In each Sectoral Conference plenary session, the Autonomous Communities participating in the Council's meetings are designated through a defined procedure. The objective of this set of rules is to guarantee the continuity and stability through the determination of an order of representation among the Autonomous Communities. This order is organised in periods of six months, thus preventing a role in negotiations once the six-month period ends. This structure also allows the Autonomous Communities holding the role to plan their representation accordingly.

The Good Practice Guide also sets a coordination scheme among these autonomous entities. The initiative is taken by the Autonomous Community participating in the Council, but it allows for the consideration of remarks from other Autonomous Communities. After the initial proposal is completed and the remarks made, an autonomic common position will be established through a meeting.

Finally, the Good Practice Guide envisages coordination between the Autonomous Communities and the central government. The competence criteria provide that, excluding some exceptions, the Council's activities in which the Autonomous Communities participate correspond to powers attributed to them by the Spanish Constitution. This implies that, for a full capacity in negotiations, the so-called autonomic "common position" has to be assumed by the central delegation and integrated within the State's Member position. In order to achieve this, the Good Practice Guide envisages a number of meetings through which the central State and the autonomic administrations try to find a common position in advance of the Council's session. However, the Spanish stance in the negotiation on the EU level is taken by the head of delegation. This standpoint will have to take into account the autonomic common position.

After the Council's meeting, the autonomic representative will inform the remainder of the Autonomous Communities of the outcome; a report will be made, in which the negotiation process is described. This will be sent to both the autonomous entities and the CARCE. More detailed information has to be transmitted to the Autonomous Community due to hold the representative role in the subsequent six-month period.

The Autonomous Communities approved the Guide of Practice as it allowed an overhaul of the cooperation mechanism in EU related issues. However, it was felt that the power of negotiation and the commitment required on the part of the autonomic representatives was too strong. This has provoked some breakdowns in the balance of representation among the Autonomous Communities because some Autonomous Communities are stronger than others, so they often impose their point of view in the negotiations. Likewise, there are still some EU Council bodies in which the autonomous entities are not represented, even if they deal with issues relating to their powers.[38]

6. The Regulation of European Affairs in Recent Reforms of the Autonomic Statutes

The new Autonomy Statutes, passed after 2006, deal with relations between the Autonomous Communities and the EU in great detail; although not all of them to the same depth.[39] The Statutes establish a number of rights which the Autonomous Communities may use when their interests or powers are affected, such as:

- They may participate in the central government position in negotiations with the EU (Art. 186 of the Catalonian Autonomy Statute; Art. 61.3 b) of the Valencian Autonomy Statute; Art 93.1 of the Aragon Autonomy Statute; Art. 110 of the Balearic Islands Autonomy Statute; Art. 62.1 of the Autonomy Statute of Castilla-León; Art. 68.3 of the LORAFNA)[40].
- They may participate in the Spanish delegation before the EU, especially before the Council of Ministers (Art. 187 of the Catalonian Autonomy Statute; Art. 234 of the Andalusian Autonomy Statute; Art. 61.4 of the Valencian Autonomy Statute; Art. 94 of Aragon Autonomy Statute; Art. 111 of the Balearic Islands

[38]For instance, the Economic and Financial Affairs Council should be open to some Autonomous Communities like Basque Country and Navarre since they have exclusive competence in relation to certain matters of taxation according to a special regional system called "*foral*". Two special economic agreements, the *Concierto económico* for the Basque Country and the *Convenio económico* for Navarre, grant the two Autonomous Communities the right to levy and collect taxes. They have to deduct an annual quota (*cupo*) from their tax income, which is paid to the central State.

[39]Ley Orgánica 6/2006, de 19 de julio, de reforma del Estatuto de Autonomía de Cataluña; Ley Orgánica 2/2007, de 19 marzo, de reforma del Estatuto de Autonomía para Andalucía; Ley Orgánica 1/2006, de 10 de abril, de Reforma de la Ley Orgánica 5/1982, de 1 de julio, de Estatuto de Autonomía de la Comunidad Valenciana; Ley Orgánica 5/2007, de 20 de abril, de reforma del Estatuto de Autonomía de Aragón; Ley Orgánica 1/2007, de 28 de febrero, de reforma del Estatuto de Autonomía de las Illes Balears; Ley Orgánica 14/2007, de 30 de noviembre, de reforma del Estatuto de Autonomía de Castilla y León. We are only referring to the "new generation" of Autonomy Statutes since the others are from before the Spanish accession to the European Communities (except those of Ceuta and Melilla adopted in 1995). This is the reason why they have no references to the European integration process and the Autonomous Communities participation in it, except some small reforms: for instance, Art 37.2 of the Canary Autonomy Statute.

[40]Ley Orgánica 13/1982, de 10 de agosto, de Reintegración y Amejoramento del Régimen Foral de Navarra. This is the special name for the Autonomy Statute of Navarra.

Autonomy Statute; Art. 63.1 of the Autonomy Statute of Castilla-León; Art 68.5 of the LORAFNA).

- They may send proposals and observations to the State relating to EU initiatives, regulatory projects and decisions that they have considered when it is felt necessary, as well as the right of being informed of such projects (Art. 186.4 of the Catalonian Autonomy Statute; Art. 233 of the Andalusian Autonomy Statute; Art 68.2 of the LORAFNA).
- They may develop and implement EU law in those matters affecting their own competences (Art. 235 of the Andalusian Autonomy Statute; Art. 61.3 (d) of the Valencian Autonomy Statute; Art. 93.2 of Aragon Autonomy Statute; Art. 109 of the Balearic Islands Autonomy Statute; Art. 62.3 of the Autonomy Statute of Castilla-León; Art. 68.4 of the LORAFNA).
- They may intervene in the control procedures of the subsidiarity and proportionality principles, when they relate to EU law proposals affecting the powers of Autonomous Communities (Art. 237 of the Andalusian Autonomy Statute; Art. 61.3 a) of the Valencian Autonomy Statute; Art. 93.3 of Aragon Autonomy Statute; Art. 112 of the Balearic Islands Autonomy Statute; Art. 62.2 of the Autonomy Statute of Castilla-León; Art 68.6 of the LORAFNA).
- They may bring cases before the European Court of Justice (Art. 191 of the Catalonian Autonomy Statute; Art. 238 of the Andalusian Autonomy Statute; Art. 95 of Aragon's Autonomy Statute; Art. 113 of the Balearic Islands Autonomy Statute; Art. 65 of the Autonomy Statute of Castilla-León; Art. 68.7 of the LORAFNA).
- They may establish Autonomous Community Delegations or Offices before the EU (Art. 192 of the Catalonian Autonomy Statute; Art. 236 of the Andalusian Autonomy Statute; Art. 61.1 of the Valencian Community Autonomic Statute; Art. 92.2 of Aragon Autonomy Statute; Art. 107 of the Balearic Islands Autonomy Statute).

It is clear that the new generation of Autonomy Statutes have endeavoured to bring about the full participation of the autonomic entities in EU affairs where they could affect autonomic competences. The Autonomous Communities now know the significance of the EU integration process and are no longer satisfied with mere "observer status", while the central government takes decisions in Brussels in areas of their competence.

III. Autonomous Communities Participation in the Implementation of EU Law

1. The Institutional Autonomy Principle and the Respect of the Internal Distribution of Competences

The institutional and procedural autonomy principle is a landmark in the States' implementation of the duties acquired through the Treaties. This means that the EU cannot intervene in the internal division of competence that may exist in any Member State. Therefore, the European institutions consider the implementation of the EU law as a responsibility belonging exclusively to every Member State, that is, to every national government. The implementation process only concerns national governments; it does not interfere in the States' internal organisation, disregarding in that sense the local and regional dimensions of the "European peoples".[41]

According to the Court of Justice, all Member States' authorities are obliged to correctly implement the EU law irrespective of their institutional organisation. Under the principle of legal certainty, a Member State has to adhere to its duties towards the Treaties and it cannot breach these duties in the name of the regions' devolved powers.[42]

In Spain, Art. 93 of the Constitution says that either the Parliament (*Cortes Generales*) or the Government are obliged (depending on the situation) to guarantee compliance with signed international treaties or resolutions. However, this does not imply that the central level can claw back the Autonomous Communities' powers on grounds that it is the only authority responsible to the EU.

This point was made clear in *Ley* 47/1985, of 27 December, allowing the Government to implement EU law. It was passed shortly before Spain entered into the European Community. Art. 1 stipulated

> For complying with the duties that Spain will assume with its entry in the European Communities, on behalf of Art. 82 of the Constitution, the Government has the power to pass rules with rank of law, within the framework of its powers...

This made it clear that in the implementation of EU law, the internal division of powers had to be respected. In fact, the Catalonian[43] and Basque[44] Parliaments passed their own delegation laws, through which they allowed their respective Governments to adapt their legislation to comply with EU law.

The Spanish Constitutional Court (*Tribunal Constitucional*) has agreed with this approach in those rulings dealing with conflicts between the central State and the Autonomous Communities regarding the implementation of EU law. In sum, the Court has stated that the central State cannot seek protection in its exclusive competence for foreign affairs (Art 149.1.3 Spanish Constitution) in order to expand its powers to all matters, relating to the development, implementation or application of EU law. The fact that Art 149.1.3 is a rule which was adopted for

---

[41]The ECJ confirmed the institutional autonomy principle, according to which the EU does not care about the internal constitutional structure of Member States, in Joined Cases 51-54/71, *International Fruit Company NV and others v. Produktschap voor Groenten en Fruit* [1971], ECR 1107. See Guillermin (1992), pp. 319–346.

[42]ECJ, Case 8/88, Germany *v.* Commission [1990] ECR 2355–2366.

[43]Ley 4/86, de 10 de marzo, de bases de delegación al Gobierno para la adecuación de las leyes de Cataluña al Derecho de las Comunidades Europeas.

[44]Ley 2/86, de 19 de febrero, de bases de la recepción del ordenamiento de las Comunidades Europeas en el ámbito de la Comunidad Autónoma del País Vasco.

compliance with EU law is not relevant when it comes to determine who the holder of the competence itself is. The implementation of international treaties affecting Autonomous Communities' competences is not a power of the central State.[45] Therefore, there is no general power of implementation of the EU law in the hands of the State.[46] Implementation of EU law is held within the responsibility of the level of government which, according to domestic law, is vested with the competence involved.

2. Guarantees for the Implementation of EU Law Decisions by the Autonomous Communities

The transposition of a directive or the implementation of another EU act requires autonomic parliaments or governments to timely adapt their legal systems in order to comply with EU law. To achieve this result, the Autonomous Communities pass new legislation or repeal earlier legislation when necessary. The 1994 CARCE Agreement set up mechanisms of "horizontal cooperation" between the Autonomous Communities in case uniform implementation of EU measures on the entire national territory is required. The following sections will focus on the mechanisms for preventing or overcoming possible breaches of the obligations arising from membership in the EU, if regional and local authorities do not implement EU law or do not do so correctly. These aspects are entirely governed by domestic law.

State Substitution Powers

The first question to deal with is on the existence of a State substitution power. Under the aforementioned principle of institutional autonomy, the sole responsibility for a breach of EU law rests with the Member State, independently of the authority that (on the domestic level) has the power of implementation. In light of this principle, can the State adopt substitution measures, that is, measures replacing the Autonomus Communities in areas of their competence, in order to put a remedy to the regional failure to comply with EU obligations? The second question (that logically follows the previous one) is whether the State substitution power can be exercised only *ex post* (that is, *after* a regional failure to comply has actually taken place), or also *ex ante* (that is, *before* a regional failure to comply has taken place, in order to prevent a non-compliance from happening).

The Spanish Constitutional Court dealt with this issue in a case regarding a competence conflict involving the European Agricultural Guidance and Guarantee Fund.[47] A given amount from this fund was granted to Spain as a Member State. Agriculture in Spain is a matter of competence of the Autonomous Communities.

---

[45]STC 79/1992, de 28 de mayo.

[46]STC 236/1991, de 12 de diciembre.

[47]STC 80/1993, de 8 de marzo.

On that occasion, the Court clarified that in case of failure to implement the EU law by the Autonomous Communities the central level (the State) is entitled to pass legislation or other measures implementing EU obligations in areas of regional competence. This means that the State can substitute the Autonomous Communities *ex post* (that is, after a regional failure to comply with EU obligations has actually taken place: e.g. upon the expiry of the deadline for the transposition of a directive). However, this State legislation would have a merely "subsidiary role" in relation to later legislation passed by the Autonomous Communities. This means that the Autonomous Communities are not deprived of their powers of implementation. If the Autonomous Communities decide to implement EU obligations, at whichever point in time they decide to do so, their laws will prevail over those of the State.

At the same time, the Constitutional Court also said: "the surveillance and control powers in order to guarantee a correct implementation [of the EU law] belong to the State, [but] these State powers cannot affect those competences that according to the Constitution have to be developed and exercised by the Autonomous Communities. Otherwise the State powers (if they implied the displacement of a competence from the Autonomous Community to the State or the *a priori* substitution by the State for the Autonomous Community) would not be merely of surveillance and control, but indeed of action". This means that *a priori* substitution (before a regional non-compliance has taken place) does not exist in Spain.

In practice, when the European Commission or the Court of Justice demand compliance with EU obligations, the central State does not normally resort to substitution of its own action for that of the Autonomous Communities in fields of autonomic competence. The normal way to resolve the problem is through cooperation between the different levels of government. However, such cooperation may turn out to be too lengthy and costly and often national Departments prefer to take the "shortcut" of a broad construction of central State's powers. By so doing, they significantly erode autonomic competences given that in such a case the national legislation would be State legislation in its full right and would not have "subsidiary role" (that is, it would not "fall" in front of later laws of the Autonomous Communities).[48] Lopez Castillo maintains that some technical regulations issued by national Departments restrict the Autonomous Communities' sphere of independent implementation of EU law and policies. He suggests that for this reason it is necessary to establish limits to the interventions by the national Departments. In his opinion, different solutions simply go against the characteristics of the Autonomic State.[49]

[48]Borrás Rodríguez (1988), pp. 61–62, here the author refers to agriculture as an example of fields where the State Administration has been overworked.

[49]López Castillo (1993), p. 174.

The Position of the Autonomous Communities in Infringement Procedures Before the EU

In those cases in which the European Court of Justice finds against Spain for a breach of their duty to implement the EU law, due to actions or omissions of the Autonomous Communities, the responsible Autonomous Communities have to comply with the findings and stipulations of the Court and pay any fine.

An Agreement signed in November 1990 deals with the Autonomous Communities' intervention rights in infringement procedures taking place before the EU Commission and the Court of Justice on matters affecting autonomic competences.[50] This Agreement sets out a collaboration mechanism for those situations in which there is a breach attributed to an Autonomous Community's action or inertia.

More specifically, under this Agreement, the Secretary of State for the Autonomous Communities is responsible for communicating to the Autonomous Communities concerned every complaint, notice letter, resolution, and any other communiqué received from the Commission. The Secretary also coordinates the Autonomous Communities' common response to the EU and files it to the Commission. In addition to this communication process, the autonomic entities can also attend those meetings of the Commission's auxiliary bodies which consider the breach committed by Spain.

The same Agreement provides that, in cases before the Court of Justice involving breaches for which the Autonomous Communities are responsible, autonomic advisors can collaborate with the national Government in order to determine Spain's position during the trial. At the request of an Autonomous Community, the Secretary of State can submit to the Court any observation in relation to an autonomic action or omission.

This collaboration mechanism respects the unity of action, which characterises every Member State, essential for defending Spain's interests in the EU, and also the distribution of competences established in the Spanish Constitution and in the Autonomy Statutes. This mechanism can only work and be fruitful if there is mutual trust between the parties (State and Autonomous Communities) involved and provided that every party is respectful of the constitutional principle of mutual loyalty. The Autonomous Communities are not hostile to the implementation of EU law; on the contrary, they are the first to be interested in it. Therefore it is necessary to find legal tools capable of making collaboration possible and productive.

[50]CARCE, *Acuerdo para regular la intervención de las Comunidades Autónomas en las actuaciones del Estado en procedimientos precontenciosos de la Comisión de las Comunidades Europeas y en los asuntos relacionados con el TJCE que afecten a sus competencia,* 29 de noviembre de 1990 (Resolución 7 de septiembre de 1992).

C. External Participation

I. Direct Participation: The Autonomous Communities and the Committee of Regions

Before the creation of the Committee of Regions, which was introduced by the Treaty of Maastricht, the Decision 88/487/CEE had created the consultative Council of regional and local entities.[51] It was the first step towards regional participation in the EU decision-making procedure. It consisted of 42 permanent members and the same number of substitutes, and Spain had three representatives and another three substitutes.

The Commission could seek its advice in every matter related to regional development and especially in the elaboration and implementation of EU regional policy and other policies with regional and local impact. This regional Council had little power and very limited impact because its opinions were not binding. Once the Committee of Regions was created, the regional Council disappeared with the Decision 94/209/CE, since the Commission judged that it was now obsolete.[52]

The main role in the creation of the Committee of Regions had been played by Germany. Spain also had a prominent position since the development of the Committee was seen to be consistent with the Autonomic State established by the 1978 Constitution.

The Autonomous Communities pleaded for a body designed exclusively to represent the regions, excluding the local level and taking into account the peculiar regional system of each Member State. It was assumed that this body would have a consultative role, although in those issues regarding territorial entities its consultation should have been compulsory. It was also felt that its association with the lawmaking institutions was of fundamental importance.[53]

Currently, Spain has 21 representatives in the Committee of the Regions. They are distributed between autonomic and local levels. Some political groups in the Spanish Parliament proposed to keep the local authorities out of the Committee and to limit the representation to the Autonomous Communities.[54] But this reform turned out not to be feasible and the 21 Spanish representatives were distributed as follows: one seat each to the Autonomous Communities and the four remaining

[51]Decision 88/487/CEE of the Commission, of the 24th June, OJ L 247, 6/9/1988, pp. 23–24.

[52]Decision 94/209/CE of the Commission, of 21st April, OJ L 103, 22/4/1994, p. 28.

[53]*Documento de trabajo del grupo técnico de la Conferencia Sectorial de asuntos relacionados con la Comunidad Europea*, prepared at the meeting of Sevilla (1 February 1991) and presented at the meeting of the *Comisión de Coordinadores de Asuntos Comunitarios Europeos* (25 February 1991). This text was the basis of the Spanish negotiation position in the Intergovernmental Conference on Political Union. About this document see Sánchez Amor (1992), pp. 309–311.

[54]In particular, the Basque Parliamentary Group, the Catalonian Parliamentary Group and the Mixed Group.

seats to the local authorities. The latter are proposed by the Spanish Federation of Municipalities and Provinces (*Federación Española de Municipios y Provincias*).

The Autonomous Communities were not satisfied with the limitation of their representation and the Committee of Regions' mixed composition. However, they judged it positively as the first step towards the development to a direct link between the EU and sub-State institutions.

II. Participation in the European Parliament: The Autonomic Members of the European Parliament

Spain has 54 Members of the European Parliament. Their electoral system is regulated by the *Ley Orgánica* 5/1985, according to which Spain is a single constituency. This implies that the internal regional structure was totally ignored. However, the law creates a system of election which *de facto* enables the presence of autonomic minorities in the European Parliament. This is very important for Spain. In fact, the presence in that assembly of the nationalities and regions composing Spain is necessary for compliance with the requirements of the Spanish Autonomic State.[55]

III. The Autonomous Communities' Presence in Brussels: The Autonomic Representation Offices

The existence of Representation Offices of the Autonomous Communities does not imply a participation in an EU institution or body. They are lobbying bodies through which the Autonomous Communities obtain information and promote their interests, especially in economic matters. The Constitutional Court has clearly stated that the establishment of autonomic offices in Brussels is not an exercise of foreign policy power by the autonomic entities, since they have no competence in international matters.[56]

[55]Art. 2 of the Spanish Constitution.

[56]STC 165/1994, de 26 de mayo. Basque Government adopted the Decreto 89/1989, of 19 April, in which the structure of the *Departamento de Presidencia, Justicia y Desarrollo Autonómico* was established. The national Government appealed to the Constitutional Court because in its opinion it was not possible for the Basque Representation Office to be run by the Basque executive power. The question was not whether the Autonomous Communities could open their own representation offices or not, but whether these could be a direct emanation of an autonomic administration. The national Government argued that, if permitted, this possibility infringed on Art. 149.1.3 of the Spanish Constitution, which grants foreign affairs competence to the central Government. The Constitutional Court allowed the Autonomous Communities to keep their Representation Offices and to run them directly through the autonomic administrations. This is not "foreign affairs", but

Following the German model, the 17 Autonomous Communities started to open their Representation Offices in Brussels. There are also Offices for sub-regional bodies, such as the Deputation of Malaga and the Insular Council of Gran Canaria.

The first Spanish Representation Office belonged to Catalonia and opened on 3 November 1986, shortly after Spain's accession to the European Communities. This was followed by the Canary Islands in 1987. Galicia and the Basque Country opened their own offices in 1988. Then came Murcia 1989 and Andalucia in 1990. In 1992, Extremadura and Castilla-León also opened their offices.

In all cases, the opening of offices was done through legal bodies which were not suitable to accomplish the autonomic objectives; Catalonia created a Patronato[57]; Galicia chose a Foundation[58]; the Canary Islands[59] and the Basque Country[60] opted for a public corporation; Murcia[61] and Andalucia[62] used Public Works Institutions (Institutos de Fomento): and finally, Castilla-León opened its Representation Office together with the French regions of Poitou-Chartres and Centre.[63]

The ruling of 1994[64] allowed the Autonomous Communities to make their offices an emanation of their respective administration. This encouraged the rest of the autonomic entities to open their own Representation Offices. Aragon opened its office in 1994 and Navarre[65] in 1995; Castilla-La Mancha and Cantabria in 1996; and finally, La Rioja in 1997. The Balearic Islands and the Council of Gran Canaria created their offices in 1996, but they achieved this through the obsolete form of corporations.[66] Some of the Autonomous Communities, which had established their offices before 1994 through corporations, such as the Valencian Community and the Basque Country, changed their offices' nature and restructured them as public institutions.

The main purpose of the regional offices is the representation of the respective Autonomous Community and of its interests. Other functions are: to give defend those interests, create territorial networks of cooperation, advice and information *ad*

"domestic affairs". The Court adopted a restrictive interpretation of Art. 149.1.3. and made it clear that it is not possible to identify every activity with external implication as "foreign affairs".

[57]Patronato Catalán Pro Europa, autonomous organism created by Decreto 237/1982, de 20 de julio.

[58]Fundación Galicia-Europa, non-profit organisation.

[59]PROEXCA S.A., a public company.

[60]INTERBASK S.A., a public corporation with only one partner, the Basque Autonomous Community.

[61]RO attached to the *Instituto de Fomento de la Región de Murcia.*

[62]Instituto de Fomento de Andalucía, public company attached to the *Consejería de la Presidencia* of the Community.

[63]From 1995, 1 January, Castilla-León has its own RO.

[64]STC 165/1994, de 26 de mayo,

[65]First it created a commercial society attached to SODENA (*Sociedad de Desarrollo de Navarra*), but now the Navarre Representation Office depends on the autonomic Government.

[66]The *Cabildo de Gran Canaria* uses a company called *EUROVÍAS* and the Balearic Islands uses a consortium.

intra (between the offices' affiliates and the regional public) and provide information *ad extra* (for the Autonomous Communities' authorities to use). The offices also offer technical support to the institutions and economic agents, make reports and publications, organise courses and conferences, support the autonomic civil servants and politicians when they have to deal with European affairs, and maintain relations with other European regions.[67]

One may agree with Hernandez Lafuente when he says that the Autonomous Communities' direct relations with EU institutions through their Representation Offices are in actual fact "unofficial relations". "Official relations" are those provided for by the Treaty or contained in EU legislative acts. These latter relations can be undertaken only by the central State.[68]

IV. Another Attempt at Participation: The "Non nato" Observer of the EU

The Observer made its first appearance in a project from the Ministry of Public Administration in 1987. The Spanish Observer was inspired by its German equivalent, the *Länderbeobachter,* but kept some substantial differences; it was a one-person post chosen by consensus among the autonomic representatives. It would become part of the Permanent Spanish Representation before the EU, with a diplomatic status. He would be allowed to attend the meetings in the Council's working groups and committees and also in those of the Commission when issues regarding autonomic competences were dealt with. If he went to those meetings, he had to defend the position of the Spanish delegation.

Many amendments were proposed to this scheme, but ultimately this project was never approved.

D. The Judicial Defence of Autonomous Communities' Competences Affected by the EU Integration Process

I. Defence Before National Courts

It has been noted that EU integration affects the distribution of competences between central State and Autonomous Communities. Therefore it seems necessary

---

[67]Olivar De Julián (2008), pp. 63–67.

[68]Hernández Lafuente (1995), pp. 201–202. This author compares the Constitutional Court case 165/1994, of 26 May, with the case 172/1992, of 29th October, which says that the *Generalitat de Cataluña* is not a valid interlocutor before the EU institutions. The direct relationship with them corresponds only to the central State administration.

to protect the rights of the Autonomous Communities on both the national and the EU level.[69]

The Autonomous Communities cannot rely on the Constitutional Court if an EU piece of legislation encroaches on their powers. An appeal of unconstitutionality (*recurso de inconstitucionalidad*)[70] cannot be used to settle these kinds of competence conflicts. If the Constitutional Court ruled over these legal disputes, it would be controlling the validity of EU secondary law. This is against the EU "orthodoxy", although some constitutional courts claim to be entitled to do so in exceptional circumstances. This is the case with the Danish Supreme Court, the German Federal Constitutional Court and the Italian Constitutional Court.[71]

A different problem is the judicial enforcement of the participation rights of the Autonomous Communities in the "ascending" and "descending" stages of the EU law-making process. For some years, the Constitutional Court strove to avoid the resolution of any competence conflict in which EU law was involved. This was due to the fact that for a substantial period the Court refused to believe that EU integration affected the internal distribution of powers between the State and the Autonomous Communities. More recently, the Constitutional Court mitigated its position and recognised the impact of EU law on the internal division of competences.[72] However, it remains controversial if cases relating to the participation rights of the Autonomous Communities have to be heard by the Constitutional Court or by ordinary courts (administrative-contentious courts).

Some legal scholars suggest that the Constitutional Court is the *only* judicial body entitled to adjudicate on competence conflicts (theory of exclusivity, *teoría de la exclusividad*).[73] Following this train of thought, the disputes arising from the violation of the participation rights of the Autonomous Communities should always be adjudicated by the Constitutional Court.

In 1989 in the *ATINA* case, the Constitutional Court took a different view (known as theory of exclusivity in weak sense, *teoría de la exclusividad en sentido debil*).[74] The Constitutional Court claimed to have jurisdiction to decide on competence conflicts between the State and the Autonomous Communities only when they regard the allocation (that is, the "*titularidad*") of the disputed powers. Instead it is beyond the responsibilities of the Constitutional Court to make decisions over

[69]Huesa Vinaixa (1986), p. 23.

[70]Art. 161 of the Spanish Constitution.

[71]See the following cases: Maastricht Ruling of the Danish Supreme Court of 6 April 1998 [in *Common Market Law Review*, Vol. 3 (1999), p. 854 ff.]; Lisbon Ruling of the German Federal Constitutional Court of 30 June 2009 (English text available at http://www.bverfg.de/entscheidungen/es20090630_2bve000208en.html, last visited on 15 June 2010); Ruling No. 183 of 27 December 1973 (*Frontini* case) of the Italian Constitutional Court.

[72]STC 33/2005, de 17 de febrero.

[73]García Roca (2002), pp. 89–110; Ortega Santiago (2005), p. 66.

[74]López Bofill (1999), pp. 60–71.

conflicts involving *how* a given power (whose allocation is not questioned) has been exercised by the State or by an Autonomous Community ("*ejercicio*" of a given power). These second types of disputes fall within the responsibility of ordinary courts.[75]

In actual fact, by bringing a case to the Constitutional Court or to an ordinary court, it is the claimant (State or Autonomous Community) who decides which court has to pronounce on a competence conflict. This is due to the fact that neither the ordinary courts nor the Constitutional Court normally decline their jurisdiction on a dispute. Both the Autonomous Communities and the central government usually bring their complaints to ordinary courts unless it is absolutely certain that a dispute concerns (only) the allocation of a power ("*titularidad*").

The only certainty in this complex distribution of responsibilities between the courts, is that the Autonomous Communities can count on a legal route to enforce their participation rights against the central government, although it is doubtful if this route is compatible with the time schedule of Union decisions. Furthermore, the infringement of the participation rights of the Autonomous Communities by the central Government would not cause the invalidity of the measures adopted by the Union.

II. Defence Before EU Courts

During the last few years, the number of cases brought before the European Court of Justice and the Court of First Instance involving sub-national authorities has significantly increased. If an act of the EU harms their self-government rights or their competences, the Autonomous Communities can bring a claim for judicial review before the Court of First Instance under Art. 263 of the Treaty on the Functioning of the European Union (TFEU, ex 230 EC). According to the established case law of the ECJ, the sub-state entities are non-privileged applicants.[76] For this reason, their claim is admissible only if they are the addressees of an EU decision. If this is not the case, then it is admissible only if they succeed in proving that an EU act concerns them directly and individually. Often these conditions are insurmountable obstacles preventing the Autonomous Communities from obtaining access to the EU courts.

The situation cannot be changed by the new Autonomy Statutes. Even if they provide the right for the Autonomous Communities to bring actions before the Court of Justice, this right is not enforceable against the EU (Art. 191 of the Catalonian Statute of Autonomy; Art. 238 of the Andalusian Statute of Autonomy; Art. 95 of the Aragon Statute of Autonomy; Art. 113 of the Balearic Islands Autonomy Statute; Art. 65 of the Autonomy Statute of Castilla-León).

---

[75] STC 88/1989, de 11 de mayo.

[76] Case C-95/97, Walloon Region *v*. Commission [1997] ECR 967 and Case C-180/97 Tuscany Region *v*. Commission [1997] ECR 3205.

As to the preliminary reference procedure of Art. 267 TFEU (ex 234 EC), one may wonder whether it could be a suitable replacement for the direct challenge of EU acts. It must be highlighted that the preliminary reference can be made only by a national court dealing with the case in which an issue involving EU law arises. This may happen only in situations in which the Autonomous Communities are not allowed to bring a direct claim for judicial review before the ECJ.[77]

It goes without saying that other EU judicial routes (extra-contractual liability and action for failure to act) are not suitable as alternative methods for the European Regions to defend their competences. Therefore, it seems realistic to conclude that regional interests can only be defended by the Member State.

This path has been established by the 1997 Agreement of the CARCE,[78] which set out a system of indirect participation for the Autonomous Communities in proceedings before the EU courts. Under this agreement, the Autonomous Communities may try to convince the Spanish Government to bring a direct action for annulment of an EU measure. The Commission of Control and Coordination[79] has the final say on whether a claim is brought before the EU courts. This Commission is a technical and political body composed of civil servants and high public officers of the central Administration, but not of Autonomous Communities' Administrations. This is a very big shortfall in the Spanish system of autonomic participation in EU related issues through the State. In spite of the constitutional rights of the autonomic entities, the bringing of a claim exclusively depends on the State's willingness to bring an action.

Some degree of regional participation is allowed in infringement procedures initiated by the EU Commission on the grounds of a breach of an EU obligation by an Autonomous Community. In this situation, the Government has to forward to the relevant Autonomous Communities all the communications dispatched by the EU Commission in the pre-judicial stage of the infringement procedure. The Autonomous Communities are entitled to respond to the allegations made by the EU Commission and can even entrust an attorney with the task to assist the national attorney before EU courts.

It is important to emphasise that two new legal routes for the protection of regional interests have recently been created on the EU level by the Treaty of Lisbon. One is the attribution of *locus standi* to the Committee of the Regions for

[77] Also when they are allowed to appeal for annulment and they have already done it. See Case-239/99, Nachi Europe *v*. Hauptzollamt Krefeld [2001], ECR 524.

[78] CARCE, *Acuerdo sobre la participación de las Comunidades Autónomas en los procedimientos ante el TJCE*, de 11 de diciembre de 1997 (BOE 2 de abril de 1998). This agreement substitutes *the Acuerdo para regular la intervención de las Comunidades Autónomas en las actuaciones del Estado en procedimientos precontenciosos de la Comisión Europea y en los asuntos relacionados con el TJCE que afecten a sus competencias*, de 29 de noviembre de 1990 (BOE 8 de septiembre de 1992).

[79] This body was created by the Council of Ministers Agreement of 13 June 1986.

the protection of its prerogatives. The second is the right of the Committee to bring an action for annulment of an EU act for breach of the subsidiarity principle.[80]

E. Conclusion

In Spain, the management of European issues initially resulted in a significant redistribution of competences between central State and regional entities. This changed the territorial balance of power to the detriment of the Autonomous Communities. However, the Autonomous Communities gradually succeeded in redressing the territorial balance of powers.

The Autonomous communities are trying to break the monopoly of the central state by pushing for cooperation with the Spanish Government in relation to the EU decision-making process. Indeed the autonomic entities want to gain direct access to the European policy arena. They want to become the only speaker within the Spanish delegation when European institutions make decisions in areas of regional competence. Even if the central State remains the major channel of influence in European policy-making process, the Autonomous communities are gaining prominence both in the formulation and in the representation of the national bargaining position. As a result of cooperation between central State and autonomic entities, the defence of regional interests takes place at European level.

Spain is a good example of the tensions which arise in light of the centralising tendency in the implementation of EU policy and legislation. The Spanish Constitution allowed for the transfer of both national and regional competences to the European level without requiring the consent of the Autonomous Communities. Consequently, these entities felt that the central State would use the implementation of EU law as an "alibi" to regain competences previously devolved to the regional level. The tension which arose as a result of this situation was finally solved by the Spanish Constitutional Court. It ruled that the implementation of European policies must not alter the internal distribution of competences between central State and the Autonomous Communities. After quite a long period of systematic intrusion in the regional sphere of autonomy, the Spanish Government must now permit regional implementation of EU law when the Autonomous Communities have the competence. The problem continues to be that the central State is responsible to the EU for any failure in implementation.

Initially, the Autonomous Communities showed little willingness to embark on cooperation with the central State in the areas of European law-making and policy-making and of implementation of EU law and policies. The Autonomous Communities' priority was to acquire the capacity for influencing the political process in Brussels without yielding to cooperation with the national Government. More

[80] Art. 263.3 TFEU and Art. 8 of the Protocol on the application of the principles of subsidiarity and proportionality.

recently, the Autonomous Communities realised that the only alternative to cooperation is their marginalisation in the European context. This explains why in the last few years cooperation between the central State and the Autonomous Communities has gradually taken place.

Selected Bibliography

Borrás Rodríguez A (1988) Comentaris sobre l'Estatut d'Autonomia de Catalunya, vol. III. Institut d'Estudis Autonomics, Barcelona

Börzel T (2002) States and regions in the European Union. Cambridge University Press, Cambridge, pp 93–102

Calongue Velázquez A (2002) Conferencia para Asuntos Relacionados con las Comunidades Europeas (CARCE). Revista de Estudios Autonómicos:231

García Roca J (2002) Conflictos entre el Estado y las Comunidades Autónomas ante el Tribunal Supremo: la competencia diferenciada entre las jurisdicciones constitucional y contencioso-administrativa. Revista Vasca de Administración Pública:89–110

Guillermin G (1992) Le principe de l'equilibre institutionnel dans la jurisprudence de la Cour de Justice des Communautés européennes. Journal de Droit International 2:319–346

Hernández Lafuente A (1995) La participación de las Comunidades Autónomas en los asuntos comunitarios europeos. MAP, Madrid, p 132

Huesa Vinaixa R (1986) La legitimación activa de las Comunidades Autónomas ante el Tribunal de Justicia de la Comunidad Europea: sus limitaciones. La Ley:23

López Bofill H (1999) Conflictos de Competencia y jurisdicción ordinaria. Marcial Pons, Madrid, pp 60–71

López Castillo A (1993) La creación y ejecución del Derecho comunitario en España, in J. Barnes Vázquez, La Comunidad Europea, la instancia regional y la organización administrativa de los Estados miembros. Civitas, Madrid, p 174

Mangas Martín A (1987) Derecho comunitario europeo y Derecho español. Tecnos, Madrid, pp 224–227

Olivar De Julián JM (2008) Las oficinas de representación de las regiones y municipios ante la Unión Europea. Thomson-Aranzadi, Pamplona, pp 63–67

Ortega Santiago C (2005) Las Comunidades Autónomas ante la jurisdicción comunitaria. Iustel, Madrid, p 66

Parejo Alonso L (1994) La participación de las Comunidades Autónomas en el proceso de adopción de decisiones de la Unión Europea. In: AA.VV., La acción exterior y comunitaria de los Länder, Regiones, Cantones y Comunidades Autónoma s (I). I.V.A.P., Vitoria, p 101

Portelli H (1993) Aux origines de la décentralisation des Etats européens: l'absence de prospective européenne. In: H. Portelli (dir.) La décentralisation française et l'Europe. Editions Pouvoirs Locaux, Paris, pp 15–20

Sánchez Amor I (1992) La participación regional en las instituciones europeas. La creación del Comité de las Regiones. In: Informe Pi i Sunyer sobre Comunidades Autónomas 1992. Barcelona, pp 309–311

Chapter 9
Austria: The Role of the "*Länder*" in a "Centralised Federal State"

Harald Eberhard

A. Introduction: The *Länder* and Austrian EU Membership

I. Austria as a Federal State in the European Union

Austria is a federal state.[1] In the Austrian federal system, regions are embodied in nine provinces (hereafter "*Länder*"),[2] which represent the intermediate level of governance[3] between the *Bund* (hereafter "Federation") and the *Gemeinden*, i.e. the local municipalities which possess the right of *Selbstverwaltung* (self-administration) and enjoy a certain amount of autonomy, as they are – within their autonomous sphere ("*eigener Wirkungsbereich*")[4] – not subject to instructions from the Federation or the *Länder*.[5] With regard to those powers which are only delegated

Dr Harald Eberhard works as scientific assistant at the Austrian Constitutional Court and teaches constitutional law and administrative law at the University of Vienna Law School.

[1]Cf. Art. 2 para 1 of the *Bundes-Verfassungsgesetz* (Federal Constitutional Law Act, hereinafter referred to as B-VG), in *Bundesgesetzblatt* (Federal Law Gazette, hereinafter referred to as BGBl., 1920/1, dating from 1920 and amended about 90 times until today).

[2]Cf. Art. 2 para 2 of the B-VG: The Federal State is composed of the autonomous *Länder* of Burgenland, Carinthia, Lower Austria, Upper Austria, Salzburg, Styria, Tirol, Vorarlberg and Vienna.

[3]About this term see – especially in the European context – Eberhard et al. (2006), pp. 35–60.

[4]These are specific fields of regulation referred to as in Art. 118 Abs. 2 und 3 B-VG.

[5]Art. 115 – 120 B-VG. Cf. especially Art. 116 para 1 and 2 B-VG: "(1) Every *Land* is divided into municipalities. The municipality is a territorial corporate body entitled to self-administration while being at the same time an administrative local district. Every piece of land must form part of a municipality. (2) The municipality is an independent economic entity. It is entitled, within the limits of the ordinary laws of the Federation and the *Länder*, to possess assets of all kinds, to acquire and to dispose of such at will, to operate economic enterprises as well as to manage its budget independently within the framework of the constitutional finance provisions and to levy taxation". See regarding the provision setting up the specific autonomy of the municipalities – Art. 118 para 4 B-VG.

H. Eberhard
Constitutional Court, Judenplatz 11, 1010 Vienna, Austria
e-mail: harald.eberhard@univie.ac.at

C. Panara and A. De Becker (eds.), *The Role of the Regions in EU Governance*,
DOI 10.1007/978-3-642-11903-3_9,

to the municipalities (*"übertragener Wirkungsbereich"*, assigned sphere of competence)[6] by the Federation and the *Länder*, they can receive instructions both from the Federation and the *Länder*. As the municipalities[7] are mere administrative bodies, they have, as opposed to the Federation[8] and the *Länder*,[9] no right to create legislation.[10] Both the Federation and the *Länder* exercise legislative and administrative powers.[11] With regard to legislation of the Federation, the Federal Parliament consists of two chambers: the *Nationalrat* (National Council) and the *Bundesrat* (Federal Council) – Art. 24 Bundes-Verfassungsgesetz (B-VG). The *Nationalrat* is directly elected by the people (Art. 26 B-VG: equal, direct, personal, free, secret elections) for a period of 5 years (Art. 27 B-VG).[12] The Members of the *Bundesrat* are elected by the *Landtage* (*Länder* Parliaments) based on the principle of proportional representation (Art. 34 and 35 B-VG). In this way, the *Bundesrat* represents the participation of the *Länder* in the legislation of the Federation. The Members of the *Bundesrat* are elected after every general election of the *Landtage* so that the *Bundesrat* – in contrast to the *Nationalrat* – is never dissolved but only partially renewed.[13] The *Länder* legislation is enacted by the *Landtage*; its members are elected by the *Länder* citizens with their main residence in the respective *Land* according to the same principles which are valid for the elections for the *Nationalrat*[14] – Art. 95 B-VG.

One can argue that the manner in which both the Federation and the *Länder* are affected by EU legislation is quite similar.[15] In general, the federal principle of the Austrian Constitution is not very strong. From the very beginning, in the 1920s, the most important powers – especially those of political and economic importance[16] – have always been allocated to the Federation. In the 1950s and 1960s, this process was enhanced by a further centralisation insofar as former *Länder* powers were transferred to the Federation.[17] From a comparative point of view, Austria can therefore be qualified as a very "centralised federal state". Nevertheless, the main

---

[6]Art. 119 B-VG.

[7]In Austria, there exist around 2,350 municipalities.

[8]Cf. Art. 24, 41 ff. B-VG.

[9]Cf. Art. 95 ff. B-VG. The legislation of the *Länder* is carried out by the *Länder* Parliaments (*Landtage*). Their members are elected on the basis of proportional representation by equal, direct, secret and personal suffrage of all male and female *Land* citizens who, in accordance with the *Land* Parliament electoral regulations, are entitled to vote.

[10]See Stelzer (2007) p. 11 f., Prakke (2004) p. 3 (pp. 60–66).

[11]About regions with such legislative powers see from a comparative perspective Gamper (2004).

[12]Art. 27 B-VG. The current *Nationalrat* is the first to last for 5 years. Before constitutional amendment BGBl. I 2007/27, the duration of a legislative period of the *Nationalrat* was 4 years.

[13]Stelzer (2007), p. 20 f.

[14]Stelzer (2007), p. 46.

[15]On the municipalities see Öhlinger (2002), pp. 1–30.

[16]See especially Art. 10 B-VG!

[17]Öhlinger (2007), pp. 50–51.

features of a federal state are clearly realised in the Austrian system; for example, the division of the state functions between the Federation and the *Länder* (see e.g. the allocation of powers in Art. 10–15 B-VG) and the exercise of these rights of participation as their own rights. These might be termed the *formal* criteria of a federal state, whereas the *material* dimension of the *Länder* powers reflects their relatively weak position.

The core of the Austrian Federal system which, according to Art. 2 para 1 B-VG, forms a basic constitutional principle protected by Art. 44 para 3 B-VG (and, in this way, has not only the status of ordinary constitutional law which can be modified by a two-thirds majority in the *Nationalrat* and the *Bundesrat* – Art. 44 para 1 B-VG) can be found in the participation of the *Länder* in the federal legislative process through their involvement in the *Bundesrat* (Federal Council)[18] and, from a political viewpoint, in the strong position of the *Länder* with regard to their participation in the federal administration (*Indirect Federal Administration*, Art. 102 B-VG[19]). In this respect, the *Land* Governors (*Landeshauptmänner*, who are the Heads of the Governments of the *Länder*[20]) play an important role.[21] In other words: the Austrian *Länder* have a strong position when it comes to administrative matters, but a relatively weak one in the legislative process.

II. The Total Revision of the Austrian Constitution in 1995

Austria's adhesion to the European Union on 1 January 1995[22] brought about the first total revision ("*Gesamtänderung der Bundesverfassung*") of the Austrian Constitutional Charter as provided for at Art. 44 para 3 B-VG.[23] This provision postulates the necessity of a referendum where a basic principle of the Constitution,

---

[18]Art. 34–37, 41 ff. B-VG.

[19]See Art. 102 para 1 B-VG: "In the sphere of the *Länder*, in so far as no federal authorities exist (direct federal administration), the Governor and the *Land* authorities subordinate to him exercise the executive power of the Federation (indirect federal administration). Insofar as federal authorities, especially Federal Police Directorates, are entrusted with the execution of matters which are performed as indirect federal administration, these federal authorities are subordinate to the Governor and bound by his instructions (Art. 20 para 1); whether and to what extent such federal authorities are entrusted with executive powers is regulated by federal laws; these may, insofar as they do not concern the mandate stated in para 2 below, only be published with the sanction of the *Länder* concerned".

[20]Art. 101 B-VG.

[21]Cf. Öhlinger (2007), pp. 143–145, Walter et al. (2007), pp. 401–404.

[22]See the adhesion treaty: BGBl. 1995/45.

[23]"Any total revision of the Federal Constitution shall upon conclusion of the procedure pursuant to Art. 42 above but before its authentication by the Federal President be submitted to a referendum by the entire Nation, whereas any partial revision requires this only if one third of the members of the National Council or the Federal Council so demand".

such as democracy, *Rechtsstaat* or federalism, will be changed in a more than marginal way.[24]

Austrian adhesion to the EU brought a change of several constitutional principles in the sense of Art. 44 para 3 B-VG. First, as a consequence of the transfer of national powers to the European Union, the basic principle of democracy (Art. 1 B-VG[25]) was modified in a more than marginal way. Furthermore, the *Rechtsstaat*, which is also seen as a basic principle, was affected. Though the Austrian model of the *Rechtsstaat* cannot be equated with either the concept of the Rule of Law as realised in the Anglo-American system[26] nor with the German *Rechtsstaat*,[27] there exist essential features of such an Austrian *Rechtsstaat* principle. The core of this principle is – apart from the binding force of legal acts over administrative acts such as ordinances and individual acts (*Legalitätsprinzip*, Art. 18 B-VG) – the legal protection system including the *Verfassungsgerichtshof* (Constitutional Court, Art. 137–148 B-VG) and the *Verwaltungsgerichtshof* (Federal Administrative Court, Art. 130–136 B-VG).[28] Insofar as the Austrian Constitutional Court is – with regard to the powers of the European Court of Justice – no longer the sole body empowered to review the law applied in Austria, the principle of the *Rechtsstaat* had been modified by adhesion to the European Union. Also, the level of the legal determination of administrative acts has been discussed as a reason for a fundamental change of the Austrian principle of the *Rechtsstaat*.[29]

III. The Federal Principle and the Transfer of **Länder** *Powers to the European Union*

Also relevant in the context of this paper is the fact that a significant modification of the Austrian federal constitutional principle has taken place. The core element of this modification consists of the transfer of *Länder* powers to the EU. This transfer, for the first time, took place at the time of the adhesion as Austria was required to accept the *acquis communautaire*. The modification of the federal principle was the basis for the creation of provisions in the B-VG aimed at involving the *Länder* in the process of European law making. This development was due to the fact that the most significant power of the EU lies in legislative initiatives[30] and participation in those areas which are also regulated, as well as exclusively, at the EU level seems to

[24]Cf. Öhlinger (2007), p. 56, Walter et al. (2007), p. 76.

[25]"Austria is a democratic republic. Its law emanates from the people".

[26]See Dorsen et al. (2003), p. 16 ff, Fleiner and Basta Fleiner (2004), p. 226.

[27]See Dorsen et al. (2003), p. 17 f, Fleiner and Basta Fleiner (2004), p. 243 ff.

[28]See for example Machacek (1994), pp. 2–28, 30–37.

[29]See in detail Eberhard (2008), pp. 49–116, especially p. 52 ff.

[30]On this aspect cf. Della Cananea (2004), p. 221 (233): the EU "uses law as a surrogate source of strength".

be a suitable instrument to compensate the loss of powers in these fields. This transfer had been legitimated by a referendum on 12 June 1994 according to Art. 44 para 3 B-VG.

For all transfers of *Länder* powers *after* 1995, several constitutional provisions have been created which dealt with the conditions of this permanent transfer up to now. In this way, we have to differentiate as follows.

1. Amendments to European Primary Law

According to Art. 48 para 3 EU, amendments of the Treaties "shall enter into force after being ratified by all the Member States in accordance with their respective constitutional requirements". The transfer of powers from the *Länder* to the EU which may occur during such revisions of European primary law, i.e. the Founding Treaties of the EU, has been taking place in Austria via special constitutional acts.[31] These acts stipulate that the signing of the respective amendment can only take place with consent both from the *Nationalrat* and the *Bundesrat* with a two-thirds majority. In a recent constitutional amendment,[32] Art. 50 para 1 Z 2 B-VG and Art. 50 para 4 B-VG have been formulated so as to require political treaties which bring about a change of the Founding Treaties of the EC and EU to be approved both by the *Nationalrat* and the *Bundesrat* with a quorum necessary to amend constitutional law[33] (i.e. a two-thirds majority of both chambers of the Parliament).

2. Amendments to European Secondary Law

All other relevant cases of "transfer" of *Länder* powers can take place only via amendments to, or creation of, EU secondary law such as regulations and directives. In this context, a number of provisions have been enacted in the B-VG along with a constitutional amendment[34] dealing with the internal procedures of Austrian participation in EU governance. These provisions can be qualified as part of the so-called *Integrationsverfassungsrecht*[35] whose task is to make the requisite amendments to Austrian constitutional law in order to ensure compliance with EU law, to the extent that Austria's participation in EU matters requires implementation of changes to procedural rules or the creation of norms with regard to its role as a federal state. The core of these provisions provide for elections for the European

[31]BGBl. I 1998/76 (Treaty of Amsterdam), 2001/120 (Treaty of Nice), 2003/53, 2005/12 and 2006/25.

[32]BGBl. I 2008/2.

[33]See Art. 44 para 1 B-VG.

[34]BGBl. 1994/1013.

[35]See Grabenwarter (2003), pp. 283–337, Winkler (2003), pp. 153–172. Furthermore, for a general overview, see Öhlinger (2007), pp. 100–104; Walter et al. (2007), pp. 136–140; Öhlinger and Potacs (2006), pp. 32–37.

Parliament and the information and participations rights of the *Nationalrat*, the *Bundesrat* and the *Länder* with regard to the Austrian role in the European process of law- and decision-making, e.g. regarding the Common Foreign and Security Policy of the European Union (Art. 23a–23f B-VG).

These provisions form – from a multi-level perspective – an essential part of the European constitutional network ("*Europäischer Verfassungsverbund*"[36]). This network consists of European Constitutional Law such as the Treaties on the one hand as well as the national constitutional provisions on the other. Due to the fact that several Member States (such as Belgium, Germany and Austria) are federal states, one aspect of this network is that attention also has to be given to procedural and decision-related aspects of the participation of federate entities in the EU law-making process.[37]

These provisions in the Austrian Constitution differ between certain forms of participation of the *Länder* in European governance. From a comparative perspective,[38] it seems to be relevant that the *Bundesrat* does not have a very strong position with regard to the participation of the *Länder* in European governance [apart from the fact that it has to approve amendments of the Founding Treaties with a two-thirds majority (Art. 50 B-VG, see before I.3.a.)]. In this respect, there is a link to the weak position of the *Bundesrat* in the national system of governance. The national legislative procedure gives the *Bundesrat*, in normal circumstances in relation to the decisions of the *Nationalrat*, only a suspensive veto, not an absolute veto (Art. 42 B-VG[39]).

Regarding this system, we can say that indirect participation of the *Länder* in EU governance takes place via the *Bundesrat* (Federal Council),[40] whereas direct participation is provided by other tools, especially the *Integrationskonferenz der Länder* (IKL, "Integration Conference of the *Länder*")[41] This "conference" is an

[36]See in particular Pernice (2001), p. 148 (p. 163 ff.).

[37]See Grabenwarter (2003), p. 335.

[38]Regarding this aspect cf. Grabenwarter (2003), p. 305 ff., especially p. 307.

[39]"Art. 42. (1) Every enactment of the National Council shall without delay be conveyed by the President to the Federal Council. (2) Save as otherwise provided by constitutional law, an enactment can be authenticated and published only if the Federal Council has not raised a reasoned objection to this enactment. (3) This objection must be conveyed to the National Council in writing by the Chairman of the Federal Council within eight weeks of the enactment's arrival; the Federal Chancellor shall be informed thereof. (4) If the National Council in the presence of at least half its members once more carries its original resolution, this shall be authenticated and published. If the Federal Council resolves not to raise any objection or if no reasoned objection is raised within the deadline laid down in para 3 above, the enactment shall be authenticated and published. (5) The Federal Council has no claim to participation in so far as National Council resolutions concern the National Council's Standing Orders, the dissolution of the National Council, a Federal finance law, a temporary provision consonant with Art. 51 para 5 or a disposal of Federal property, the assumption or conversion of a Federal liability, the contraction or the conversion of a Federal monetary debt, the sanction of a final Federal budget account".

[40]See below B.III.2.

[41]See section "*Integrationskonferenz der Länder* (IKL, Integration conference of the *Länder*)".

institution consisting of the *Landeshauptmänner* (Governors) and the Presidents of the *Länder* Parliaments. Its function is to observe common interests of the *Länder* in European Integration matters and to deliberate on important questions of integration policy. Another important instrument is the "*Landeshauptmännerkonferenz*" (Conference of the Governors of the *Länder*) which serves as a platform to formulate the common points of view in all relevant matters.[42] Although this "conference" is an informal institution, it has enormous importance in the Austrian political reality.

B. Constitutional Law Regarding European Integration ("*Staatliches Integrationsverfassungsrecht*")

I. Information Rights of the Länder

According to Art. 23d para 1 B-VG, the Federation must inform the *Länder* without any delay regarding all EU legislative proposals ("*Vorhaben*") which affect the *Länder*'s autonomous sphere of competence or could otherwise be of interest to them and it must give them the opportunity to present their views within a reasonable timeframe to be fixed by the Federation.[43] Such statements shall be addressed to the *Bundeskanzleramt* (Federal Chancellery).[44] In this way, the *Bundeskanzleramt* plays a central role as well as the *Bundeskanzler* (Federal Chancellor) who is appointed by the directly elected *Bundespräsident* (Federal President, Art. 60 B-VG); he has a very important political and essential coordinative function in his role as chairman of the *Bundesregierung* [Federal Government, which is composed of all *Bundesminister* (ministers) and *Staatssekretäre* (State Secretaries), Art. 69 B-VG]

The categories of proposals and what type of notification must be given are defined in detailed provisions of an agreement between the Federation and the *Länder*[45]: Accordingly, the term "project" encompasses documents, reports and other (formal) information from all institutions of the EU, documents about informal meetings of ministers, information about procedures at the European Court of Justice, as well as reports of the Austrian Representation in the EU. It has been highly controversial in recent years whether modifications to the Founding Treaties (EC[46] and EU[47]), especially the adhesion of new Member States, can also be seen as

---

[42]See below B.III.1.

[43]See Öhlinger (1999a), Rz 6.

[44]The Austrian Federal Chancellor is the head of government (Art. 69 B-VG, however, he does not have the authority to direct the other members of the Cabinet) and the leader of the Federal Chancellery which has the status of a Federal Ministry (Art. 77 B-VG).

[45]See below footnote 72.

[46]Treaty establishing the European Community.

[47]Treaty of the European Union.

a project in this sense.[48] Projects within the framework of the European Union which "could otherwise be of interest to them" encompass those which touch the financial interests of the *Länder* as well as their administration in private forms.[49]

A similar information right is granted to the *Bundesrat*. According to Art. 23e para 1 B-VG, the competent member of the *Bundesregierung* (Federal Government) shall without delay inform the *Nationalrat* and the *Bundesrat* about all projects within the framework of the European Union and give them the opportunity to present their opinion.

One special Austrian characteristic is the strong role of the *Gemeinden* (municipalities) irrespective of the fact that they have no legislative function but only administrative powers.[50] Regarding this administrative function, they possess the right of *Selbstverwaltung* (self-administration) and are, in this way, autonomous institutions. This explains how they can formulate their point of view if their own spheres of administrative powers or other important interests are affected.[51]

II. Articulation of the **Länder** *Position in European Governance*

These rights trigger the obligation of the Federation to integrate the *Länder* into EU legislative procedure under certain conditions. If the Federation is in possession of a uniform statement of the *Länder* on an EU legislative proposal which is within the competence of the *Länder* (which means that this is, in most cases, an object of Art. 15 para 1 B-VG[52]),[53] the Federation is bound in negotiations with and voting in the EU institutions. This could also be true of proposed EU regulations[54] which are to operate within the remit of a *Land's* competence because of the direct applicability of these legal acts.[55] In these cases, the statement of the *Länder* has binding force as a regulation could totally replace a *Länder* competence.

[48]In this way confirming Öhlinger (1999a), Rz 8. See also Öhlinger (2004), pp. 225–227; Lenzhofer (2006), pp. 83–107.

[49]See Öhlinger and Potacs (2006), p. 34.

[50]See supra I.1.

[51]The representation of these bodies is incumbent upon the *Österreichischer Städtebund* (Austrian Association of Cities and Towns, Austrian Municipal Federation) and the *Österreichischer Gemeindebund* (Austrian Association of municipalities, Austrian Communal Federation). See Art. 115 para 3 B-VG.

[52]See below footnote 106.

[53]In such areas which affect powers both of the Federation and the *Länder* (e.g. the area of land use planning) the binding character of such a statement would be restricted with the aspect of the *Land* power: see Öhlinger (1999a).

[54]Art. 288 para 2 TFEU.

[55]Cf. Öhlinger and Potacs (2006), p. 36.

The binding character of such statements relates to Austrian participation in the European Council,[56] but also to proposals of the European Council[57] and preparatory acts for decisions of the Council like decisions in the Coreper.[58,59]

There are certain conditions for a uniform statement. Firstly, five *Länder* must assent, with no *Land* making a dissenting vote.[60] In that respect, a uniform statement does not have to be created unanimously.[61] The Federation may only deviate therefrom for "compelling foreign and integration policy reasons". The Federation must advise the *Länder* of these reasons without delay (Art. 23d para 2 B-VG). The term "compelling foreign and integration policy reasons" is, at its core, not really a justiciable one.[62] Theoretically, the respective federal minister is responsible vis-à-vis the *Länder* when he or she deviates from a uniform statement without the above-mentioned basis. Therefore, despite a uniform statement of the *Länder*, the interests of the whole state, in the European context, take precedence ("*gesamtstaatliche Verantwortung*"[63]). In other words, the uniform statement of the *Länder* has no absolute value in the process of negotiations and voting at the EU level. A statement of the *Nationalrat* only has absolute value if the projected legislative acts of the EU would require an amendment to the Federal Constitution.[64]

---

[56] Art. 16 ff. TEU.

[57] Art. 15 TEU.

[58] *Comité des représentants permanents*. Cf. Art. 240 TFEU.

[59] See Öhlinger (1999a), Rz 13.

[60] To this term cf. section "*Integrationskonferenz der Länder* (IKL, Integration conference of the *Länder*)"

[61] Cf. the parliamentary materials regarding the amendment BGBl. 1994/1013, RV 27 BlgNR 19. GP, p. 9: a uniform statement implicates that all *Länder* were integrated into the decision process and this fact is clear from the point of view of the Federation.

[62] Cf. the preparatory materials regarding the amendment BGBl. 1994/1013, RV 27 BlgNR 19. GP, p. 9: such reasons exist if this assumption is "peremptory" for the perception of essential Austrian interests in the EU. See also Öhlinger (1999a), Rz 14; Öhlinger (1999b), Rz 12.

[63] See in the context of the German legal situation (Art. 23 para 5 Bonner GG) Grabenwarter (2003), p. 306.

[64] See Öhlinger (1999b), Rz 14. Cf. Art. 23e para 2 B-VG: "If the competent member of the Federal Government is in possession of an opinion by the National Council about a project within the framework of the European Union which shall be passed into Federal law or which bears upon the issue of a directly applicable juridical act concerning matters which would need to be settled by Federal legislation, then the member is bound by this opinion during European Union negotiations and voting. Deviation is only admissible for imperative foreign and integrative policy reasons.", and Art. 23e para 3 B-VG: "If the competent member of the Federal Government wishes to deviate from an opinion of the National Council pursuant to para 2 above, then the National Council shall again be approached. In so far as the juridical act under preparation by the European Union would signify an amendment to existing Federal constitutional law, a deviation is at all events only admissible if the National Council does not controvert it within an appropriate time".

III. Representation of the Länder

1. Forms of Direct Involvement of the Regions in EU Law and Policy Making

Direct Participation of the *Länder*

The *Länder* are also integrated in European governance via forms of a direct participation. Insofar as an EU legislative proposal affects matters within the competence of the *Länder*, the *Bundesregierung* (Federal Government) can assign a representative nominated by the *Länder* to participate in the decision-making of the Council of the European Union (Art. 23d para 3 B-VG). In this way, this representative is, in the wording of Art. 16 para 2 TEU, such one "at ministerial level, who may commit the government of the Member State in question and cast its vote".[65]

This provision applies only in respect of the Council of the European Union (Art. 16 TEU), not the European Council (Art. 15 TEU).[66] However, the *Länder* have no legal claim to participate in this way.[67]

In this respect, it is not necessary that the matter is one of an exclusive *Länder* competence (Art. 15 B-VG), so that the *Länder* also – as a general rule – have to take care of Federal interests.[68] The exercise of this authority will be affected by cooperation and, which seems to be somewhat unclear,[69] coordination with the competent member of the *Bundesregierung* [the respective *Bundesminister* (Federal Minister)]. In matters pertaining to federal legislation, the *Länder* representative is responsible to the *Nationalrat*,[70] whereas in matters pertaining to *Länder* legislation he is responsible to the *Landtage* (*Länder* Parliaments) in accordance with the provision which deals with legal responsibility.[71]

---

[65]Cf. Öhlinger (1999a), Rz 21.

[66]Cf. the preparatory materials regarding the amendment BGBl. 1994/1013, RV 27 BlgNR 19. GP, p. 9.

[67]Öhlinger (1999a), Rz 22.

[68]See the preparatory materials regarding the amendment BGBl. 1994/1013, RV 27 BlgNR 19. GP, p. 10.

[69]Öhlinger (2007), p. 102; Öhlinger (1999a), Rz 22.

[70]This means a criminal responsibility, but not such one in a political dimension. See Art. 142 B-VG: "(1) The Constitutional Court pronounces on suits which predicate the constitutional responsibility of the highest Federal and *Land* authorities for legal contraventions culpably ensuing from their official activity.

(2) Suit can be brought:

...

c) against an Austrian representative in the Council for contravention of law in matters where legislation would pertain to the Federation: by a vote of the National Council for contravention of law in matters where legislation would pertain to the *Länder*: by identically worded votes of all the *Länder* parliaments; ...".

[71]Cf. Art. 142 B-VG. According to this provision the relevant persons are legally responsible to the Constitutional Court with regard to the breach of Austrian Constitutional Law. This form of

An institutional influence on European governance can also be seen in the right of the *Länder* to participate in the appointment of the 12 Austrian Members of the Committee of the Regions (Art. 305 TFEU). According to Art. 23c para 5 B-VG, Austrian participation in the nomination of members of the Committee of the Regions and their deputies shall be affected on the basis of proposals from the *Länder* as well as from the *Österreichischer Städtebund* Austrian Association of Cities and Towns (Austrian Municipal Federation) and the *Österreichischer Gemeindebund* (Austrian Communal Federation). In this context, the *Länder* shall propose one representative each, and the *Österreichischer Städtebund* and the *Österreichischer Gemeindebund* jointly propose three representatives.

Both institutions have their constitutional basis in Art. 115 para 3 B-VG which says that they are "competent to represent the interests of the municipalities". The *Österreichischer Städtebund* is involved in the preparation of national legislation and, among other issues, comments from the point of view of local government on some 100 federal regulations every year as the cities and municipalities see it. Moreover, representatives of the *Österreichischer Städtebund* are active in a number of advisory bodies in fields such as the environment or welfare. It presents statements regarding new legislation and discusses the implementation of new policies. The *Österreichischer Gemeindebund* represents – in the same way – the smaller local authorities.

Other important means of participation are provided by the integration of *Länder* representatives in numerous working groups of the Council and boards of the European Commission.

Agreement Between the Federation and the Länder *According to Art. 15a B-VG*

The detailed provisions of the modalities of the participation of the *Länder* are laid down in an agreement between the Federation and the *Länder*,[72] based on Art. 15a B-VG.[73] This agreement was, in a chronological view, the forerunner of the provisions of Art. 23d B-VG.[74]

---

responsibility has to be differed from the political responsibility to the *Nationalrat* (National Council, Art. 76 B-VG).

[72]Published in BGBl. 1992/775.

[73]See in special Art. 15a para 1 B-VG: "The Federation and the *Länder* may conclude agreements among themselves about matters within their respective sphere of competence. The conclusion of such agreements in the name of the Federation is, depending on the subject, incumbent on the Federal Government or Federal Minister. Agreements which are to be binding also on the authorities of the Federal legislature can be concluded by the Federal Government only with the approval of the National Council. Art. 50 para 3 shall by analogy be applied to such resolutions of the National Council; they shall be published in the Federal Law Gazette".

[74]Parts of the agreement became in a first step part of Art. 10 B-VG with the amendment of the B-VG BGBl. 1992/276. See in detail Öhlinger (1999a), Rz. 4.

Integrationskonferenz der Länder (IKL, Integration Conference of the *Länder*)

With the agreement between the *Länder* about common decision-making in matters of European integration[75] a so-called *Integrationskonferenz der Länder* (hereafter: IKL, "integration conference of the *Länder*") has been established.[76] Its function is to observe common interests of the *Länder* in European Integration matters and to deliberate on important questions of integration policy (Art. 1 of the agreement). In this respect, the IKL substitutes the function of the *Bundesrat* in these issues.[77] Some *Länder* have implemented the IKL in their constitutional statutes.

In this conference, all *Länder* are represented by the *Landeshauptmänner* (Governors, Heads of the *Länder* Governments who are elected by the *Land* Parliaments – Art. 101 B-VG) and the *Landtagspräsidenten* (Presidents of the *Länder* Governments). The President of the *Bundesrat* has the right to participate in the sessions of the conference. Each *Land* has one vote which is exercised by the *Landeshauptmann*. Uniform statements in the sense of Art. 23d para 2 B-VG are adopted if five *Länder* agree, unless one *Land* makes a dissenting vote (Art. 3 of the agreement). The practical irrelevance of this conference is exemplified by the fact that so far it has only met twice.[78]

The *Land* Parliaments established their own committees for matters of European integration.[79] These were a kind of compensation for the restriction of legislative competences of the *Länder* which resulted from EU directives and regulations.

Other Instruments

Besides participation in the IKL, the Austrian Regions have established a coordination office in Vienna ("*Verbindungsstelle der Bundesländer*"). This office also represents a binding element between national institutions and the Austrian Delegation at the European Union in Brussels. Another important, but more or less informal, instrument can be seen in the *Landeshauptmännerkonferenz* (Conference of the Governors of the *Länder*/Heads of *Länder* Governments), which in the political as well as constitutional reality of the Austrian federal system has a strong function with regard to the demands of the *Länder*.[80] The meetings of this conference are instruments for the articulation of a common position of the *Länder* at an early point in time vis-à-vis the Federation.

---

[75]Published in Wiener LGBl. (Vienna Law Gazette) 1992/29.

[76]Öhlinger (1999a) Rz 14 ff.; Grabenwarter (1995), p. 166 (p. 171).

[77]About this aspect from a comparative perspective Grabenwarter (2003), p. 307.

[78]Öhlinger and Potacs (2006), p. 36.

[79]Cf. Sonntag (2008), pp. 45–48.

[80]Öhlinger (2007), p. 148, Walter et al. (2007), p. 406.

2. Forms of Indirect Involvement of the Regions in EU Law and Policy Making

Forms of indirect involvement of the *Länder* can be seen insofar as the Austrian *Länder* participate in federal legislation by their representation in the second chamber of the Austrian Parliament, the *Bundesrat*.[81] According to Art. 24 of the B-VG, the legislative power of the Federation is exercised by the *Nationalrat* jointly with the *Bundesrat* in which the *Länder* are represented in proportion to the number of nationals[82] in each *Land* (Art. 34 B-VG).[83] The members of the *Bundesrat* are elected by the *Länder* parliaments based on the principle of proportional representation.[84]

The participation of the *Bundesrat* in the EU law-making process is based on the constitutional provision of Art. 23e para 6 B-VG. When the competent member of the Federal Government possesses an opinion of the *Bundesrat* regarding an EU legislative proposal which imperatively needs to be implemented by a Federal law that would in accordance with Art. 44 para. 2 B-VG[85] require the agreement of the *Bundesrat*, the member is bound by this opinion during European Union negotiations and voting. Deviation is only admissible for compelling foreign and integration policy reasons. The maintenance of the *Bundesrat* competences pursuant to Art. 23e B-VG and the respective details are settled by the Standing Orders of the *Bundesrat* (*Geschäftsordnung des Bundesrates*).[86] Therefore, the extent to which a specifically designated committee of the *Bundesrat* shall be competent for the treatment of projects within the framework of the European Union instead of the *Bundesrat* is settled, along with the extent to which the maintenance of the *Bundesrat* competences is reserved to the *Bundesrat* itself.

IV. Judicial Defence of the Regions' Competences at the National and European Levels with Regard to an Invasion of Competences of the Regions by the EU

It can be seen as an essential element of the *Rechtsstaat*[87] that legal remedies have to be available where secondary legislation does not comply with primary law.

[81]See supra I.1.

[82]Austrian nationals with an Austrian main residence.

[83]See Prakke (2004), pp. 34–39.

[84]See in detail Stelzer (2007), p. 20 f.

[85]"Constitutional laws or constitutional provisions contained in ordinary laws restricting the competence of the *Länder* in legislation or execution require furthermore the approval of the Federal Council which must be imparted in the presence of at least half the members and by a two thirds majority of the votes cast".

[86]See §§ 13a and 13b *Geschäftsordnung des Bundesrates*, BGBl. 1988/361.

[87]Haltern (2005), pp. 151, 157 ff.

In light of the restrictions, which exist for individuals bringing an action before the European Court of Justice under Art. 263 para 4 TFEU,[88] Member States are privileged applicants when initiating such an action (Art 263 para 2 TFEU[89]), whereas the Austrian *Länder*, can bring such an action only under the conditions of Art. 263 para 4 TFEU. The Austrian Constitutional Law contains significant provisions which allow the *Länder* to participate in the privilege of Art. 263 para 2 TFEU. The rationale of these provisions is to compensate the curtailed possibilities of the *Länder* filing a lawsuit at the Courts of the EU.

According to Art. 10 para 1 of the Agreement about the right of the *Länder* and the municipalities to participate in matters of European integration dating from 1992,[90] the Federation has an obligation to file a lawsuit before the European Court of Justice under certain circumstances.[91] This provision possesses constitutional status. Such written requests must be made to the *Bundeskanzleramt* (Federal Chancellery) and have to contain the relevant and constitutive contents of such a lawsuit according to the provision of EU Law (Art. 10 para 2 leg cit).

If certain (allegedly unlawful) acts of institutions of the European Union affect the *Länder*'s autonomous sphere of competence, the Federation has to file a lawsuit at the request of a *Land*, unless another *Land* disagrees, or there exist some compelling foreign and integration policy reasons.[92] This provision has a more or less symbolic and political function, since there does not exist any specific procedure to overcome possible disagreements regarding the points of view of the Federation and the *Länder* concerning a certain legal act of the European Union. This is shown by the fact there has so far not been any reference to this provision.

V. The Fulfilment of EU Obligations in the Internal Sphere

The European Union is frequently thought to be blind regarding federalism in its Member States (Hans Peter Ipsen).[93] If an EU Member State, or a part of it, fails to fulfil an obligation deriving from the Treaties, the Federation is responsible for it.[94] Nevertheless, it is possible for the Federation to enact rules about the integration of

---

[88]"Any natural or legal person may, under the same conditions, institute proceedings against a decision addressed to that person or against a decision which, although in the form of a regulation or a decision addressed to another person, is of direct and individual concern to the former".

[89]Art. 263 para 2: "It shall for this purpose have jurisdiction in actions brought by a Member State, the European Parliament, the Council or the Commission on grounds of lack of competence, infringement of an essential procedural requirement, infringement of this Treaty or of any rule of law relating to its application, or misuse of powers".

[90]Supra note 72.

[91]See in detail Öhlinger (1999a), Rz 35 ff.

[92]In this case, the Federation is not committed to file a lawsuit: Öhlinger (1999a), Rz 37.

[93]See Öhlinger (1999a), Rz 23 with further references.

[94]See Öhlinger and Potacs (2006), p. 31 f.

the *Länder* given the case that the Federation has to accept punitive consequences deriving from such breach of the Treaties.

The Austrian system of the allocation of powers between the Federation and the *Länder* is – in its main points[95] – laid down in Art. 10 to 15 B-VG.[96] This system is also relevant when it comes to the necessity of implementing European Law. The system of the allocation of powers is, in this way, an essential instrument of the fulfilment of obligations deriving from EU Membership.

Regarding the implementation of EU Law, the national legislator (with regard to Austria: the Federal Parliament, consisting of the *Nationalrat* and the *Bundesrat* – Art. 24 B-VG) is bound twice (so-called *"doppelte Bindung"*).[97] On the one hand, it has to comply with EU law, and on the other hand, EU law can grant a flexible scope with regard to its implementation. Within this scope, and regarding the special modalities of implementation,[98] the national legislator has to face the regular binding character of the national constitutional provisions (e.g. those concerning the allocation of powers between the Federation and the *Länder*). In this context, it had been pointed out by a much discussed decision of the Austrian Constitutional Court[99] that it would be necessary for the Constitution to be modified if there is no explicit constitutional base for federal provisions, but European Law requires a uniform provision. This seems significant, as, with regard to single constitutional provisions, the Constitutional Court decided that they would be "displaced"[100] if they contradicted EU law (*Anwendungsvorrang*).[101] However, this option fails in the case that European law postulates certain provisions and the Austrian Constitution does not give the relevant powers to the Federation or the *Länder*.[102]

If a provision of EC law has to be implemented by the *Länder*, then they are responsible for this procedure. According to Art. 23d para 5 B-VG, the *Länder* must take measures which are necessary within their autonomous sphere of competence for the implementation of juridical acts within the framework of the European Union. If an EU Court (which practically means the European Court of Justice) finds against Austria on the grounds that a *Land* has failed to punctually comply with its obligations under EU law,[103] the competence for such measures, in

[95]There also exist constitutional provisions about the division of powers outside from the B-VG.

[96]Öhlinger (2007), pp. 118–132; Walter et al. (2007), pp. 154–160.

[97]Cf. Official Collection of the Decisions of the Constitutional Court (VfSlg) 14.863/1997, 17.022/2003.

[98]Cf. the so called "principle of institutional and procedural autonomy". Öhlinger and Potacs (2006), pp. 140–144. See also Art. 288 para 3 TFEU ("procedure, choice of form and methods").

[99]Official Collection of the Decisions of the Constitutional Court (VfSlg) 17.022/2003.

[100]This effect means no derogation, but the obligation of the single organ not to apply this provision in the respective context. Regarding the supremacy of EU Law as a structural principle cf. ECJ, Costa v. ENEL [1964] ECR 585, 593. See also Öhlinger and Potacs (2006), p. 58 f.

[101]Official Collection of the Decisions of the Constitutional Court (VfSlg) 15.427/1999.

[102]See Korinek (2004) p. 131 (p. 137 ff.).

[103]This could only be relevant in the case that there exists a judgment of the ECJ in a procedure according to Art. 258 ff. TFEU. See Öhlinger (1999a), Rz 32.

particular the issuance of the necessary laws, passes temporarily to the Federation. A measure taken by the Federation pursuant this provision, in particular the issue of such a law or the issue of such an ordinance, becomes invalid as soon as the *Land* has taken the necessary action.[104] In these cases, a devolution of the competences takes a place which is limited to that period of time during which the *Länder* do not provide for the respective provisions.[105]

C. Main Areas of Overlap Between the Competences of the Regions and Those of the EU

First, the "centralised" dimension of the Austrian federal system must be emphasised once again. Though the *Länder* have – by means of the blanket clause of Art. 15 para. 1[106] of the B-VG – all powers which are not those of the Federation, the most important areas of legislation operate under federal powers.[107] Typical as well as traditional powers of the *Länder* affect law in the fields of hunting (*Jagdrecht*), nature conservation (*Naturschutz*), fishery (*Fischereirecht*), as well as construction laws (*Baurecht*). In these areas, a potential influence of European law can be seen. In particular, the interconnection between national provisions of nature conservation and the respective acts of EU law is clearly visible (e.g. "Natura 2000" areas).[108]

The influence of EU law is also significant in relation to the provisions regarding agriculture in general as well as the trade in agricultural real estate (*Grundverkehrsrecht*).[109] Another important area of influence can be seen in the provisions in the field of social welfare.[110]

---

[104] Art. 23d para 5 last sentence B-VG.

[105] Cf. Öhlinger (1999a), Rz 32.

[106] "Insofar as a matter is not expressly delegated by the Federal Constitution to the legislation or the execution of the Federation, it remains within the autonomous sphere of competence of the *Länder*".

[107] See supra I.1. and the profound ruling in Art. 10 B-VG where can be found all powers of the Federation in the field of legislation as well as administration.

[108] The Natura 2000 network encompasses the Council Directive 92/43/EEC on the conservation of natural habitats and wild fauna and flora as well as the Council directive 79/409/EEC on the conservation of wild birds. The Birds Directive provides for the creation of "Special Protection Areas" and the Habitat Directive for the creation of "Special Areas of Conservation".

[109] Öhlinger (1999a), Rz 2.

[110] See e.g. § 7a of the Vienna Social Welfare Act (Wiener LGBl. [Vienna Law Gazette] 1973/11 as amended 2006/58) which regulates the conditions under which (foreign) citizens of the Union are equated with Austrian citizens regarding the claim of social welfare. This provision transforms several EU directives, e.g. the directives 2003/109/EC concerning the status of third-country nationals who are long-term residents, 2004/38/EC on the right of citizens of the Union and their family members to move and reside freely within the territory of the Member States and 2004/83/EC on minimum standards for the qualification and status of third-country nationals or stateless persons as refugees or as persons who otherwise need international protection and the content of the protection granted.

Besides the sphere of sovereign acts, a specific overlap of competences of the *Länder* and those of the EU can also be seen with regard to provisions dealing with private law acts of the state, e.g. the directives on Public Procurement law (*Vergaberecht*).[111]

D. Representation Offices of the Regions in Brussels

Most of the Austrian *Länder* have installed representation offices in Brussels and a common *Länder* representation at the Delegation (Embassy, Permanent Mission) of Austria to the EU in Brussels. These can be qualified as institutions of an essential

---

[111]Cf. Art. 14b B-VG, which set up the competences in this field as follows:

"(1) Legislation regarding public procurement, to the extent not covered by para. 3, is a power of the Federation. (2) Execution regarding matters of para 1 is

1. Federal power regarding

...

2. *Länder* power with regard to

a) the award of contracts by one of the *Länder*, the municipalities and the municipality associations;

b) the award of contracts by endowments, funds and institutions in terms of Art. 127 para 1 and Art. 127 a paras 1 and 8;

c) the award of contracts by enterprises in terms of Art 126b para 2, to the extent that it is not subject to para 1 subpara c, as well as the award of contracts by enterprises in terms of Art. 127 para 3 and Art 127a paras 3 and 8;

d) the award of contracts by self governing corporate bodies instituted by *Länder* legislation;

e) the award of contracts by legal entities not contained in para 1 subparas a through d;

aa) financed by one of the *Länder* or jointly with the Federation or other *Länder*, to the extent the award is not subject to para 1 subpara e sublit aa;

bb) subject to *Länder* supervision of their management, to the extent that the award is not subject to para 1 subpara e sublit aa or bb or sublit aa;

cc) the administrative, management or supervising bodies which consist of members appointed by one of the *Länder*, to the extent the award is not subject to para 1 subpara e sublit aa through cc or sublit aa or bb;

f) the joint award of contracts by the Federation and the *Länder*, to the extent it is not subject to para 1 subpara f, as well as the joint award of contracts by more than one of the *Länder*.

Irrespective of the size of their population, municipalities are considered legal entities which in terms of para 1 subparas b and c and para 2 subparas b and c are subject to the jurisdiction of the Federal Board of Audit. Within the scope of para 1 subparas b, c, e and f, purchasers in terms of para 1 are considered to belong to the Federation and purchasers in terms of para 2 are considered to be part of the respective *Länder*. If in terms of para 2 subparas c, e or f more than one of the *Länder* is involved, the jurisdiction for execution shall depend on the relative weight of the characteristic which in terms of the respective subpara (sublitera) of para 1 is or would be relevant for the subdivision of the jurisdiction for execution between the Federation and the *Länder*, furthermore on purchaser's domicile, on the domicile (main residence) of the awarding authority, if however it is still not possible to define the jurisdiction, it shall rest with such *Land* which at the time of institution of the award procedure holds the chair or most recently held the chair of the Federal Council.

(3) Power of the *Länder* is the legislation and execution in matters of review within the scope of contract awards by purchasers in terms of para 2 subpara 2. ...".

and – from a practical point of view – very effective informal influence in the system of European Governance ("lobbying"). They have no explicit basis in Austrian constitutional law, but do in the agreement between the Federation and the *Länder* about the right of the *Länder* and the municipalities to participate in matters of European integration dating from 1992.[112] According to Art. 9 of this agreement, the *Länder* have the right to delegate representatives of the Austrian Delegation (Embassy, Permanent Mission) at the EU at their own expense. Finally, the *Verbindungsstelle der Bundesländer*, a kind of coordination office of the *Länder*, cooperates with the Austrian Delegation at the EU in Brussels.

E. Conclusion

European Governance today consists of governing on several levels (multi level governance). The Austrian *Länder* are players in this system, but one has to keep in mind that – with regard to the national level – EU law *prima facie* does not affect the national allocation of powers because of the autonomous sphere of the Member States in general. In a certain way, a trend towards a centralisation of powers in order to facilitate the system of implementation of EU law can be seen.[113] The reform discussion of the federal system in Austria cannot be characterised as very successful because of repeated failure in recent years.[114] But the Austrian federal system includes not only special *Länder* competences but also the participation of the *Länder* in both Federal legislation and administration in Federal matters. In this way, the *Länder* also participate in the implementation of EU law in these areas and, in that respect, have a certain amount of influence.

Apart from that, the participation of the Austrian *Länder* in European governance at the EU level, especially in the European Parliament and in the Committee of the Regions, set up a system of governance which has strengthened the role of the Austrian *Länder* at the European level. *Prima facie*, the participation of the *Länder* in European governance at the national level, i.e. regarding the activities of the Federal Government, has a detailed and – in a comparative view[115] a strong – legal basis in the core constitutional document, the B-VG. However, in legal reality, the position of the *Länder* derives its functionality mainly by informal ways [especially via the *Landeshauptmänner* (Governors)]. In summary, one can say that this system has been quite successful during the last 14 years of Austrian EU Membership.

---

[112]See supra note 72.

[113]Often, it is seen critically that there exists nine different regulations concerning building law in the *Länder*.

[114]Eberhard (2007), pp. 789–802; Eberhard and Lachmayer (2008), pp. 112–123.

[115]Grabenwarter (2007), p. 137 ff.; Scholz (1997), p. 1013 (p. 1022 ff.).

Selected Bibliography

Della Cananea G (2004) Procedures in the new (draft) constitution of the European Union. European Review of Public Law/Revue Européenne de Droit Public 1:221 (233)

Dorsen N, Rosenfeld M, Sajó A, Baer S (2003) Comparative Constitutionalism. Thomson West, Minnesota, pp 16

Eberhard H (2007) Die Entwicklung des österreichischen Bundesverfassungsrechts im Gefolge des Österreich-Konvents. European Review of Public Law/Revue Européenne de Droit Public 19(3):789–802

Eberhard H (2008) Das Legalitätsprinzip im Spannungsfeld von Gemeinschaftsrecht und nationalem Recht. Stand und Perspektiven eines ,europäischen Legalitätsprinzips. ZÖR (Zeitschrift für öffentliches Recht): 49–116

Eberhard H, Lachmayer K (2008) Constitutional Reform 2008 in Austria. Analysis and perspectives. Vienna Online J Int Constitut Law 2(2):112–123 (www.icl-journal.com, last checked on 15 June 2010)

Eberhard H, Konrath C, Trattnigg R, Zleptnig S (2006) Governance – zur theoretischen und praktischen Verortung des Konzepts in Österreich. Journal für Rechtspolitik (JRP): 35–60

Fleiner T, Basta Fleiner LR (2004) Allgemeine Staatslehre, 3rd edn. Springer, Berlin

Gamper A (2004) Die Regionen mit Gesetzgebungshoheit. Eine rechtsvergleichende Untersuchung zu Föderalismus und Regionalismus in Europa. Peter Lang, Frankfurt

Grabenwarter C (1995) Änderungen der österreichischen Bundesverfassung aus Anlaß des Beitritts zur Europäischen Union. ZaöRV (Zeitschrift für ausländisches öffentliches Recht und Völkerrecht) 55:166–190

Grabenwarter C (2003) Staatliches Unionsverfassungsrecht. In: von Bogdandy A (ed) Europäisches Verfassungsrecht. Springer, Berlin, pp 283–337

Grabenwarter C (2007) Landtage und Bundesrat in der Europäischen Union. In: Lienbacher G, Thanner T, Tschirf M, Weiss K (eds.) Ein Leben für Staat und Gesellschaft, Festschrift für Jürgen Weiss. NVW, Wien, Graz, pp. 137–154

Haltern U (2005) Europarecht. Dogmatik im Kontext. Mohr Siebeck, Tübingen

Korinek K (2004) Die doppelte Bedingtheit von gemeinschaftsrechts-ausführenden innerstaatlichen Rechtsvorschriften. In: Hammer S, Somek A, Stelzer M, Weichselbaum B (eds) Demokratie und sozialer Rechtsstaat in Europa, Festschrift für Theo Öhlinger. Facultas. WUV, Wien, p 131

Lenzhofer S (2006) Hätten der Nationalrat, der Bundesrat oder die Länder die Aufnahme von EU-Beitrittsverhandlungen mit der Türkei verhindern können? ZÖR (Zeitschrift für öffentliches Recht): 83–107

Machacek R (1994) Austrian Contributions to the Rule of Law. Engel, Kehl

Öhlinger T (1999a) Art. 23d B-VG. In: Korinek K, Holoubek M (eds) Österreichisches Bundesverfassungsrecht, Kommentar. Springer, Wien, New York

Öhlinger T (1999b) Art. 23e B-VG. In: Korinek K, Holoubek M (eds) Österreichisches Bundesverfassungsrecht, Kommentar. Springer, Wien, New York

Öhlinger T (2002) Die österreichischen Gemeinden und die Europäische Union. In: Österreichischer G, Österreichischer S (eds) 40 Jahre Gemeindeverfassungsnovelle 1962. Manz, Vienna, pp 1–30

Öhlinger T (2007) Verfassungsrecht, 7th edn. Facultas, Vienna, pp 100–104

Öhlinger T (2004) Kann der Nationalrat zur Aufnahme von Verhandlungen der EU mit der Türkei über einen Beitritt verbindlich Stellung nehmen? JRP (Journal für Rechtspolitik): 225–227

Öhlinger T, Potacs M (2006) Gemeinschaftsrecht und staatliches Recht. Die Anwendung des Europarechts im innerstaatlichen Bereich, 3rd edn. LexisNexis, Vienna

Pernice I (2001) Europäisches und nationales Verfassungsrecht. VVDStRL (Veröffentlichungen der Vereinigung der Deutschen Staatsrechtslehrer) 60:148–193

Prakke L (2004) The Republic of Austria. In: Prakke L, Kortmann C (eds) Constitutional Law of 15 EU Member States. Kluwer, Deventer, pp 3–70

Scholz R (1997) Bundesstaaten in der Europäischen Union – Deutschland und Österreich im Vergleich. In: Haller H, Kopetzki C, Novak R, St. Paulson L, Raschauer B, Ress G, Wiederin E (eds) Staat und Recht. Festschrift für Günther Winkler. Springer, Wien, New York, pp 1013–1029
Sonntag N (2008) Europaausschüsse in Bund und Ländern, FÖDOK (Föderalismusdokumente) 29. Institut für Föderalismus, Innsbruck
Stelzer M (2007) Introduction to Austrian Constitutional Law. LexisNexis, Vienna
Walter R, Mayer H, Kucsko-Stadlmayer G (2007) Grundriss des österreichischen Bundesverfassungsrechts, 10th edn. Manz, Vienna, pp 136–140
Winkler R (2003) Integrationsverfassungsrecht. Springer, Wien, New York

Chapter 10
France: Centre, Regions and Outermost Regions: The Case for a New French and European Governance

Jacques Colom

A. Introduction

Following the French Revolution, the Jacobins and then later Napoleon Bonaparte created a unitary and centralised state. In contrast, the nineteenth and twentieth centuries were characterised by a slow process towards recognition of local autonomy.[1] The 1958 Constitution founded the Fifth Republic under which France continued to be a unitary centralised state. This remained in existence until the Act of 2nd March 1982 on Rights and Liberties of the Regions, the Departments and the Municipalities (hereafter referred to as the 1982 Act).

The 1982 Act instituted the Regions as collective territorial entities.[2] By so doing, it transformed France into a unitary decentralised state with Overseas Departments and Overseas Regions (Réunion, Martinique, Guadeloupe, French Guyana). At the same time, Corsica obtained special status as a Region. This Region was later (in 1991) transformed into the Territorial Collectivity of Corsica (*Collectivité Territoriale de Corse*).

Since 1982, decentralisation has continued in metropolitan France as well as in the Overseas Departments. The specific status of the Overseas Departments was

[1]The Act of 21 March 1831 reintroduced the election of Municipal Councils. The Acts of 22 June 1833, 10 August 1871 and 5 April 1884 did the same for the election of the Departments (first two Acts) and of the Mayors and their Adjuncts (last Act). Cf. Auby et al. 2008, pp. 8–14. The difficult evolution towards more decentralization may be illustrated by mentioning the evolving thoughts of the influential French public lawyer Maurice Hauriou. He believed strongly in decentralisation before the First World War, while after the First World War he defended a centralist opinion. In his view, centralisation was the only option to defend the State against a major crisis. See on this topic F. Fournié, *Recherches sur la décentralisation dans l'œuvre de Maurice Hauriou*, Paris, LGDJ, p. 245.

[2]In 1969, the French president de Gaulle called a referendum on the introduction of Regions. The outcome of the referendum was negative for the President. However, 3 years later, the Act of 5 July 1972 did institute the Regions as simple public territorial entities.

J. Colom
Faculté de Droit et Économie, Université de La Réunion, 15 Avenue René Cassin 97715 Saint-Denis, La Réunion
e-mail: mila.colom@orange.fr

C. Panara and A. De Becker (eds.), *The Role of the Regions in EU Governance*,
DOI 10.1007/978-3-642-11903-3_10, © Springer-Verlag Berlin Heidelberg 2011

confirmed by Article 74 of the French Constitution, which was introduced in the French Constitution by the Constitutional Act No. 92-554 of 25 June 1992 (hereafter referred to as the 1992 Constitutional Act).[3]

Over the last three decades, the French constitutional framework has evolved towards more autonomy for the territorial entities. At the same time, France, as one of the founding states of the European Communities, has developed its constitution in order to comply with the advancement of the European integration.[4] This contribution will focus on the constitutional status of the French territorial entities,[5] with special attention to the Regions and the four Overseas Departments.

The Overseas Departments were colonies until 1 January 1947, on which date they were granted the status as Overseas Departments (*départements d'outre-mer*) pursuant to the Act of 19 March 1946. Later, they were defined as Overseas Departments by the 1992 Constitutional Act and as Overseas Regions (*Régions d'outre-mer*) by the 1982 Act. Since the Treaties of Maastricht and Amsterdam, these Overseas Departments and Regions are also recognised within the European context as the outermost regions of the European Union.[6]

Decentralisation in France did not grant as many powers to the decentralised entities as it is the case in some regional states (such as Italy and Spain) or federal states (such as Austria, Belgium and Germany). This is also reflected by the fact that the French Regions are rather weakly involved in the decision-making process of the European Union.

B. Post 1982 Decentralisation in France

The 1982 legislative reform initiated the decentralisation process in France through the creation of 21 metropolitan Regions, four Overseas Departments and the Region of Corsica.[7] The executive power in the areas devolved to the competence of the Regions was transferred from the prefects (*les préfets*; authorities appointed by the

---

[3]The English translation of the French Constitution used in this paper can be found at http://www.assemblee-nationale.fr/english/8ab.asp#XV (last visited on 21 March 2010).

[4]The 1992 Constitutional Act introduced a new Title in the Constitution of 1958: "The European Communities and the European Union".

[5]Apart from the Territorial Collectivity of Corsica, 21 Metropolitan Regions and 4 Overseas Regions are currently in existence. Furthermore, there exist 100 Departments, among which the 4 Overseas Departments. Finally, there are 36,565 Municipalities. Of those, three (Paris, Lyon and Marseille) are endowed with a special status.

[6]These provisions were foreseen in Article 227(2) and later in Article 299(2) of the EC Treaty. The specific measures for the outermost regions can be currently found in Article 349 of the Treaty on the Functioning of the European Union (TFEU).

[7]The 21 metropolitan Regions are those in continental France: Alsace, Aquitaine, Auvergne, Bourgogne, Centre, Champagne-Ardennes, Franche-Comté, Île de France, Languedoc-Rousillon, Limousin, Lorraine, Midi-Pyrénées, Basse-Normandie, Haute-Normandie, Nord-Pas-de-Calais, Pays de la Loire, Picardie, Poitou-Charentes, Provences-Alpes-Côte d'Azur, Rhône-Alpes.

central government to represent the State in the Departments and in the Regions) to the Presidents of the Regions.[8] However, the powers of the Regions were and still are very limited; the main areas falling within their responsibility are school education[9] and urban and economic development.

The 1982 reform removed administrative control (la *tutelle administrative*) over the actions of territorial entities. The 1992 reform of Article 72 of the Constitution installed the principle of free administration (*principe de libre administration*)[10] for territorial entities, but no indication of what this principle might include was given. Furthermore, the constitutional principle of free administration did not originally apply to the Regions but only to Municipalities, Departments and Overseas Territories. It was only as late as 2003 that the second wave of decentralisation (Constitutional Act of 28 March 2003) granted explicit constitutional recognition to the Regions. The current version of Article 72, after the 2003 amendment, allows the creation by the Parliament (through statute) of further territorial entities.[11]

Some distinctions need to be made between the different regional entities in the French system. The metropolitan Regions include a number of Departments, whereas the Overseas Regions correspond with one Department. This means that the Overseas Regions and the Overseas Departments are *geographically* the same. However, there are two different Assemblies (one for the Region and one for the Department).[12] The only exceptions are two *pays et territoires d'outre-mer* (PTOM). These are New Caledonia and French Polynésia, who since 1958 have had a single assembly common to the Region and the Department. In St. Pierre et Miquelon and Mayotte (Communauté d'outre–mer) departments do not yet exist, however a department is currently in the process of being created in Mayotte.

The 2003 reform, which enjoyed strong support in the Senate, has granted better protection to the Regions through their explicit recognition in Article 72 of the Constitution. This made the Regions no longer a 'constitutional orphan' and they became a part of the French decentralised model. The French Parliament drew inspiration from Italy and Spain, two regionalised countries, in introducing the new

---

[8]Articles L 4231-1 to 4231-9 of book 10, third title of the General Code on territorial entities (Code général des collectivités territoriales – in acronym CGCT).

[9]The exact divide of competences between the State and the Regions in the area of education is regulated by Articles from L 214-I to L 214-17 of the Educational Code (*Code de l'Education*).

[10]See Article 72.3 of the French Constitution and Article L 1111-1 of the General Code on territorial entities.

[11]Cf. Douence 1992, p. 469.

[12]In 1982, a legislative proposal was made to merge the two Assemblies. The *Conseil Constitutionnel* (The French Constitutional Court) judged that this initiative was in breach of the Constitution. Cf. Conseil Constitutionnel Decision of 2nd December 1982. On 8 June 2010, the National Assembly passed a legislative bill merging the two assemblies (starting from 2014). The bill is still awaiting examination by the Senate (the discussion is scheduled for the end of June 2010). The single territorial assembly will be elected through the two-round system (currently territorial assemblies are elected with the proportional system). The change from proportional representation to the two-round system is likely to advantage the party of the incumbent President Nicolas Sarkozy.

principles.[13] These are the principles of free administration and subsidiarity' as well as general aspects of the distribution of competences.[14] However, the final outcome of the reform was not the creation of a truly regionalised system granting constitutional, legislative and administrative autonomy to regional entities.

There is a lack of uniformity between the institutions that have been established. The constitutional provisions which are currently in force open up the possibility to create differences in the decentralisation process with the result that territorial entities enjoying specific status may be created. For example, the French Parliament passed the Act of 13 March 1991 which transformed Corsica into a territory with a special status (Territorial collectivity of Corsica).

Despite the increasing importance of decentralisation, the central government still takes the lion's share of power. This is due to a number of elements. First, although the Regions enjoy some financial autonomy, some of their financial competences continue to be exercised under the influence of the State.[15]

Second, the decentralised entities' experimental regulatory powers are significantly limited.[16] These entities can derogate from State legislation only for limited purposes and for a limited duration. More specifically, the Constitution only authorises the experiment if a State act or regulation enables the territorial entities to derogate from statutory or regulatory provisions governing the exercise of their competences (cf. Art. 72.4 of the French Constitution and Art. LO 1113-1 of the General Code on Territorial Entities, *Code Général des Collectivités Territoriales*, hereafter CGCT). Territorial entities tend not to use this opportunity very much.[17]

Third, the prefects retain a power of supervision over the legality of the administrative action of the Regions. Prefects can challenge the validity of regional administrative measures before administrative courts. This supervisory power has the potential to be abused by the national government.

Fourth, constitutional review over the actions of the Regions is exercised by the *Conseil Constitutionnel* (the French constitutional court). In general, the *Conseil Constitutionnel* decides very often in favour of the central State, and its jurisprudence tends to be influenced by a tradionalist and centralised mindset.[18]

The autonomy currently enjoyed by the Regions remains a merely administrative autonomy. The report of the Committee for the reform of local entitities (which was appointed on 22 October 2008 by the French President Nicolas Sarkozy), also known as *Comité Balladur* (named after former French Prime Minister Édouard Balladur who presided over the Committee), expressed no desire to strenghten the autonomy of the Regions. On the contrary, the final report of the Committee (with

[13]Annuaire 2004 des collectivités locales, "Réforme de la décentralisation, réforme de l'Etat, régions et villes en Europe", CNRS, 2004.

[14]Ponthier 2006, 365–394.

[15]Cf. Waline 2008, p. 102; Chavrier 2008, p. 1657.

[16]Long 2008, p. 1625.

[17]Lapouze 2006, p. 1050.

[18]Roux 2005, pp. 1397–1389.

the title "It is time to decide"), which was published on 5 March 2009, questions the general clause on their competences provided in Article L 2121-29 of the General Code on territorial entities for the municipalities, in Article L 4221-1 for the Regions and in Article L 3211-1 for the Departments of the General Code on Territorial Entities. This general clause foresees that territorial assemblies are competent to deal with local issues. The report of the Committee furthermore questions the number of Regions and the political representation of the Regions and of the Departments.[19]

The political Left, which is currently in the opposition at national level, is the ruling party in 21 out of the 22 French Regions. Therefore, it is no surprise that the Regions currently argue for the development of a third phase (after the 1982 and the 2003 phases) in the decentralisation process. The most significant aspect of their proposals concern a reform of the Senate. The functioning of the Senate should, in their view, resemble the functioning of the German *Bundesrat*.[20] Needless to say, these ideas are not shared by the current right wing majority, which believes in the need to preserve the sovereignty of the State.

The Senate currently defends the interests of all territorial entities and is not solely a body representing the Regions. Given the procedure for the election of Senators, this broad focus seems to be understandable. The Senate is elected by indirect suffrage by approximately 150,000 elected officials ("*grands électeurs*"), including regional councillors, department councillors, mayors, city councillors and their delegates in large towns, and deputies of the National Assembly. The Senate has control over fewer competences than the directly elected National Assembly, *Assemblée Nationale*, the other House of the French national Parliament. Nonetheless, it has the power to block drafts of constitutional reforms during the parliamentary phase. Article 89 of the French Constitution provides that both House of national Parliament need to adopt the same text before it is submitted to a referendum. In practice, this confers on the Senate the power to prevent the passage of constitutional reforms.[21] The other side of the coin is that the National Assembly has an equal power to block drafts of constitutional reforms. Therefore, an extension of the regional competences requires an agreement between the two Chambers as well as between the Centre-Right and the Left.

---

[19]Report of the Comité Balladur pour la réforme des collectivités locales "Il est temps de décider". This report was submitted to the President on the 5th of March 2009.

[20]Carcasonne 2005, p. 104.

[21]Le Lidec (2004), pp. 15–24. The author estimates that the Senate played a preponderant role in the 2003 constitutional reform which led to the constitutional recognition of the Regions.

C. The Transfer of Powers of the Regions to the EU

Title XV of the French Constitution on the European Communities and the European Union does not mention the Regions and the other territorial entities. From this point of view, the French Constitution seems to be distant from the spirit of the Treaty of Lisbon. The Treaty of Lisbon makes many references to the Regions and strengthens the Committee of the Regions. It clearly intends to promote decentralisation in the EU.[22]

Article 88-1 of the French Constitution stipulates that "The Republic shall participate in the European Union constituted by States which have freely chosen to exercise some of their powers in common by virtue of the Treaty on European Union and of the Treaty on the Functioning of the European Union, as they result from the treaty signed in Lisbon on 13 December 2007".

Title XV grants the Senate and the National Assembly an important role in the process of transferring powers to the EU and in the ratification process of treaties on the accession of new Member States to the European Union.

The territorial entities are (if it is accepted that the Senate truly represents them) indirectly involved through the Senate in the ratification process of the European treaties transferring powers to the EU.

Article 88-5 of the French Constitution stipulates that the ratification of a treaty providing the accession of a new Member State to the European Union should be in principle submitted to a referendum. However, the second paragraph of the same Article allows for an exception in case both the National Assembly and the Senate consent to the ratification by a three-fifths majority. Therefore a bill providing the accession of a new Member State to the Union can be passed without necessarily being submitted to a referendum.

It is interesting to highlight an inconsistency within the French Constitution. The prior consultation of voters is also foreseen in Article 72-4 of the Constitution when a change of status of the territorial entities is proposed. This implies that the transfer of powers of the territorial entities to the State is always submitted to consultation of the local population while the transfer of powers to the EU level is not always submitted to a referendum.

D. Direct and Indirect Participation by the Territorial Entities in the Council

French law does not provide any indirect participation of the territorial entities in determining the French position in the Council. The only situation in which the territorial entities play a more enhanced role is through the Committee of Local

[22]Cf. Committee of the Regions (2009), p. 59.

Financing. This body is constituted in part of representatives of the Regions and the Departments and has to be consulted on EU legislative drafts which could cause financial implications for them.[23] In any other case, the territorial entities can use informal political means to try to influence the French position in the Council.

Given the non-existence (apart from the afore-mentioned exception) of a hard legal basis for the territorial entities to intervene *indirectly*, it appears absolutely logical that these entities cannot *directly* represent France in the Council pursuant to Article 16, paragraph 2, of the Treaty on the European Union (TEU; ex Art. 203 EC). The Regions are not represented in the French delegation to the Council, in the Coreper, in the committees of experts linked to the Coreper or in any other EU comitology committee.

The principle of *indivisibilité* of the sovereignty of the French Republic, as it was affirmed at the time of the French Revolution, is not the only explanation for the current lack of participation rights of the Regions in EU law and policy making. The *Conseil Constitutionnel* gave its contribution to the preservation of the status quo. The French Parliament in the Articles 42 and 43 of the *Loi d'Orientation pour l'Outre-Mer* (Act of the Orientation of the Overseas) of 13 December 2000 granted some competences on international relations to Corsica and to the Overseas Regions by allowing them to independently sign international agreements.[24] However, the *Conseil Constitutionnel* limited the scope of these provisions and stated that these Regions should act with the authorisation and in the name of the State.[25]

In 2003, the *Conseil d'Etat* (a body of the French national Government that provides the executive branch with legal advice and acts as the administrative court of last resort), indicated that it is unlikely that forms of direct involvement of the territorial entities in negotiations within the EU institutions will be introduced in the near future. The countries which involve their territorial entities are mainly decentralised regional and federal states. In some of those countries, the territorial entities have some competences in international relations (this is the case in Belgium and Germany). According to the *Conseil d'Etat*, the French situation is not comparable with that of these countries due to the centralism which traditionally characterises the French system. At the same time, the *Conseil d'Etat* expressed the fear that informal contacts between the European Commission and the territorial entities would multiply in cases where the original refusal of a direct and indirect involvement is retained. To tackle the issue of territorial participation, the *Conseil d'Etat* proposed to create an entity coordinating the national Government and the territorial entities in EU-related matters.[26]

[23]Article L1211-4 of the General Code on Territorial Entities.

[24]Article L1115-4 of the General Code on Local Entities (lastly modified by the Law No. 2008-352 of 16 April 2008).

[25]Decision 2000-435 of 7 December 2000.

[26]Report of the General Assembly of the *Conseil d'Etat*: "Collectivités territoriales et obligations du droit communautaire", 58, 23 October 2003.

The fear expressed by the *Conseil d'Etat* has proven well founded; over the last few years, informal contacts flourished. In order to ensure some territorial participation in matters of the European Union, the French Prime Minister issued in December 2005 a *circulaire* (a ministerial letter giving instructions to the government offices on how to interpret a law and how to comply with legal requirements).[27] This *circulaire* provides the obligation for the offices of the national Government to enter in contact with the territorial assemblies before every Council dealing with matters of their competence.[28] The *circulaire* also provides that a better collaboration between the French representation in the Coreper and territorial entities should be established. However, a *circulaire* is not a legal basis capable of founding a complaint of the territorial entities before the *Conseil d'Etat* in cases where their participation rights are not respected in full. This is due to the fact that a *circulaire* is only binding for the offices of the national Government to which it is addressed and it cannot in principle be relied on by other parties.

The lack of direct or indirect involvement of the territorial entities in EU law and policy making is certainly a matter of concern. The situation of the Overseas Regions is of even greater concern. They (like all other Regions) are not integrated into the French delegation to the Council. This happens despite the fact that Articles L. 3441-5 and 4433-4-4 CGCT authorise the Presidents of the Overseas Regions and of the Overseas Departments to become part, on their request, of the French delegation. It is envisaged in cases where negotiations are undertaken with the EU over specific measures setting out the prerequisites for the application of Article 349, paragraph 2, of the Treaty on the Functioning of the European Union, TFEU. This provision allows for the adaptation of EU law to the specific situation of the Overseas Regions with the aim of facilitating the integration of the geographical areas in the common market.

The General Code on Territorial Entities also authorises the French Overseas Regions to express their opinion on proposals for agreements on regional cooperation. These projects concern different types of cooperation between France and the neighbouring states of the Overseas Regions on economic, social, technical, scientific, cultural, civil security[29] and environmental cooperation (see Article 2233-4 of the CGCT). Therefore, there is a strong case for the involvement of the Overseas Regions in French foreign policy as far as it concerns matters within their competence.

The *circulaire* of the Prime Minister of 22 November 2005 introduced the duty of the national Government to communicate EU proposals to the Houses of Parliament. In practice, the Government has often delayed the transmission of these proposals and has sometimes failed to transmit them or given only partial transmission. The constitutional reform of 2008 introduced a similar obligation at

[27] *Circulaire* of the Prime Minister of 19 December 2005 on the association of Parliament, territorial entities, social partners and the civil society in the EU decision-making process.

[28] See paragraph 2 of the *circulaire*.

[29] This concerns the preservation of security of the French population.

Article 88-4 in the French Constitution.[30] This provision obliges the French Government to inform the Parliament of EU proposals. However, the French negotiators at the EU level do not have a legal duty to take into account the positions expressed by the Houses of Parliament. The *circulaire* does not contain clear indications regarding the involvement of territorial assemblies. It only provides that the local assemblies should be involved in the debate on European issues when their competences are at stake.

According to *Protocol on the application of the principles of subsidiarity and proportionality*, annexed to the Treaty of Lisbon, the Commission, the European Parliament and the Council have the obligation to send draft legislative acts to the national parliaments. Article 88-6 of the French Constitution gives both Houses of Parliament the right to issue an opinion as to the conformity of these draft acts with the principle of subsidiarity.[31] This opinion has to be addressed by the President of the Senate or of the National Assembly to the Presidents of the European Parliament, the Council of the European Union and the European Commission. The Government has to be informed about the content of the opinion.

Under Article 88-6, each House of Parliament may institute proceedings before the European Court of Justice against an EU legislative act for non-compliance with the principle of subsidiarity. Such proceedings shall be transmitted to the Court of Justice by the Government.

---

[30]Constitutional Act No. 2008-724 of 23 July 2008. Article 88-4 states: "*The Government shall lay before the National Assembly and the Senate drafts of or proposals for Acts of the European Communities and the European Union containing provisions which are of a statutory nature as soon as they have been transmitted to the Council of the European Union. It may also lay before them other drafts of or proposals for Acts or any instrument issuing from a European Union Institution.*"

[31]Article 88-6: "*The National Assembly or the Senate may issue a reasoned opinion as to the conformity of a draft proposal for a European Act with the principle of subsidiarity. Said opinion shall be addressed by the President of the House involved to the Presidents of the European Parliament, the Council of the European Union and the European Commission. The Government shall be informed of said opinion.*

Each House may institute proceedings before the Court of Justice of the European Union against a European Act for non-compliance with the principle of subsidiarity. Such proceedings shall be referred to the Court of Justice of the European Union by the Government.

For the purpose of the foregoing, resolutions may be passed, even if Parliament is not in session, in the manner set down by the Rules of Procedure of each House for the tabling and discussion thereof. Such proceedings shall be obligatory upon the request of sixty Members of the National Assembly or sixty Senators."

E. Liaison Offices, Lobbying and Networking by the French Regions in Brussels

To overcome the problem of their lack of participation in the EU law and policy making, the French Regions established liaison offices in Brussels and began lobbying and networking at the EU level.

Currently 21 French Regions run a liason office in Brussels. Some Regions established an office in common. This is the case of Brittany/Pays de la Loire/ Poitou-Charente and of Auvergne/Centre/Limousin.

The liaison offices are not the only initiative taken by the Regions. In 1973, the *Conférence des Régions Périphériques et Maritimes* (CRPM, Conference of the Regions of the Periphery and of the Coastal Regions) was created. In 1995, the *Conférence des Presidents des Régions UltraPériphériques* (RUP, Conference of the Presidents of the Outermost Regions) was created with the support of the CRPM on an initiative of the representatives of La Réunion. In May 2010, the EU Commission, along with the support of Spain, Portugal and France (three Member States who participate in the RUP) set up a European RUP forum. This will take place every two years. Its objective is to strengthen the links between the EU, the three above-mentioned Member States and the RUP. The Spanish, Portuguese, and French Governments are currently trying to encourage the involvement of other EU Member States with outermost regions (UK, Netherlands, Denmark, and Finland).

Some Regions have gone even further in the use of lobbying mechanisms. More specifically, they have associated with other strong Regions in order to develop interregional axes. This is the case of the Region Rhône-Alpes which associated with three other economically developed European regions (known as the 'locomotives of the European economy'): Baden-Württemberg (Germany), Lombardy (Italy) and Catalonia (Spain).

Some other developments should be underlined. For instance, in 1986 the *Fédération des entreprises d'outre-mer* (literally: federation of the overseas companies) was created, and in 1989, the pressure group *Europe et Départments d'outre-mer* (literally: Europe and Overseas Department, EURODOM) was created.[32]

These networks function effectively and generally permit good collaboration between the Regions and the European Union. However, they do not escape criticism insofar as the French Government often argues that it is necessary for France to speak with a single voice at the European level.

F. The French Presence in the Committee of the Regions

The 24 French representatives and 24 alternates in the Committee of the Regions are appointed by the Prime Minister upon a proposal from the Minister of Interior.

[32]Janus (1995), p. 326.

The Minister of Interior has to consult the Association of French Mayors, the Assembly of French Departments and the Association of French Regions.

The 24 French representatives (and alternates) are internally distributed as follows: 12 representatives of the Regions, 6 of the Departments, and 6 of the Municipalities. There is no guarantee that the Overseas Departments are represented in the Committee of the Regions. The presence of these Departments in the French delegation depends on the current political climate.

At present, only the incumbent President of the Conseil Général of the Réunion Department (Nassimah Dindar) is an alternate member in the French delegation to the Committee. But her appointment seems to have more to do with the fact that she is a member of the government party (*Union pour un movement populaire*, UMP) than with her being an overseas representative.

G. The Peculiar Position of the Overseas Regions in the EU Context

The specific situation of the French Overseas Regions reveals a very difficult legal problem. The Overseas Regions enjoy a priviliged status as 'outermost regions' under EU law (cf. Article 349 TFEU[33]). However, they have not enjoyed any particularly privileged treatment. For the Overseas Regions, such as Réunion, situated at 10,000 km distance from Europe, it is unfortunate that this specific status has not yet been put into effect. This problem has become more pressing due to the fact that Réunion has an unemployment rate of nearly 50% in certain areas and among certain communities.[34]

The current priviliged status in the EU is a consequence of long political, social and legal debates. The Overseas Departments became part of the EEC upon the signing of the Treaty of Rome in 1957. Article 227 of the original Treaty foresaw that provisions of Community law could be adapted to the specific situation (of Algeria) and of the Overseas Departments.[35]

The 1951 Treaty of Paris took a different approach. It foresaw the application of its provisions only on European territory. In 1978 the decision of the ECJ in Hansen

[33]According to Art. 349(1) TFEU the Outermost Regions of the EU are: Guadeloupe, French Guiana, Martinique, Réunion, Saint-Barthélemy, Saint-Martin, the Azores, Madeira and the Canary Islands.

[34]The Overseas Regions had a specific historical development. Their colonial status was retained after the Act of 19 March 1946 on departmentalisation. Cf. N. Schmidt, "La France a-t-elle aboli l'esclavage?" in Guadeloupe-Martinique-Guyane 1830–1935, 2009.

[35]Article 227 of EEC-Treaty: "Concerning Algeria and the French Overseas Departments, the specific and general provisions on the free movement of goods, on agriculture with the exception of article 40 paragraph 4, on the free movement of services, on competition, on protection as foreseen in the articles 108, 109 and 226, on the institutions are applicable after the entry into force of the present Treaty".

left such partial application of the Treaty behind and installed the principle of integration of the Overseas Departments into the Treaty.[36]

In general, EU law fully applies to the Overseas Departments. These Departments can be excluded from some provisions. Instead, some other provisions only receive application in the Overseas Departments. Such differentiated application of the law usually arises from an initiative of the French Government. For example, until July 1990, the French Government excluded the Overseas Regions from the application of most directives concerning the liberalisation of air transportation. Paradoxically, the 1986 judgement of the ECJ in the case *Nouvelles Frontières*, which constituted the basis for the establishment of a common policy in this field, concerned a conflict on air transportation between metropolitan France and the Overseas Departments. This case broke the monopoly of the public company Air France on French air transportation.[37]

Another interesting case study as to the impact of the European integration on the French overseas territories is the French octroi de mer (sea charge). This is a duty (originating from the pre-1789 era) which is levied on goods imported from third countries to the overseas territories. The revenue is devolved to the Municipalities, Departments and Regions in these territories. This duty is indispensable to the Overseas Regions – who have the right to impose an additional import (*additionnel à l'octroi de mer*) and to decide on the exemptions from its application. In a number of cases the ECJ found that the *octroi de mer* is in breach of the principle of free movement of goods within the Union.[38] The rulings of the ECJ obliged French authorities to reform the *octroi de mer* and consequently led to a reduction of regional autonomy. Sea charges currently apply in an indifferentiated way to imported products and to products manufactured in the overseas territories. This is the result of two pieces of legislation: the first is the Act of 17 July 1992 and the second is the Act of 2 July 2004 (implementing EU Decision 2004/162/EC). The 2004 Decision and the 2004 Act are emblematic of the challenge brought by the common market to the autonomy of the overseas territories.

H. The Fulfilment of EU Obligations in the Domestic Sphere

In France, it is accepted that the Regions, like any other legal person under French law, are subject to EU law on the basis of Art. 55 of the Constitution ("Treaties or agreements duly ratified or approved shall, upon publication, prevail over Acts of

[36]C-148/77, *Hansen*, Rec. 1787, 10 October 1978. Cf. Faberon and Ziller 2007, 543 p., see p. 116.

[37]Judgement of the ECJ of 30 April 1986, Joined Cases from 209 to 213/84 *Ministére Publique v. Lucas Asjes and Others (Nouvelles Frontières)*, ECR [1986] 1425.

[38]See the Cases 2 and 3/69 of 31 December 1969 *Social Fonds voor de Diamantarbeiders v. SA Ch. Brachfeld and Sons* [1969] ECR 211 and the Case C-163/90 of 16 July 1992 *Legros et al.* ECR [1992] p. I-4685. On the *additionnel à l'octroi de mer* see the Case C-363/93 of 9 August 1994 *Lancry* ECR [1994] p. I-3957 and the Case C-126/94 of 7 November 1996 Cadi surgelés [1996] ECR I-5647. In the legal scholarship cf. Custos (2008), pp. 34–42.

Parliament, subject, with respect to each agreement or treaty, to its application by the other party"). The Regions and the other territorial entities must therefore comply with all the obligations arising from EU law. However, they do not have any responsibility for the transposition of EU directives. The State is the only entity which is responsible for their transposition. This is a striking difference between France and regional states, like Italy or Spain, or federal states, like Belgium or Germany.

Alsace is the only Region in France currently entitled to manage structural funds. It would be preferable if this competence were generalised.[39] In its 2003 report, the *Conseil d'Etat* indicated that the transfer of this power would make official the growing contacts between the European Commission and the French Regions. It also pointed out that further measures should be taken to oblige the Regions to take the responsibility for problems which are linked to their actions.[40]

The proposal made by the *Conseil d'Etat* is to make the territorial entities pay the financial consequences of their non-compliance with EU law in order to push them to be more compliant with Union law. The *Conseil d'Etat* underlined that it could also be a powerful and meaningful symbol if the French territorial entities were involved in the pre-litigitious stage of the infringement procedures initiated by the European Commission against France. This should happen any time one or more territorial entities are directly responsible for an infringement of an obligation arising from EU law.

An interesting example of situation in which the territorial entities caused public spending is the Council Directive of 25 May 1991 (91/271/EEC) on urban waste water treatment. This piece of legislation imposed fairly strict standards for waste water treatment plants. Many French Municipalities have not complied with the European standards. For this reason, France has been condemned for the first time by the ECJ in 2004 and has been issued a final warning by the Commission in 2008.[41] On 20 November 2009, the Commission brought an action against France before the ECJ for failure to comply with the previous ECJ judgement. The decision of this case is still pending. The French law currently in force provides the State with legal means to put pressure on those territorial authorities which do not respect the law. The prefect can actually threaten the incompliant territorial authorities to bring a case against them before the administrative court. In its 2003 report, the *Conseil d'Etat* proposed the strengthening of these instruments by enabling the State to exact a refund of the fines paid to the EU from those Municipalities which are responsible for a breach. According to this proposal the Public Prosecutor should be given the power to institute criminal proceedings against the Mayors of those Municipalities who intentionally delay the payment.

[39]French Senate, Information report, 2008–2009, No. 471. See also Krattinger and Gourault (2009).

[40]Report of the General Assembly of the *Conseil d'Etat*: "Collectivités territoriales et obligations du droit communautaire", 23 October 2003, p. 82.

[41]See the Case C-280/02 of 23 September 2004 *Commission v. France* [2004] ECR p. I-08573. The final warning was issued in January 2008 (see the Commission press release of 31 January 2008).

The substitution power can be used by the national Government only in exceptional circumstances; for example, if a Mayor refuses to use his police powers against a serious disturbance of public order, or if the security of the citizens is under threat or any other time the law exceptionally authorises the State to do so (cf. for example Art. L 216-1 and 216-13 of the environmental code). In light of these rules it seems unlikely that the national Government would be able to substitute its direct action for that of a territorial entity in case of non-compliance with the EU law.

I. The Defence of the Competences of the Regions on the Judicial Level

The French Regions are very desirous to obtain the standing to bring a direct action for annulment before the EU Courts. This would enable them to ensure respect for their competences, particularly in the areas of economic development and aid to development.

The refusal of the European Court of Justice to grant the Regions and other sub-state entities the status of privileged applicants under former Article 230 EC (current Article 263 TFEU) has caused some difficulties. This constitutes a part of the paradoxical treatment of the Regions by the EU. On the one hand, they are considered to be valuable partners in the full development of the EU. On the other hand, they are not considered to be equal players when it comes to the need to take decisions and to judicially defend their legal interests.

J. Conclusion

The legal evolution of the French Regions should be analysed in light of the parallel evolution of EU integration. According to French legal scholars, the European Union has to some extent contributed to the empowerment of the French Regions.[42] However, their status remains fragile both at national and EU level.[43] The best legal solution to this problem would be to introduce genuine multilevel governance capable of integrating the regional and the other territorial entities fully into the EU law and policy making process.

It would be desirable to introduce full multilevel governance based upon the democratic principle and the principle of accountability. This would help convince the EU to further integrate its outermost regions within the union. For example with the inclusion of Réunion the EU would be linked to the African continent, and to India, China and Australia.

[42] Auby et al. (2008), pp. 332–333.

[43] Savy (2007), p. 1122; Michalon (2006).

Selected Bibliography

Auby J-B, Auby J.-F, Noguellou R (2008) Droit des collectivités locales. Themis, Paris, pp 8–14
Bordes M (1972) "L'administration provinciale and municipale en France au XVIIIe Siècle", SEDES
Bourjol (1969) Les institutions régionales de 1789 à nos jours. Berger Levrault
Carcasonne G (2005) Pour un bundesrat français. In X (ed) *Pouvois locaux*. nr. 67, p 104
Chavrier G (2008) Quel avenir pour la région dans l'organisation dans l'organisation territoriale française. *AJDA*, p 1657
Committee of the Regions (2009) Les Quinze and du Comité des régions de l'Union européenne: adoption de la loi "Declaration de mission". *Revue Lamy des collectivités territoriales,* p 59
Custos D (2008) Champ d'application territorial du droit communautaire et de l'Union. *Jurisclasseur Europe Traité,* No. 472, pp 34–42
Daniel JD (ed) (2007) "L'outre-mer à l'épreuve de la décentralisation: nouveaux cadres institutionnels et difficultés d'adaptation", L'harmattan
Douence J-C (1992) Le statut constitutionnel des collectvités d'outre-mer. *RFDA*, p 469
Faberon J-Y, Ziller J (2007) Droit des collectivités d'outre-mer, LGDJ
Faure B (2009) "Droit des collectivités territoriales", Dalloz
Gohin O (2006) Institutions administratives (5th edn), LGDJ
Janus M (1995) EURODOM: un lobby original des régions ultraperiphériques de la Communauté européenne. *Revue du Marché Commun et de l'Union européenne,* p 326
Krattinger Y, Gourault J (2009) Faire confiance à l'intelligence territoriale, 17 June 2009
Lapouze P (2006) L'expérimentation par les collectivités territoriales. *JCPA*, p 1050
Lavroff DG (ed) (2003) La République décentralisée, L'Harmattan
Le Lidec P (2004) Pourquoi une nouvelle étape de la décentralisation? Modernisation politique et compétition politique. In X, *Annuaire 2004 des collectivités locales,* pp 15–24
Long M (2008) L'expérimentation: un premier bilan décevant pour les collectivités territoriales. *AJDA,* p 1625
Loughlin J, Mazey S (ed) (1995) The End of the French Unitary State? Ten Years of Regionalization in France 1982–1992, Franck Cass
Luchaire F (1992) *Le statut constitutionnel de la France d'Outre-Mer,* Paris, Economica, p 104
Mélanges Moreau (2003) Les collectivités locales. Economica, 2003.
Mélanges Douence (2006) La profondeur du droit local, Dalloz
Michalon T (2006) La république et sa periphérie. La légitimité par la décentralisation. In *Mélanges offertes à Jean-Claude Douence: le profondeur du droit local,* Paris, Dalloz
Fr. Olivier-Martin (1991) Histoire du Droit Français des origines à la révolution, CNRS
Ponthier JM (2006) Nouvelles observations sur la clause générale de compétence. In *La profondeur du droit local*, pp 365–394
Roux A (2005) Constitution, Décentralisation et libre administration des collectivités territoriales. In X (ed) Mélanges offerts à Francis Delperée, Brussels, pp 1397–1389
Rubio N (2000) L'avenir des départements antillais, La Documentation française
Savy R (2007) Vingt ans après ou les régions françaises au milieu du gué. In *Mélanges offertes à Jean-François Lachaume Le droit administratif: permanences et convergences.* Paris, Dalloz, p 1122
Verpeaux M (2008) Droit des collectivités territoriales (2nd edn), PUF
Waline J (2008) *Droit administratif.* Paris, Dalloz, p 157

Selected Bibliography

Chapter 11
Belgium: The State and the Sub-State Entities Are Equal, But Is the State Sometimes Still More Equal Than the Others?

Alexander De Becker

A. Introduction

In 1957, Belgium founded the European Communities with the Netherlands, Luxemburg, France, Germany and Italy. In those days, Belgium was still a unitary but to some extent decentralised state. The aspect of decentralisation did not, however, imply any form of federalism; instead, it implied that the local entities had a constitutionally founded autonomy. Articles 41 and 162 of the Belgian Constitution provide that the municipalities have autonomy in matters of local interest.[1]

The constitutional concept of local autonomy has remained intact. The Belgian institutional framework has, however, undergone a profound reform since 1957. Belgium has become a federal State with six different sub-state entities; it has seen an important diverging process. At the same time, Belgium has (or more precisely the major Belgian politicians have) always remained one of the major supporters of "European integration".[2] Belgium can therefore be considered as a country with a paradox. On the one hand, it undergoes a continuous evolution towards regionalisation, while on the other hand, it undergoes an evolution towards integration in the EU.

This contribution aims to guide a foreign reader through the apparent ambiguous evolution of Belgian federalism. It starts with an introduction to the current Belgian institutional framework, followed by a description of its interesting but complex evolution. It will consider how the reformers have attempted to combine the internal disintegration with an integration of the different sub-state entities in the institutions of the European Union.

---

[1]On this topic: Deom and de Kerckhove (1980), pp. 147–205 and Mast et al. (2002), pp. 486–488.

[2]Read the pro-European books of two former Belgian Prime Ministers Jean-Luc Dehaene and Guy Verhofstadt: Dehaene (2004), p. 237 and Verhofstadt (2006), p. 76.

A. De Becker
Faculteit recht en criminologie, Vrije Universiteit Brussel, Pleinlaan 2, 1050 Brussel, Belgium
e-mail: alexander.de.becker@vub.ac.be

C. Panara and A. De Becker (eds.), *The Role of the Regions in EU Governance*,
DOI 10.1007/978-3-642-11903-3_11, © Springer-Verlag Berlin Heidelberg 2011

B. Introduction to the Complex Belgian Federalism

I. *The Evolution from a Unitary State to a Federal State*

Belgium has legally been a federal State since 1993; however, analysis of the Belgian transition with regard to EU governance has to start earlier. The State reform of 1993 was a next step in the continuous Belgian evolution towards more autonomy for the sub-state entities.

This contribution therefore starts with a brief historical description of the evolution of the Belgian national institutional framework since 1970. This description is necessary to understand the role of the Belgian sub-state entities in European governance and in a broader sense to understand the role of the Belgian sub-state entities in international organisations.

According to the current Article 1 of the Constitution, Belgium is a federal State which is composed of Communities and Regions. The current Article 1 of the Constitution was introduced by the Constitutional Reform of 1993. Between 1970 and 1993, Belgium was legally a decentralised country, although it had many characteristics of a federal state.[3]

The evolution of the Belgian institutional framework can best be described as a centrifugal evolution. The sub-state entities (more precisely, the Communities and Regions) within the Belgian institutional landscape received and have kept on receiving more and more competences.[4]

In 1970, the Belgian institutional transformation started. The first State reform in 1970 introduced a double devolution of powers. As a consequence of Flemish demand (the northern part of the country), new Cultural Communities were created, which received legislative powers to enact "décrets" (Acts enacted by the Parliaments of the Communities) concerning cultural and some educational and linguistic issues.[5] The Walloon part (the southern part of the country) simultaneously demanded the creation of regions to execute some socio-economic competences. Three Cultural Community Councils were created in 1970 [the Dutch speaking (later the Flemish), the French speaking and the German speaking].

The Regions were theoretically created in 1970, but it took until 1980 and even 1988 (as a part of the second and third State Reforms) before the exact competences of the Regions were defined. The Regions became competent for socio-economic issues (such as economy, transport, country planning, housing policy, etc.) while the Communities became in 1980 competent for personal matters as a consequence of the second State reform.

---

[3]See Melchior (1987), p. 330.

[4]Alen et al. (1992a), p. 123 and Alen (1994), p. 167.

[5]Alen et al. (1992a), pp. 18 and 125.

In 1980 (the year of the Second State Reform), two Regions became operative (the Flemish and the Walloon). The competences of the Communities were also enlarged in 1980; they became not only competent for cultural issues but also for more person-linked competences (health, social aid), which meant that the Cultural Communities were reformed into (full) Communities. The Communities and the Regions got their own Council [which later became a (full) Parliament] and their own government. The third Region (the Brussels-Capital Region) was theoretically founded in 1970, but it took until 1988 (the year of the third State Reform) before the institutions of this Region (Parliament and Government) were introduced.

The third State reform of 1988 created a full, complete and consistent double path federalism by installing the Council and the Government of the Brussels-Capital Region. This means that since the State reform of 1988 three Communities and three Regions were operative in bipolar federal Belgium (the Flemish Community, the French speaking Community and the German speaking Community and the Flemish Region, the Walloon Region and the Brussels-Capital Region).

The territorial boundaries of the Flemish Community and the Flemish Regions do not correspond, they overlap.[6] The Flemish Community can execute its power in personal matters in Brussels; however, the Flemish region has got no (socio)-economic power in the territory of Brussels. The socio-economic aspects within the Brussels' region are regulated by the Brussels-Capital Region. The French Community can similarly execute its power in the Brussels-Capital Region concerning personal matters in Brussels. However and moreover, the French Community cannot execute its competences within the territory of the German speaking Community (in the total East of the country).[7] The Walloon Region cannot execute any (socio-economical) power in Brussels, but it can execute these competences in the territory of the German speaking Community.[8]

---

[6]Craenen (2001).

[7]Rimanque (1993), pp. 165–194.

[8]Some aspects of the asymmetrical state structure have to be underlined: the institutions of the Flemish Community and the Flemish Region were in fact merged in 1980 (although the six representatives of Brussels in the Flemish Parliament are not entitled to vote concerning regional matters). Legally they remain two separate entities: the Flemish Community and the Flemish Region.

The French speaking Community transposed some of its powers to the Walloon Region and to the French speaking members of the Parliament and the government of the Region Brussels-Capital. The Walloon Region transposed some of its powers to the German speaking Community. On this topic: Rimanque (1993), pp. 189–193.

Schematically, the Belgian federal State is composed as follows[9]:

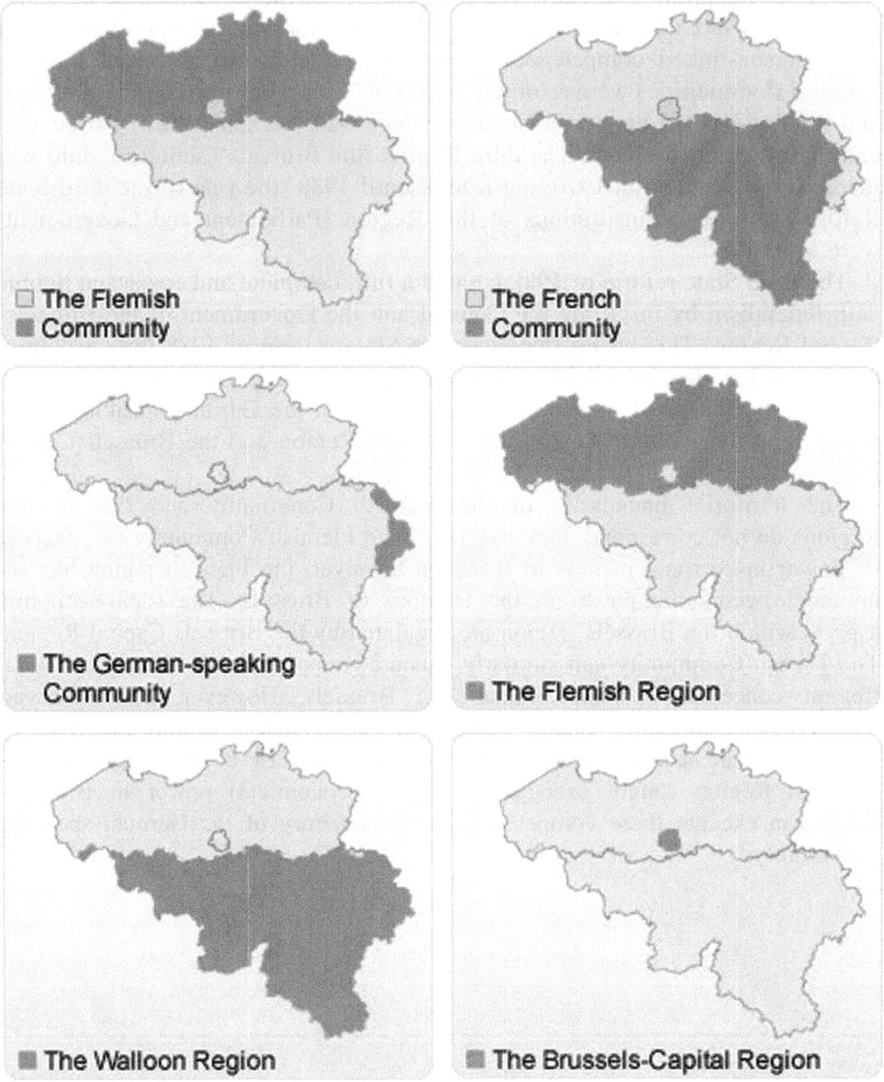

The fourth State reform of 1993 formally transformed Belgium into a federal state. Article 1 of the Constitution was modified and the Communities and the Regions got their own directly elected Parliaments and their own governments with specific powers.

---

[9]This map can be consulted at http://www.belgium.be/en/about_belgium/government/federale_staat/map/ last consulted on 15 June 2010. The author acknowledges the FEDICT for its willingness to let him use these maps.

The competences of the Regions were enlarged in the State reforms of 1988, 1993 and 2001. Currently, they are (mainly)[10] competent for country planning, environmental issues, nature policy, housing policy, agriculture and fisheries, economy, energy, some aspects of employment policy, infrastructure and transport, external trade and administrative control of local entities. The Communities are competent for health policy, person-linked matters (family policy, social welfare, integration of foreigners, policy towards disabled persons, youth, policy for elderly people, social aid to prisoners...) and scientific research.[11]

Presently, political discussions have been pending for a year and a half concerning a new State Reform. The Flemish part of the Kingdom requires at least the regionalisation of labour market policy and bigger fiscal autonomy for the sub-state entities, while the Walloon part desires a consolidation of the existing State organisation.

It is important to keep this complex institutional framework in mind when this contribution is read.

II. Some Specificities of Belgian Federalism

Some more aspects of the Belgian federal framework have to be underlined before we can start to answer the question concerning the participation of the sub-state entities in European governance.

The Parliaments of the Communities and Regions exercise their powers by the enactment of *décrets* (with the exception of the Brussels-Capital Region which enacts *"ordonnances"*)[12] which have (in principal) an equivalent legal power as an Act of federal Parliament.

Each Community and each Region has now got enumerated powers, which it normally executes exclusively.[13] The Belgian institutional framework is organised

---

[10]It is important to indicate that some competences are not fully transferred to the Regions. This is for example the case for economy. Multilateral trade policy, guarantees against import - and export risks and the import, trade and export of weapons for military and police aspects (where the Conduct code of the EU concerning the export of weapons has to be respected) are still federal competences. In principal, however, economy belongs to the competences of the regions.

[11]A similar remark has to be made concerning the competences of the Communities as for the competences of the Regions. Some parts of their competences which interfere with federal competences lead to a difficult repartition of the competences between the federal State and the Communities.

[12]The "ordonnances" of the Parliament of the Region Brussels-Capital can, to some extent, be declared unconstitutional by a judge and even be suspended by the federal government, in contrast to the principal of equality between the decrees of the Parliaments of the Communities and the Regions and the Acts of the federal Parliament. On this issue: Alen et al. (1992b), pp. 154–155.

[13]Article 35 of the Constitution provides that the Communities and the Regions exercise residual powers, and that the federal authority is only competent to exercise those powers which are constitutionally enumerated. However, that article only applies when a Special Act is enacted; this Special Act indicates the date when Article 35 will become applicable. On the same date the

based upon the basic principle of strictly exclusive competences.[14] Concurrent powers, with priority given to the central authority, do not in principal exist in the Belgian federal institutional framework.[15] The Belgian adoption of strictly exclusive powers was considered to result in fewer possibilities for conflicts of competences.[16] The national exclusivity of competences must, in the vein of the Belgian State reform, be transferred to the execution of "external powers". This approach implies that, vis-à-vis foreign affairs, the Communities and the Regions need to be able to execute the same competences as they do for national affairs. This parallel between the execution of powers within the Belgian framework and outside the Belgian framework is mostly described with the following adage "*in foro interno et in foro externo*".[17]

Moreover, Belgium has got a bicameral system on the federal level (with a Chamber and a Senate). Neither federal chamber can be considered to fully represent the sub-state entities. To some extent, the Senate has partially got a composition which represents the different sub-state entities, but the role of the Senate is not comparable with the role of the German *Bundesrat*[18]; in contrast, each sub-state has got a unicameral system with only one directly elected Parliament.

Finally, it is important to point out that most of the institutional reforms were effected by the Constitution, but mainly by an Act which was to be approved by a special majority in Parliament. Such a "Special Act" is adopted by two-thirds of the present Members of the federal Parliament and by a majority of the Members of Parliament in each linguistic (Dutch speaking and French speaking) group. Also, there exists a quorum for the adoption of a Special Act; a majority of the Members of the federal Parliament have to be present in Parliament when the Act is adopted.

C. The Transfer of Powers from the Communities and the Regions to the EU

I. Constitutional Provisions

Now that the complex bipolar federal structure of Belgium has been made clear, it is possible to describe how the Communities and the Regions interact with the governance of the EU. This part considers the role which the Communities and the Regions play when powers are transferred to the European level.

---

se enumerated federal competences need to be constitutionally underpinned in order to make Article 35 of the Constitution applicable. On this issue: Velaers (2007), pp. 1631–1641.

[14]Pas (2006), pp. 57–58.

[15]To some extent there exist some possibilities of parallel powers, concurrent powers and implied powers in the Belgian institutional framework. On this issue: Alen et al. (1992b), pp. 128–129.

[16]A. Alen et al. (1992b), p. 128.

[17]Velaers (2006), pp. 3–86.

[18]Concerning the German Bundsrat, read the constribution of Carlo Panara in this book, C. Panara, "A Cooperative solution to the Challenge of European integration".

Article 34 of the Belgian Constitution provides that the execution of some powers can legally be transferred to supranational institutions by way of Treaty or by Statute. This article was introduced in the Belgian Constitution as a result of the growing role of supranational entities in international public law. It is important to stress that this article to some extent devalues the concept of "national sovereignty" which played a key role in the conception of the Belgian Constitution and to a larger extent in all European continental constitutional texts which were enacted in the nineteenth century.[19]

The concept of "national sovereignty" which played and actually still plays a key role in Belgian constitutional law is linked to the concept of a nation state.[20] Article 33 of the Belgian Constitution provides that all powers emanate from the Nation and they are exerted in the manner established by the Constitution. This is a typical provision based upon the concept of national sovereignty.[21] Article 34 is the basis of the growing concept of the transfer of power to a supranational level.[22] However, it remains necessary to underline that, within the actual constitutional concept, only the exercise of certain powers can be transferred. More precisely, only the exercise of certain, well-determined powers can be transferred. According to the advisory opinions of the advisory body of the Council of State (a section of the Supreme Administrative Court in Belgium which grants advice to the government, and in some cases to Parliaments, on drafts or projects of statutes), it is impossible to transfer an unclear, defined, number of competences.[23]

The stipulation of Article 34 was introduced into the Belgian Constitution in 1970. One of the major consequences is, of course, that the exercise of certain well-enumerated powers can be transferred to the institutions of the EU by signing and promulgating EU-Treaties.

Article 34 of the Constitution does not provide a specific procedure for the Communities and the Regions' transference of power to the EU. The application of the principle "*in foro interno et in foro externo*" should, however, lead to the conclusion that exclusive competences which are bestowed on the Communities and the Regions can be transferred by a sub-state entity itself via a Treaty or a *décret*. An advisory opinion concerning the installation of the *Nederlandse Taalunie* (a supranational entity which endeavours to promote the use of the Dutch language) states that sub-state Parliaments can, without any doubt, transfer the exercise of certain powers to supranational institutions.[24]

---

[19]Rimanque (2005), p. 106. Concerning the concept of national sovereignty in Belgium, read Leroy (1992), vol. I, pp. 91–106.

[20]Tilleman and Alen (1992), pp. 12–13.

[21]Uyttendaele (2001), p. 102.

[22]Valticos (1982), pp. 9–22; Tilleman and Alen (1992), pp. 12–13.

[23]Parliamentary Documents, Senate, session 1988–1989, number 651/1. See also Velaers (1999), p. 236.

[24]Parliamentary Document, Flemish Parliament, session 1994–1995, number 728/1. See also Velaers (1999), p. 237.

Thus, Article 34 of the Constitution has to be read within the framework of the principle "*in foro interno et in foro externo*". This principle is currently underpinned by Article 167 Section 1 of the Belgian Constitution. This section stipulates the basic approach for the application of the principle "*in foro interno et in foro externo*". It explicitly establishes the power for the Communities and the Regions to sign treaties. This section stipulates literally:

> The King manages international relations, without prejudice to the ability of Communities and Regions to engage in international co-operation, including the signature of treaties, for those matters within their responsibilities as established by the Constitution and in virtue thereof.

This article contains, at first glance, a certain paradox. The first clause of this section indicates that the King (the federal executive power) manages the international relations while the second clause consolidates the primary power of the Communities and the Regions to engage in international co-operation and to sign treaties. It is useful to add that Articles 127 § 1, 3°, 128 § 1 and 130, 4° explicitly confirm, above this stipulation, the power of the Communities to co-operate internationally concerning culture, education and personal matters.[25]

As was mentioned before, in 1993 the Belgian institutional regulators opted for a solution where the internal repartition of powers of the Communities and the Regions also had to be transferred to an external level.[26] This means that, if a sub-state entity can execute certain competences in the internal framework, it should be able to execute the same competences for foreign affairs. The text of the Constitution explicitly recognises the power of the Communities and the Regions to sign treaties, but it is commonly accepted that the competences concerning the foreign affairs of the Communities and the Regions go a lot further than just the signing of treaties. It also includes, for instance, the accession into supranational entities (of course only if such an accession is limited to competences which are attributed to the Communities and the Regions).[27]

The combination of both articles delivers a clear answer to the question of how the transfer of powers from the Communities and the Regions to the European Union has to be done. The relevant Treaty has to be signed by the Communities and Regions concerned. The signing and promulgation of such a Treaty has to be executed in two phases. Firstly, an international treaty between the Member States has to be signed; and secondly, the signed Treaty can only enter into force if the sub-state Parliament expresses its consent. The representation of the Communities and the Regions within the institutions of the EU plays a key role in facilitating the operation of this constitutional framework. The details concerning the representation rules of the representatives of the Communities and the Regions in the EU institutions will be developed further.

---

[25]Velaers (2006), p. 7.

[26]Craenen (1993), p. 82.

[27]Velaers (2006), p. 7.

Consent for the Treaty itself has to be given by an Act of (the sub-state) Parliament. The "constitutional" treaties of the EU have got mainly a mixed character. This means that they invoke a transfer of powers from the federal level to the EU level as well as a transfer of powers from the Communities and/or the Regions towards the EU level.

The application of the principle "*in foro interno et in foro externo*" leads to the conclusion that each Parliament has to express its consent for such constitutional treaties.[28] These treaties transfer federal competences as well as competences of the Communities and the Regions. Therefore, each Parliament is required to give its assent to the signing of the Treaty. This procedure means that Belgium needs a considerable amount of time for ratification. For example, the Treaty of Lisbon had to be approved by six Belgian Parliaments (the federal, the Flemish,[29] the Parliament of the Walloon Region, the Parliament of the French speaking Community, the Parliament of the German speaking Community and the Regional Parliament of Brussels-Capital). Since the fourth State Reform of 1993, each "constitutional" treaty of the European Communities has been approved by all the different Parliaments. This was also the case for the ratification of the Treaty of Amsterdam, the Treaty of Nice and the Treaty of Lisbon. It may be worth recapitulating that the Constitutional Treaty was also ratified by all the different Belgian Parliaments.

II. Procedure to Diminish the Internal Democratic Deficit

The important role of the sub-state Parliaments in approving EU treaties (whether or not they transfer powers to the EU) does not fully reconcile the problem of the democratic deficit.

Article 168 of the Constitution protects the respective federal Chambers from being confronted with a signed Treaty before the national government has consulted or even informed Parliament of the ongoing negotiations. This article states that "the Chambers are informed from the beginning of negotiations concerning any revision of treaties establishing the European Community in addition to treaties and acts. They are aware of the planned treaty prior to signature". Similarly, Article 16 Paragraph 2 of the Special Act of 8 August 1980, as modified by the Special Act of 27 March 2006, provides that the sub-state parliaments, each to the extent that they are concerned, have to be informed from the beginning of negotiations concerning any revision of constitutional EU treaties in addition to treaties and acts[30]

---

[28]Velaers (2006), p. 51.

[29]Flanders has merged the Parliaments of the Flemish Community and the Flemish Region although their territorial competences are slightly different. On this issue: Rimanque (1993), p. 189.

[30]Velaers (2006), p. 51.

The above procedure has not, however, been followed in relation to the Flemish Parliament during the negotiations and the adoption of the Treaty of Lisbon.[31] No sanction is foreseen in Article 16 Paragraph 2 of the Special Act of 8 August 1980, as modified by the Special Act of 27 March 2006. This led the Flemish Parliament to ratify the Treaty of Lisbon, irrespective of the fact that Article 16 Paragraph 2 of the Special Act had been violated.[32]

D. Representation of the Sub-State Entities in European Institutions

I. Representation in the Council of Ministers

Until the fourth State Reform of 1993, Belgium had difficulties in the representation of the Kingdom in the Council of Ministers.[33]

Before 1993, this led to the fact that the Belgian delegation, given the limited territorial competences of the Communities and the Regions, had to be presided over by a member of the federal government. The Ministers of the governments of the Communities and the Regions could advise the federal Minister and could consult with the federal Minister. However, alone, the federal Minister had the right to vote.[34]

The fourth State reform of 1993 formally established the federal state. This new institutional concept enabled better development of the principle of "*in foro interno et in foro externo*". The Belgian regulation was modified firstly to allow Ministers of sub-state entities to represent Belgium and secondly to allow them to execute the right to vote for the whole Belgian nation. The reasons why Belgium can only, since 1993, be represented by a member of Government of a sub-state entity are, however, not only based upon national law. The actual text of Article 203, which stipulates that each Member State in the Council of Ministers is represented by a Minister who is to commit the Member State's government, was only introduced into the EC Treaty by the Treaty of Maastricht, which entered into force on 1 November 1993.[35] The new formulation grants a sub-state entity the opportunity to be represented by its own Minister. Moreover Article 203 of the EC Treaty grants the opportunity to externalise the federal structure of a Member State within the framework of the EU institutions. It may be useful to recapitulate that Article I-23

[31]*Parliamentary Documents,* Flemish Parliament, session 2007–2008, nr. 1653/3, pp. 3–5.

[32]*Parliamentary Documents,* Flemish Parliament, session 2007–2008, nr. 1653/5, p. 2.

[33]Ingelaere (2006), p. 149.

[34]Ingelaere (2006), pp. 149–150.

[35]Belgium and Germany (as federal states) were strongly defending a revision of Article 203 of the EC Treaty in order to make it possible to be represented in the Council by sub-state Ministers, see Velaers (2006), p. 52.

§ 2 of the proposed European Constitution foresaw that the Minister of a sub-state entity who represented a Member State also had the power to vote.[36]

Depending on the agenda of the European Council, Belgium can be represented by: (1) a federal Minister; (2) a Minister of a sub-state government; (3) a federal Minister assessed by a Minister of a sub-state government; or (4) a Minister of a sub-state government assessed by a federal Minister.[37]

The Council of the European Community often has a "mixed" agenda (which means that some aspects of the agenda belong to the powers of the federal authority and some belong to the powers of the Communities and the Regions). The re-partition of competences between the different Councils at the European level does not correspond of course with the national re-partition of competences between the federal State and the sub-state entities in Belgium. Therefore, it was necessary that Belgium made national regulations concerning its representation in the Council of Ministers.

Article 81 § 6 of the Special Act of 8 August 1980, as modified by the Special Act of 16 July 1993, provides that a government (of the Communities and the Regions) can bind the State within the Council of the European Communities, as long as its representation conforms to a cooperation agreement, as stipulated in Article 92 bis § 4 bis of the Special Act.

Article 92 bis § 4 bis of the same Special Act of 1980, as modified by the Special Act of 16 July 1993, stipulates that the federal authority, the Communities and the Regions have to sign a cooperation agreement concerning the representation of Belgium within international and supranational organisations and concerning the procedure which has to be followed to provide a common position. If no consensus can be reached, a cooperation agreement has to clarify how the Belgian representative must act during the meetings at the international or supranational levels.[38]

On 8 March 1994, the Cooperation Agreement between the federal authority, the Communities and the Regions concerning the representation of the Kingdom of Belgium in the Council of Ministers of the European Union was signed.[39]

This Cooperation Agreement chiefly provides the rules for the coordination of a joint Belgian opinion in the Council of the European Union. The coordination of the Belgian joint opinion is organised by the *Directory General for European Affairs and Coordination* of the Public Service of Foreign Affairs.[40] A meeting to

---

[36]Ingelaere (2006), p. 150.

[37]The Council meetings concerning fisheries constitute the exception to this rule. Belgium will in these councils always be represented by the Flemish Minister giving the fact that the Belgian Coast lies entirely in Flemish territory. The other exception concerns the Council meetings on Agriculture. In the Council meetings on Agriculture, the national Minister will always be assisted by the Flemish and the Walloon Minister.

[38]Ingelaere (2006), p. 151.

[39]Published in the *Belgian Moniteur,* 17 November 1994.

[40]The Federal Public Service for Foreign Affairs used to be known as the Ministry for Foreign Affairs. The new name is a consequence of the big reform of the Belgian federal public employment status. On this topic: de Becker (2007).

coordinate a Belgian joint opinion is organised before each session of the Council of Ministers, irrespective of the issues which are foreseen on the agenda of the Council of Ministers. The meetings are thus not only organised when the Council for General Affairs meets, but each time that a Council meeting is scheduled.

This implies that, before each meeting of a Council, the following actors are invited: the representatives of the (federal) Prime Minister, the federal Vice-Prime Ministers, the federal Minister competent for European Affairs, the Minister-Presidents of the Communities and the Regions, the Ministers of the Communities and the Regions competent for international affairs, the Permanent Representation in the EU and the representatives of the Communities and the Regions in the Permanent Representation in the EU. According to the matters which will be dealt with by the specialised Councils, the members of the different governments can be substituted by the Ministers competent for the matters which will be dealt with by the specific Councils.[41]

If no joint opinion concerning the Belgian opinion in the Council is reached during such a meeting, the director of the Directory General for European Affairs and Coordination has to direct the issue to the Secretary of the Inter Ministerial Conference for Foreign Policy within a maximum period of three days. The Inter Ministerial Conference for Foreign Policy consists of all Belgian Ministers, responsible for foreign policy, on all different levels (national and sub-state).[42]

The president of the Inter Ministerial Conference for Foreign Policy (a consultation committee) has the duty to organise as soon as possible a meeting concerning the problem. However, no rules are provided in cases where no joint opinion can be reached within the framework of the Inter Ministerial conference for Foreign Policy.

The commentary which is annexed to the Cooperation Agreement of 8 March 1994 and which, according to Article 13 of the Cooperation Agreement,[43] constitutes an integral part of this Agreement, provides that the Inter Ministerial Conference for Foreign Policy must remember that an abstention in the European Council is not a neutral vote. If a Council decision requires an unanimous vote, an abstention is considered to be a positive vote. If a decision requires a qualified majority, an abstention is considered to be a negative vote. Therefore, in reality, the coordination meeting has the obligation to reach a consensus concerning the Belgian joint opinion.[44]

Article 7.2 of the Cooperation Agreement of 8 March 1994 provides that for those powers which are exclusively conferred to the Communities and the Regions, the sub-state entities have to represent Belgium in the European Council. This operates on a rotational basis. The Communities and the Regions agree among each

[41]Ingelaere (2006), pp. 152–153.

[42]*Parliamentary Question*, Flemish Parliament, session 2003–2004, 1, to be consulted on http://jsp.vlaamsparlement.be

[43]Velaers (2006), p. 57.

[44]Point 5 of the commentary concerning the cooperation agreement, *Moniteur belge*, 17 November 1994. See also Le Hardy de Beaulieu (1994), pp. 831–833.

other upon a system where a well-balanced rotation of their representation is guaranteed.[45] The currently agreed rotation system includes four main principles:

1. A rotation per semester, which means a rotation after each new EU presidency.
2. A balance between the representatives of the Communities and the Regions whether they act as minister-assessor or as minister.
3. Continuity: if more than one Council is held during a period of six months, the rotation per semester system continues. This means that the semesterial president remains president for the other Council Meetings.[46]
4. If no Council is organised during a semester, the presidency is retained until the next Council-meeting in the next semester.

One can see that there exists a difference between the Councils in which the Ministers of the Communities and the Regions can assist the Council of Ministers and those where they fully represent Belgium. In fact, there exist four different sorts of representation models for Belgium in the Councils. Firstly, on some Councils, Belgium is just represented by a federal Minister. These Councils deal with matters which are internally conferred to the federal authority. This is the case for the following Councils:

- Council for General Affairs and External Relations
- Council for Economic and Financial Affairs
- Council for Employment, Social Policy, Health and Consumer Affairs (as far as it concerns Consumer Affairs)
- Council for Justice and Home Affairs (as far as it concerns Justice and Civil Protection)
- Council for Transport, Telecommunications and Energy (as far as it concerns telecommunications)

Secondly, on some Councils, Belgium is represented by a federal Minister with an assessor representing the sub-state entities. This structure applies to Councils which are dealing with "mixed" matters, which concern mainly federal competences. The assessor can address himself to the Council for those subjects for which the sub-state entities are internally competent. He must also communicate with other sub-state governments in case the development of the negotiations requires an actualisation of the Belgian joint opinion.[47] This is the case for the following Councils:

[45]The negotiations for such an agreement take place under the presidency of the German Community (as the smallest player in the sub-state field). The agreement also contains guarantees that the Flanders (implying the Flemish Community as well as the Flemish Region) is represented as often as the French speaking Community and the Walloon Region together. The Flemish Community and the French speaking Community represent Belgium twice as often as the German speaking Community. Furthermore, there is aimed to give the Regions an opportunity to represent Belgium. See for more specific aspects concerning the agreement Ingelaere (2006), p. 153.

[46]A consequence of this rotation system is that, during the Belgian EU presidency in 2001, for the first time, Ministers of sub-state entities presided over the Council of Ministers.

[47]Ingelaere (2006), p. 153.

- Council for Competitiveness (as far as it concerns the internal market)
- Council for Employment, Social Policy, Health and Consumer Affairs (as far it concerns Social Policy and Health)
- Council for Transport, Telecommunications and Energy (as far as it concerns Transport and Energy)

In these Councils, however, the federal Minister retains the right to vote. During the vote, the federal Minister has to respect the consensus which has been achieved within the framework of the coordination meeting.

The third category of Council is where Belgium is represented by a Minister of a government of a Community or a Region, with a federal minister as an assessor. This concerns the following Councils:

- Council for Competitiveness (as far as it concerns Industry and Research)
- Council for Environment

Here the federal Minister can address a message to the Council, with consent of the sub-state Minister concerning those issues which nationally belong to the federal competences, but the right to vote is executed by the Minister of the sub-state entity. Again, the Minister of the sub-state entity has to respect the consensus reached in the coordination meeting.

The fourth category of Council deals only with competences which are internally transferred to Communities and the Regions. Given the Belgian structure, this essentially means that Belgium is only represented by a Minister of a sub-state entity. This form of exclusive representation of Belgium by Ministers of the Communities and the Regions exists within the following Councils:

- Council for Education, Youth and Culture
- Council for Competitiveness (as far as it concerns Tourism)

The Council for Agriculture and Fisheries constitutes an exception to the general representation rules. There is no rotation system for this Council, although Belgium will always be represented by a Minister of a sub-state entity.

If the Council for Agriculture and Fisheries is dealing with issues concerning fisheries, the Flemish Region will represent Belgium, given the fact that: (1) the Regions are, since 2001, competent for fisheries; and (2) that the Flemish Region is the only coastal region.

If the Council for Agriculture and Fisheries is dealing with agriculture issues, which is (since 2001) also a regional competence, the Flemish and Walloon Region prepare the Belgian opinion. However, Belgium is represented in the Council by a federal Minister, assisted by the Flemish and the Walloon Ministers competent for agriculture.[48]

---

[48]If no consensus can be reached among the Regions concerning the Belgian opinion, the Belgian federal Minister has the duty to abstain during the vote in the Council. See Ingelaere (2006), pp. 156–157.

It can be observed that the Belgian sub-state governments are currently trying to develop further. In Belgium (mainly in Flanders), there is some lobbying taking place to introduce the so-called "split vote" within the Council. Actually, the result of the current coordination meetings implies that the sub-state entities, even if they represent Belgium in the Council, have to vote in accordance with the consensus reached in the coordination meetings. Therefore, the Flemish government declared in 1999 that it was its ambition to get a direct representation in the institutions of the European Union by introducing a mechanism of "split vote" in the Council of Ministers for the exclusive competences of the Communities or the Regions.[49] This "split vote" would imply that each sub-state entity (with or without the federal government, according to the repartition of the competences) gets a part of the votes of Belgium in the Council which they may exercise independently.[50] The Flemish government repeated this ambition in 2004.[51]

The Flemish government has not yet convinced many other actors within the EU. This is logical, because a coalition of different regions, using their "split votes", might fundamentally reform the existing balances in the EU.[52] However, the "split vote" remains a hot topic on the Flemish institutional agenda.

II. Representation in the Permanent Representative of the Communities and the Regions

The Cooperation Agreement of 8 March 1994 considers only the representation of Belgium in the Council.

However, the rotation system has also been introduced into the meetings of the Committee of Permanent Representatives (Coreper) where the representatives of the Communities and the Regions may speak on behalf of Belgium to the extent that it concerns competences of the sub-state entities. The representatives of the Communities and the Regions participate in the meeting of the Coreperfor the competences which nationally (and indeed at the EU level) belong to the sub-state entities. The Belgian group is presided by the Adjunct-Permanent Representative for meetings within the Coreper1 and by the Permanent Representative for meetings within the Coreper2.[53]

The composition of the Belgian delegation within the scope of the Belgian Permanent Representation is more complex. A Cooperation Agreement of 18 May 1995 between the federal State, the Communities and the Regions concerning

[49] Ingelaere (2006), pp. 157–158.

[50] *Parliamentary Documents,* Flemish Parliament, session 1995–1996, nr. 265/1.

[51] Regeerakkoord van de Vlaamse regering (2004–2009)", Vertrouwen geven, verantwoordelijkheid nemen", 80 to be consulted on http://www.docs.vlaanderen.be. See also Ingelaere (2006), p. 158.

[52] Ingelaere (2006), pp. 158–159.

[53] Ingelaere (2006), p. 159.

the legal status of the representatives of the Communities and the Regions in diplomatic and consular posts deals with the appointment of the representatives of the sub-state entities. The representatives of the Communities and the Regions are appointed by the sub-state entities, however they remain under the diplomatic hierarchic authority of the Head of the Diplomatic Post, who is himself appointed by the Belgian federal State.[54] On the one hand, the representatives of the sub-state entities receive their tasks and missions from the sub-state authorities, but, on the other hand, those diplomats represent Belgium within the European institutions. They remain under the hierarchic authority of the Head of Department.

This double "personality" leads to an awkward situation for these representatives. They are not considered to be members of a "regional lobby group", but are (considered to be) full members of the representative organs of a Member State,[55] which normally facilitates their access to important information channels.

III. Representation Offices of the Sub-State Entities in Brussels

Although the sub-state entities participate directly in the European institutions and although that they can represent Belgium within the Council and the Coreper, some sub-state entities still consider it to be fruitful to open a representation office in Brussels.

On 22 July 2005 the Flemish government decided to create the *Vlaams-Europees verbindingsagentschap* (VLEVA) (the liaison agency Flanders-Europe) to improve the visibility of the Flemish presence on the European decision-making level. The agency aims also to promote Flemish interests. The office is a public–private partnership where a lot of businessmen get the opportunity to network in the European institutions.[56]

Wallonia and Brussels integrated their permanent representation into one entity. The *delegation Wallonie-Bruxelles auprès l'UE* (the delegation of Wallonia and Brussels by the EU) is however integrated into the Permanent Representation of Belgium in the Coreper.

The Region of Brussels-Capital has itself established two important representation offices (the Brussels-Europe liaison-office and the representation of the Brussels-Capital Region in the EU). The latter is integrated into the Permanent Representation of Belgium. The former, however, aims to promote Brussels as the capital of the EU and seat of key European institutions as well as informing residents of the important role played by Europe in the well-being and the prosperity of the Region.[57]

[54] Ingelaere (2006), p. 160.

[55] Ingelaere (2006), pp. 159–160.

[56] Huysseune and Jans (2008) p. 8.

[57] Huysseune and Jans (2008), p. 9.

The German speaking Community also has a representation office in Brussels, which was founded before the German speaking Community was integrated into the rotation system to represent Belgium at Councils and in the Coreper.[58]

IV. The Committee of the Regions[59]

The Committee of the Regions was established in 1994 as a consequence of the Treaty of Maastricht. It currently has 344 members and 344 substitutes Belgium has currently 12 representatives (and 12 substitutes) within the Committee.

All Belgian members and alternates are directly elected representatives in the Parliaments of the Communities and the Regions. Flanders has 5 or 6 representatives, the Walloon Region 3 or 4, Brussels-Capital Region 2 and the German Speaking Community 1. There exists a mid-term rotation between Flanders and the Walloon Region to ensure the seat of the German speaking Community.

All members are appointed for a period of four years. It is important to note that Belgium is the only Member State without any local representative within the Committee of the Regions. The local entities (municipalities and provinces) are not directly represented in the Belgian delegation of the Committee of the Regions. In each other delegation, some members represent the municipal level.

E. Defence of the Competences of the Communities and the Regions at the Judicial Level

I. Direct Challenge before the European Court of Justice

Until now, this contribution has focused upon how the Belgian sub-state entities participate in the EU institutions. This part focuses on the means of defence for the Communities and the regions to ensure their own competences.

The scope of the problem becomes clear in light of the jurisprudence of the European Court of Justice. A direct challenge of an Act of the EC can only be undertaken by a European institution or a Member State. The European Court of Justice decided in *Région Wallonne v. Commission*, a case which was introduced by the Walloon Region,[60] that sub-state entities and local entities can only request the

[58]Huysseune and Jans (2008), p. 10.

[59]Further information concerning Belgian representation and concerning the Committee of the Regions in general can be found at the following website www.cor.europa.eu.

[60]ECJ, 95/97, Région wallonne v. Commission, 21 March 1997, *ECR*, I-1787. This jurisprudence was later confirmed in ECJ, 180/97, Regione Toscana v. Commission, 1 October 1997, *ECR*, I-5245. See also Raccah (2008), p. 99.

annulment of a regulation or a decision made by a European institution if it were directly addressed to them, or, if it were intended for other entities, concerned them directly and individually.[61]

Belgium has got a specific national regulation to ensure that the Communities and the Regions can act against regulations or decisions of the institutions of the EC. Article 81 § 7 of the Special Act of 8 August 1980, as modified by the Special Act of 16 July 1993, provides that the State has to issue an action against an international legal entity before an international or supranational Court at the request of a government or governments of the Communities and the Regions for those matters which belong to the competences of the Communities and the Regions. Such a request has firstly to be debated in the Inter Ministerial Conference for Foreign Policy. The Conference decides within a period of 30 days by way of consensus. If no consensus can be reached, the King (the federal executive power) must immediately issue an action The procedure in the Inter Ministerial Conference for Foreign Policy may never prevent the King to summon within the procedural delay.[62]

If the request contains mixed aspects (whereby federal as well as sub-state competences are engaged), the federal State issues an action against the international legal entity. A Co-operation Agreement of 11 July 1994 describes the procedure which has to be followed if such a "mixed" action is requested by at least one sub-state government. The federal government or the concerned sub-state government that wishes to summon a European institution has to inform the Inter Ministerial Conference for Foreign Policy. As a consequence of this request, the Inter Ministerial Conference must install a task force "judicial action, which verifies whether it concerns indeed a "mixed" action If the task force agrees that it concerns a "mixed" action, one federal civil servant shall be appointed to coordinate the further proceedings.[63] If the task force does not agree upon the mixed character, Article 81 § 7 of the Special Act of 8 August 1980, as modified by the Special Act of 16 July 1993, becomes applicable.

II. New Rules Concerning the Principal of Subsidiarity in the Treaty of Lisbon

The Treaty of Lisbon, of 13 December 2007, provides some regulation which enlarges the guarantees of the principle of subsidiarity. This principle, which is already exists in Article 5 of the EC Treaty, provides that, in areas in which the EU has no exclusive competence, the EU shall act only and insofar as the objectives of

[61]Some initiatives were taken to allow regional entities to defend their rights before the European Court of Justice in case their prerogatives were directly affected by regulation of decisions of the European institutions, see European Parliament, *A5- 427/2002*. On this issue see also van Nuffel (2001), p. 880.

[62]Ingelaere (2006), pp. 178–179.

[63]Ingelaere (2006), pp. 179–180.

a proposed action cannot be sufficiently achieved by a Member State, either at the central level or at the regional or local level.

Yet the EC Treaty does not have any control mechanism in place to ensure that national and sub-state competences are protected against a disproportionate action of the EU, which is in breach of this principle of subsidiarity.

The principle of subsidiarity will in the future be controlled by National Parliaments, according to the new Article 3b, as modified by the Treaty of Lisbon. The protocol on the application of the principles of subsidiarity and proportionality seeks to provide legal assurance that political actions are to be taken as closely as possible to the citizens of the Union. Therefore, the Commission shall consult widely before proposing legislative acts and the Commission, the European Parliament and to some extent the Council shall send their draft legislative acts and, later, amendments, to the national Parliaments for consultation.

Declaration 51, which is annexed to the Treaty of Lisbon, is of specific application for Belgium. This declaration concerning the Belgian national parliaments states that:

> It wishes to make clear that, in accordance with its constitutional law, not only the Chamber of Representatives and Senate of the Federal Parliament but also the parliamentary assemblies of the Communities and the Regions act, in terms of the competences exercised by the Union, as components of the national parliamentary system or chambers of the national parliament.[64]

This statement implies that Parliaments of the different Communities and Regions can act as components of the National Belgian Parliament.

What is the legal impact of this declaration? Does it imply that the European Commission, Parliament and (sometimes) the Council shall forward their legislative drafts and their amended drafts to the Parliaments of the Communities and the Regions? Article 4 limits the obligation to forward such a drafts and amended drafts to the National Parliament. The declaration of Belgium that the Parliaments of the Communities and the regions act as branches of the national parliament, in terms of competences exercised by the EU, seems to be difficult to reconcile with Article 6 of the Protocol which provides that "it will be for each national parliament or each chamber of a national parliament to consult, where appropriate, regional parliaments with legislative power". It seems that Declaration 51 concerns mainly Article 6 of the Protocol which grants any national Parliament the possibility to send a reasoned opinion stating why it considers that the draft does not comply with the principle of subsidiarity.

This EU approach is inconsistent with the Belgian federal framework which tries to develop a legal parity between the federal State and its sub-state entities. However, when seen from an international public law angle and more specifically when seen within the European framework, the Belgian declaration is inconsistent with the fact that the EU is composed of Member States. The co-operation

[64]Conference of the Representatives of the Governments of the Member States, convened in Brussels on 23 July 2007 to be consulted on http://eur-lex.europa.eu/en/treaties/dat/12007L/htm/C2007306EN.01023101.htm.

agreement of 19 December 2005 which was a consequence of the draft of Constitutional Treaty, however, indicates a very important and fare going consequence of this Declaration (which Belgium has also annexed to the draft of Constitutional Treaty). This co-operation agreement indicates that each sub state entity can represent Belgium before the ECJ. The other Parliaments can claim that the Parliament aiming to start action before the ECJ is not competent to do so. The Parliament claiming the incompetence can ask an advice of the Council of State. If this advice indicates that, according to the Council of State, a problem of competences does exist, a Conference composed of the seven presidents of the distinct Parliaments has to provide a solution. The question remains whether this new regulation can enter into force without modification of the existing Belgian regulations. Furthermore, a new internal co-operation agreement seems the only solution to make this declaration applicable. This new co-operation agreement has, however, not yet been reached.[65] In the actual stand of the situation, this Co-Operation Agreement of 19 December 2005 cannot enter into force since it was provided that it would only resort legal effects when the Constitutional Treaty entered into force. In order to execute internally Declaration 51 annexed to the Treaty of Lisbon, Belgium needs at least a new Co-operation Agreement and presumably also a reform of the Special Act of 8 August 1980.[66] The Communities and the Regions can probably take advantage of the newly created possibility of bringing actions before the ECJ on the basis of infringement of the principle of subsidiarity by legislative acts. Those actions have to be brought before the ECJ by the Member State, but, in the light of Declaration 51, it may reinforce the judicial control for respecting the competences of the Communities and the Regions.

The Communities and the Regions may, indirectly, also take advantage of the enlarged role of the Committee of the Regions to act before the ECJ. In relation to legislative acts, the EU Treaty provides that the Committee of the Regions can bring actions before the ECJ if the EU Treaty provides that the Committee had to be consulted.[67]

F. Fulfilment of EU Obligations in the Internal Sphere

Finally, an answer has to be delivered to the question of how Communities and Regions fulfil their EU obligations. The fulfilment of EU obligations implies the duty of the Member States to implement and/or execute regulations or decisions which were promulgated at the EU level.

[65] *Parliamentary Questions,* Flemish Parliament, session 2008–2009, 4 November 2008 to be consulted on http://jsp.vlaamsparlement.be/website/htm-vrg/534355.html.

[66] Advice of the Belgian Council of State, *Parl. Doc.*, Belgian Senate, nr. 568/1 to be consulted on www.senate.be consulted on 1 November 2009.

[67] It is worth noting that the Committee of the Regions can deliver an opinion on its own initiative, which to some extent undermines the usefulness of this provision.

In principal, there exist only exclusive competences in the Belgian Institutional Framework. This aspect, combined with the principle "*in foro interno et in foro externo*", implies that the Communities and the Regions have the obligation to implement or apply EU law themselves, through their own institutions, within the remit of their exclusive competences.[68]

This repartition of obligations becomes more complicated when they are approached from another angle. According to the jurisprudence of the ECJ, a Member State may not invoke its national law to rectify the non-implementation of EU law.[69] The federal state remains responsible for the non-implementation of EU law even if the competences belong to sub-state entities at the national level.[70]

The principle "*in foro interno et in foro externo*" significantly complicates the situation. It is therefore not surprising that Belgium is seen as a bad pupil in relation to the implementation of EU law.[71] Nevertheless, this conclusion also causes a paradox with the fact that sub-state entities are fully involved in EU law making. This situation does not appear to be suitable for guaranteeing an adequate fulfilment of EU obligations.

The Belgian Constitution provides an exceptional procedure for cases in which a Community or a Region fails to fulfil its EU obligations. Article 169 of the Constitution provides a possibility for federal institutions (legislative and executive) to substitute the legislative or the executive power of the concerned Community or Region if the ECJ found that Belgium had violated EU law or had not fulfilled its EU obligations. The ECJ must have delivered a decision *erga omnes*; a decision concerning a prejudicial question is not considered to be a finding against a Member State. This last decision only clarifies how EC law has to be applied or whether the EC law is valid or not.[72] It does, however, not include a clear indication that the implementation of the EC rule by a sub-state entity is invalid or in breach of EC-law.

The Special Act of 5 May 1993 put the substitution procedure on a statutory footing. Article 16 § 3 of the Special Act of 8 August 1980, as modified by the Special Act of 5 May 1993, provides the procedure which has to be followed if an institution of the federal State decides to substitute itself for an institution of the Communities and the Regions in order to fulfil its European obligations. The federal State can only start this procedure after a formal finding against the Community or the Region for a violation of EC law.

Moreover, the substitution procedure can only be set up if three cumulative conditions are fulfilled. First of all, the federal State has to grant formal notice[73] three months before the formal substitution (which normally means directly after

[68]Velaers (2006), pp. 66–67.

[69]ECJ, *Commission v. Belgium,* 2 February 1982 and ECJ, *Commission v. Belgium,* 14 January 1988. See also Lenaerts and van Nuffel (2003).

[70]Schaus (1994), p. 79.

[71]Ingelaere (2006), pp. 173–174.

[72]*Parliamentary Documents,* Senate, Extra Ordinary Session, 1991–92, 457/3, p. 2.

[73]Bribosia (2004), p. 803.

the ECJ's ruling). Secondly, the Community or Region concerned had to be involved in the whole procedure during the litigation to find a solution for the pending case. Thirdly, the Cooperation Agreement concerning the representation of the Belgian State in litigations before supra-national courts has to be respected.[74]

The substitution by the State concerns only the necessary measures for the execution of the *juris dictum* of the decision (Article 16 § 3, first section of the Special Act of 8 August 1980, as modified by the Special Act of 5 May 1993). The federal State has to consider the principle of proportionality and has to estimate the federal loyalty towards the sub-state entities.[75]

Substitution constitutes, according to Belgian doctrine, mainly a symbolic measure.[76] It is chiefly an exception to the general rule "*in foro interno et in foro externo*" which is normally consistently and consciously respected in Belgium. Therefore, the procedure is also very cumbersome; it has not yet been applied. Some authors have argued that the federal State should be able to substitute the sub-state entities before they are condemned.[77] Such an *a priori* substitution, however, has the disadvantage that, until the final ruling against a sub-state entity, it remains uncertain whether they have indeed acted in breach of EC law.[78] Therefore, no proposals for an *a priori substitution* have been become hard law.

G. Conclusion

Belgium is for many reasons a peculiar federal State within the European Union.

The main principle of Belgian federalism is "*in foro interno et in foro externo*". This means that the Belgian Communities and Regions are fully competent to exercise their exclusive competences at the national level as well as at the EU level. Shaping this principle in international and European public law is, however, very difficult. The European Union normally only recognises its Member States as constituting "elements" of the European construction.

Nevertheless, Belgium has achieved many goals when it concerns the participation and the integration of the Communities and the Regions into European governance. Ministers of the Communities and the Regions can, in applying Article 203 of the EC Treaty, represent Belgium in the Council of Ministers. Representatives of the Communities and the Regions are fully part of the Permanent Representation at the EU. However, this integration process at the EU level demands a lot of internal organisation and cooperation.[79] A lot of cooperation agreements have been concluded in a spirit of federal loyalty.

[74] Ingelaere (2006), p. 182.

[75] *Parliamentary Documents,* Chamber, 1992–93, nr. 798/3, p. 7. See also Velaers(2006), p. 65.

[76] Louis and Alen (1994), pp. 102–103.

[77] Louis and Alen (1994), p. 100.

[78] Melchior (1987), p. 334.

[79] See Andersen (1993), p. 152.

The Belgian (and certainly the Flemish) sub-state entities continue to demand more direct participation rights in the European Union. For example, the concept of the "split vote" within the Council of Ministers has been demanded, as well as a full possibility to challenge an act of a European institution before the European Court of Justice. The application of the principle "*in foro interno et in foro externo*" constitutes a continuous search of balances between the principles which are governing European public law and those governing the internal Belgian repartition of competences. Currently, the federal state is still more equal on the European level than the sub-state entities.

However, Belgian federalism is evolving daily. The centrifugal power within the Belgian federal construction remains extremely active. This stems from the fact that Belgium is used to searching for flexible solutions for its internal evolution. Belgium has evolved from a unitary nation towards a federation of regions. It is the conviction of many Belgians that such an evolution would help the EU to overcome its current image of being too bureaucratic and too distant from the people. A centrifugal power (including stronger regionalisation) brings, in their opinion, power closer to the EU citizen.

Selected Bibliography

Alen A (1994) Het Belgisch federalisme. In: Federalisme. Maklu, Antwerp

Alen A, Tilleman B, Meersschaut F (1992a) The state and its subdivisions. In: Alen A (ed) Treatise on Belgian constitutional law. Kluwer, Deventer

Alen A, Tilleman B, Meersschaut F (eds) (1992b) Treatise on Belgian Constitutional Law. Kluwer, Deventer

Andersen R (1993) Les compétences. In: Delperee F (ed) La Constitution fédérale du 5 mai 1993. Bruylant, Brussel, p 152

Bribosia D (2004) Fédéralisme et traités internationaux: de la Belgique aux Balkans. In: Liber Amicorum Jean-Pierre De Bandt. Bruylant, Brussel, p 803.

Craenen G (1993) België en het buitenland: de nieuwe regeling van de buitenlandse betrekkingen. In: Alen A, Suetens LP (eds) Het federale België na de vierde staatshervorming. die Keure, Brugge, p 82

Craenen G (2001) The Institutions of Federal Belgium: an introduction to Belgian public law. Acco, Leuven

de Becker A (2007) De overheid en haar personeel: juridische grondslagen van de rechtspositie van de ambtenaar. die Keure, Brugge

Dehaene JL (2004) De Europese uitdaging: van uitbreiding tot integratie. Van Haelewyck, Leuven

Deom D, De Kerckhove G (1980) "L'intérêt communal". Ann Dr:147–205

Huysseune M, Jans T (2008) Brussels as the capital of Europe of the regions? e-Journal Brussels Studies. www.brusselsstudies.be, last visited 30 April 2010

Ingelaere F (2006) De Belgische deelstaten en de Europese Unie. In: Judo F, Geudens G (eds) International betrekkingen en federalisme. Larcier, Brussels

Le Hardy de Beaulieu L (1994) Fédéralisme et relations internationales en Belgique. La réforme de 1993–1994. Revue internationale de droit comparé:831–833

Lenaerts K, Van Nuffel P (2003) Europees recht in hoofdlijnen. Maklu, Antwerp

Leroy M (1992) Requiem pour la souveraineté, anachronisme pernicieux. In: Présence du droit public et des droits de l'homme – mélanges offertes à Jacques Velu, vol. I. Bruylant, Brussels, pp 91–106

Louis JV, Alen A (1994) La Constitution et la participation à la Communauté européenne. Revue belge de droit international:102–103
Mast A, Dujardin J, Van Damme M, Vande Lanotte J (2002) Overzicht van het Belgisch administratief recht. Kluwer, Mechelen, pp 486–488
Melchior M (1987) Constitution et organisations internationals. Le problème de la supranationalité. In: Le nouveau droit constitutionnel. Bruylant, Brussels, p 330
Pas W (2006) The Belgian national Parliament from the perspective of the EU Constitutional Treaty. In: Kiiver P (ed) National and Regional Parliaments in the European Constitutional Order. Europa Law Publisher, Groningen, pp 57–58
Raccah A (2008) L'accès aux normes de l'Union européenne, composante de leur application directe. Jurisdoctoria 1:99
Rimanque K (1993) De instellingen van Vlaanderen, de Franse Gemeenschap en het Waalse Gewest. In: Alen A, Suetens LP (eds) Het federale België na de vierde staatshervorming. die Keure, Brugge
Rimanque K (2005) De Grondwet: toegelicht, gewikt en gewogen. Intersentia, Antwerp
Schaus A (1994) L'exécution des traités. Revue belge de droit international:79
Tilleman B, Alen A (1992) General introduction. In: Alen A (ed) Treatise on Belgian Constitutional law. Kluwer, Antwerp
Uyttendaele M (2001) Précis de droit constitutionnel. Bruylant, Brussels
Valticos N (1982) Expansion du droit international et Constitutions nationales, un cas significatif: le transfert de pouvoirs à des organisations internationales et la Constitution belge. In: Evolution constitutionnels en Belgique et relations internationales: Hommage à Paul De Visscher. Pedone, Paris, pp 9–22
Van Nuffel P (2001) What's in a Member State? Central and Decentralized Authorities before Community Courts. Common Market Law Rev:880
Velaers J (1999) De Grondwet en de Raad van State: afdeling wetgeving. Kluwer, Antwerp
Velaers J (2006) In foro interno et in foro externo: de internationale bevoegdheden van de gemeenschappen en de gewesten. In: Judo F, Geudens G (eds) Internationale betrekkingen en federalisme. Larcier, Brussels
Velaers J (2007) 'Het recht van de wetgever': beschouwingen over de voorbehouden en de residuaire bevoegdheden". In: Itinéraires d'un constitutionnaliste: en hommage à Francis Delperée, Bruylant, Brussels, pp 1631–1641
Verhofstadt G (2006) The United States of Europe. Federal Trust, London

Chapter 12
Devolution and European Representation in the United Kingdom

Mike Varney

A. Introduction

All traditional views of the British constitution, the most famous being those of Dicey[1] or Bagehot,[2] noted that the sovereign power of the UK had only one *locus* – the Westminster Parliament.[3] Parliament was deemed to be sovereign, and the *locus* of executive power was located in the largest party in Parliament, which formed the executive. From a legal perspective, this traditional constitutional orthodoxy remains in place even today – devolution of power to Scotland, Northern Ireland and Wales was achieved via an Act of the Westminster Parliament, and from a legal perspective, the Westminster Parliament would be free to take away the powers granted to the devolved governments via another Act should it so wish.[4] This situation is a result of the clear position in UK constitutional law that one Parliament is not in a position to bind its successors.[5] It is important to note that, while the constitutional position grants the Westminster Parliament a power to repeal and remove the regional government which exists in the UK in Scotland, Wales, Northern Ireland and London, it is most unlikely that such a move would be politically feasible.

The position outlined above places the UK in a rather different situation from those states in Europe which have a federal structure, or which have a written constitution in which the powers of central and sub-national governments are often enumerated in a rigid constitutional structure, rather than being subject to the

[1] Dicey (1960).

[2] Bagehot (1963).

[3] For a helpful modern account of this issue see King (2007), chapter 8.

[4] It is notable that Laws LJ described the Acts of Parliament which brought about devolution in the UK as 'constitutional statutes' which cannot be subject to implied repeal by a later Act. There was, however, no suggestion that these Acts could not be subject to express repeal by a later Act. See *Thoburn* v. *Sunderland City Council* [2002] EWHC 195 (Admin), [2003] Q.B. 151 at [62].

[5] It is important to note that this might be subject to some qualification, though the general principle remains. See Bradley and Ewing (2007), pp. 62–65.

M. Varney
Law School, University of Hull, Yorkshire, UK

C. Panara and A. De Becker (eds.), *The Role of the Regions in EU Governance*,
DOI 10.1007/978-3-642-11903-3_12, © Springer-Verlag Berlin Heidelberg 2011

legislative will of Parliament. Until the passage of the Scotland Act 1998, the Northern Ireland Act 1998, and the Government of Wales Act 1998 (now largely repealed and replaced by the Government of Wales Act 2006), there was no legislative or executive power in the hands of sub-national authorities (SNAs) in the UK, and other than the Scottish, Welsh and Northern Ireland Offices, which were emanations of the central Westminster government, there were no institutions in place to represent the interests of these regions. It is important to emphasise that all areas of the UK were and remain represented in the Westminster Parliament, and Members of Parliament from the Scotland, Wales and Northern Ireland are able to represent the views of their constituents on that basis.

The devolution of power in the UK is a radical constitutional change, which has required significant changes to the UK's constitutional arrangements. The Acts of Parliament which devolved powers to the regions create only a general framework for the devolution process. Each of the Acts outlines the institutions of the devolved governments, processes for election to the devolved legislatures, sets out some of the powers and features of the executives of the devolved administrations and deals with a range of other procedural issues. The Acts also define the competences which are to be passed to the devolved governments, certain financial issues and the process for judicial resolution of disputes over the division of competence. This means that a great many issues over the day-to-day exercise of governmental power and the interface between the Westminster Parliament and the devolved administrations is left to less formal arrangements, such as constitutional conventions and agreements which are not intended to be legally binding, known as Concordats.

As an unwritten constitution, the United Kingdom constitution has always been reliant on such informal arrangements. Maitland noted that these conventions are a vital part of the United Kingdom constitution, and that these 'moral' rules, which are not intended to be legally binding, are often as important, or possibly more important, than those rules of our constitution which are legally enforceable in the courts.[6] Modern treatments of the constitution continue to reflect this position – constitutional conventions and other informal rules, customs and practices are an important part of the United Kingdom constitution.[7] These conventions and informal rules are crucial to the operation of devolved government in the United Kingdom, and are central to the interface between the devolved governments, the Westminster government and the European Union.

The purpose of this paper is to examine the law and practice existing in the United Kingdom that shape and govern the involvement of the devolved governments in European policy making. Its focus will be on the position of the devolved governments in Scotland, Wales and Northern Ireland, though a brief consideration will be given to the endeavours of the devolved government in London, and in particular the Mayor and his executive, to wield influence on European policy-making. In addition to the examination of the legal and constitutional arrangements,

---

[6]Maitland (1908), pp. 527–528.

[7]See Bradley and Ewing (2007), pp. 12–32 or Turpin and Tomkins (2007), pp. 156–179.

the paper will also consider the endeavours of the devolved governments to wield political power in the European Union policymaking process – all the devolved governments have deployed not only the direct methods granted to them via official means to influence the EU policy-making process, but have also endeavoured to enhance their involvement in European policy making through the use of indirect mechanisms, particularly via political influence and political networks.

B. The Legal Position: Devolved Government and European Union Policy Making

Devolution in the UK is described as an 'asymmetric' process, as the powers devolved to each of the SNAs differ.[8] Furthermore, prior to the passage of the Government of Wales Act 2006, the power devolved to Wales was solely executive in nature – the Welsh Assembly did not enjoy the legislative powers which were enjoyed by the Scottish Parliament and Northern Ireland Assembly. The Welsh Assembly does now enjoy some legislative power, which renders it more likely that European Union law making might overlap with devolved competences. The position in the UK is not aided by the fact that each piece of devolution legislation uses slightly different terminology for the powers which are retained by the Westminster Parliament.[9] Given the differences in the way that power is devolved, and the complex web of legislation that is involved, this section of the paper will treat each of the devolved authorities in turn, examining the powers which have been devolved, and the provisions which apply to EU law and EU policy making. The purpose of this section is to offer a detailed analysis of the devolution legislation for Scotland, Northern Ireland and Wales. A detailed discussion of the legislation which grants powers to the Mayor of London and the London Assembly will not be considered in such detail.

The regional government in London does not share all the characteristics of the devolved administrations in Scotland, Wales and Northern Ireland. In particular, the Greater London Authority and the Mayor have a far more limited sphere of competence than the other devolved governments, and all the powers devolved to London are administrative – the London Assembly does not enjoy law-making power in the same way as Scotland, Wales and Northern Ireland.

C. The Position under the Scotland Act 1998

The Scotland Act 1998 introduced devolution of power to Scotland, and created the Scottish Parliament. Section 28 of the Scotland Act 1998 empowers the Scottish Parliament to pass legislation. In the Act, this legislation is described as an "Act" of

---

[8]Burrows (2000), pp. 90–91.

[9]Burrows (2000), pp. 90–91

the Scottish Parliament. There is some debate over whether this legislation should be considered akin to an Act of the Westminster Parliament, but this is largely an issue of constitutional theory rather than practical importance.[10] Section 28 of the Act provides that the Parliament is free to make law subject to the restrictions in section 29. Section 29(1) of the Act provides that "An Act of the Scottish Parliament is not law so far as any provision of the Act is outside the legislative competence of the Parliament". Section 29(2) then offers detail of what is outside the competence of the Scottish Parliament. For the purposes of this discussion, the relevant limitations are set out in section 29(2)(b) – the Scottish Parliament may not pass any legislation in relation to a 'reserved' matter, and also in section 29(2)(d) – no law may be passed which is incompatible with the European Convention on Human Rights, or with EU Law.

An examination of Schedule 5, which lists the 'reserved' matters (i.e. those matters over which the legislative power remains with the Westminster Parliament) offers a clear exposition of the legal position of the Scottish Parliament and executive with regard to EU policy making. Paragraph 7 of Schedule 5 provides that "International relations, including relations with territories outside the United Kingdom, the European Communities (and their institutions)...are reserved matters". The result of this is that all involvement in negotiations over European policy making are reserved matters, and are thus controlled by the United Kingdom executive in Westminster. The Scottish Parliament has the responsibility for adopting implementing measures for EU Law in its devolved competence, as section 53 and Paragraph 7(2) of Schedule 5 of the Scotland Act 1998 make it clear that "observing and implementing" EU Law obligations is not reserved to the Westminster Parliament. It is important to clarify the approach taken in section 53 of the Act at this point. The approach in section 53 of the Act is to pass all powers which would have been exercised by a Minister of the Crown in Westminster to the Scottish Executive, insofar as these powers relate to devolved competences.

It was noted above that the Scottish Parliament does not have the power to pass legislation which is contrary to EU law by virtue of section 29(2)(d) of the Scotland Act 1998. The Act also provides a mechanism which ensures that EU law obligations are met – as the UK government is still responsible for a failure to meet EU law obligations, section 57 of the Scotland Act 1998 provides that the executive power devolved under section 53 of the Act may also be exercised by a Minister of the Crown in Westminster. There might be two reasons why this could be necessary. First, it is possible that the devolved administrations may all agree that a particular measure is best implemented by delegated legislation at Westminster which has application throughout the UK. The other possibility is that it may be necessary to exercise this concurrent power to implement EU law obligations should the devolved administration in Scotland fail to do so. Evidently, the United Kingdom government is ultimately responsible for ensuring that the UK meets its EU law obligations, and should the Scottish government refuse to implement a

[10]For analysis, see Burrows (2000), pp. 57–65.

piece of EU law, it will be necessary for the UK government to have recourse to the power found in section 57 of the Act.

The formal legal framework under the Scotland Act 1998 does not create any potential for the devolved government to be involved in EU law making or policy making, as all these matters are reserved to the Westminster government. Nonetheless, European obligations can have a significant impact on a number of spheres where competence has been devolved to the Scottish institutions. A recent report by the Scottish government has identified certain spheres where EU policy which are of particular interest and importance for the Scottish government. These include fisheries and aquaculture, agriculture and energy policy.[11] All matters relating to the formal representation of the Scottish government at EU level and cooperation between the Westminster government and the Scottish government in relation to EU policy making are dealt with by Concordat and convention, rather than through legislation. The detail of these Concordats and conventions will be discussed below.

D. The Position Under the Northern Ireland Act 1998

The Northern Ireland Act 1998 introduced devolution of power to Northern Ireland. The process of devolution in Northern Ireland has considerable complexity due to the history of violence in the province. Devolution in Northern Ireland is designed to implement the Good Friday Agreement, which was negotiated between the parties involved in Northern Ireland politics at the time, including the United Kingdom government and the government of the Republic of Ireland.[12] Devolution in Northern Ireland has faced greater difficulties than the devolution process in Scotland and Wales due to the entrenched political disagreements which exist within the political system. Devolution in Northern Ireland has been subject to two relatively lengthy periods of suspension, one from February to May 2000 as a result of the IRA's failure to provide information on the decommissioning of weapons,[13] and for a lengthier period between October 2002 and May 2007 as a result of a political impasse which arose due to accusations that certain of Sinn Fein's support staff within the Northern Ireland administration were gathering intelligence on behalf of the IRA.[14] There have also been two 24-h suspensions of devolution in Northern Ireland, one on 10 August 2001, and another on 22 September 2001. When devolution in Northern Ireland is suspended, all powers

[11]Scottish Government (2008), pp. 6–8.

[12]See Burrows (2000), pp. 12–15 for further detail on this issue. Helpful accounts can also be found in Hadfield (1998, pp. 599–616, 1999, pp. 3–31).

[13]D. McKittrick, "IRA Offers Deal for Arms 'to be Put Beyond Use' as Assembly Suspended", *The Independent*, available at http://www.independent.co.uk/news/uk/this-britain/ira-offers-deal-for-arms-to-be-put-beyond-use-as-assembly-suspended-726470.html (12 February 2000).

[14]See M. Purdy, "Stormont Conspiracy Theories Continue", *BBC News Online*, available at http://news.bbc.co.uk/1/hi/northern_ireland/4511566.stm (8 November 2005).

return to the Westminster government. This is significant, as due to political differences and suspensions, the institutions have not operated for as long as, or completed as much government business as, the devolved institutions in Scotland and Wales. This may be relevant, particularly when the Northern Ireland government's endeavours to participate in European Union policy making are considered.

The devolution legislation in Northern Ireland takes a similar approach to the Scotland Act 1998. The Northern Ireland Act 1998 provides that the Northern Ireland Assembly may pass Acts by virtue of section 5. Section 6(1) then provides that "A provision of an Act is not law if it is outside the legislative competence of the Assembly". Section 6(2) then offers the circumstances in which legislation will be outside the competence of the Assembly. For the purposes of this discussion, the relevant limitations of the Assembly's competence are found in s. 6(2)(b) – the legislation relates to an 'excepted matter', or s. 6(2)(d) – the legislation in question would be incompatible with EU law. The terminology in the Northern Ireland Act differs from the Scotland Act 1998 in the sense that what is a 'reserved matter' under the Scotland Act 1998 is treated as an 'excepted matter' under the Northern Ireland Act.

Paragraph 2 of Schedule 3 of the Northern Ireland Act 1998 states that "International relations including relations with...the European Communities (and their institutions)" are excepted matters, and remain with the Westminster government. Paragraph 3(c) of Schedule 2 provides that the Northern Ireland government is responsible for implementing EU law obligations within the sphere of its devolved competence. The legislative framework offers similar provisions to those under the Scotland Act 1998. Section 24 of the Northern Ireland Act 1998 prohibits a Northern Ireland Minister from creating subordinate legislation or doing acts which would be incompatible with EU law, and section 25 prohibits Northern Ireland Ministers from engaging in subordinate legislation which deals with excepted matters. Finally, section 26(1) of the Act provides that the Secretary of State for Northern Ireland (a Minister in the Westminster Government) may take steps to prevent any action by a Northern Ireland Minister which is incompatible with international obligations. In addition, section 26(2) allows the Secretary of State for Northern Ireland to take any step which would ordinarily be exercised by a Northern Ireland Minister should it be required to meet an international obligation. It appears likely that this power might be used in the same way as that under the Scotland Act 1998, either with the agreement of the Northern Ireland Ministers should it be desirable for a United Kingdom implementation of a EU law measure, or in a case where the Northern Ireland government have failed to take the necessary action to implement EU law.

The above discussion illustrates that the positions under the Scotland Act 1998 and the Northern Ireland Act 1998 are broadly similar when representation of the devolved governments at the European level is considered. The Northern Ireland government is charged with implementing European law which arises in areas within devolved competence, but there is no procedure in legislation for the representation of the devolved government's interests at the European level. The most recent European strategy produced by the Northern Ireland executive suggests that policy issues such as agriculture, fisheries, economic development, education and culture are viewed as high priorities for the devolved government.[15] As with the Scottish government, all matters of formal representation of the Northern Ireland government are dealt with by convention and Concordat, rather than in legislation.

E. The Position Under the Government of Wales Act 2006

Devolution was first introduced in Wales by the Government of Wales Act 1998. This Act introduced a form of devolution to Wales which was purely executive – the Welsh Assembly did not enjoy the power to pass legislation in the same way as the Scottish Parliament and the Northern Ireland Assembly.[16] Section 31 of the Government of Wales Act 1998 creates a framework for the Secretary of State for Wales (a Minister in the Westminster Parliament) to consult with the Welsh Assembly about any legislation which is to be passed by the Westminster Parliament and which has an impact on Wales. Furthermore, s. 33 empowered the Welsh Assembly to "consider, and make appropriate representations about, any matter affecting Wales". It is evident that these provisions gave the Welsh Assembly considerably less power than that possessed by the Scottish and Northern Irish institutions, and the Welsh Assembly's freedom to promulgate new policy was limited accordingly. The Westminster government's practice under ss. 31 and 33 of the Government of Wales Act 1998 does, however, offer an interesting insight on its willingness to cooperate with the Welsh government.[17] In 2000, the interface between the Westminster Parliament and the Welsh Assembly was formalised by a Protocol which committed the Westminster Parliament and government to engage in broad consultation over legislation which impacts on Wales.[18] This formalisation of the discretion granted by ss. 31 and 33 of the Act appears to demonstrate that the use of agreements as part of the devolution settlement has proven to be an effective means of facilitating cooperation between Westminster and the devolved governments.

Given the Welsh Assembly's relatively limited powers under the Government of Wales Act 1998, its role in implementing EU obligations was more limited than its Scottish and Northern Irish counterparts.[19] Insofar as the Welsh Assembly had responsibility for implementing EU obligations, the Government of Wales Act 1998 contained similar provisions to the Scottish and Northern Irish legislation, providing for the Westminster government to also implement EU measures.

Almost all of the Government of Wales Act 1998 has now been repealed by the Government of Wales Act 2006. This Act came about as a result of considerable

[15]Office of the First Minister and Deputy First Minister 2006.

[16]See Burrows (2000), p. 55 and pp. 78–82 for details of the Welsh Assembly's powers.

[17]For some detail on how this came about see Osmond (1999), chapter 5.

[18]Department for Constitutional Affairs (2005).

[19]A full account will not be given here due to the repeal of the Government of Wales Act 1998. For a full account, see Burrows (2000), pp. 134–135.

interest in Wales for a more extensive devolution of power to the Welsh Assembly. In 2004, the Welsh Assembly Government appointed Lord Richard to lead a Commission to investigate a number of issues, including possible expansion of the Assembly's powers.[20] The Richard Report took an expansive view of the future for the Welsh Assembly, advocating a progression to a set of fully devolved law-making powers akin to those of Scotland and Northern Ireland in due course.[21] In its White Paper[22] leading to the passage of the Government of Wales Act 2006, the UK government did not follow such a radical proposal, preferring instead a more limited expansion of the Assembly's law-making and executive powers.[23]

The ultimate position under the Government of Wales Act 2006 is that the Welsh Assembly has been granted power to pass legislation known as "Assembly Measures".[24] These measures do not have the same legislative status as the "Acts" of the Scottish Parliament or Northern Ireland Assembly, although these powers are still considerably greater than those previously enjoyed under the Government of Wales Act 1998. Section 94(1) provides that "Subject to the provisions of this Part, an Assembly Measure may make any provision that could be made by an Act of Parliament". Despite this relative breadth, the legislative competence of the Welsh Assembly is more limited than its Scottish and Northern Irish counterparts.

Rather than a devolution scheme where power is devolved to the sub-national authorities and certain matters are reserved to the Westminster parliament, section 94(3) and 94(4) provide that Assembly Measures are only within the competence of the Assembly if the Measure relates to one of the matters listed in Part 1 of Schedule 5 of the Act. In essence, this is the opposite approach to that which is taken in the Scottish and Northern Irish legislation – the Welsh Assembly has power to legislate only in areas where power has been expressly granted by Westminster, rather than having a general power to legislate with certain matters reserved to the Westminster Parliament. The powers granted to the Assembly in Part 1 of Schedule 5 are relatively broad, and include, amongst other things, matters such as agriculture, culture, economic development and matters relating to education and health. It is important to note at this point that the Government of Wales Act 2006 does envisage "full" devolution for the Welsh Assembly. Part 4 of the Government of Wales Act 2006 provides for a framework for the passing of Acts by the Welsh Assembly – essentially the same powers as the Scottish and Northern Irish institutions. These will be brought into force if approved in a referendum of the Welsh people to take place in due course.

---

[20]For the Report see Commission on the Powers and Electoral Arrangements of the National Assembly for Wales, available at http://www.richardcommission.gov.uk/content/finalreport/report-e.pdf, 2004, accessed 15 June 2010.

[21]Richard Report 2004, chapter 13.

[22]Cm 6582, *Better Governance for Wales*, London: TSO, 2005.

[23]For commentary see Rawlings (2005), pp. 824–852.

[24]For a more detailed account of the new legislative powers see Trench (2006), pp. 687–696.

Insofar as the Welsh Assembly has the power to implement EU measures, the legislative framework is similar to that under the other devolution regimes in the UK. Section 94(6)(c) of the Government of Wales Act 2006 provides that the Assembly cannot pass a measure which is incompatible with EU law. Section 80 of the Act provides that the Welsh Ministers have an obligation to implement EU law obligations where the obligation could be complied with by the exercise of any of their functions. Section 80(8) provides that the Welsh Ministers do not have the power to make subordinate legislation, or to take any other action which would be contrary to EU law. Finally, section 82 provides that the Secretary of State for Wales might oblige or prevent actions by the Welsh Ministers insofar as these might be necessary in order to ensure that international obligations are complied with. There is no provision for devolution in relation to international affairs in Schedule 5 of the Act, so it is clear that the Westminster government retains power to represent Wales in the European policy-making process.

At present, the Welsh government has not a published European strategy, unlike the Scottish and Northern Irish governments. There, is, however, a section on the Welsh government's website concerning the role of Wales in the European Union.[25] It seems likely that the more limited European endeavours of the Welsh government are a result of the limited powers granted to the Assembly prior to 2006, which did not necessitate such an active role in European policy making. It is likely that the Welsh government will seek to extend and expand its role in European policy making as its powers expand.

F. The Impact of European Law on Devolved Powers

It is rather difficult to obtain a clear picture of the overall impact of European law and policy on the devolved powers granted to the SNAs in the UK. However, there is some evidence that European policy making and European law have a considerable impact on the exercise of devolved powers. The first source of such evidence can be found in the Richard Report, where it is noted that the most significant constraint on the exercise of powers in relation to agriculture and rural development is not imposed by the devolution legislation in the UK but by the constraints imposed by EU law.[26]

A similar position arises when the report of the Calman Commission is considered. This report reviewed Scottish devolution, and it notes that, in fields such as health and safety and environmental protection, European law has placed considerable constraints on the Scottish government's freedom of action.[27] This view is

[25]See http://wales.gov.uk/topics/international/europeanunion/?lang=en (accessed 15 June 2010).

[26]See the Richard Report 2000, pp. 103–105.

[27]Commission on Scottish Devolution, *The Future of Scottish Devolution within the Union: A First Report*, Edinburg: Commission on Scottish Devolution, paras. 5.35 and 5.38.

augmented by the Scottish government's recent European strategy, which notes the importance of a number of European policy areas to the role of the Scottish government.[28] A recent study into the implementation of European environmental law in Scotland and Wales suggests that in most cases there will be few significant substantive differences in implementation of European Directives, though there are frequently minor differences to allow for differing institutional arrangements for enforcement.[29] It is acknowledged that these minor differences could constitute a more significant divergence of environmental policy between the devolved governments and Westminster over time.[30]

Material from political scientists also suggests that the devolved governments see the impact of European policy on their devolved powers as a significant issue, and have been anxious to ensure that they are adequately represented in the European policy-making process.[31] In a speech in 2004, the then First Minister, Jack McConnell MSP, suggested that 75% of devolved powers were affected by European policy making.[32] Given that the general powers devolved to Northern Ireland are broadly similar to those devolved to Scotland, and that after the Government of Wales Act 2006 the Welsh government also possesses a similar range of competences, it is likely that all devolved governments see a similar impact on their powers.

G. The Arrangements for Representation of Devolved Governments in EU Policy Making

I. The General Framework for Cooperation

It was noted above that the method of permitting devolved governments to participate in the EU policy process in the UK was through the use of constitutional conventions, Concordats and other 'soft law' agreements. The Memorandum of Understanding between the Westminster government and the devolved governments provides the general framework for relations between the governments.[33] The Memorandum addresses a number of issues, including communication and consultation between the governments, the provision of information and statistics and the arrangement of Parliamentary proceedings. Paragraph 17 of the

---

[28]Scottish Government 2008, p. 2.

[29]Reid et al. (2008), pp. 39–41.

[30]Reid et al. (2008), p. 41.

[31]See e.g. Burch et al. (2005), pp. 465–475; Bulmer and Burch (2002), pp. 114–136.

[32]J. McConnell MSP, "First Minister's Speech to the Consular Corps", available at http://www.scotland.gov.uk/News/News-Extras/189 (20 January 2004).

[33]Cm 5420, *Memorandum of Understanding and Supplementary Agreements between the United Kingdom Government, Scottish Ministers, the Cabinet of the National Assembly for Wales and the Northern Ireland Executive Committee* London: TSO, 2001.

Memorandum of Understanding deals with international relations and relations with the European Union, where it states:

> As a matter of law, international relations and relations with the European Union remain the responsibility of the United Kingdom Government and the UK Parliament. However, the UK Government recognises that the devolved administrations will have an interest in international and European policy making in relation to devolved matters, notably where implementing action by the devolved administrations may be required. They will have a particular interest in those many aspects of European Union business which affect devolved areas, and a significant role to play in them.

This is complemented by paragraph 19 of the Memorandum, which provides:

> The UK Government will involve the devolved administrations as fully as possible in discussions about the formulation of the UK's policy position on all EU and international issues which touch on devolved matters. This must, obviously, be subject to mutual respect for the confidentiality of those discussions and adherence to the resultant UK line, without which it would be impossible to maintain such close working relationships.

Part B of the Memorandum document then contains the Concordats on the coordination of European policy issues. There are separate Concordats between the UK government and the Scottish, Welsh and Northern Ireland governments, respectively. The content of each of these Concordats is broadly similar. In essence, they each provide a general framework in which the devolved governments and the UK government might co-operate on the development and influence of European policy making. The Concordats provide for three key principles. The first is that the devolved governments should be able to participate on a full and continuing basis in the negotiations on European policy which might impinge on devolved powers. The second principle is that coordination methods should ensure that the UK can negotiate its policy position effectively in fast-moving negotiations, and third is that coordination should ensure that EU obligations are implemented consistently.[34] There is then a 'Common Annex' to the Concordats between the UK government and the devolved governments that lays down the methods of cooperation between the UK and devolved governments.

The first issue to be addressed by the Common Annex is that of the provision of information. Here, the UK government is to provide information about all European legislative proposals likely to be of interest to devolved administrations "as early as possible".[35] Similar obligations are imposed on the devolved administrations should they become privy to information that might be of interest to the UK government. The Annex then moves on to set out a general position that the UK government will ensure that devolved administrations are fully involved in the

[34]See para. B 1.4 of the Memorandum of Understanding, *Supplementary Agreements between the United Kingdom Government* in relation to Scotland. Identical provisions can be found in para. B. 2.4 for Wales and B 3.4 for Northern Ireland.

[35]See para. B 1.4 of the Memorandum of Understanding, *Supplementary Agreements between the United Kingdom Government* in relation to Scotland. Identical provisions can be found in para. B. 4.2 for Wales and B 3.4 for Northern Ireland.

formulation of the UK's position in EU policy matters.[36] The document then moves to the methods through which there might be Ministerial involvement in European policy making. The approach adopted here is flexible, in the sense that such involvement might be via written consultation in some matters where this is deemed to be appropriate, or via negotiation between officials in the UK and devolved administrations.[37] Should agreement not be reached by officials, then the negotiations will be escalated to Ministerial level for further discussion. It is acknowledged that agreement may not be reached in all cases, and in circumstances where agreement cannot be reached, the matter will be referred to the Joint Ministerial Committee (JMC) for further negotiations.[38] The role of the JMC will be considered later in this section. The next part of the Annex sets out a set of principles for the full involvement of civil servants from the devolved governments in the negotiation of the UK's position on European matters.[39]

The Annex then deals with an area of particular interest – the potential for Ministers and officials of the devolved governments to be involved in the negotiations in the Council of Ministers and other relevant events. The basic principle is set out in paragraph B 4.12, where the document states "Ministers and officials of the devolved administrations should have a role to play in relevant Council meetings, and other negotiations with EU partners". The later paragraphs in this section then make it clear that it is the UK Minister who remains in control of the selection process for the negotiating team,[40] and that the key focus of all negotiations will be to achieve a coherent UK line on matters of policy.[41] While these provisions do not seem to grant a right for representatives of the devolved authorities to attend negotiations in the Council of Ministers, they appear to create a strong presumption that the devolved authorities will have a role in such negotiations. Ultimately, however, the decision over who might be involved in negotiations on issues, even where they pertain to devolved competence, remains with the leading Minister in

[36]See para. B 1.4 of the Memorandum of Understanding, *Supplementary Agreements between the United Kingdom Government* in relation to Scotland. Identical provisions can be found in para. B. 4.4 for Wales and B 3.4 for Northern Ireland.

[37]See para. B 1.4 of the Memorandum of Understanding, *Supplementary Agreements between the United Kingdom Government* in relation to Scotland. Identical provisions can be found in para. B. 4.6 for Wales and B 3.4 for Northern Ireland.

[38]See para. B 1.4 of the Memorandum of Understanding, *Supplementary Agreements between the United Kingdom Government* in relation to Scotland. Identical provisions can be found in para. B. 4.7 for Wales and B 3.4 for Northern Ireland.

[39]See para. B 1.4 of the Memorandum of Understanding, *Supplementary Agreements between the United Kingdom Government* in relation to Scotland. Identical provisions can be found in para. B. 4.9–4.11 for Wales and B 3.4 for Northern Ireland.

[40]See para. B 1.4 of the Memorandum of Understanding, *Supplementary Agreements between the United Kingdom Government* in relation to Scotland. Identical provisions can be found in para. B. 4.13 for Wales and B 3.4 for Northern Ireland.

[41]See para. B 1.4 of the Memorandum of Understanding, *Supplementary Agreements between the United Kingdom Government* in relation to Scotland. Identical provisions can be found in para. B. 4.14 for Wales and B 3.4 for Northern Ireland.

Westminster. Where officials of the devolved administrations attend negotiations, their overriding responsibility will be to "support and advance the single UK negotiating line which they will have played a part in developing."[42] A result of this is that, where the UK government and the Westminster government are unable to agree on a policy line in the JMC, it seems that representatives of the devolved governments would be obliged to pursue the policy line of the UK government should they still attend the Council of Ministers.

The remainder of the Annex deals with, *inter alia*, the framework for cooperation on the implementation of EU measures,[43] the procedure to be adopted where the UK is subject to infraction proceedings,[44] and some general principles on the scrutiny of EU legislation by devolved administrations.[45] This Concordat is designed to provide the basis for all cooperation between the UK government and devolved governments on the issue of European policy.

In addition to the Concordats outlined above, there is a range of policy-making guidance for officials and Ministers in both the UK and devolved governments. None of this addresses only the issue of European policy making, but it does address issues such as common working arrangements between the devolved and UK governments, and also some guidance for UK government departments on the appropriate procedures to be adopted where UK legislation could have an impact on devolved powers.[46] There is also a concise guide for officials, with the title *Devolution: A Guide for Officials*.[47] This leaflet seeks to enhance cooperation between officials in the UK government and those in devolved administrations by setting out some examples of good administrative practice which ought to be followed. Once again, none of this guidance is aimed specifically at European policy making, although some of the principles, such as the requirement that there ought to be "enough time for proper circulation and consideration of papers and proposals" and "consulting the Devolved Administrations early on anything which bears on their interests", are clearly principles which should bear heavily on matters relating to European policy in light of the Concordat.

---

[42]See para. B 1.4 of the Memorandum of Understanding, *Supplementary Agreements between the United Kingdom Government* in relation to Scotland. Identical provisions can be found in para. B. 4.15 for Wales and B 3.4 for Northern Ireland.

[43]See para. B 1.4 of the Memorandum of Understanding, *Supplementary Agreements between the United Kingdom Government* in relation to Scotland. Identical provisions can be found in paras. B. 4.16–4.20 for Wales and B 3.4 for Northern Ireland.

[44]See para. B 1.4 of the Memorandum of Understanding, *Supplementary Agreements between the United Kingdom Government* in relation to Scotland. Identical provisions can be found in paras. B. 4.22–4.28 for Wales and B 3.4 for Northern Ireland

[45]See para. B 1.4 of the Memorandum of Understanding, *Supplementary Agreements between the United Kingdom Government* in relation to Scotland. Identical provisions can be found in paras. B. 4.31–4.33 for Wales and B 3.4 for Northern Ireland.

[46]See http://www.justice.gov.uk/guidance/devolutionguidancenotes.htm (accessed 15 June 2010).

[47]Ministry of Justice (no date) *Devolution: A Guide for Officials* London: Ministry of Justice. Available at: http://www.justice.gov.uk/docs/devolution_guide_officials.pdf (accessed 15 June 2010).

II. The Role of the Joint Ministerial Committee (JMC)

It was noted above that where officials cannot reach agreement on a common line on European policy, and where such matters cannot be resolved via correspondence, the Concordat states that matters should be referred to the Joint Ministerial Committee.[48] The JMC is the body that has been created where Ministers of the UK government and those of the devolved administrations can meet and discuss matters of policy. The constitution and rules of operation of the JMC are set out in Annex A of the Memorandum of Understanding. The JMC has four terms of reference, of which two are of particular interest for the purposes of this discussion. The first term of reference is "to consider non-devolved matters which impinge on devolved responsibilities and devolved matters which impinge on non-devolved responsibilities".[49] The second term of reference of interest is "to consider disputes between the administrations".[50] Annex A then goes on to offer a particular consideration of the JMC's role in European policymaking, when it states in para. A 1.9:

> The JMC – chaired for this purpose by the Foreign Secretary (or his representative) – will also operate as one of the principal mechanisms for consultation on UK positions on EU issues which affect devolved matters. The fact that rapid decisions have to be taken on EU issues to meet the timetable of negotiations in the Council of Ministers, as well as the Government's own wish to involve the devolved administrations as fully as possible in discussions on the formulation of UK policy positions, necessitates a mechanism which enables the lead UK Minister where necessary to consult other UK Government Ministers and their counterparts in the devolved administrations simultaneously. In this functional format, it is likely that the majority of business will be conducted through correspondence, although meetings will also be convened where necessary.

The JMC has been the subject of considerable scrutiny by political scientists in the UK, as its role in the devolution process is considered to be central.[51] In general, the role of the JMC in its European guise has been deemed to be a success, although the use of it and the manner in which it has been used to disseminate information to the devolved administrations has varied with the approach taken by various Foreign Secretaries in the UK government. As an example, Bulmer et al. found that when Jack Straw was Foreign Secretary he made considerable use of the JMC to provide information and foster debate between the UK and devolved governments.[52] The JMC's role has delivered considerable cooperation between

---

[48]See para. B 1.4 of the Memorandum of Understanding, *Supplementary Agreements between the United Kingdom Government* in relation to Scotland. Identical provisions can be found in para. B. 4.7 for Wales and B 3.4 for Northern Ireland.

[49]See para. B 1.4 of the Memorandum of Understanding, *Supplementary Agreements between the United Kingdom Government* in relation to Scotland. Identical provisions can be found in paras. A. 1.2(a) for Wales and B 3.4 for Northern Ireland*Ibid.* para. A 1.2(a).

[50]See para. B 1.4 of the Memorandum of Understanding, *Supplementary Agreements between the United Kingdom Government* in relation to Scotland. Identical provisions can be found in paras. A. 1.2(a) for Wales and B 3.4 for Northern Ireland*Ibid.* para. A 1.2(d).

[51]See, in particular, Burch et al. (2005) and Bulmer et al. (2006), pp. 75–93.

[52]Bulmer et al. (2006), p. 83.

the UK and devolved governments[53] and the broader framework has allowed for the devolved governments to have access to UKRep, the UK's team of civil servants engaged in European policy matters.[54] In their final analysis of the role and impact of the JMC, Bulmer et al. argue that

> Within the key relationship between the [devolved governments] and UK central government...there has been a major recalibration of the pre-existing arrangements for making EU policy within the United Kingdom, one that has involved a measure of give and take between both parties.[55]

It is important to note at this stage that the JMC has no formal legal status beyond that given to it in the Memorandum of Understanding and the relevant Concordats. It is not provided for in the Acts of Parliament that create the formal legal framework for the devolution settlement. This has the advantage of creating a considerable degree of flexibility and fluidity in what is a dynamic relationship between the UK and devolved governments, but has the disadvantage that the devolved governments have few entrenched legal rights to consultation on European policy making. It has been argued that the main route for devolved governments to pursue their interests in EU policymaking is via the UK's official representation to the European Union. The devolved governments' access to EU policy making via such formal channels has been described as "conditional and dependant".[56] In order for the devolved governments to be successful in pursuing their policy interests via the formal route using the UK's formal representation to the EU, they must "balance their policy interests with the rules of engagement imposed on them via the prevalent Whitehall culture".[57]

III. The Potential Role of the Courts

The system of devolution in the UK does not envisage a significant juridification of the relationship between the devolved governments and the UK government. The Memorandum of Understanding and Concordats on the issue of European policy making are clear on this matter. Paragraph 2 of the Memorandum of Understanding states:

> This Memorandum is a statement of political intent, and should not be interpreted as a binding agreement. It does not create legal obligations between the parties. It is intended to be binding in honour only.

---

[53]It is important to note that the literature reflects the interface between the UK and Scottish and Welsh devolved governments, as the Northern Ireland government has been suspended in the period when much of this research took place.

[54]See Burch et al. (2005), p. 471.

[55]Bulmer et al. (2006), p. 83.

[56]Bulmer et al. (2006), p. 86.

[57]Bulmer et al. (2006), p. 86.

Furthermore, in paragraph 3 of the Memorandum of Understanding, it is provided that

> ...the four administrations may prepare Concordats or make other less formal arrangements to deal with the handling of procedural, practical or policy matters between them. Concordats are not intended to be legally binding, but to serve as working documents.

It is clear, then, that neither the Memorandum of Understanding nor the Concordats on coordination of European Union policy issues are intended to be legally binding. It is undoubtedly the case that political pressure may be exerted to ensure that both sides adhere to the requirements of the documents, but litigation on the content or adherence to the Memorandum of Understanding or Concordats seems to be most unlikely. Rawlings suggested that it might be possible to argue that the Memorandum of Understanding and Concordats create a legitimate expectation that might be enforced by the courts,[58] or alternatively that a failure to adhere to the terms of a Concordat could provoke judicial review on the grounds of irrationality[59] or failure to take account of a relevant consideration (i.e. the existence of the commitment in the Concordat itself).[60]

The issue which has the most potential to arise in a judicial review claim is probably that of legitimate expectation. To what extent can it be said that the Memorandum of Understanding and the Concordats engender a legitimate expectation that they will be enforceable in the courts, particularly in light of the paragraphs quoted above? Even though the Memorandum of Understanding and the Concordats themselves may not create a legitimate expectation that will be enforced by the courts, it may be that the continued practice of adherence to the terms of them could create such an expectation.[61] The potential for such an expectation to be enforced in the context of the Memorandum of Understanding and Concordats is highly uncertain, and the courts are not generally willing to interfere in intergovernmental matters. Rawlings and Scott both consider that the courts are unlikely to intervene significantly in the intergovernmental processes that are in some way codified by these 'soft law' instruments.[62]

Given that there is unlikely to be significant recourse to the courts in this relationship between the devolved and UK governments, and also given the focus placed on confidentiality of negotiations and cooperation between the parties, there

---

[58]Rawlings (2000), pp. 257–286 at pp. 283–284.

[59]Rawlings (2000), p. 283. The classic case on judicial review of irrational decisions is *Associated Provincial Picture Houses* v. *Wednesbury Corporation* [1948] 1 KB 223.

[60]Rawlings (2000), p. 283. The case of *R* v. *Human Fertilisation and Embryology Authority, ex p Blood* [1997] 2 WLR 806.

[61]Although there are no cases on this point in relation to Concordats etc. there are a number of cases which assert that the adoption of a particular practice can lead to an enforceable legitimate expectation. See, e.g., *R (BAPIO Action Ltd.)* v. *Secretary of State for the Home Department* [2008] UKHL 27, [2008] 2 WLR 1073 is a recent example of a decision by the House of Lords asserting such a principle. See Fordham (2008) , para. 41.2.1 and 41.2.3.

[62]Rawlings (2000), pp. 283–284 and Scott (2001), pp. 21–48, esp. pp. 31–32.

are significant concerns about the lack of transparency and accountability in the regime created by the Memorandum of Understanding and Concordats.[63] Although the relationship between the devolved and UK governments requires a degree of confidentiality, there may be some concern over the general lack of clarity about the operation of the Concordat and the roles of the various parties in influencing the UK's line on European policy. The Westminster Parliament appears to have taken relatively little interest in the operation of the Concordats, with no investigation by the Public Administration Select Committee, though there is evidence of the Scottish Parliament's European and External Relations Committee taking a somewhat stronger interest in this issue.[64]

There is one area where the courts retain a potential role in matters relating to European policy. It was noted above that, although the issue of official representation to the EU is retained by the UK government, the implementation of European legislation where the issue concerned is a devolved competence lies with the devolved governments. There is, of course, potential for a disagreement between the UK government and devolved governments over whether a particular matter falls within a devolved competence or is retained by the Westminster Parliament. Where such a dispute arises, the devolution legislation provides for a judicial solution.[65] In essence, where there is a question of competence, this might be referred to the courts and might ultimately be appealed or remitted to the Judicial Committee of the Privy Council as the final court of appeal on devolution issues.[66] The potential for this to happen in relation to European matters is clearly envisaged by paragraph B 4.8 of the Common Annex to the Concordats.

H. Devolved Competences and the European Court of Justice

Little consideration appears to have been given in the legislation leading to devolution or in the concordats to the potential role of the devolved governments before the European Court of Justice. It is possible that the European Union could encroach on devolved competences, and yet it is clear from Art. 263 TFEU (ex 230 EC) that the devolved governments do not enjoy privileged standing before the European Court of Justice, and so they may only challenge the legality of European

---

[63] Scott (2001), pp. 21–48, esp. pp. 31–32 and Rawlings (2000), pp. 281–282.

[64] See Scottish Parliament, *Report on an Inquiry into the Scrutiny of European Legislation*, Edinburgh: Scottish Parliament, 2007, Scottish Parliament Paper 783. Available at: http://www.scottish.parliament.uk/business/committees/europe/reports-07/eur07-02.htm (accessed 15 June 2010).

[65] This is provided for in Schedule 6 of the Scotland Act 1998, Schedule 10 of the Northern Ireland Act 1998 and Schedule 9 of the Government of Wales Act 2006. See Burrows 2000, chapter 6 for a more detailed account of the process and procedure.

[66] The role of the Judicial Committee of the Privy Council will be removed and it will be replaced by the UK's new Supreme Court when this comes into being in October 2009. See section 40(4)(b) and Schedule 9 of the Constitutional Reform Act 2005.

measures if these measures are of "direct and individual concern" for the purposes of Art. 263(4) (ex Art. 230(4) EC). This means that the devolved governments are unlikely to find themselves in a position to launch a direct challenge before the European Court of Justice, other than insofar as a decision might be addressed directly to one of the devolved governments themselves. There are no examples at present of the devolved administrations in the UK bringing an action before the European Court of Justice.

In many other countries, where regional governments enjoy exclusive competences, there is no doubt that this would be a highly problematic issue. However, it is important to remember that, in the UK, the Westminster Parliament must implement all European measures for England, while the devolved authorities have responsibility for implementation in their territories. As such, the Westminster government will have a strong interest in challenging any European legislation that it believes to be unlawful, as it will be responsible for its implementation in England.

Should one of the devolved governments wish to launch a challenge to the legality of a particular piece of EU legislation that is considered to be unlawful, it seems most likely that the government would need to enter into discussions about a possible challenge under Art. 263 TFEU (ex 230 EC) by the UK government.

I. Representation in the Committee of the Regions

Scotland, Northern Ireland and Wales all have representatives in the Committee of the Regions. In total, the UK has 24 full seats in the Committee of the Regions, with 4 allocated to Scotland, 2 to Wales and 2 to Northern Ireland.[67] Paragraph B 3.29 of the Common Annex to the Memorandum of Understanding places an obligation on the devolved governments to nominate persons for their share of the Representatives in the Committee of the Regions. Such nominations are then subject to approval by the Foreign Secretary in the UK government, although it is unlikely that any nomination would be rejected, other than in exceptional circumstances. London makes recommendations to the UK government in accordance with the arrangements for England[68] and presently has five members of the Committee of the Regions.

[67]See Department for Communities and Local Government (No Date) *Procedure for Selecting Persons to be Proposed as English Members of the 2006/2010 Committee of the Regions* London: Department for Communities and Local Government. Available at http://www.communities.gov.uk/localgovernment/360902/international/localgovernanceinternationally/theeuropeanunion/procedureselecting/ (accessed 15 June 2010).

[68]See Department for Communities and Local Government (No Date) *Procedure for Selecting Persons to be Proposed as English Members of the 2006/2010 Committee of the Regions* London: Department for Communities and Local Government. Available at http://www.communities.gov.uk/localgovernment/360902/international/localgovernanceinternationally/theeuropeanunion/procedureselecting/ (accessed 15 June 2010).

J. Alternative Methods of Influence: Representative Offices and Other Means

It was noted in the introduction to this paper that the devolved governments are not restricted solely to formal representations to the EU via the formal mechanisms described above. Paragraph B 4.27 of the Common Annex to the Concordats expressly states that the devolved governments are free to open a representative office in Brussels provided that they do not endeavour to alter the UK's formal arrangements for representations to the EU. Each of the devolved governments has chosen to open such an office.[69] These offices have been viewed as an important mechanism for devolved governments to become involved in the complex web of lobbying and policy influencing that is required in order to exercise influence in European Union policymaking.[70] Other than insofar as the issue is addressed in the common Annex to the Concordats, there is no further legal or quasi-legal regulation of the ability of the devolved administrations to engage in what Bomberg and Peterson have characterised as "non-institutional channels of influence".[71]

Bulmer et al. suggest that these regional offices have generally operated within the broad framework laid down by UKRep, though they have also served a number of other purposes. In particular, the Brussels offices have often been used to create coalitions of Members of the European Parliament representing the devolved areas on issues of common interest, and also to create similar coalitions of members of the Committee of the Regions.[72] These offices have had evident value for the devolved administrations, permitting them to influence policy making outside the formal channels and also creating a base in Brussels where the activities of the devolved administrations can have their focus.

In addition to the representative offices, the devolved governments have engaged in a number of other mechanisms that have permitted them to exercise influence on European policymaking. In particular, all the devolved governments have joined RegLeg,[73] a network of sub-national authorities with legislative power in the European Union. These policy networks offer an alternative route to influence European policy making, and also allow for the building of co-operative strategies with regions from other countries that might possess common interests.

There are no formal provisions for the representation of the Greater London Authority in European Union policy making. Nonetheless, there is evidence that the

[69]See information on the Scottish office at http://www.scotland.gov.uk/Topics/Government/International-Relations/Europe/Scotland-in-Brussels (accessed 15 June 2010), the Welsh office at http://wales.gov.uk/topics/international/europe/?lang=en (accessed 15 June 2010) and Northern Ireland at http://www.ofmdfmni.gov.uk/index/promoting-ni/onieb/about-the-onieb.htm (accessed 15 June 2010).

[70]See *e.g.* Bomberg and Peterson (1998), pp. 219 – 235, *esp.* pp. 228–232.

[71]Bomberg and Peterson (1998), p. 228.

[72]Bulmer et al. (2006), p. 84.

[73]For more information see http://www.regleg.eu/ (accessed 15 June 2010).

Greater London Authority has endeavoured to engage in the indirect influence of European policy. It has a representative office in Brussels,[74] and also makes use of its five members of the Committee of the Regions.

There is evidence that the regional governments in the UK have been willing to engage in a variety of different activities and policy networks in order to achieve their European policy objectives. The devolved governments have not only concentrated on formal methods of representation via the UK government, but have also joined coalitions of interest and regional groupings where this has aided their policy objectives.

K. Conclusions

The discussion above has aimed to show that the position of the devolved governments in the United Kingdom is somewhat different to that of many of their European counterparts. In particular, the devolved governments have no formal constitutional status or rights beyond those granted by the Acts of the UK Parliament that created the devolved system of government. Ultimately, this is a result of the UK's lack of a written constitution and its constitutional practice, which is in stark contrast to most other EU member states. Furthermore, the courts in the UK have an extremely limited role in the devolution process: there is potential for litigation on the scope of the devolved competences, but it is clear that the 'soft law' elements of the relationship between the UK and devolved governments will see little, if any, judicial involvement.

The discussion above has demonstrated that all relations between the UK government and devolved governments on the issue of European policy making and representation is dealt with through 'soft law' and formal and informal agreements. The Memorandum of Understanding and Concordats provide a general framework for the relationship between the UK and devolved governments, and within that framework is a need for cooperation and understanding between the UK and devolved administrations. The formal channels of influence are very much in the control of the UK government, though there is considerable evidence that the MoU and Concordats have created a framework through which devolved governments have been able to participate effectively in European policy making. The devolved governments have also demonstrated the ability to build capacity to influence European policy through informal methods, such as the creation of Brussels offices and participation in regional policy networks.

Analyses of the system of UK government suggest that the issue of European policy making has led to changes in the general structure of UK governance. Prior to devolution, the UK's strategy towards European policy was considered to be

---

[74]See http://www.london.gov.uk/london_house/index.jsp for more information on London's Brussels office. (Accessed 15 June 2010).

centred only in Westminster, with relatively little regard for regional interests.[75] Since 1997 and the advent of the Labour government in the UK, and the devolution process in 1998, it appears that the UK itself has become more engaged in European policy making.[76] Furthermore, there is some evidence from policy outcomes that regions have been able to influence European policy far more effectively since the advent of devolution.[77] It is clear, however, that the UK government retains considerable power over European policy making. As Gamble notes

> ...the constitutional basis of the United Kingdom has changed in a federal direction, yet in comparative terms it remains a federacy rather than a federation. The supremacy of the Westminster executive has been qualified but not removed.[78]

Within this context, considerable challenges and questions remain. In light of the considerable reliance on cooperation between the devolved governments and the UK government on the issue of European policy, a particular issue of interest will be how the differences in political viewpoint will be dealt with. At the time when devolution was brought about, the Labour party enjoyed a considerable majority in the Westminster Parliament and also controlled the devolved Scottish and Welsh institutions due to its majorities in the Scottish Parliament and Welsh Assembly. Things have now changed, with the Scottish National Party leading a coalition government in Scotland and Labour now in a position whereby it is in coalition with Plaid Cymru (a Welsh nationalist party) in Wales. In these circumstances, it may be that political differences put the present constitutional arrangements under greater strain than when Labour held majorities in the UK and Scottish Parliaments and the devolved assemblies.

Selected Bibliography

Bagehot W (1963) The English constitution. Collins, London

Bomberg E, Peterson J (1998) European Union decision making: the role of sub-national authorities. Polit Stud:219–235; 228–232

Bradley AW, Ewing KD (2007) Constitutional and administrative law, 14th edn. Harlow, Pearson, pp 62–65

Bulmer S, Burch M (2002) British devolution and European policy making: a step-change towards multi-level governance. Polit Européenne:114–136

Bulmer S, Burch M (2005) The Europeanization of UK government: from quiet revolution to explicit step-change? Public Admin:861–890

---

[75]Bulmer and Burch (2005), pp. 861–890.

[76]Bulmer and Burch (2005)

[77]Bulmer et al. 2006, p. 89. This seems to be supported by the Scottish Parliament's recent report on transposition of European legislation, which suggests that Scotland was able to have an effective role in the creation of certain European Directives relating to environmental protection. See Scottish Parliament, *Report on an Inquiry into the Transposition of EU Directives* Edinburgh: Scottish Parliament, 2008, Scottish Parliament Paper 89. Available at: http://www.scottish.parliament.uk/s3/committees/europe/reports-08/eur08-01.htm#3 (accessed 15 June 2010).

[78]Gamble (2006), pp. 19–35 at page 33.

Bulmer S, Burch M, Hogwood P, Scott A (2006) UK devolution and the European union: a tale of cooperative asymmetry? Publius:75–93

Burch M, Gomez R, Hogwood P, Scott A (2005) Devolution, change and European Union policy-making in the UK. Reg Stud:465–475

Burrows N (2000) Devolution. Sweet and Maxwell, London

Department for Constitutional Affairs (2005) Devolution guidance note 9: post-devolution primary legislation affecting Wales. Department for Constitutional Affairs, London

Dicey V (1960) Introduction to the study of the law of the constitution, 10th edn. Macmillan, London

Fordham M (2008) Judicial review handbook, 5th edn. Hart Publishing, Oxford, para. 41.2.1 and 41.2.3

Gamble A (2006) The constitutional revolution in the United Kingdom. Publius:19–35

Hadfield B (1998) The Belfast agreement, sovereignty and the state of the union. Public Law:599–616

Hadfield B (1999) The nature of devolution in Scotland and Northern Ireland: key issues of responsibility and control. Edinburgh Law Rev:3–31

King A (2007) The British constitution. Oxford University Press, Oxford, Chapter 8

Maitland FW (1908) The constitutional history of England: a course of lectures delivered. Cambridge, Cambridge University Press, pp 527–528

Office of the First Minister and Deputy First Minister (2006) Taking our place in Europe: Northern Ireland's European strategy. Office of the First Minister and Deputy First Minister, Belfast

Osmond J (1999) Devolution 'a dynamic and settled process'? Institute of Welsh Affairs, Cardiff, Chapter 5

Rawlings R (2000) Concordats of the constitution. Law Q Rev:257–286

Rawlings R (2005) Hastening slowly: the next stage of Welsh devolution. *Public Law:*824–852

Reid CT, Ross A, Nash H (2008) Producing a real difference? The transposition of community environmental directives in post devolution Scotland and Wales. Scots Law Times:39–41

Scott A (2001) The role of concordats in the new governance of Britain: taking subsidiarity seriously? Edinburgh Law Rev:21–48

Scottish Government (2008) Action plan on European engagement. Edinburgh, Scottish Government, pp 6–8

Trench A (2006) The government of Wales Act 2006: the next steps in devolution for Wales. Public Law:687–696

Turpin C, Tomkins A (2007) British government and the constitution, 6th edn. Cambridge, Cambridge University Press, pp 156–179

Conclusion
The Role of the Regions in the European Union: The "Regional Blindness" of Both the EU and the Member States

Carlo Panara and Alexander De Becker

Introduction

The recent Reform Treaty signed by the EU Member States in Lisbon on 13 December 2007 (hereafter also Treaty of Lisbon or ToL) constitutes a new step in the European integration process.[1] New institutional mechanisms have been installed and new powers have been transferred to the EU level by this Treaty. The process of European integration has always involved the transfer of powers from the Member States to the Union, and the constitutional impact of such a transfer of powers has always been the subject of considerable debate.[2]

Carlo Panara is Senior Lecturer in EU and Public Law at the School of Law at Liverpool John Moores University, UK. Alexander De Becker is part-time Professor at the University of Amsterdam in Public Law and Labour Law, Lecturer in Public and Labour Law at the Faculty of Law and Criminology of Vrije Universiteit Brussel (VUB), Belgium, and Postdoctoral researcher of the Belgian Scientific Research Foundation. The authors wish to express their gratitude to Alicia Chicharro Lázaro, Jacques Colom, Harald Eberhard, Mike Varney and Stefano Villamena for their precious advice and help. The authors remain solely responsible for any errors.

[1]The ToL entered into force on 1 December 2009 after ratification by the 27 Member States.

[2]The recent ruling of the German Federal Constitutional Court on the compatibility of the ToL with the Basic Law can be cited as an example of this tension. In this ruling ("Lisbon ruling") the Court stressed that the transfer of powers from the Federal Republic of Germany to the EU may not be so far going that the Member States lose their space and opportunity to develop political initiatives upon economical, cultural and social issues. See the ruling of 30 June 2009 (the English translation is available at http://www.bverfg.de/entscheidungen/es20090630_2bve000208en.html, last checked on 30 October 2009).

C. Panara (✉)
School of Law, Liverpool John Moores University, John Foster Building, 98 Mount Pleasant, Liverpool L3 5UZ, UK
e-mail: c.panara@ljmu.ac.uk

A. De Becker
Faculteit Recht en Criminologie, Vrije Universiteit Brussel, Pleinlaan 2, 1050 Brussel, Belgium
and
Faculteit rechtsgeleerdheid, Universiteit van Amsterdam, Oudemanhuispoort 4-6, 1012 Amsterdam, The Netherlands
e-mail: alexander.de.becker@vub.ac.be

C. Panara and A. De Becker (eds.), *The Role of the Regions in EU Governance*,
DOI 10.1007/978-3-642-11903-3,

Such a transfer of powers becomes particularly complicated when the Member State is a federal or a regional state. Indeed, in such cases, the competences transferred to the EU level may well be, at the domestic level, within the domain of those sub-state entities we call "Regions".[3]

On a Member State level, the problem arises of how to put the latter in the condition to participate in decision-making regarding the transfer of their powers. The problem is not an easy one to tackle in that the powers are normally transferred to the EU through international treaties, whose stipulation and ratification are, as a rule, the task of the Member States' central organs.[4]

On the EU level, once the competences of sub-national authorities have been assigned to the EU, it carries them out by means of its own institutions which consist of individuals who are independent of the Member States (Commission and Parliament) or of representatives of the latter (Council). This specific duality is linked to the EU being an intergovernmental and a supranational organisation at the same time. For a long time, this situation – which has been described by Hans-Peter Ipsen as the "*Landesblindheit*" (regional blindness) of the Community[5] – has made the governments of the Member States, represented in the Council by their ministers, the protagonists in the Community decision-making process. This occurred even when issues on the Council's agenda were not within the province of the central government but of sub-national entities when considered from the perspective of the domestic level.

This, along with the transfer of state powers to the EU level, is a crucial problem for a decentralised state participating in the European "federalising process".[6] Without adequate forms of participation for sub-national entities in the making of EU law, we are faced with a real paradox. Due to the fact that powers have been transferred to the supranational level, a significant proportion of the competences reserved for such entities by the national constitution will ultimately be exercised in Brussels. They will be exercised (in conjunction with all other Member States' governments) by the central government which the state constitution sought to

[3]Note that in this article we call "Regions" not only the Regions in regional states, but – in a way which is consistent with the European primary law – the level of government that, both in regional and federal settings, is at the intermediate level between the state and the local authorities. Accordingly, we call "Regions" the German and the Austrian *Länder*, the Italian, Belgian, and French Regions, the Belgian Communities, the Spanish *Comunidades autónomas*, and the authorities with devolved powers in Scotland, Wales and Northern Ireland. In the case of Italy, the term "Region" covers also the Autonomous Provinces of Trento and Bolzano which have powers very similar to those of the Regions.

[4]The simplified revision procedure introduced by the ToL at Art. 48(6) TEU (Treaty amendments passed by the European Council by unanimity) cannot be used to confer more powers on the EU. Such "simplified" amendments can furthermore enter into force only after their approval by all the Member States in accordance with their respective constitutional requirements.

[5]Ipsen (1966), p. 256.

[6]On the concept of federalising process see Friedrich (1968). On the concept of federal state and regional state as a form of government in the framework of the type of decentralised State see Volpi (1995), p. 367 ff. and spec. p. 407 ff.

exclude from certain fields. But what sense is there in maintaining the regional level of government if regional powers have to a large extent been absorbed by the Union?

A further problem is that sub-national entities, under Art. 263 TFEU (ex 230 EC), do not have a privileged status regarding action for the annulment of EU acts before the Court of Justice. This results in a situation where the defence of their prerogatives against possible invasions of competence by EU institutions are entrusted to their national government. However, the national government may have no intention of seeking recourse: the national government, by going to Brussels to play its role in the EU legislative process, might take the opportunity to usurp powers that are not granted to the national level in the state's constitution.

Once issued by EU institutions, EU law must be applied and directives must be implemented. The central state or the sub-national entities will generally do so in conformity with the distribution of powers at the domestic level. Problems also arise in this context: what is to be done in the case when a sub-state entity does not comply with such obligations stemming from the Treaties? From the point of view of the Union, the responsibility for a lack of respect for EU obligations falls on the Member State and not on its constituent sub-state entities.

An answer to the issues under scrutiny has come both from EU law and the constitutional laws of the different Member States. This study will focus on the solutions adopted by the EU and by the most representative decentralised Member States (Austria, Belgium, France,[7] Germany, Italy, Spain, and UK) to allow the participation of the Regions in EU law and policy making. The objective is to assess whether the mechanisms set up at national and at EU level represent an adequate answer to the aforementioned problems, or whether unresolved issues remain.

While evaluating this system, one must be aware that there is not only the need to safeguard the rights of the Regions, but there is also the need to prevent their rights of participation from becoming an excessive constraint for the national government, capable of precluding it from conducting negotiations within the Council in an effective way. The need to safeguard the rights of the Regions must be reconciled with the requirement for proper institutional mechanisms on both the domestic level and the EU level. Striking a balance between proper governance of the "EU of twenty-seven" and introducing legal instruments assuring the rights of the Regions or, at least, recognising their role, is an extremely difficult task.

Research on the participation rights of the Regions in the EU decision-making process is vital in order to understand the current and future developments of the EU. Important documents emphasise sub-state entities' role in European governance and outline a system of multilevel governance in which the sub-state level

[7]Notwithstanding its strong Jacobin tradition as "unitary centralised state", France has undertaken during the last three decades a progressive transformation of its constitutional setting into a "unitary decentralised state". The French Regions have formally been established by the Act of 2 March 1982. Note on this topic Gatti-Montain (1985), pp. 285–320. It will become clear in this article that the French decentralisation still presents fundamental differences from the legal status of the Regions in the other researched federal and decentralised countries.

operates besides the EU and the Member States. These documents include the Commission's 2001 *White Paper on European Governance* and the more recent 2009 Committee of the Regions' *White Paper on Multilevel Governance*.[8]

The ToL added even more interest to the research in this particular field.[9] Art. 5 TFEU (ex 5 EC) expressly recognises the important role of the Regions and of the local levels of government. It actually states that "in areas which do not fall within its exclusive competence, the Union shall act only if and insofar as the objectives of the proposed action cannot be sufficiently achieved by the Member States, *either at central or at regional and local level*, but can rather, by reason of the scale or effects of the proposed action, be better achieved at Union level".[10] This provision constitutes the legal basis of the subsidiarity principle. In order to comply with subsidiarity, the EU needs to take into account not only the national level but also the sub-national levels of government within the Member States.

The Transfer of Powers of the Regions from the National Level to the EU

It is undisputed that at the present stage of the European integration membership of the EU belongs only to States and not to the Regions.[11] However, many powers conferred on the EU are powers that under national constitutions fall, *entirely or in part*, within the sphere of competence of the Regions. Such a transfer of powers to the EU has the potential to alter the balance of powers between state and sub-state entities enshrined by the national constitutions in each Member State.

Belgium is the Member State where the rights of the federate entities are guaranteed on a maximum level according to the constitutional principle "*in foro interno et in foro externo*".[12] From this principle derives that the Belgian sub-state

[8]Commission of the European Communities (2001). Committee of the Regions (2009). The Committee of the Regions' *White Paper* suggests that "The conditions for good multilevel governance actually depend on the Member States ... The principles and mechanisms of consultation, coordination, cooperation and evaluation recommended at Community level must firstly be applied within the Member States" (p. 7).

[9]This topic is to regard as one falling within the area of the European public law, as defined by Birkinshaw (2001), p. 4: "The impact of EU law and the ECHR on the laws of Member States, and the impact in turn, of the law of Member States on EU law, in particular, as well as on each other. This is what I have in mind when speaking of European Public Law".

[10]Emphasis added.

[11]Lenaerts et al. (2005), pp. 520–531.

[12]Art. 167(3) of the Belgian Constitution provides the following: "The Community and Regional Governments conclude each one in so far as it is concerned, treaties regarding matters that fall within the competences of their Parliament. These treaties take effect only after they have received approval of the Parliament".

entities shall be able to decide on the allocation to supranational organisations of the exclusive powers they enjoy on the domestic level. A treaty transferring powers of the Belgian Regions or Communities to the EU can only enter into force in Belgium if the parliaments of *all* the sub-state entities concerned consent to it as far as their competences are at stake in the given treaty.[13] As a result, every sub-state parliament has a veto power regarding the ratification of the treaty by Belgium.

The Belgian arrangement is unique among the EU Member States. If we consider Germany, another federal state, we find participation rights of the *Länder* in the decision on the transfer of powers to the EU. Each single *Land* does not, however, possess a veto power. In the case of Germany, a new Treaty requires the passage of a law with the consent of the *Bundesrat*, which is the constitutional body representing the *Länder* at the federal level. Normally a two-thirds majority within the *Bundesrat* (as well as within the *Bundestag*) is required.[14] This legal position implies the recognition of an indirect participation of the *Länder* – i.e. participation through the *Bundesrat*. This also means that the *Länder* are involved in the decision on the transfer of powers as a "layer of government" rather than as individual entities.

The German pattern is similar to the solution introduced in Austria in 2008. Treaties amending the founding Treaties require the approval of both the *Nationalrat* and the *Bundesrat*[15] with a quorum necessary to amend the Federal Constitution – i.e. two-thirds majority in both chambers of the Parliament.[16]

[13]The Belgian federal construction foresees a double divide of the sub-national entities. In Belgium there are three Communities (Flemish, French speaking and German speaking), which are competent for person-bound matters (culture, education, etc.), and three Regions (Flemish, Walloon and Brussels-Capital). The Regions are competent for territorial matters, such as economy, fisheries, agriculture, labour market, etc.

[14]Art. 23(1) of the Basic Law (henceforth BL, the German constitution of 1949; the name "Basic Law" is the literal translation of *Grundgesetz*). The *Bundesrat* (meaning "Federal Council") is a constitutional body where the Executives of the 16 *Länder* are represented at federal level. The members of the *Bundesrat* are not elected but appointed by the various *Länder* cabinets. Each *Land* is allocated a number of votes (from a minimum of three to a maximum of six) on the basis of the size of the respective population. The *Bundesrat* participates in federal legislation and administration and in matters related to the EU. The *Bundestag* (meaning "Federal Assembly") is instead a democratically elected chamber representing the people.

[15]According to Art. 24 of the Federal Constitutional Law (*Bundes-Verfassungsgesetz*, henceforth also referred to as B-VG), the Federal Parliament in Austria consists of two chambers: the *Nationalrat* (meaning "National Council") and the *Bundesrat* (meaning "Federal Council"). The *Nationalrat* is directly elected by the people for a period of 5 years (Arts. 26 and 27 B-VG). The members of the *Bundesrat* are elected by the *Landtage* (meaning "Regional Assemblies"). The *Länder* are represented in the *Bundesrat* in proportion to the number of nationals in each *Land* (Arts. 34 and 35 B-VG).

[16]See Art. 50 paras. 1 and 4 of the Federal Constitutional Law. Before the new provision entered into force at the beginning of 2008, special constitutional acts (passed by a 2/3 majority in both chambers) were enacted for each amendment to the founding Treaties. The 2008 constitutional amendment formulated the qualified majority requirement as a general rule.

The main difference between the German pattern and the position in Austria is that the Austrian *Bundesrat* consists of representatives elected by the Regional Assemblies (*Landtage*). Furthermore, these representatives enjoy a free mandate and are not bound – unlike the *Länder* representatives in the German *Bundesrat* – by any instruction from the *Land* Executive. Therefore, the position of a *Land* representative within the Austrian *Bundesrat* may depart from that of its Executive.

The participation of the Spanish *Comunidades autónomas* in the decision on the transfer of powers to the EU is weak when compared to that of the German and Austrian *Länder*. The Spanish Senate is not a full "chamber of the regions" like the German or the Austrian *Bundseräte*, and the representation of the *Comunidades autónomas* as a proportion of the membership of the Spanish Senate is not significant.[17] Furthermore, although the Senate is involved in the ratification of new treaties, the Congress[18] still retains the power to overcome the Senate's possible veto by absolute majority, or even, but only after 2 months, by simple majority.[19] Thus, the involvement of the *Comunidades autónomas* in the decision on the transfer of powers to the EU is therefore not particularly significant.

A similar situation prevails in France, where foreign affairs are largely within the domain of the President of Republic. In principal, both Chambers of the Parliament, i.e. the National Assembly and the Senate, are involved in the ratification process of a treaty. However, the vote of the Senate – where the territorial communities of the Republic are represented – can be overruled. In a case where the Senate opposes the ratification of a treaty, the Government can, as a matter of last resort, confer the right of final say to the directly elected National Assembly.[20] Furthermore, the President can actually limit the number of treaties undergoing "authorisation" by the Parliament: according to Art. 11 of the Constitution, the President can submit the ratification of a treaty to referendum on a proposal of the Government. This is a deviation from the normal functioning of the institutions. The President exercised this constitutional right in the case of the Accession Treaty of 1972, the Treaty of Maastricht and the Treaty Establishing a Constitution for Europe. In most cases, however, the *Conseil Constitutionnel* (the French constitutional council) has required a constitutional revision prior to ratification.[21] In the context of a constitutional

---

[17]The Spanish Senate consists of 264 members. 208 members are directly elected by popular vote. The other 56 are appointed by the regional legislatures.

[18]It may be worth to note that the Spanish Council of State (the Government's supreme advisory body) proposed in 2006 to reshape the Spanish Senate in a way similar to the German and the Austrian *Bundesräte*. This bid has, however, not been translated yet into any political initiative. On this issue read Rubio Llorente and Alvarez Junco (2006).

[19]Art. 90 of the Spanish Constitution.

[20]Art. 45(4) of the French Constitution.

[21]Art. 54 of the French Constitution provides a specific regulation. In the case where the entry into force of a Treaty demands the modification of some constitutional provisions, the ratification process can only start after the revision of the Constitution. The competences of the *Conseil Constitutionnel* include consultative tasks as well as judicial tasks.

amendment, the Senate would act on a par with the National Assembly and would therefore have a veto power. This approach was adopted in the cases of the Treaties of Maastricht, Amsterdam, and Lisbon. Such an approach was not, however, followed for the Treaty of Nice.[22]

The French Senate's aim in the framework of the constitutional amendment procedure has traditionally been the defence of its own constitutional prerogatives rather than the defence of the interests of the territorial communities. We have to bear in mind that, like the Spanish Senate, the French Senate is not a "chamber of the regions". The representatives of the Regions are a minority among the "*grands électeurs*" of the Senate in comparison to those representing other levels of government.[23] In sum, the representation of the Regions in the Senate is too weak and therefore the French Regions are not significantly involved in the decision on the transfer of their powers to the EU. This state of affairs has not been modified by the constitutional reform in 2008.[24]

In Italy and in the UK, there exists no legislative basis for regional involvement. The Italian Senate is in fact elected on a regional basis but it does not consist of regional representatives. In the UK, foreign relations are under the exclusive control of the Westminster Parliament and of the British Government. Such an arrangement is perfectly consistent with the fact that all the powers of the devolved authorities stem from legislation passed by the Westminster Parliament, so only the Westminster Parliament has the right to transfer powers to the EU.

[22]Given the fact that the *Conseil d'Etat* did not identify any constitutional threat in the text of the Treaty of Nice, the French Government decided that the consultation of the *Conseil Constitutionnel* was not necessary. Art. 54 of the French Constitution does not foresee an obligation to consult the *Conseil Constitutionnel* in any case when a Treaty is ratified. However, until 2001, the *Conseil Constitutionnel* was always consulted in the ratification process of European treaties [read Rozenberg and Lequesne (2000), p. 451]. Since the constitutional reform of 4 February 2008, every Treaty which foresees the accession of new Member States to the EU will be submitted to a referendum (Art. 88(5) of the French Constitution). The French Parliament (National Assembly and Senate) can derogate from this principle with a 3/5 majority. Art. 88(5) of the French Constitution provides also that a referendum cannot be organised for those accessions which are a consequence of an intergovernmental convocation prior to 1 February 2004.

[23]Senators are elected indirectly by approximately 150,000 local elected officials ("*grands électeurs*"), including regional councillors, department councillors, mayors, city councillors and their delegates in large towns, and deputies of the National Assembly. Until September 2004, the Senate had 321 senators, each elected to a 9-year term. On that date, the term was reduced to 6 years, while the number of senators will progressively increase to 346 in 2010 to reflect changes in the country's demographics. Senators were elected in thirds every 3 years; this will also change to one-half of their number every 3 years.

[24]The constitutional reform of 4 February 2008 modified Title XV of the French Constitution to update it with necessary innovations due to the ratification of Treaty of Lisbon. A second constitutional reform of 23 July 2008 focused mainly on the role of the President and the Parliament. This second reform strengthened the role of French citizens through the use of referendum.

The Expansion of the EU Sphere of Competence in Ways Other than a Treaty Amendment

An expansion of EU competences can be achieved without a Treaty amendment. First of all this may happen by means of the "flexibility clause" contained in Art. 352 TFEU. This provision performs the role which was previously that of Art. 308 EC. Art. 352(1) applies when EU action is required to achieve one of the objectives set out in the Treaties but the Treaties have not provided the necessary powers. In such a situation, the Council can adopt a measure by acting unanimously on a proposal from the Commission and after obtaining the consent of the European Parliament. Do the Regions in decentralised Member States have a say if the measure in question touches upon their powers? And is their contribution to the adoption of this measure truly influential? The answer largely depends on the quality of the regional participation rights in the EU law-making phase recognised by each individual Member State. Participation rights are the focus of Sect. C below. In this section, we will be looking at those EU and national provisions specifically dealing with the problem posed by the "flexibility clause".

At the EU level, any chamber of a national parliament can play a role in the framework of the so-called "early warning mechanism".[25] Each chamber can submit to the Commission a reasoned opinion on the non-compliance of a proposal with the principle of subsidiarity. By so doing, the chamber can try to persuade the Commission to withdraw the proposal or to amend it in a way that makes it respectful of the principle.[26] But we have already noted that only Germany and Austria, among the Member States, have an authentic "chamber of the regions", whereas in other decentralised Member States, there is no representation of the Regions in the national parliament (Italy and UK) or this representation is weak (Belgium,[27] Spain and France). Furthermore, there is no guarantee that the Commission will take the opinion on board.

At present, only Germany has legislation specifically tackling the issue of Art. 352 TFEU. This legislation was passed to comply with the requirements of the "Lisbon ruling" of the Federal Constitutional Court.[28] In this ruling, the Court established that the ToL is compliant with the BL provided that the national legislative bodies (*Bundestag* and *Bundesrat*) are given sufficient participation rights in the EU law-making and Treaty amendment procedures. German approval

[25]On the early warning mechanism, see Sect. K below.

[26]Arts. 6 and 7 of the Protocol on the Application of the Principles of Subsidiarity and Proportionality (henceforth Protocol on Subsidiarity) attached to the ToL.

[27]The Belgian Senate may not be considered to be a Chamber of the Regions. 21 of the 74 Senators (including three "Royal" Senators: the Princes Philip and Laurent and Princess Astrid) are appointed by the Parliaments of the Communities. 40 Senators are directly elected in "federal" elections. 10 are appointed by the 61 elected Senators themselves. Some proposals have been made to make of the Senate a full Chamber of the Regions but they have not yet been carried forward.

[28]Ruling of the German Federal Constitutional Court of 30 June 2009.

of a measure under Art. 352 (as well as German abstention on it) requires the passing of an act in accordance with Art. 23(1) BL (i.e. an act where the consent of the *Bundesrat* is required). In the absence of such an act, the German representative in the Council must vote against the measure.[29]

Germany is a completely isolated case study. An ad hoc legislation tailored on the "flexibility clause" does not (yet) exist in any of the other Member States subject to our research. This is probably due to the fact that other decentralised Member States prefer to tackle this issue through the provision of participation rights for the Regions in "normal" EU law making (see Sect. C below).

Another way to expand the sphere of competence of the EU without amendments to the Treaty is on the basis of the so-called "bridging clauses". These provisions allow the European Council (or the Council) to pass a procedural change without a Treaty amendment. Such a modification may significantly affect the position of the Regions when it consists in a shift from unanimity to qualified majority voting in the Council. If single Member States lose their veto power in the Council, regional participation rights would be weakened as a result. The Regions should therefore be involved in the decision on the bridging clause if a matter of regional competence is at stake.

Among the national patterns that are subject to analysis, only Germany has introduced specific provisions in this regard. This happened in the wake of the Lisbon ruling. Once again, the other Member States prefer to tackle this issue through the regional participation rights in normal EU lawmaking (see Sect. C below). In line with its approach to the flexibility clause, German approval of the proposed procedural change (as well as the German abstention) requires the passage of a law in accordance with Art. 23(1) BL.[30] This rule applies to the general bridging clause of Art. 48(7) TEU.[31] This provision creates the basis for a shift from unanimity to qualified majority voting in the Council in the area of common security and defence policy and in all policy areas covered by the Treaty on the Functioning of the EU.[32]

---

[29]§ 8 of the Law on the Responsibility of the *Bundestag* and the *Bundesrat* for the European Integration, *Integrationsverantwortungsgesetz* (in acronym, *IntVG*), in *BGBl.*, 2009, I, p. 3022.

[30]§ 4 of the *IntVG*.

[31]The same regime applies to Art. 81(3) TFEU.

[32]The German law (§ 5 and 6 of the *IntVG*) also covers the so-called "special bridging clauses" that is, those bridging clauses, whose scope is sufficiently defined and for which no law under Art. 23 (1) BL is required. They imply the shift from unanimity to qualified majority voting in the Council or the shift from a "special" legislative procedure to the "ordinary" procedure. In these cases, only the approval by the *Bundestag* is normally required. In addition, the approval by the *Bundesrat* is also necessary if the BL requires the consent of the *Bundesrat* to pass a law in that specific area, or it is an area belonging to the legislative competence of the *Länder*. "Special bridging clauses" are provided at: Art. 31(3) TEU (re CFSP); Art. 312(2) TFEU (re the multiannual financial framework); Art. 153(2) TFEU (re social policy); Art. 192(2) TFEU (re environment); Art. 333(1) TFEU (re enhanced cooperation).

Main Areas of Overlap Between the Competences of the Regions and Those of the EU

The Regions from different Member States have different powers. Therefore, the main areas of overlap between the powers of the Regions and those of the EU vary from Member State to Member State. In one of the states that is analysed (the UK), there is considerable *asymmetry* among powers granted to the different regions. Asymmetries are to some extent also present in Spain, Belgium, Italy and France. Thus, it is somewhat difficult to consider the Regions as an homogeneous level of governance with a clear physiognomy of their own within the EU.

It is important at this stage to address one major issue of terminology. Within the framework of this chapter, most of the countries that are subject to our research use the term "concurrent powers". However, the term does not convey the same meaning in all jurisdictions. In general, it always concerns a situation where there is an overlap between the exercise of powers by the national authorities and the exercise of similar powers by regional authorities. Therefore, within the scope of the present article, the term "concurrent powers" is used with reference to the typical meaning it has in the Member States under consideration.

Throughout the Member States subject to our analysis, the impact of EU law and policies is notable above all in the following areas which fall within the competence of the Regions in many of the national patterns addressed in this volume: education and culture (Belgium, Germany, UK and France); building regulation insofar as the EU might be competent to pass regulations in this matter (Belgium, Germany, Austria and Italy); hunting (Belgium, Austria and Italy); fisheries (Belgium, Spain, Italy, Austria and UK); environment (Austria, Spain and Italy); agriculture (Belgium, Austria, Spain, Italy and UK). These subjects fall within the responsibility of the following Council configurations: Education, Youth and Culture; Environment; Agriculture and Fisheries; Competitiveness.

Other important areas of overlap are: social welfare (Austria and Spain); radio/TV (Belgium and Germany); energy (Belgium and UK); economic development (Belgium, UK and France); public procurement law (Austria and Italy); economic planning, industry, transport, health, taxation, and consumer protection (Belgium and Spain).

The Participation of the Regions in the EU Law and Policy Making: The Regions in the Council

The presence of the Regions in the Council, perhaps better described as their representation in the Council, is closely linked to the constitutional evolution that has taken place in many Member States since the establishment of the European Community. A considerable wave of decentralisation seems to have passed through the Member States between the 1970s and the early years of the new century. Major examples of this are the Italian Regions becoming operational in 1970, the full transformation of Belgium into a federal state in 1994, the progressive creation of a "unitary decentralised state" in France since 1982, the introduction of devolution in the UK in 1997, and the constitutional reforms aiming at "re-federalising" Germany in 1994 and 2006.[33]

The original idea that the EU, as an intergovernmental organisation, should not be influenced by the internal organisational structure of its Member States has come under significant pressure due to this evolution. The current attitude of the EU vis-à-vis the representation of the Regions in the Council is totally different from the approach in the past. The original EEC Treaty did not explicitly provide that it was necessary for a Member State to be represented by a member of its national government.[34] The EU institutions interpreted this provision as implying that the representation of the Member States was formally linked to the post of member of a national cabinet.[35]

It was only with the entry into force of the Treaty of Maastricht in 1993 that a new form of representation of the Member States was introduced. The representation of the Member States in the Council should now consist of a representative of each Member State "at ministerial level", authorised to commit the government of that Member State.[36] Due to this modification, there is no longer a doubt on the validity of the representation of a Member State by a minister of a regional government, provided that the representative may commit the Member State and cast its vote.

This new approach, characterised by the fact that the Treaty starts to take into account (some aspects of) the internal organisation of the Member States, opens up new possibilities for the representation of the decentralised Member States in the Council. The Treaty leaves it to the Member States to deal internally with the issue of ensuring adequate representation of its constituent authorities in the Council. The Member States obtain two different sorts of possibilities to organise their representation in the Council: the *internal* cooperation of central government and regional entities, on the one hand, and the *external* representation of the latter in the Council, on the other. Both forms can be and are often used cumulatively.

---

[33]It is also important to also mention the democratisation of Spain and its transformation into a decentralised regional state (*Estado autonómico*) in the 1978 Constitution. Both Belgium and Italy passed significant state reforms in 2001.

[34]Art. 146 of the EEC Treaty provided the following: "The Council shall be composed of representatives of the Member States. Each Government shall delegate to it one of its members".

[35]On this point see Lenaerts et al. (2005), p. 414.

[36]See Art. 16(2) TEU (ex 203 EC). This modification was introduced in the Treaty of Maastricht mainly due to Belgian and German pressure, which desired that their internal federal framework could be hinted at EU-level. On this issue see Lenaerts et al. (2005), p. 414.

Internal Cooperation

Internal cooperation means that the national government and the executive powers of the sub-state entities liaise before a meeting of the Council in order to adopt – if this is possible – a common position. Forms of internal cooperation can be found in all the national case studies that are considered when Council meetings deal with matters belonging to the competence of the Regions.

Three patterns can be isolated. The first pattern ascribes an equal weight to the positions of the national government and of the sub-state governments in establishing a common position.

Belgium is the only example of this first pattern and it can be considered as unique from the comparative point of view. Belgian constitutional law does not recognise a hierarchical relationship between the national authority and the regional authorities. The national government[37] and the regional governments are considered to be "equal partners" in the domestic debate. This has significant consequences. The Belgian representative can only express standpoints in the Council if they have been subject to prior coordination[38] on the domestic level.[39] All Councils on regional matters have to be preceded by a coordination meeting, where each national, regional and community government of Belgium is represented, as well as the Permanent Representative of Belgium to the EU and the attachés of the Communities and the Regions in the Permanent Representation.[40] Once a common position is achieved, the Belgian standpoint will be communicated via the Permanent Representation to the EU and to the federal, regional and community Ministers.[41] The Permanent Representation of Belgium is bound by the common position which is reached in the coordination meeting.

Austria, Germany and Spain may be regarded as a second pattern. The Austrian and the German *Länder*, as well as the Spanish *Comunidades autónomas*, play a significant role in reaching a common position at the domestic level, but they are not treated as complete equals of the national government. This

[37]The term "national government" is used throughout this text to describe what is known in Belgium as the "federal" government.

[38]"Coordination" is the, perhaps unfortunately chosen, official term for the discussion and necessary agreement between the national state government and the regional governments. The term "coordination" is used both in the Dutch and the French versions of the Cooperation Agreement of 8 March 1994 between the Federation, the Communities and the Regions (*Accord de coopération entre l'Etat fédéral, les Communautés et les Régions, relatif à la représentation du Royaume de Belgique au sein du Conseil de Ministres de l'Union européenne*; published in *Moniteur Belge* of 17 November 1994; hereinafter this document will be referred to as Cooperation Agreement). It may be worthwhile to emphasise that no solution is foreseen in cases where no common position can be reached.

[39]Art. 2(5) of the Cooperation Agreement.

[40]Art. 2(2) of the Cooperation Agreement.

[41]Art. 5 of the Cooperation Agreement.

pattern entails the obligation for the national government to consult the Regions. The position of the Regions resulting from this consultation may bind the national government.

In a case where the Austrian *Länder* have adopted a common position the national government is bound to uphold this stance in the Council. The government can only depart from the common position in circumstances where there is a pressing issue of foreign policy or European integration.[42] The common position is outside the scope of the formal competence of the *Bundesrat*. The *Länder* negotiate their common position within the informal framework of an organisation linked to the *Bundesrat* (*Verbindungsstelle des Bundesrats*).

In Germany, the cornerstone of the internal participation system is Art. 23(2) BL. According to this provision, the *Länder* have the right to participate through the *Bundesrat* in matters concerning the EU ("*Angelegenheiten der Europäischen Union*"). The *Bundesrat* has to be involved in EU-related decisions in two circumstances. The first is when the topics on the agenda of the Council are, at the domestic level, topics on which the *Bundesrat* has the right to intervene. The second is when the matter dealt with in the Council falls within the competence of the *Länder*.[43] The weight of the position of the *Bundesrat* varies according to the circumstances. The first possible situation is when an EU proposal affects the interests of the *Länder* without touching on their legislative powers. In such a case, the position does not have binding character and *it must be only taken into account* ("*berücksichtigt*") by the Federal Government. This means that the Federal Government may depart from the position if it considers it appropriate to do so. But there are situations in which the position of the *Bundesrat* acquires a quasi-binding (if not a fully binding) value. This happens when an EU proposal focuses on a matter falling within the legislative competence of the *Länder*, the structure of their authorities or their administrative procedures. The BL says that in such a case the position of the *Bundesrat* must be given "the greatest possible respect" ("*maßgeblich zu berücksichtigen*") by the Federal Government.[44] Whether this expression means that the position of the *Bundesrat* is binding is the subject of some controversy. Attaching binding character to the position may have serious shortcomings. The Federal Government would have its hands too tied when conducting negotiations at the EU level and it could not act with the necessary flexibility. Therefore, it seems preferable to embrace the thesis that the Federal Government would have to do what it can to act in accordance with the opinion of the *Bundesrat*, but that it is allowed to diverge from it when this proves to be in the best interests of the Federal Republic. However, it should be noted that this entire debate on the binding or non-binding character of the *Bundesrat*'s positions has a rather academic character. In practice, it has always been possible to find political

---

[42]Art. 23 d of the Austrian Constitution. The Austrian government has departed from a common position on only three occasions.

[43]Art. 23(4) BL.

[44]Art. 23(5) BL.

solutions capable of preventing a full clash between the *Bundesrat* and the national government.[45]

Spain has a system of internal cooperation which shows similarities with Germany. The Spanish government has to take account of the common position of the *Comunidades autónomas* in matters which are within the competence of the latter. In the meetings of the Council, the national government can be assisted by regional representatives. The Spanish government should normally respect the position agreed in the preparatory meetings with the *Comunidades autónomas*. However, it can exceptionally sacrifice this common position if this is required during the negotiation process in the Council.

The third pattern can be found in Italy and the UK where the role of the regional entities in the search towards a common position is restricted to the consultation of the Regions by the national government.

The role of the Italian Regions in the preparation of Council meetings is rather limited. The Regions may request the examination of EU proposals touching upon matters falling within the legislative competence of the Regions by the State–Regions Conference (a body where the national and the regional executives are represented).[46] However, if no agreement is reached within the Conference, the Government is free to depart from the position expressed by the majority of the Regions. The Regions are also allowed to participate in the meetings of the *Comitato Interministeriale per gli Affari Comunitari Europei* (Interdepartmental Committee for EC Affairs, CIACE in acronym). Within this body, EU issues are discussed in order to determine the negotiating position of the Government.[47] But once again there is no way the Regions can bind the Government to uphold their position in the Council.

The UK is the youngest pupil in the class when we consider the establishment of a link between foreign affairs and devolved entities. In the UK, there is no formal legal basis for the consultation of the devolved entities. The UK government and

---

[45]§ 5(2) of the *Gesetz über die Zusammenarbeit von Bund und Ländern in Angelegenheiten der Europäischen Union* (Act on the Cooperation of the Federation and the *Länder* in Matters related to the EU, EUZBLG in acronym) provides for a conflict resolution mechanism. It establishes that in the case of an insurmountable disagreement with the Federal Government, the *Bundesrat* can confirm its initial position by two-thirds majority. The position would in this way become "decisive" ("*maßgebend*"), probably intended, in this context, as synonymous with "binding". The conflict resolution mechanism of § 5(2) EUZBLG has found no application so far. There has only been one occasion, involving Directive 96/61/CE of 24 September 1996 on integrated pollution prevention and control, when the conflict was so difficult to overcome that the *Bundesrat* was close to confirming its position by two-thirds majority. On that occasion, an agreement was ultimately found.

[46]The Italian Constitutional Court pointed out the State–Regions Conference "is the privileged forum for the discussion and negotiation of policy between the State and the Regions" (Ruling No. 116 of 1994).

[47]This is a body composed of the Prime Minister, the Minister for European Affairs, the Foreign Affairs Minister, the Minister for Regional Affairs and Local Autonomy, and the other Ministers with responsibility for topics on the agenda of individual CIACE meetings. See Art. 2 of the so-called (after its proponent) "Buttiglione Act" (Act No. 11 of 4 February 2005).

Westminster Parliament remain the solely responsible for the relations with the EU. There are, however, quasi-legal agreements in place which require the UK government to consult with the devolved governments where EU measures have an impact on devolved competences. The devolved administrations are involved in such discussions, but are not in a position to bind the national government to act in conformity with their position.[48]

Finally, France does not have a legally binding system of consultation in the preparation of Council meetings. The decentralised entities are not involved in the preparation of common positions which are later defended in the Council. Only in some circumstances, where the Committee of Local Financing (which is constituted in part of representatives of the Regions and the Departments) needs to be consulted on EU legislative drafts which might cause financial implications for them, do the decentralised entities have a more enhanced role.[49]

Aspects of loyalty play an important role in the federal and decentralised countries subject to our analysis. It is therefore worthwhile to underline that each national government has a legal duty to provide its Regions with timely information in relation to those EU proposals which touch upon regional competences.

External Representation in the Council

The second form of regional participation is the external representation of the Regions in the Council. It was noted above that the Member States can be represented in the Council by a Minister of a sub-state entity. Art. 16(2) TEU provides the following: "The Council shall consist of a representative of each Member State at ministerial level, who may commit the government of the Member State in question and cast its vote".

Four patterns are identifiable in this regard.

The first, comprising Belgium and to a lesser extent Germany, is based upon a *full representation* of the country by one of its Regions in cases where they are competent for the matter which is dealt with by the Council.

Belgium may be considered to be the country with the most far-reaching regulation concerning the external participation of the Regions in Council meetings. This is of course linked to the fact that Belgian federalism does not recognise, in principle, concurrent competences. The Belgian system foresees three possible forms of representation in the Council: an exclusive national representation for exclusive federal competences; an exclusive representation by the Communities

[48]The Memorandum of Understanding between the Westminster government and the devolved governments provides the general framework for their relations. Para. 19 of the Memorandum provides the following: "The UK Government will involve the devolved administrations as fully as possible in discussions about the formulation of the UK's policy position on all EU and international issues which touch on devolved matters".

[49]Art. L1211-4 of the *Code général des collectivités territoriales*.

and by the Regions for those competences which exclusively belong to the Communities and the Regions; and finally a mixed representation. The mixed representation recognises two sub-forms: a national representation with an assessor[50] from the Regions and the Communities and a representation by the Regions and the Communities with a federal assessor. The mixed representation tools find application when there are matters which belong partly to the (exclusive) power of the national government and partly to the (exclusive) power of the Regions or the Communities on the Council agenda. The composition of the Belgian representation to the Council varies accordingly with the issues which are dealt with by the Council. It is the role of an Inter Ministerial Conference to decide over the composition of the Belgian representation. A rotation system decides which Community or which Region may represent (or act as an assessor for) Belgium.[51] The representative of the Region or Community, whether he acts as the full representative of Belgium or as an assessor, does not only represent his own Region or Community but acts for Belgium as a whole.

The German system foresees the representation of Germany in the Council by a regional Minister when draft EU acts which primarily concern the exclusive competences of the *Länder* in the areas of education, culture or radio/TV are dealt with.[52] The right to represent Germany belongs to a representative of the *Länder* designated by the *Bundesrat*. The representative of the *Länder* – who becomes the representative of the entire Federal Republic and not only of a single *Land* – must act "with the participation of and in coordination with" the Federal Government. "Participation" implies that the representatives of the Federation have the right to participate in all meetings and official contacts in which the *Länder* representative engages.[53] "Coordination" is more difficult to construe. According to the bicameral commission which drafted Art. 23 BL, "coordination" is something less than an "agreement", but something more than simple "respect for the other's point of view".[54] It is arguable that the representative of the

[50]In this composition, the leading Minister is the spokesman. The assessor (who is a national or regional Minister) does not have a say in the meeting but he can assist the leading national or regional representative. He can speak at the meeting but he has to do this in coordination with the Minister who represents Belgium. The Minister who represents Belgium has the final say over the Belgian point of view.

[51]Council meetings on fisheries constitute an exception to this rule. Belgium will in these meetings always be represented by the Flemish Minister. This is due to the fact that the Belgian Coast lies entirely in the Flemish territory. Council meetings on agriculture are another exception. In these meetings the national Minister will always be assisted by the Flemish and the Walloon Minister competent for Agriculture. This is due to the fact that agriculture constitutes (to some extent) a concurrent power between national and regional authorities.

[52]Art. 23(6) BL.

[53]ROJAHN (2001), p. 169 (Rn. 75); Streinz (2007), p. 923 (Rn. 117).

[54]See the report made by the *Gemeinsame Verfassungskommission* of the *Bundestag* and of the *Bundesrat* on the draft constitutional law which gave rise to the 1992 constitutional amendment (*Drucksache des Bundestages*, 12/6000, p. 24; 12/3896, p. 20). On this point see Scholz (1996); Streinz (2007), p. 923 (Rn. 117).

Länder should pay the greatest possible respect to the position of the Federal Government.[55]

The second pattern entails the *potential* to permit the Member State to be represented in the Council by a regional Minister. This may happen when the issue on the Council agenda concerns a matter of regional competence or affects vital interests of the Regions. Currently, only Austria adopts this approach. Germany did so until the constitutional amendment in 2006.

Prior to 2006, the direct participation mechanism of the German *Länder* provided for by Art. 23(6) BL, instead of being limited only to the three aforementioned areas (education, culture, radio/TV), embraced all fields of exclusive legislative competence of the *Länder*. The Federation was in principal obliged to transfer the exercise of Germany's rights to a representative of the *Länder*, but it was able, in exceptional circumstances, to withhold such rights on the grounds of national interest. The direct participation in Council meetings was therefore a mere possibility for the *Länder*. Furthermore, the pre-2006 rule had sometimes led to disputes between the *Bundesrat* and the Federal Government as to whether or not the focus of a given EU proposal concerned a matter of exclusive competence of the *Länder*. These disputes were normally settled extra-judicially by granting, as a sweetener, to the representative of the *Länder*, the right to issue statements during the Council sessions at which the proposals were dealt with.[56]

The Austrian Constitution provides that, if a matter (concurrent or not) which belongs to the competence of the *Länder*, or which is of interest to them, is dealt with at European level, the national government *can* (!) allow a regional Minister to represent Austria in the Council. This Minister will have to collaborate with the representative of the Federation, and, like the federal Minister, he will be bound by the common position of the *Länder*.[57] In line with the position in Germany and Belgium, the regional representative does not represent his *Land* but the whole Member State. Up to now, this participation opportunity has never been invoked by the *Länder*. They seem to have preferred to participate in Council meetings under the auspices of the Austrian delegation.

The third pattern, which is constituted by Italy and Spain, is characterised by the fact that the Regions can become a *part of* the national delegation to the Council.

Italy offers, in theory, a significant possibility that representatives of the Regions will be included in the external representation of Italy in the Council. The direct participation of the Regions in the EU decision-making process is based on Art. 117(5) of the Constitution. According to this provision, the Regions shall

[55]For matters other than education, culture or radio/TV, but which concern essential interests of the *Länder*, even if outside the scope of their competences, or for which the *Bundesrat*'s intervention is envisaged at the national level, the *Länder* can request to be consulted during negotiations within advisory bodies of the Council (and of the Commission) and can also, with the consent of the Federal Government, state their opinion during the meetings of such advisory bodies. See § 6(1) and (2) of the EUZBLG.

[56]Müller-Graff (2007), p. 717.

[57]Art. 23d (1) of the Austrian Constitution.

participate in any decision about formation of European law in their fields of competence. The so-called (after the name of its proponent) "La Loggia" Act provides for the participation of the Regions in the meetings of the Council and the working groups and committees of the Council and of the Commission. The same Act specifies that such participation takes place in the framework of the Government's delegations and that the President of a Region may even be appointed as head of the delegation when a matter of "residuary" (i.e. exclusive in principal) legislative competence of the Regions is on the agenda.[58] The true and actual weight of such participation is restricted, though, by the *indivisibility* of the Italian delegation before the EU. This is due to the need to guarantee the unitary position of the Italian Republic and the need to speak with a *single voice* in the international and supranational arena.

Spain follows the traditional pattern according to which only the national government can represent the State externally. This means that representation at the EU level remains limited to a single Spanish delegation. A representative of the *Comunidades autónomas* is admitted into this delegation for matters of regional interest. With some exceptions, the Council's activities in which the *Comunidades autónomas* participate correspond to powers attributed to them by the Constitution. The involvement of the *Comunidades autónomas* implies an important consequence: that during the negotiations the Spanish delegation has to take account of the common position of the Autonomous Communities. The final say on the Spanish position remains with the head of delegation.

The fourth pattern, which includes the UK, foresees only that the Regions have to *play a role* in the UK representation at the meetings of the Council.

Ministers and officials of the devolved administrations have to play a role in Council meetings at which substantive discussion is expected on matters likely to have a significant impact on their devolved responsibilities.[59] However, decisions on ministerial attendance at these meetings are taken on a case-by-case basis by the competent UK Minister. It is he who takes the overall responsibility for the negotiations and determines how each member of the team can best contribute to secure the agreed position. This suggests that the UK Minister can consider it appropriate that the regional Minister speaks for the entire country in the Council or that, even in a case where the matter has a significant impact on the devolved authorities; the regional Minister should not have a role to play.[60] Most frequently,

---

[58]The head of the Italian delegation is appointed by the Government with the agreement of the State-Regions Conference. A regional representative has never led the Italian delegation at the time of writing. Furthermore it is important to highlight the fact that a President of a Region is not a "minister" under Italian constitutional law and that to make him the head of the Italian delegation to the Council would be problematic given that Art. 16(2) TEU requires the Member State representative in the Council to be of "ministerial level". The "La Loggia" Act is the Act No. 131 of 5 June 2003.

[59]It concerns mainly the following Councils: Agriculture and Fisheries; Environment.

[60]Concordat on Coordination of European Union Policy Issues: Common Annex, December 2001, par. B4.12-14.

Scotland has participated as an observer or, sporadically, as a spokesperson for the UK. This is explained by the fact that its Executive has more resources than those of Wales and Northern Ireland. Moreover, Scotland has more devolved powers than the other devolved authorities and Scottish participation in the Council was already well established prior to devolution.

France constitutes the exception to the rule. It is not foreseen that Regions or local entities are to play a role within the French representation in the Council. The specific rules concerning the Overseas departments (or outermost regions) in the TFEU seem nevertheless to imply that the French government should at least consult those specific department.[61] Art. 349 TFEU foresees that the Council can adopt specific measures with the objective of laying down the conditions of application of the Treaties to those regions. This happens on a proposal of the European Commission and after consultation with the European Parliament. However, these provisions do not impose a requirement that France should consult its internal "territorial" Regions (i.e. the Regions within continental France) to reach a common position in preparation for an EU Council.[62]

A "Constitutional Myth": The Enforcement of Regions' Participation Rights in Domestic Courts

The Regions' participation rights provided for by national law are in principal judicially enforceable in the national patterns under consideration – with the exceptions of the UK and France. In practice, it is only on rare occasions that the Regions have filed a lawsuit in a domestic court in order to enforce their participation rights.

In Germany, the *Bundesrat* can bring a case against the Federal Government with the aim of enforcing the constitutional participation rights of the *Länder*, and the *Länder* can bring a case against the Federation before the Federal Constitutional Court.[63]

Italian Regions are entitled to obtain the enforcement of their rights by bringing a case before the Constitutional Court reliant upon Art. 134(2) of the Italian Constitution (the suit is called "*conflitto di attribuzione tra Stato e Regioni*", i.e. competence conflict between State and Regions). This is possible only when such rights are "constitutional" (i.e. explicitly provided for, or at least "rooted", in the Constitution)

[61]2007 Report of the French Council of State *L'administration française et l'Union européenne? Quelles influences? Quelles stratégies?*, p. 309, available at http://www.conseil-etat.fr/cde/media/document//rapportpublic2007.pdf (last checked on 19 October 2009).

[62]The *Secretariat général des affaires européennes* with a very limited number of regional representatives is the only body in existence. However, no hard law provision exists to include the views of the Regions in the position of France in the Council.

[63]See Art. 93(1) No. 1 and No. 3 BL. See also Streinz (2007), p. 924 (Rn. 120).

and their infringement stems from non-legislative (i.e. administrative) acts.[64] If an information or participation right is "sub-constitutional" (i.e. it is provided for by a sub-constitutional law and is not "rooted" in the Constitution), the Regions could file a suit to a court in order to obtain the setting aside of the administrative act or regulation of the Executive that infringes on their rights.[65]

In Belgium, the Communities and Regions are entitled to bring a case against the Federal Government and against the other Communities and Regions before the Constitutional Court should this be necessary. The Constitutional Court rules on conflicts of powers. It judges whether an Act (passed in National Parliament) or Decree (passed by Parliaments of Communities and Regions) or Ordinance (passed by Parliament of Brussels Capital-Region) has been enacted in respect of the constitutional and legal rules concerning the division of powers.[66]

The participation rights of the Austrian *Länder* imply an enormous political margin of appreciation for the representatives of the Federation; it is sufficient to think that the Federation can depart from a common position of the *Länder* on grounds of "imperative foreign and integration policy reasons": Art. 23 d(2) B-VG. Therefore, the likelihood that these rights could be actually "enforced" by the *Länder* is rooted more strongly in theory than in practice. The *Länder* are not able to file a suit before the Constitutional Court if the Federation is ignoring their participation rights. There are also no other remedies in domestic courts. The ultimate – but totally theoretical – sanction lies in the constitutional responsibility of the members of the Federal Government. The Austrian Constitution provides for two different types of responsibility: political (Art. 74 B-VG) – focusing on the no-confidence vote against the Federal Government – and legal (Art. 76 and 142 B-VG). Regarding the latter, the Constitutional Court has the competence to pronounce on suits predicating the legal responsibility of the highest federal and regional authorities where they are culpable for contraventions ensuing from their official activity. It is arguable that an infringement of the participation rights of the *Länder* may give rise to the legal responsibility of the Government. However, there is no precedent in this regard, given that all the

[64]The relevant constitutional provision is Art. 117(5) of the Italian Constitution: "Regarding the matters that lie within their field of competence, the Regions and the Autonomous Provinces of Trento and Bolzano participate in any decisions about the formation of EU law". If this constitutional provision were violated by a legislative act (e.g. by a Parliament statute), the Regions could file a suit before the Constitutional Court in order to obtain a declaration of invalidity of this act under Art. 127(2) of the Italian Constitution ("Whenever a Region regards a State law, another act of the State having the force of law, or a law of another Region as infringing on its own sphere of powers, it may raise the question of its constitutionality before the Constitutional Court within sixty days of the publication of said law or act").

[65]Pending the case, an urgent remedy aimed at preventing the occurrence of an "imminent and irreparable damage" is available under Art. 700 of the Italian Civil Procedure Code.

[66]Art. 142 of the Belgian Constitution.

Länder-Federation conflicts have always been settled in an informal (i.e. non-judicial) way.[67]

In Spain, the participation rights of the *Comunidades autónomas* are theoretically judicially enforceable before the Constitutional Court or ordinary courts (contentious-administrative).[68]

In the framework outlined above, France and the UK constitute exceptions. In these two countries, no remedy is offered in cases where the regional participation rights are infringed.

Devolved governments in the UK do not have a right to bring a case before a domestic court to defend their participation rights. Such rights are in fact provided for by agreements between the devolved authorities and the Westminster Government. Such agreements are not intended to be legally binding and only have political effect. The Memorandum of Understanding, for instance, defines itself as "a statement of political intent" and as "binding in honour only".[69] The same document states that Concordats signed by Westminster and devolved governments "are not intended to be legally binding, but to serve as working documents".[70] It seems therefore unlikely that courts will intervene in the intergovernmental procedures codified by such "soft law" instruments.[71]

The main problem with judicial enforcement of the participation rights of the Regions is that, should a domestic court find that a right provided for by domestic law has not been complied with, that court would not in any case be entitled to declare the invalidity (or the inapplicability) of the EU measure. The invalidity of EU legislation can – according to an "orthodox" EU law perspective – be declared *only* by European courts.[72] In March 1995, the Federal

[67]Art. 142(2) lit. b B-VG provides for that a suit can be brought against members of the Federal Government (and the authorities placed on an equal footing with them with regard to responsibility) for contravention of the law. This may happen by a vote of the National Council but not by one of the *Länder* Assemblies. The information and participation rights of the *Länder* could therefore be enforced only in an indirect manner: i.e. if the National Council passes a vote according to Art. 142(2) lit. b B-VG. According to lit. c of the same article, a suit can also be brought by a vote of the National Council against an Austrian representative in the Council for contravention of law in matters where legislation belongs to the Federation. In matters where legislation belongs to the *Länder*, a suit could be brought by identically worded votes of all the *Länder* Assemblies. This last mentioned competence of the Constitutional Court refers to the case in which the Federal Government assigns participation in the Council to a representative designated by the *Länder*.

[68]Art. 161(1) of the Spanish Constitution. See the Ruling of the Spanish Constitutional Court No. 88 of 9 May 1988. Cf. García Roca (2002), pp. 89–110.

[69]Para. 2. Cm 5420, *Memorandum of Understanding and Supplementary Agreements between the United Kingdom Government, Scottish Ministers, the Cabinet of the National Assembly for Wales and the Northern Ireland Executive Committee*, London, TSO, 2001. The Memorandum provides the general framework for relations between the central government and the devolved governments.

[70]Para. 3.

[71]Rawlings (2000), pp. 283–284, and Scott (2001), pp. 21–48, esp. pp. 31–32.

[72]Lenaerts et al. (2005), pp. 445–446.

Constitutional Court declared the Federal Government's behaviour as illegitimate for not having involved the *Bundesrat* in the adoption of Directive 89/522/EEC regulating television.[73] However, this declaration of illegitimacy did not result, *nor could it*, in the invalidity of the above-mentioned directive. This is due to the fact that the impact of a national ruling is confined to the domestic jurisdiction.

The practical operation of the systems that are subject to the national case studies demonstrates that, with regard to the matter of the participation rights, the extra-judicial settlement of disputes is generally preferred by the Regions in the analysed countries. This is due to the principle of loyal cooperation between the different levels of government. This is also due to the fact that a ruling in favour of the Regions in a domestic court would not produce the invalidity of the contested EU measure. Furthermore, it would require some time for a domestic court to pass a ruling on the judicial enforcement of regional participation rights. It is doubtful that this would be compatible with the time schedule of the Union decision-making. This situation is the symptom of a residual "*Landesblindheit*" ("regional blindness") of the Union. This regional blindness surely limits the effectiveness of national provisions regulating sub-state entities' participation rights. Although these problems remain national at first sight, questions rise whether this regional blindness of the European institutions in general does not (to some extent) cause or, at least, feed the feeling of a democratic deficit.

A way to overcome this problem may be resort to Art. 46 of the 1969 Vienna Convention on the Law of the Treaties in order to grant to the ECJ the power to declare invalid an EU measure which is in breach of Regions' participation rights. In order to reach this conclusion, though, it would be necessary to accept that a violation of participation rights of the Regions amounts to a "manifest" violation of "a rule of internal law of fundamental importance".[74] This conclusion is far from straightforward given the very complicated provisions governing Regions' participation rights in each of the Member States. So long as an EU act remains within the scope of the competences outlined in the Treaties, it is questionable whether and to what extent the breach of a domestic rule may be invoked to obtain a declaration of invalidity of that act by the ECJ. This makes it rather difficult to consider such national regulations as "rules of fundamental importance" concerning the external relations of the State.

---

[73]The text of this case can be read in *Entscheidungssammlung des Bundesverfassungsgericht* (hereinafter *BVerfGE*), Vol. 92, p. 203 ff.

[74]This is the text of Art. 46 of the 1969 Vienna Convention on the Law of the Treaties: "(1) A State may not invoke the fact that its consent to be bound by a treaty has been expressed in violation of a provision of its internal law regarding competence to conclude treaties as invalidating its consent unless that violation was manifest and concerned a rule of its internal law of fundamental importance. (2) A violation is manifest if it would be objectively evident to any State conducting itself in the matter in accordance with normal practice and in good faith".

The Intervention of the Constitutional Court in the Event of an Encroachment by the EU on Competences of the Regions

Can the Regions rely on some kind of judicial protection *at the national level* against EU measures vitiated by incompetence (i.e. in breach of the distribution of competences between the Union and the Member States established in the Treaties)? From an "orthodox" EU law perspective, the answer would certainly be negative. EU law provides that the national courts must refer to the Court of Justice *all* issues concerning the validity of European measures. Under no circumstance is a domestic court allowed – even if it were a constitutional court – to declare the invalidity of an EU act and/or to set that act aside on its own initiative. This would not be permitted even when it seems to the domestic court that the invalidity is totally manifest.[75]

Some of the analysed national patterns depart from the EU "orthodoxy" described above. In the "Maastricht ruling" of 12 October 1993, the German Federal Constitutional Court stated that the acts of the EU have no legal effect at the national level, if they are adopted *ultra vires*.[76] The Court re-affirmed in its recent "Lisbon ruling", released on 30 June 2009, that it is vested with the authority to exercise an *ultra vires* review ("*Ultravireskontrolle*") on EU measures. The Court also pointed out that such review can result in legal instruments of the EU being declared inapplicable in Germany if they transgress the confines of EU competences or are not compliant with the principle of subsidiarity.[77] It must be noted that the Court has so far never used its review power. This is due – among other things – to the fact that the impact of a declaration of non-applicability could be devastating for the relationship of Germany with the EU (and for the Union!). It is therefore highly likely that the Court will seldom exercise *ultra vires* review in the future.

In Italy, the only limits which remain in force today to the prevalence of EU law over domestic law are those involving the inviolability of the "supreme principles" of the republican legal system and of the "inviolable rights of the human being". This is the so-called "*controlimiti* doctrine" ["*controlimiti*" meaning "limits against" or, better, "limits to (the prevalence of Community law)"] elaborated by

---

[75]The "*acte clair* doctrine" of the ECJ does not confer to domestic courts the right to declare invalid an EU piece of legislation. This remains an exclusive prerogative of the ECJ according to the Case 314/85 *Firma Foto-Frost* v. *Hauptzollamt Lübeck-Ost* [1987] ECR 4199. Furthermore the ECJ maintains that the EU law prevails over *any* national norm including constitutional ones. See the Case 11/70 *Internationale Handelsgesellschaft mbh* v. *Einfuhr- und Vorratsstelle für Getreide und Futtermittel* [1970] ECR 1125.

[76]*BVerfGE*, Vol. 89, p. 188.

[77]In the same ruling, the Court pointed out that it also had the competence to carry out an "identity review" ("*Identitätskontrolle*"): that is, that it had the right to declare EU legislation infringing on the "inviolable core content of the constitutional identity of the Basic Law" ("*unantastbare Kerngehalt der Verfassungsidentität des Grundgesetzes*") non-applicable in Germany, pursuant to Art. 23(1), last sentence, and Art. 79(3) BL.

the Italian Constitutional Court since 1973.[78] It is extremely unlikely that the Constitutional Court would, on this ground, declare as inapplicable a piece of EU legislation encroaching on a regional matter. In fact, the Constitutional Court could do so *only if* that EU legislation would infringe so heavily on the legal position of the Regions that the constitutional principle of local autonomy – which can be regarded as a "*controlimite*" – could be considered as being violated.[79]

Both the German and the Italian positions are (although the Italian to a lesser extent) in opposition to the declared position in EU law. It is, however, extremely unlikely that one or other Court will in the future declare the inapplicability at national level of an *ultra vires* legal instrument of the EU. Furthermore, such an "activist" approach is proclaimed only in Germany and to a lesser extent in Italy.[80] The only protection for the Regions common to all the analysed countries is a direct claim for judicial review to the EU. But is it a viable solution?

The Never-Ending Question of the *Locus Standi* of the Regions

As regards the direct challenge of EU acts before EU courts, Art. 263(2) TFEU only recognises the European institutions listed in it and the Member States as having the status of privileged applicant. Sub-state entities do not have the status of privileged applicant and, as regards their *locus standi*, according to the established case law of the ECJ, they are on the same level as natural and private legal persons.[81]

This implies that the Regions can challenge decisions addressed to them, as well as regulations or decisions intended for other entities, but which concern them "directly and individually".[82] It is widely acknowledged that these requirements represent an almost insurmountable obstacle to the recognition of the legitimacy to

---

[78]See the *Frontini* Ruling No. 183 of 27 December 1973 and, providing more clarity, the *Granital* Ruling No. 170 of 8 June 1984 (both available at http://www.giurcost.org). In the legal scholarship see Sorrentino (2002), pp. 1355–1361, and Tizzano (2007), pp. 734–744. See also Panara (2008), pp. 158–159.

[79]This principle is provided for by Art. 5 of the Italian Constitution: "The Republic, one and indivisible, recognises and promotes local autonomy; it fully applies administrative decentralisation of state services and adopts principles and methods of legislation meeting the requirements of autonomy and decentralisation".

[80]The French *Conseil Constitutionnel* stated in its decision No. 2007-560 DC (20 December 2007) that in case a European Treaty contains a clause running counter to the Constitution, calls into question constitutionally guaranteed rights and freedoms, or adversely affect the fundamental conditions of the exercise of national sovereignty, the authorisation to ratify such measures requires the prior revision of the Constitution. A similar conclusion was reached by the Belgian Council of State in its advisory opinion concerning the Treaty of Lisbon (see Parl. Doc., Senate, nr. 4-568/1, session 2007–2008). The Austrian Constitutional Court accepted primacy of EU Law, see Öhlinger (2008), pp. 11–23.

[81]See the landmark decision of the ECJ of 21 March 1997 in the case C-95/97, *Région Wallonne* v. *Commission*, in ECR, 1997, at I-1787.

[82]Art. 263(4) TFEU.

impugn EU measures. The result is that only "government authorities of the Member States"[83] are actually permitted to appeal to EU courts to obtain the annulment of a regulation or a directive "on grounds of lack of competence, infringement of an essential procedural requirement, infringement of the Treaties or of any rule of law relating to its application, or misuse of powers" in the vast majority of cases.[84] This element is another form of regional blindness of the EU. The defence of regional powers has no alternative but to be fulfilled at the EU level by the national governments of the Member States.

The first point to make is that the fact that an EU act impinges on a matter falling within the sphere of competence of a regional authority is insufficient to demonstrate that that Region is "individually concerned". The division of legislative and regulatory powers within a Member State is seen as "solely a matter for the constitutional law of that State [with] no effect from the point of view of assessing the possible effects of a Community legal measure on the interests of a territorial body".[85]

Furthermore, if an EC measure affects specific interests of a Region or its political objectives, this is not sufficient for establishing "individual concern". In the *Cantabria* case, the CFI held that "any general interest the applicant [Region] may have, as a third person, in obtaining a result which will favour the economic prosperity of a given business and, as a result, the level of employment in the geographical region where it carries on its activities, is insufficient, on its own, to enable the applicant to be regarded as 'concerned' [...], nor, *a fortiori*, as being individually concerned".[86] This has been confirmed in several cases since.[87]

Even in a case such as *Região autónoma dos Açores*, where under the old Art. 299 EC (now Art. 349 TFEU) there was a recognised "obligation for the Council to adopt specific measures for the outermost regions, taking into account the special characteristics and constraints of those regions", the CFI held that the fact that a regional authority is entitled to specific protection under EC law is not sufficient to give it standing under Art. 230(4) EC (now Art. 263(4) TFEU.[88] The CFI concluded

---

[83]C-95/97, *Région Wallonne* v. *Commission*, fn. 80 above, para. 6.

[84]See Art. 263(2) TFEU. In this regard see Van Nuffel (2001), pp. 871–901; Dani (2004), p. 181 ff.

[85]See the decision of the CFI in the case T-417/04, *Regione autonoma Friuli-Venezia Giulia* v. *Commission*, in ECR, 2007, at II-641, para. 62. This decision has been challenged on appeal and the appeal is still pending. See also the case T-37/04, *Região autónoma dos Açores (Portugal)* v. *Council*, Judgment of 1 July 2008, in [2008] ECR II-103*, Summ.publ., para. 39.

[86]T-238/97, *Comunidad Autónoma de Cantabria* v. *Council* [1998] ECR II-2271, para. 49 (the contested regulation concerned State aid to certain shipyards); see also T-609/97, *Regione Puglia* v. *Commission and Spain* [1998] ECR II-4051, para. 21 (the contested regulation concerned production aid payable to producers of olive oil).

[87]T-609/97, *Regione Puglia* v. *Commission and Spain* cit., para. 22; C-142/00 P, *Commission* v. *Nederlandse Antillen* [2003] ECR I-3483, para. 69; Order of the President of the CFI of 7 July 2004 in T-37/04 R, *Região autónoma dos Açores (Portugal)* v. *Council* [2004] ECR II-2153, para. 118; T-417/04, *Regione autonoma Friuli-Venezia Giulia* cit., para. 61.

[88]T-37/04, *Região autónoma dos Açores* cit., para. 54 et seq.

that "the applicant has not put forward arguments which enable it to be held that the contested provisions will entail harmful effects for the fish stocks and for the marine environment in the Azores and, consequently, for the survival of the fishing sector in the region".[89]

The judicial approach is different in cases concerning State aid. In this area, the "Community judicature has accepted the right of regional authorities to challenge Community acts which either prevent [sub-national entities] from adopting [aid] measures which they may legitimately adopt if there is no Community intervention or require them to withdraw those measures and to take certain action".[90] In *Vlaamse Gewest*, for example, the CFI acknowledged that "The contested decision has a direct and individual effect on the legal position of the Flemish Region [since] [such decision] directly prevent[ed] [that Region] from exercising its own powers, which [. . .] consist[ed] of granting the aid in question, as it [saw] fit".[91] In *Freistaat Sachsen and Volkswagen* v. *Commission* and in *Friuli Venezia Giulia* v. *Commission*, the CFI recognised the standing of the applicant Region and relied in particular on the fact that the decision required the Region to recover aid from the beneficiaries.[92] In 2000, the Sicily region challenged a Commission decision which stated, *inter alia*, that the State aid established pursuant to a regional law in favour of undertakings operating in the agriculture or fisheries sector was incompatible with the common market and required Italy to withdraw the aid in question. The Commission did not seek to argue that the measure was not of direct and individual concern to the applicant, and the CFI held the action admissible after assessing only whether the applicant had commenced action within the time limit for bringing an action.[93] In many cases since, the whole question of *locus standi* in actions

---

[89]T-37/04, *Região autónoma dos Açores* cit., para. 78. An appeal against this decision has brought on 8 October 2008 is still pending before the ECJ: see the Application in O.J. 2008 C 327/15 (Case C-444/08 P).

[90]See T-37/04, *Região autónoma dos Açores* cit., para. 82, referring, to: T-214/95, *Vlaamse Gewest* v. *Commission* [1998] ECR II-717, para. 29; Joined Cases T-346/99 to T-348/99, *Diputación Foral de Álava and Others* v. *Commission* [2002] ECR II-4259, para. 37; Joined Cases T-366/03 and T-235/04, *Land Oberösterreich and Austria* v. *Commission* [2005] ECR II-4005, para. 28. The CFI pointed out in *Região autónoma dos Açores*, at para. 82, that the cases listed above concerned decisions on "aid paid by the applicant local bodies, so that the lawfulness of that aid depended on the outcome of the proceedings".

[91]T-214/95, *Vlaamse Gewest* cit., para. 29. This was in line with previous cases concerning a decision affecting, *inter alia*, a Region's power to grant state aid, in which the admissibility of the action had not been contested by the Commission, see Cases 62 and 72/87, *Exécutif regional wallon* v. *Commission* [1988] ECR 1573, paras. 6 and 8.

[92]Joined Cases T-132/96 and T-143/96, *Freistaat Sachsen* v. *Commission* [1999] ECR II-3663, paras. 84–86; T-288/97, *Friuli Venezia Giulia* v. *Commission* [1999] ECR II-1871, paras. 31 and 32.

[93]T-190/00, *Regione Siciliana* v. *Commission* [2003] ECR II-5015, paras. 29–33 (dismissed as unfounded).

brought by Regions in the area of State aid was not even addressed explicitly by the EU judicature.[94]

The ECJ is instead reluctant to admit the standing of the Regions in cases regarding decisions on the ending or restriction of financial assistance or contributions previously granted under the Structural Funds. As such, the ECJ overturned the judgement of the CFI in *Regione Siciliana* v. *Commission* and held that nothing supports the conclusion that the Sicily region was directly concerned in its capacity as the authority responsible for the implementation of an ERDF (European Regional Development Fund) project.[95]

As for cases regarding financial assistance granted under the Cohesion Fund, the position of the Courts seems to be even stricter. On 10 September 2008, for instance, the CFI by Order dismissed as inadmissible, due to lack of direct concern, an application brought by the Município de Gondomar (Portugal) for the annulment of a Commission Decision on the cancellation of the financial assistance for the Project concerning the Redevelopment of Grande Porto Sul – Subsistema de Gondomar.[96]

In an Order of 8 October 2008, the CFI also rejected as inadmissible, due to lack of direct concern, an action brought by the Community of Grammatikou (Athens, Greece) against the Commission Decision relating to the grant of assistance from the Cohesion Fund for the project "Construction of a Landfill Site at the Integrated Waste Management Facility of North-East Attica at the location 'Mavro Vouno Grammatikou', in the Hellenic Republic".[97] The applicant had claimed to be directly and individually concerned by the Decision "because it is a public body

[94]See, e.g. Joined Cases T-228 and 233/99, *Westdeutsche Landesbank and Land Nordrhein-Westfalen* v. *Commission* [2003] ECR II- 435; T-369/00, *Département du Loiret* [2003] ECR II-1789, and [2007] ECR II-851; T-318/00, *Freistaat Thüringen* v. *Commission* [2005] ECR II-4179; Joined Cases T-211 and 215/04, *Gibraltar and the UK* v. *Commission*, Judgment of 18 December 2008. Still pending is T-394/08, *Regione autonoma della Sardegna* v. *Commission*, O.J. 2008 C 285/52.

[95]C-15/06, *Regione Siciliana* v. *Commission* [2007] ECR I-2591, para. 32. This ruling overturned the CFI's ruling in T-60/03, *Regione Siciliana* v. *Commission* [2005] ECR II-4139. The CFI held also held a direct action of annulment brought by a public-law consortium (comprising the Italian State, the Campania Region, the Province of Naples and a number of municipalities located in the area of the Vesuvius volcano), whose object is to protect and improve the complex sites of the *Ville Vesuviane* (that is the towns around Vesuvius) to be admissible. See T-189/02, *Ente per le Ville Vesuviane* v. *Commission*, not published in the ECR, information at [2007] ECR II-89*. However, the Court of Justice recently overruled this decision, see C-445/07 P, 10 September 2009, OJ C, 267/11.

[96]T-324/06, *Município de Gondomar* v. *Commission*, Order of 10 September 2008, not yet published in the ECR, paras. 37–52. The applicant brought an appeal before the ECJ on the basis that the CFI erred in law when denying the applicant's direct concern. The ECJ rejected the appeal as unfounded in its Order of 24 September 2009 (not published yet): C-501/08 P, *Município de Gondomar* v. *Commission*; see the Application in O.J. 2009, C 19/18.

[97]T-13/08, *Koinotita Grammatikou* v *Commission*, Order of the CFI of 8 October 2008, see O.J. 2009, C 32/35.

responsible for the protection of public health and the environment in the area where the project that being financed is located".[98] No appeal has been brought against this decision.

A la recherche of a Way Out: Are Art. 277 TFEU and Art. 267 TFEU Viable Alternatives to a Direct Challenge?

It is commonly recognised in legal scholarship that the legal protection afforded to non-privileged applicants in EU law is far from satisfactory.[99] This is not the view of the EU judicature. The CFI in *Região autónoma dos Açores* pointed out that regional authorities are able "either indirectly to plead the unlawfulness of such [EU] acts before the Community judicature under Art. 241 EC [now Art. 277 TFEU] or to do so before the national courts and ask them ... to make a reference to the Court of Justice for a preliminary ruling [under Art. 234 EC now Art. 267 TFEU] as to lawfulness".[100]

This standpoint of the CFI – which echoes earlier rulings of the ECJ[101] – does not seem to resolve the problem. According to Art. 277 TFEU, it is possible to invoke the "inapplicability" of a regulation in the context of other proceedings brought to the Court. Art. 277 TFEU only applies if the applicant is entitled by Art. 263 TFEU to bring a challenge against a decision implementing an (allegedly unlawful) earlier regulation. Therefore, if an applicant is not recognised as having *locus standi* to challenge the given decision, or if such a decision does not exist, there would be no judicial defence against that regulation.

As to Art. 267 TFEU (ex 234 EC), much as in the case for individuals, it is unlikely that adequate judicial protection could be provided through preliminary rulings initiated in domestic courts. The judicial protection of the Regions would in fact end up depending on the existence of an action in domestic law, and such cases would not be as straightforward as a direct challenge. A Region may even have to voluntarily place itself in breach of an EU obligation – e.g. it may have to decide not to implement a European norm – in order to enable itself to challenge its validity. Furthermore, domestic courts inevitably act as a "filter" which could prevent the plea for invalidity of an EU measure from being referred to the ECJ. As a result, the applicant Region may have to pursue its claim through more than one national court.

[98]See for Application O.J. 2008, C 79/29.

[99]See Craig and De Búrca (2008), p. 525 ff.

[100]T-37/04, *Região autónoma dos Açores* cit., para. 92.

[101]See Case C-50/00 P *Unión de Pequeños Agricultores* v. *Council* [2002] ECR I-6677 and Case C-263/02 *Jégo-Quéré* v. *Commission* [2004] ECR I-3425.

New Developments After Lisbon?

An important question in relation to the *locus standi* of the Regions is whether anything has changed with the entry into force of the ToL. The rephrasing of Art. 263 TFEU (ex 230 EC) deserves some attention.

The current Art. 263(4) provides the following: "Any natural or legal person may . . . institute proceedings against an act addressed to that person or which is of direct and individual concern to them, *and against a regulatory act which is of direct concern to them and does not entail implementing measures*" (italics not in the original). This provision has to be compared to the old Art. 230(4) EC: "Any natural or legal person may . . . institute proceedings against a decision addressed to that person or against a decision which, although in the form of a regulation or a decision addressed to another person, is of direct and individual concern to the former".

The new wording seems to suggest that it is sufficient that a "regulatory act" is of direct concern to a Region in order to give it *locus standi* before the ECJ. It appears that no individual concern needs to be shown if no implementing measure is required.

The key question lies in the definition of the expression "regulatory act" within the framework of Art. 263(4) TFEU. Within the framework of the Constitutional Treaty, regulatory acts were secondary norms in the hierarchy of the European norms. The Constitutional Treaty made a distinction between laws, framework laws, regulations, decisions, recommendations and opinions. Laws would have replaced what were previously regulations. Framework laws would have replaced what were previously directives. Regulations would have been non-legislative acts of general application for the implementation of legislative acts and certain provisions of the Constitutional Treaty. Decisions would have been non-legislative acts binding in their entirety. Recommendations and opinions would have had no binding force.[102]

The new Treaty, however, does not adopt this distinction. Art. 288 TFEU returns to the traditional distinction between regulations, directives, decisions, recommendations and opinions. Questions may arise on how the EU courts are going to interpret the words used in the new Art. 263(4) TFEU.[103] In the case where the provision might be construed in light of its historical background, the outcome would be that this provision does not imply any modification. However, from a strictly legal point of view, a combined and literal application of the articles 263(4) TFEU and 288 TFEU might lead to a totally different conclusion.

This latter conclusion, although unlikely, would open up an unprecedented scenario and would grant new strength to the *locus standi* of the Regions (and

---

[102] Art. I-33(1) of the Treaty establishing a Constitution for Europe.

[103] The applicant in the Case T-417/04, *Regione autonoma Friuli-Venezia Giulia v. Commission* [2007] ECR II-641, argued that the draft of the Constitutional Treaty should be taken into account. The CFI rejected this argument since the TFEU had not yet entered into force.

more, in general, to individuals) before the EU courts. Should this be the construction adopted by the CFI and the ECJ, a major element of the "regional blindness" of the EU would finally be overcome.

A Pragmatic Approach: The Judicial Defence of the Rights of the Regions at EU Level Through the National Government

It is far from certain whether the ECJ will adopt the latter interpretation. The enormous restrictions which face sub-state entities bringing an action before the ECJ under Art. 263(4) TFEU will probably remain – at least in the near future. As we noted above, neither the preliminary reference procedure of Art. 267 TFEU (ex 234 EC), nor that of Art. 277 TFEU (ex 241 EC), offer a suitable alternative to the direct challenge route. Therefore, it is important to ask: what is the position of domestic law if one or several Regions assume that an EU act is unlawful? The analysis of the national systems under consideration allows the identification of three different patterns regarding the bringing of a claim for judicial review under Art. 263 TFEU.

The first pattern is based on the right of a *single* regional authority to *oblige* the central government to bring a claim for judicial review under Art. 263(2) TFEU. Two federal states adopt this approach: Belgium and Austria. In both countries, the State is under a legal obligation to bring a claim if an EU act concerns a matter belonging to the competence of a regional entity.[104]

Belgium will go even further (based upon Declaration 51 annexed to the Final Act of the Intergovernmental Conference which adopted the ToL) in the near future. Belgium attached the following statement on National Parliaments to its signing of the ToL:

> Belgium wishes to make clear that, in accordance with its constitutional law, not only the Chamber of Representatives and Senate of the Federal Parliament but also the parliamentary assemblies of the Communities and the Regions act, in terms of competences exercised by the Union, as components of the national parliamentary system or chambers of the national parliament.

This declaration is linked to the interpretation of the term "national parliament" throughout the Treaty. Some major questions remain unanswered in this context. The EU regards Declaration 51 as a unilateral declaration by a Member State which is not binding on the EU itself. However, Belgium is internationally bound by its unilateral declaration. A declaration can be defined as a notification by which a state

[104]See the Belgian Cooperation Agreement of 11 July 1994 and the Cooperation Agreement of 19 December 2005. These two documents are available at http://www.vlaamsparlement.be (last checked on 26 November 2009). On Austria see Art. 10(1) of the 1992 Agreement concerning the right of the Austrian *Länder* and Municipalities to participate in matters of European integration, published in *Bundesgesetzblatt* (Federal Law Gazette, *BGBl.* in acronym) 1992/775.

clarifies the meaning or the scope it gives to a treaty or to a provision, or by which a state sets down the reasons for becoming a party.

On the internal level, Belgium should, by preference, adapt its legal framework and its existing legislation, in accordance with the advice of the Belgian Council of State, to make clear how it intends to execute this unilateral declaration in the Belgian institutional framework. This means that the Special Act of 8 August 1980 needs to be revised.[105]

In the case of Austria, it must be emphasised that the Federation is not under an obligation to challenge an act on behalf of a single *Land*, if another *Land* disagrees, or if there are compelling "foreign and integration policy reasons". This "safety clause" weakens the position of the *Länder* since no procedure exists to overcome possible disagreements with the Federation. Hitherto, no direct challenge has been brought by Austria on the basis of a request stemming from the *Länder*.

The second pattern is based on the right of the *majority of the regional authorities* to *compel* the central government to challenge an EU act under Art. 263(2) TFEU. Germany and Italy adopt this approach. In Germany, the *Bundesrat* can oblige the Federal Government to make use of the remedies offered by EU law.[106] The *Bundesrat* has this authority in relation to EU acts which affect issues falling within the legislative competence of the *Länder*. There is, however, a "safety clause" in favour of the Federal Government which could allow it to ignore a request of the *Bundesrat* on grounds of its "responsibility for the whole state" and of considerations of "foreign, defence, and integration policy".[107] Once a challenge has been made, the *Länder* can also contribute to the development of the Federal Government's strategy in the proceedings, which must be agreed on with the *Bundesrat*.[108] In Italy, given the absence of a "chamber of the Regions", it is the absolute majority of the Regions (and of the Autonomous Provinces of Trento and Bolzano) within the State–Regions Conference that may oblige the national Government to bring a claim under Art. 263(2) TFEU.[109]

The third pattern recognises the right of regional authorities to *request* the central government to bring a claim against an EU act, *without the central government being under any legal obligation to do so*. This approach is taken by Spain, France,

[105]Advice of the Belgian Council of State, *Parl. Doc.*, Belgian Senate, No. 568/1, session 2007–2008, to be consulted on www.senate.be (last accessed on 1 December 2009). A first initiative was taken by the previous Belgian Prime Minister and current Chairman of the European Council, Herman Van Rompuy: see Proposal to modify the Special Act of 8 August 1980, *Parl. Doc.*, Belgian Chamber of Representatives, session 2007–2008, nr. 1263/001. This proposal has not been adopted by the Belgian Chamber or the Belgian Senate.

[106]See § 7(1), first subparagraph, of the EUZBLG.

[107]See § 7(1), second subparagraph, of the EUZBLG.

[108]See § 7(3) of the EUZBLG.

[109]Art. 5(2) of the "La Loggia" Act. Consultation of the official web site of the State-Regions Conference (http://www.statoregioni.it) does not reveal any direct action for annulment filed by the Italian Government under Art. 5(2) of the "La Loggia" Act since the entry into force of the Act (last checked on 2 January 2010).

and the UK. In these three countries, one or more regional authorities may ask the national government to bring a claim for judicial review, but it will ultimately be for the national government to decide whether to file or not the action.[110] The potential for a sub-state entity to succeed in convincing the central government to take action might well depend on its political weight and on its capacity for "mobilising" public opinion.

It is important to stress that the first pattern is highly unlikely to be adopted in larger federal or decentralised states with a large number of regions like Germany, Italy, Spain and the UK. The difference between the second and the third patterns seems to be linked to the fact that those countries belonging to the third pattern are not full federal states. The overall impression is that the mechanisms set up at national level are not able to compensate entirely for the lack of the status as privileged applicants of the Regions. Even in Austria, where in principal, a single *Land* has the right to compel the Federation to file a claim on its behalf, or in Germany, where a majority within the *Bundesrat* has the same right, there are "safety clauses" which could allow the Federal Government to refuse to file a claim for judicial review. The Belgian solution set out above and based upon their Declaration 51 seems to offer better protection for the interests of a single Region. This development would include a competence for regional parliaments to bring an action before the Community Courts based upon the infringement of the principles of subsidiarity and proportionality in accordance with what is prescribed under Art. 8 of the Protocol on the application of the principles of subsidiarity and proportionality. However, it remains impossible to evaluate the Belgian proposal given that the necessary reforms within the Belgian internal legal system have not been undertaken.

The position of the German *Länder* in this respect has been strengthened by the 2008 constitutional amendment.[111] According to that amendment, the *Bundestag* and – more importantly for our purposes – the *Bundesrat* are entitled to require a direct claim for judicial review before the ECJ against EU legislation on grounds of an infringement of the principle of subsidiarity. This provision mirrors what is provided for in the *Protocol on the Application of the Principles of Subsidiarity and Proportionality*, annexed to the ToL, that any national Parliament, or – for our purposes – "any chamber thereof", will be entitled to require the respective Member State to "notify", on their behalf, a direct action for annulment of EU legislative acts, on grounds of an infringement on the subsidiarity principle.[112] The effectiveness of

[110]In Spain, the matter is regulated by the *Acuerdo sobre la participación de las Comunidades Autónomas en los procedimientos ante el TJCE* of 11 December 1997 (published in *Boletín Oficial del Estado*, *BOE* in acronym, of 2 April 1998). Neither the Memorandum of Understanding nor the Concordats between the UK and its devolved entities seem to contain a provision which includes a possibility for the devolved entities to oblige the Westminster Government to commence an action before EU Courts. On this topic note Lenaerts (2008), p. 10. In France, no specific legal provision is in place.

[111]See Art. 1 of the Constitutional revision act of 8 October 2008 (in *BGBl.*, I, p. 1926). This provision adds a new paragraph 1a to Art. 23 BL.

[112]Art. 8(1) of the Protocol.

this provision of the Protocol in the different Member States will largely depend on its implementation in the different national systems.

A Jiminy Cricket for the EU: The "Early Warning" System

The lack of privileged applicant status is not the only problem for the Regions. Should the ECJ confirm its traditional "light touch" approach to the application of the principle of subsidiarity this may affect the effectiveness of the rephrased Art. 5 TFEU (ex 5 EC).[113] Given that an *ex post* evaluation of compliance with the principle of subsidiarity has proven difficult for the ECJ to carry out, the drafters of the *Protocol on Subsidiarity* created the "early warning" system. The rationale for this new tool is to strengthen consideration of the principle of subsidiarity in the legislative process (i.e. *ex ante*). The "early warning" system has already been mentioned above at Sect. B.I of this chapter. However, the scope of this section differs from the approach taken in Sect. B.I. Here, the "early warning" system will be approached from the specific perspective of the EU institutions.

The important aspect for the Regions is that any national Parliament *or any chamber thereof* is entitled, within 8 weeks from the date of transmission to it of a draft EU legislative act, to send to the political institutions a reasoned opinion stating why it considers that the draft in question does not comply with the principle of subsidiarity (early warning).[114] This allows the chambers of the regions to communicate with the EU institutions and to play a role in the development of legislation.

Where reasoned opinions on non-compliance of a proposed piece of legislation with the principle represent at least one-third of all the votes allocated to national

[113]ECJ, C-233/94, *Germany v. European Parliament and Council,* 13 May 1997 [1997] ECR I-2405; ECJ, C-377/98, *Netherlands v. European Parliament and Council,* 9 October 2001 [2001] ECR I-7079; ECJ, C-491/01, *British American Tobacco (Investments) and Imperial Tobacco*, 10 December 2002 [2002] ECR I-11453; ECJ, C-114/01, *Avesta Polarit Chrome Oy,* 11 September 2003 [2003] ECR I-264. Read also the recent conclusion of the Advocate General in C-58/08, *Vodafone Ltd.,* 1 October 2009, to be consulted on http://curia.europa.eu (last checked on 11 December 2009). Read on this topic Van Nuffel (2000), pp. 412–424 and Konig and Lorz (2003), pp. 167–173.

[114]Art. 6 of the *Protocol on Subsidiarity* provides that it will be for each national parliament or each chamber of a national parliament to consult, where appropriate, regional parliaments with legislative powers. The Constitutional Treaty provided a similar reinforcement of the principle of subsidiarity. Within the Member States, time will tell how the early warning mechanism will function. Only Belgium has so far given an important indication in the creation of the aforementioned Declaration 51. In Belgium, a new Cooperation Agreement has to be concluded to ensure the submission of the drafts to the regional parliaments. This Cooperation Agreement did not enter into force due to the Dutch and French rejection of the Constitutional Treaty. As yet, no new Cooperation Agreement has been concluded to execute Art. 6 and Art. 8 of the *Protocol on Subsidiarity*. However, there is a view that it is likely that a similar Co-operation Agreement will be adopted.

parliaments (each parliament has two votes and each chamber of bicameral parliaments one), the draft will have to be reviewed, but not necessarily amended or withdrawn.[115]

The early warning power of the national parliaments is potentially more influential where the "ordinary legislative procedure" (that is the former co-decision procedure, that became the norm under the ToL) applies. In such a case, if reasoned opinions on the non-compliance of a proposed legislative act represent at least a simple majority of the votes allocated to national parliaments, the proposal has to be reviewed by the Commission. If the Commission decides to maintain the proposal, it has to justify, in a reasoned opinion, why it considers such a proposal to be compliant with the principle of subsidiarity. This reasoned opinion, as well as the reasoned opinions of the national parliaments, will have to be submitted to the Parliament of the EU and the Council for consideration in the legislative process. Therefore, the national parliaments' opinions may form the object for discussion and are likely to have influence on the EU legislator.

But all that glitters is not gold. The "early warning" might turn out to be like Jiminy Cricket talking to Pinocchio: there is no guarantee at all that he will be listened to. And the position of the Regions is not necessarily particularly strong given that only two chambers among the analysed national patterns – the German and Austrian *Bundesräte* – can be regarded as proper "chambers of the regions". It seems therefore far from easy for single Regions or groups of regions to be able to build a majority around their position. What position could the regions ever agree on? The Regions have different powers in the different Member States. What may hurt the interests of the Belgian Regions or Communities may not impact on those of the Italian Regions or the Austrian *Länder*.

Authorities at Home, Lobbyists in Brussels: The Liaison Offices of the Regions in Brussels and Other Forms of Contact with the EU Institutions

Most Regions throughout the EU have opened representation offices in Brussels over the last 25 years. The offices are not a only a creation of "full" Regions – some local entities (e.g. major cities) have got representatives in Brussels. The liaison offices lobby the EU institutions in Brussels in the interests of the regional governments.

It is difficult to estimate the influence of these offices on the EU legislative process. But the large number of such offices and the considerable budget allocated to some of them seems to confirm their utility from the point of view of the Regions they represent.

Their major tasks are the following:

[115] This threshold shall be a quarter in the case of a draft legislative act of the Commission or of a quarter of the Member States in the area of freedom, security and justice (Art. 7(2), second subparagraph, of the *Protocol on Subsidiarity*).

- Representation of the Region
- Promotion of the Region's image and interests
- Networking

In Germany and Spain, the liaison offices initially created some legal concern, and in France, they found the criticism of the national Government. This is due to the fact that their existence has the potential to give rise to regional mini-foreign policies disconnected from the foreign policy of the state (German scholars talk of "*Nebenaußenpolitik*" of the *Länder*, i.e. foreign policy on the side). But this concern has proven unjustified given that the liaison offices operate only in regional matters and have no diplomatic status.[116]

The function of the Observer on behalf of the German *Länder* in Brussels (called *Länderbeobachter*) is somewhat different. This office has existed since 1959. The Observer is appointed by the Conference of the Ministers of the *Länder* for European Affairs (EMK, *Europaministerkonferenz*) and works closely with the Permanent Representation of the Federal Republic of Germany in the EU. The Observer is able to attend the EU advisory and institutional bodies' meetings but he is not allowed to participate in discussions or to vote. His task is to pass all useful information in relation to the EU to the *Länder*.

In 2003, the French *Conseil d'Etat* expressed the fear that the lack of involvement of the French territorial entities in the EU law and policy making would multiply informal contacts with the European Commission.[117] Indeed, the use of the liaison offices and the undertaking by the Regions of other informal contacts with the European Union institutions (e.g. through associations of regions) can be seen as a by-product of the "regional blindness" of the Member States.

The Committee of the Regions: An Upgraded Role for a Consultative Body

The role of the Committee of the Regions (hereinafter CoR) was upgraded by the ToL with the aim of the reduction of the democratic deficit and the widespread feeling that the EU institutions are too far divorced from European citizens. The CoR was created by the Maastricht Treaty as a consultative body representing local and regional authorities within the EU.[118] Its competences were originally limited to an advisory body ancillary to the political institutions.

---

[116]See the Ruling of the Spanish Constitutional Court No. 165 of 26 May 1994.

[117]Report of the General Assembly of the *Conseil d'Etat* entitled *Collectivités territoriales et obligations du droit communautaire*, 23 October 2003, p. 58.

[118]Art. 300(3) TFEU establishes that "*The CoR shall consist of regional and local bodies who either hold a regional or local authority electoral mandate or are politically accountable to an elected assembly*". In all the analysed national patterns the regional and local authorities within the Member States are involved in the choice of the members of the CoR directly or through their associations.

The ToL offered the CoR the opportunity to play a more prominent political role. The CoR has to be consulted on more topics than in the past. The consultation is mandatory (even though the resulting opinion is not binding) in those fields of intervention that are more closely linked to the interests of local and regional authorities.[119] The CoR can be consulted on any other topic if the political institutions regard it as appropriate.[120] The CoR can also draft opinions on its own initiative and present them to the Council, the Commission and the Parliament.[121]

The *locus standi* of the CoR has been significantly expanded by the ToL. The CoR became a "semi-privileged" applicant since it is now entitled to bring actions before the ECJ for the purpose of protecting its prerogatives.[122] The CoR has thus obtained *locus standi* in those situations where it must be consulted under the Treaties. In addition, Art. 8(2) of the Protocol on subsidiarity provides that the CoR can bring direct actions against the infringement of the principle of subsidiarity provided that it is a matter in which it had the right to be consulted.

Given the increased powers of the CoR under the ToL, the Regions might be able to reinforce their influence within the institutional framework of the EU. More than ever before, the CoR is the "subsidiarity watchdog".[123] In the fields in which the consultation of the CoR is mandatory, the EU acts in the exercise of shared competences, where, according to Art. 5(3) TEU (ex 5 EC), the subsidiarity principle plays a decisive role. It is likely that among the aspects the CoR will focus upon, the respect of the subsidiarity principle by the lawmaking institutions within the EU will occupy an important place. Over the next few years, the CoR might contribute significantly to the development and keeping of the right balance of powers between the Union, the Member States and the sub-national entities.

[119]Consultation of the CoR is mandatory for the following areas: Transport (Art. 91(1) TFEU); Employment (Art. 148(2) and 149(1) TFEU); Social policy (Art. 153(2) TFEU); Education, vocational training, youth and sport (Art. 165(4) and 166(4) TFEU); Culture (Art. 167(5) TFEU); Public health (Art. 168(4) TFEU); Trans-European networks (Art. 172 TFEU); Economic, social and territorial cohesion (Art. 175(3), 177(1) and 178(1) TFEU); Environment (Art. 175(1), (2) and (3) TFEU). All the aforementioned subjects were within the sphere of competence of the CoR before the entry into force of the ToL. The ToL increased the number and range of policies in which the opinion of the CoR is required. More specifically the ToL added the following areas to the aforementioned ones: sea and air transport (Art. 100(2) TFEU; within the framework of the Transport policy); a number of measures aimed at protecting public health (Art. 168(5) TFEU; within the framework of the Public health policy); extension of the ordinary legislative procedure to some areas of environmental protection (Art. 192(2) TFEU; within the framework of the Environment policy); Energy policy (Art. 194(2) TFEU).

[120]Art. 307(1) TFEU (ex 265 EC).

[121]Art. 307(4) TFEU (ex 265 EC).

[122]Art. 263(3) TFEU (ex 230 EC). The category of "semi-privileged" applicants includes those bodies which are entitled to bring a direct claim *only* in order to protect their own prerogatives. The Court of Auditors and the European Central Bank also belong to this category.

[123]Among others, consider the report pertaining to the 95th meeting of the Bureau of the Committee of the Regions, 7 July 2006, p. 5 and the press release of the Committee of the Regions of 4 December 2009 http://www.cor.europa.eu/pages/PressTemplate.aspx?view=detail&id=decfa388-ecd6-4cc0-9d0d-dc9ae2584112 (last checked on 15 June 2010).

The Fulfilment of EU Obligations in the Domestic Sphere

A Member State cannot invoke its national law to justify the non-implementation of EU obligations.[124] Therefore, a Member State remains responsible for the non-implementation even if a given competence belongs to its sub-state entities.[125] On the other hand, the EU cannot alter the distribution of competences that exists in a Member State, since the European construction must not interfere in the Member States' internal organisation: this is the institutional and procedural autonomy principle stated by the ECJ.[126]

This principle finds full support in the Member States. The Austrian Constitutional Court, for instance, elaborated the concept of "*doppelte Bindung*".[127] The domestic legislator is actually "bound twice", because on the one hand, it has to comply with EU law, and on the other, with the norms of the national Constitution – above all those concerning the distribution of powers between Federation and *Länder*. The consequence is that the *Länder* have the constitutional *right* and at the same time the *duty* to implement EC measures falling within their sphere of competence.

This constitutional right and duty of implementation is not an Austrian peculiarity. It is instead a well-established principle in all the constitutional patterns considered in this chapter. This principle is in fact *explicitly* (the case in Austria,[128] UK,[129] Italy[130]) or *implicitly* (the case in Germany,[131] Belgium,[132] Spain[133]) embodied in all the national constitutions under consideration except France.

In France, the situation is partly different. It is indeed accepted that the Regions, like any other legal person under French law, are subject to EU law (cf. Art. 55 of the Constitution: "Treaties or agreements duly ratified or approved shall, upon

---

[124]See the Case 72/81 *Commission* v. *Belgium* [1982] ECR 183, and the Joined Cases 227–230/85 *Commission* v. *Belgium* [1988] ECR 1. See also Case 8/88 *Germany* v. *Commission* [1990] ECR I-2321 at 2355–66. In the legal scholarship see Lenaerts et al. (2005), pp. 535–537.

[125]In this regard see Schaus (1994), p. 79.

[126]See ECJ, Joined Cases 51–54/71, *International Fruit Company NV and others* v. *Produktschap voor Groenten en Fruit* [1971] ECR 1107. See Guillermin (1992), pp. 319–346.

[127]See the decisions of the Austrian Constitutional Court published in the Official Collection of the Decisions of the Constitutional Court (*Erkentnisse und Beschlüsse des Verfassungsgerichtshofes*, in acronym *VfSlg.*) 14.863/1997 and 17.022/2003.

[128]Art. 23d(5) B-VG.

[129]Section 53 and Para. 7(2) of Schedule 5 of the Scotland Act 1998; Para. 3(c) of Schedule 2 of the Northern Ireland Act 1998; section 80 of the Government of Wales Act 2006.

[130]Art. 117(5) of the Italian Constitution.

[131]See Degenhart (2007), p. 1424 (Rn. 6). The right of the *Länder* to implement the EU law in matters of their competence can be drawn from Art. 30 BL, according to which the exercise of state powers and the discharge of state functions is a matter for the *Länder*, unless otherwise provided or permitted by the BL.

[132]The principle "*in foro interno et in foro externo*" is linked to the provisions in Art. 92 bis of the Belgian Special Act of 8 August 1980. In this regard, see Velaers (2006), pp. 66–67.

[133]In Spain this principle can be drawn from Art. 1 of Act No. 47 of 27 December 1985 passed at the time of the Spanish accession to the EEC. The principle has been finally confirmed by the Constitutional Court in the decisions No. 236 of 12 December 1991 and No. 79 of 28 May 1992.

publication, prevail over Acts of Parliament, subject, with respect to each agreement or treaty, to its application by the other party"). In light of this provision, the French Regions (and any other French territorial authority) must therefore comply with all the obligations arising from EU law. However, they do not have any responsibility for the transposition of EU directives in the areas falling within their competence. The State is the only entity entitled to discharge that task. This is a striking difference between France and the other examined regionalised and federal states.

It is important to make reference to a ruling of the Austrian Constitutional Court. According to this ruling, it would be necessary for the Constitution to be modified if the EU law required uniform implementation provisions issued at national level in a field where there is no explicit constitutional basis for federal intervention.[134] In other words, the requirement for uniformity arising from the EU does not justify the recognition of "implied powers" for the Federation. This is notwithstanding the fact that the Constitutional Court had already affirmed the "*Anwendungsvorrang*" principle: that single constitutional provisions should be set aside in the event of a conflict with EU law.[135]

The opinion that the federal or regional structure of a Member State may delay or possibly have a negative impact on the correct implementation of the EU law is widespread. For example, according to some, the principle "*in foro interno et in foro externo*" leads Belgium to be a "bad pupil" in relation to the implementation of EU law.[136] In Germany, there are scholars who point out that the implementation of EU measures is often problematic due to the federal structure of the state.[137] Recent studies show that the Italian Regions are often responsible for the infringement of EU obligations in matters relating to the internal market, public procurement, and the environment.[138]

All of this begs the following question: what is going to happen if a Region does not comply with obligations stemming from the Treaties? From the point of view of the Union, the responsibility shall fall exclusively on the Member State and not on the incompliant sub-national – regional or local – entity. This is due to the fact that, as we know, only states are members of the EU. Therefore, we have to investigate

[134]See the ruling of the Austrian Constitutional Court in *VfSlg*. 17.022/2003.

[135]See the ruling of the Austrian Constitutional Court in *VfSlg*. 15.427/1999. See also Öhlinger and Potacs (2006), p. 58 ff.; Korinek (2004), p. 137 ff.

[136]Ingelaere (2006), pp. 173–174.

[137]Huber (2007), p. 217. It is also worth mentioning the repeal of the power to enact framework legislation ("*Rahmengesetzgebung*") by the 2006 constitutional reform ("*Föderalismusreform*"), provided for by the previous Art. 75 BL. This framework legislation was characterised by the fact that, in sectors subject to it, the Federation was competent to lay down rules of principle, while the *Länder* were competent to issue further regulations integrating the federal framework law. First of all, the *Rahmengesetzgebung* was repealed owing to its excessive complexity (where did the Federation's competence end and where did the *Länder*'s begin?), but also because it was a source of delays and non-compliance when implementing EU secondary law.

[138]See Parodi and Puoti (2006); De Maio (2006), pp. 147–182.

the Member States' mechanisms aimed at preventing (or punishing) breaches of their duties caused by regional authorities.

Financial Liability of the Regions

In some of the national patterns, financial liability of the Regions is provided for in cases of violation of EU law or EU obligations. Such arrangements perform a deterrent function insofar as the Regions are aware that the failure to implement or the incorrect implementation of EU law or any other breach of EU obligations may cost them money.

Germany is the "champion" of this approach. The 2006 reform of the BL ("*Föderalismusreform*") established the principle that any costs deriving from Germany's violation of "supranational" or "international" obligations must be borne by the responsible *Länder* in proportion to the respective quota of responsibility.[139]

In Austria, the financial burdens following from the regional breach of the duty to implement the EU law are covered at first by the Federation. This is due to the fact that the Federation is the only entity responsible to the EU. Austrian law contains the obligation for the *Länder* and the local communities to bear those costs which derive from judgments of the ECJ in relation to breaches of EU law.[140] In cases where there is a disagreement on the attribution of the financial responsibility to the sub-state entities, the conflict has to be decided by the Constitutional Court (Art. 137 B-VG).

Similarly, in Spain, when the ECJ finds against Spain for a breach in the implementation of EU law due to the actions or omissions of the autonomous communities, the responsible *Comunidades autónomas* must comply with the findings of the Court and pay any fine. Also, in the UK, it is clearly stated in the Memorandum of Understanding that where any breach of EU obligations is due to the devolved governments, they will be liable to pay all of the related costs.[141] In Italy, a mechanism peculiar to its system was recently introduced. This is the "right of redress" ("*diritto di rivalsa*") of the State against the Regions for financial

[139]Art. 104a(6), first subparagraph, BL.

[140]2008 Financial Equalisation Act (*Finanzausgleichsgesetz* 2008, in acronym FAG 2008). Published in Federal Law Gazette (*BGBl.*) I 2007/103.

[141]Para B4.25 of the Memorandum of Understanding states that "To the extent that financial costs and penalties imposed on the UK arise from the failure of implementation or enforcement by a devolved administration on a matter falling within its responsibility, or from the failure of a devolved administration to meet its share of an EC quota or obligation, responsibility for meeting these will be borne by the devolved administration".

damages resulting from rulings served by the ECJ on grounds of a Region's failure to comply with EU obligations.[142]

A few years ago, the French *Conseil d'Etat* expressed the view that it would be highly desirable to introduce a mechanism allowing the State to recover from the territorial communities – including the Regions – the pecuniary sanctions issued by the Community.[143] The legislator followed the same path and introduced the mechanism at Art. L 1511-1-1 of the General Code of the Territorial Communities.[144] This mechanism does not include the financial consequences of any failure to comply with EU law. It only covers the financial consequences which arise from the non-acceptance by the ECJ of a state aid program put into operation by a territorial community.

Under Belgian law, in cases where the national authority needs to exercise its substitution power, the costs of the procedure and potential damages linked to the intervention of the national authority can be claimed from the sub-state entities. The national authority may recover these expenses by withdrawing parts of the yearly budget paid by the national authority to the responsible Region.[145]

State liability may also arise from an action or a failure to act of a sub-state entity. The ECJ in *Konle* and *Haim* affirmed that in such cases the reparation of the damage or the loss can be made by the sub-state entity.[146]

Substitution Powers of the State: "Trojan Horse" for Surreptitious Re-Centralisation or Tool for "Sustainable Integration"?

Another tool often provided for by domestic law is the recognition of substitution powers to the central government of the State. The practical meaning of such substitution is that the power to enact implementation measures passes *temporarily*

---

[142]See Art. 16-*bis* (added in 2007) of the "Buttiglione" Act. This measure is criticised because it is labelled as a "right of redress"; so it would not be an *obligation* of the State but a *right*. Having foreseen a right in favour of the State seems to have allowed for a certain amount of discretion in the proposition of the action. This may result in decreased effectiveness of this new tool. The same Act establishes that the State has a similar "right of redress" against the Regions (and other public bodies) responsible for a violation of the European Convention on Human Rights (ECHR).

[143]Report adopted by the general assembly of the *Conseil d'Etat* on 23 October 2003: *Collectivités territoriales et obligations du droit communautaire*.

[144]Art. L 1511-1-1 of the General Code of the Territorial Communities (*Code Général des Collectivités Territoriales*) states at para. 3 that: "*Les collectivités territoriales et leur groupements supportent les conséquences financières des condamnations qui pourraient résulter pour l'Etat de l'exécution tardive ou incomplète des décisions de récupérations. Cette charge est une dépense obligatoire au sens de l'article L 1612-15*".

[145]Article 16 § 3 of the Special Act of 8 August 1980. Ingelaere (2005), p. 183. These withdrawals cannot be disproportionate.

[146]Case C-302/97 *Konle* v. *Austria* [1999] ECR I-3099, paras. 61–64, and case C-424/97 *Haim* v. *Kassenzahnärtztliche Vereinigung Nordrhein* [2000] ECR I-5123, paras. 31 and 32.

to central authorities (whether executive or legislature). The non-compliant Region retains the right to implement at a later stage, that is the right to replace the implementation measure issued by the central government with a regional measure (Italian scholars describe this phenomenon in terms of "*cedevolezza*", i.e. pliability, of the substitute measure). The current "*Landesblindheit*" of the EU forces some Member States to provide substitution powers in order to comply with the decisions of the ECJ. This *ultimum remedium* is necessary to break the potential unwillingness of a sub-state entity to abide by EU law. The substitution power is a good example of EU integration greatly interfering with the internal distribution of powers in the Member States.

Theoretically we can distinguish an *a priori* from a *post facto* substitution. *A priori* substitution would take place before the non-fulfilment of an EU obligation in order to prevent it from occurring (e.g. before the expiry of the term for transposing a directive). *Post facto* substitution would take place after the non-fulfilment of an EU obligation (e.g. after the expiry of the term for transposing a directive).

A priori substitution is clearly incompatible with the principle of institutional and procedural autonomy and with the right and duty of the Regions to implement EU measures in matters of their competence. The Spanish Constitutional Court dealt with this issue in a case regarding a competence conflict concerning the European Agricultural Guidance and Guarantee Fund.[147] The Court established that the central government has the right to issue substitute norms implementing the EU law in areas of regional competence *only after the non-fulfilment of an EU obligation has actually taken place*. This standpoint is absolutely logical: the constitutional distribution of powers between the central government and the regional level would be seriously undermined if the substitution power were exercisable *a priori*.

Only a *post facto* substitution is generally accepted. But there are exceptions. In the UK, for example, the devolved authorities and the Westminster Government may agree that a particular EU act would be best implemented by national measures receiving uniform application throughout the UK.[148] The prerogatives of the devolved authorities are anyway respected given that their *a priori* replacement by the Westminster Government can only be undertaken by agreement.

The other exception is Italy. The national Government is entitled to implement EU directives on a yearly basis under the so-called "*legge comunitaria*" in *all* areas (including the areas falling within the sphere of legislative competence of the Regions).[149] This is an *a priori* substitution exercisable by the Government via

[147]Ruling of the Constitutional Court No. 80 of 8 March 1993.

[148]This possibility rests on section 57 of the Scotland Act 1998, section 26(2) of the Northern Ireland Act 1998 and section 82 of the Government of Wales Act 2006 respectively.

[149]The "*legge comunitaria*" (law for the implementation of Community law) is a special statute passed by the Parliament every year in order to ensure Italian legislation is in conformity with all EU directives and regulations issued the year before.

delegated legislation. The substitute norms issued by the State are characterised by the aforementioned pliability ("*cedevolezza*"). This means that, if the State substitutes its norms for those of the Regions, then, at a later stage, the Regions may replace such norms with their own legislation and regain control over the areas of their competence.[150]

Often, substitution can take place *only after a judicial decision has been issued by EU courts against the Member State*. This is the case in Austria and in Belgium. In Austria, substitution is possible only if an EU court finds against Austria on grounds that a *Land* has failed to comply with obligations arising from EU law within the requisite time limit.[151] Similarly, in Belgium, the Constitution provides for a substitution procedure for situations in which a Region or a Community fails to fulfil EU obligations and the ECJ has delivered a decision.[152]

In other Member States, the *post facto* substitution is possible even *in the absence of (or before) a judicial decision*, if there is a lack of, or there is an incorrect implementation of, EU obligations. Such is the case of the UK, where the Scotland Act 1998, the Northern Ireland Act 1998, and the Government of Wales Act 2006 entrust a Minister in the national government with substitution power if there is a failure to implement EU obligations, *irrespective of whether there has already been a judgement of the ECJ*. The matter has formed the object of a scholarly and political debate in Belgium, where some scholars suggested that the State should be able to substitute the sub-national entities which have failed to comply before a condemnation by the EU.[153] Such a substitution, however, would have the clear disadvantage that, before the decision of the ECJ, it would remain uncertain whether the regional authority has really acted in breach of EU law.[154]

In Italy, the problem of *when* the substitution power can be exercised by the State (i.e. before or after a final condemnation has been issued by the ECJ) has been addressed neither by the legislator nor by legal scholarship. So far, the only example of exercise of substitution powers (apart from the "ordinary" *ex ante* substitution taking place on the basis of the "*leggi comunitarie*" through delegated legislation of the Government) is the suspension in 2006 by a Government Decree Law of the application of a statute of the Liguria Region. This statute was in breach

---

[150]The Regions do not "repeal" the State law. In actual fact they "derogate" from it. Should the Region repeal its own statute without replacing it with a new one, then the State law previously in force would be brought back into effect and fill the gap (this phenomenon is known as the "*reviviscenza*", i.e. "revival", of the State law).

[151]See Art. 23d(5), last sentence, B-VG. This could only be relevant in the case of a judgment of the ECJ in a procedure according to Art. 258 TFEU (ex 226 EC) et seq. In this regard see Öhlinger (1999).

[152]Art. 169 of the Belgian Constitution. In this regard it must be noted that a preliminary ruling under Art. 234 EC is not considered as a finding against a Member State: in fact this type of ruling only clarifies the question of the interpretation or validity of EC law.

[153]Louis and Alen (1994), p. 100.

[154]Melchior (1987), p. 334.

of Directive 79/409/EEC of 2 April 1979 on the conservation of wild birds.[155] On this occasion, the State intervention followed an Order of the President of the ECJ issued in the context of an infringement case against Italy.[156]

Without any doubt, the exercise of substitution powers by central governments is an exception to the "normal" constitutional distribution of powers. Therefore, in order to respect the decentralised structure of the state, the substitution procedures must be inspired by principles such as federal comity, loyal cooperation, respect for regional autonomy and proportionality. In Belgium, for instance, the State can only commence the procedure following a formal finding by the ECJ of a violation of EC law. Moreover, three cumulative conditions must be fulfilled. First, formal notice shall be given to the Community or Region concerned, in order to grant sufficient time to conform to EU obligations before the substitution takes place; second, the Community or Region concerned must be involved in the whole procedure during the litigation to find a solution for the pending case; third, the substitution shall entail only those measures which are strictly necessary to comply with the *juris dictum* of the ECJ's ruling (proportionality).[157] In Belgium, this very cumbersome procedure has so far not found any application. *Bundestreue* (that is federal loyalty) still seems to be strong enough not to need this procedure.

In a similar way, in Italy, the substitution procedure takes account of the rights of the Regions. Like in Belgium, the national Government must assign a proper timescale to allow the Regions to act, and *only* in the absence of their activity will it intervene with the necessary measures. The Head of the Executive of the Region concerned has the right to participate in the session of the Council of Ministers deciding on the adoption of the substitute measure. Finally, once again like in Belgium, consideration of the principle of proportionality is required, and the State measure by means of which the substitution is carried out must respect the limit of the "mildest possible means".[158]

The same cooperative approach is adopted in Spain. The simple awareness by regional authorities that their powers may be exercised by the national government is generally sufficient to persuade them to cooperate and comply with the EU obligations.

---

[155]See the Decree Law No. 297 of 27 December 2006 suspending the regional statute No. 36 of 31 October 2006. After about 2 months of suspension, the Liguria Region repealed regional statute No. 36 by means of regional statute No. 4 of 2 February 2007. The Government had previously made another attempt to exercise its substitution power on the basis of Art. 8 of the "La Loggia" Act through the Decree Law No. 251 of 16 August 2006 in order to ensure the implementation of the Directive 79/409/EEC on the protection of wild birds. This Decree Law, however, lost effect given that the Parliament did not confirm it within the term of 60 days provided for by Art. 77 of the Constitution.

[156]Order of the President of the ECJ in the Case C-503/06.

[157]Art. 16 § 3 of the Special Act of 8 August 1980, as modified by the Special Act of 8 August 1988.

[158]The substitution procedure is regulated by Art. 8 of the "La Loggia" Act. The substitute measure should be adopted with the participation of the competent regional body: this is the view of Villamena (2008), p. 127.

In Germany, there is no way the Federation could step in and substitute a *Land*. An intervention of the federal power in Germany would be theoretically possible under Art. 37 BL in order to coerce the *Länder* to comply with their duties (that is, the so-called "*Bundeszwang*", federal execution). It must be pointed out, however, that Art. 37 BL has never been applied since the entry into force of the BL; the application of this article would in fact be too time-consuming and politically costly.[159]

The French State, given the significantly lower degree of decentralisation in France in comparison to the other countries subject to our study, does not need a full substitution power vis-à-vis the Regions (nor vis-à-vis other territorial entities). This is linked to the fact that the State is the only authority responsible for the transposition of EU directives and more generally to the fact that it performs a largely predominant role in implementing EU law.

Defence of the Regions in the Infringement Procedure

If the Commission initiates an infringement procedure under Art. 258 TFEU against a Member State on the grounds of the missed or faulty implementation of an EU obligation by a sub-state entity, and if, in all the Member States, the Regions will suffer in one way (financial liability) and/or another (substitution) the consequences of their supposed non-compliance, the question arises of which rights of defence the Regions have in the infringement procedure. The traditional "regional blindness" of the EU is quite apparent in this area. This is due to the fact that the infringement procedure is directed against the Member State and not against the responsible sub-state entity. It is necessary to examine on one more occasion the way each of the Member States considered ensures participation rights to the Regions. The analysis showed that participation rights exist in Belgium, Spain, UK and Germany.

In Belgium, Spain and the UK, the Community, Region or devolved authority concerned is *individually* involved in the whole litigation process. This includes both the pre-judicial and the judicial phase of the infringement proceedings. If a case is brought to the ECJ against Belgium, Spain or the UK (judicial phase of the proceedings), the Community, Region or devolved authority will contribute to determining the position of the Member State in the judicial proceedings.[160]

Unlike Spain, Belgium and the UK, German law does not recognise a right of defence to a single *Land*. It recognises instead a *collective* right of the *Länder* –

---

[159] On this point see Huber (2007), p. 217.

[160] The relevant legal provisions are: in Belgium, Art. 16 § 3 of the Special Act of 8 August 1980; in Spain, Art. 11 of the Agreement (*Acuerdo sobre la participación de las Comunidades Autónomas en los procedimientos ante el TJCE*) of the *Conferencia de Asuntos relacionados con las Comunidades Europeas* (CARCE) of 11 December 1997; in the UK, Paras. B4.22–B4.24 of the Memorandum of Understanding.

through the *Bundesrat* – to influence the action of the Federal Government. The Federal Government needs to agree its defence strategy with the *Bundesrat* in infringement proceedings brought against the Federal Republic of Germany on grounds of a breach caused by the *Länder*.[161]

In the remainder of the national patterns we have examined, nothing is provided as to the participation rights of the Regions in infringement proceedings. This is the case in a federal state like Austria, in a regional state like Italy, and in a centralised system like France. This is one of those situations in which the lack of protection of the rights of the sub-state entities is not due to the "regional blindness" of the EU but to that of (some of) the Member States.

Concluding Remarks

The second half of the twentieth century witnessed the evolution towards a supranational European level. Initially, the European construction did not take any account of sub-state levels of government. At the time of the signing of the Treaty of Rome, West Germany was the only Member State where a federal system was in force. Since 1957, all the Member States have undergone profound constitutional transformations. Belgium, France and Italy have decentralised powers to Regions and other sub-state entities. The UK and Spain, which acceded the Community at a later stage (1973 and 1986, respectively), underwent a similar evolution. Austria was already a federal state when it joined the EU in 1995.

Given the trend towards regionalisation, it is of fundamental importance to assess whether the original "regional blindness" of the EU still exists and to what extent. The loss of authority by sub-state entities may reinforce the feeling of a democratic deficit within the EU.[162] In fact the political process in Brussels is largely influenced by lobbies and corporations which represent private and particular interests. In this context, the Regions are institutions which democratically represent the citizens and which can give them a voice in the promulgation of EU legislation and policy.

The EU has kept its original supranational character, and its members are and will be in the foreseeable future only states. From this point of view, it is perfectly logical that the EU is still in some measure "regionally blind". Regions and other sub-national entities can play a role in European governance, but they are not in a position to obtain EU membership. Furthermore, the Regions are currently excluded from the hard core of the Union's power. This is because the focus of the Union is still on economic issues, whereas the Regions' main focus (apart from

---

[161]See § 7(3) of the EUZBLG.

[162]White Paper on European Governance, 25 July 2001, pp. 13–14, to be consulted on http://eur-lex.europa.eu/LexUriServ/site/en/com/2001/com2001_0428en01.pdf (last checked on 11 December 2009).

agriculture) is on areas in which the Union has only limited responsibility (e.g. school education and culture). The impression is that those who yearn for a "Europe of the Regions" are likely to remain disappointed for a long time to come.

Over the last two decades, the EU has made important steps to recognise the existence and role of the Regions. Since the entry into force of the Treaty of Maastricht, regional Ministers can sit in the Council on behalf of a Member State. The same Treaty instituted the Committee of the Regions as an advisory body to the political institutions, and extended the application of the subsidiarity principle to all shared Community powers. Recently, the ToL reshaped this principle in a way which implies stronger consideration for sub-national entities. But there still remain profiles of "regional blindness" that should be addressed. Major examples are the lack of *locus standi* of the Regions in direct challenges and the traditional "light touch" approach of the ECJ in matter of subsidiarity. In reality, the Regional policy of the EU focuses on the allocation of the Structural and Cohesion Funds to the Member States or to designated Regional Development Agencies within the Member States. They take care of further distribution of the European funding to sub-national administrations. Regions and other territorial authorities cannot directly access funds and benefit from the thrust of the EU Regional Policy.

But there is a further complexity. The Regions are not a homogeneous level of government. Their powers and constitutional status vary enormously from Member State to Member State (and often even within an individual Member State). For this reason, the discourse on the Regions as the "third level" within the Union is an oversimplification which is at odds with reality. It is impossible for the EU to fully grasp and take into account regional diversity. A clear example is the Committee of the Regions. A weakness of the Committee is not only that it is just an advisory body, its effectiveness is principally affected by the representation of a plethora of different sub-state entities (both regional and local) with little in common apart from being sub-state.

Another example is the principle of subsidiarity. The huge difference between the Regions makes proper application of the principle very difficult to interpret. It might be extremely difficult to judge whether an action of the EU takes sufficient account of the prerogatives of the Regions (and of other sub-state authorities) in *all* the Member States. This explains why Art. 2 of the *Protocol on Subsidiarity* provides for a wide consultation round by the Commission before a legislative proposal is formulated. From the beginning of the decision-making process, the Commission shall endeavour to strike a balance between the heterogeneous interests of sub-national entities in the different Member States.

In sum, the "regional blindness" of the EU has not yet disappeared. To an extent, this is understandable given the supranational context and the heterogeneity of the regional level. One may introduce palliatives and corrections, but at least in the foreseeable future it will be impossible to reshape the very nature of the Union.

The participation of the Regions in EU law and policy making does not depend only on EU law. This participation is "filtered" by the Member States, and its scope varies significantly from Member State to Member State. For example, the Belgian Regions have a veto right on the transfer of their powers to the Union, whereas in other countries the Regions are not involved in this decision at all (Italy and UK). The spectrum is just as broad in the field of external representation of the Regions in the Council. Belgian Regions and Communities and German *Länder* have the full right to sit in the Council when issues of their exclusive competence are on the agenda. At the other end of the spectrum, France does not provide any regional participation in the Council whereas in the UK there is no binding legal framework for the participation of devolved authorities. In the field of internal preparation for Council meetings, there are countries where common positions achieved by the regional authorities prior to Council meetings are legally binding (this is the case in Belgium) or quasi-binding (Austria, Germany, and Spain). There are others where the Regions are merely consulted (Italy and UK) or not involved at all (France).

In sum, there are Member States which are at the forefront of regional participation (especially Belgium and Germany) and others which do not involve their Regions so much (especially France and UK). If the Regions in some Member States are still incapable of performing a sufficiently important role, this is due to the national law rather than to the Union. In other words, there exists a "regional blindness" of the Member States above and beyond that of the EU.

The consequence of this mix of national and supra-national "regional blindness" is the increasing importance of extra-institutional channels of communication between the EU and the regional level. An example is the use of liaison offices by single Regions to lobby the Commission. Another example is offered by the intensification over the last few years of direct contacts between associations of sub-state entities and the Commission in the wake of the 2001 White Paper.

In addition to the area of regional participation rights in EU law and policy making, there are further profiles of "regional blindness" at the Member States' level. Once again, the conclusion that the role of the Regions largely depends on national law is fully confirmed. An example is the absence of ad hoc legal remedies for the enforcement of regional participation rights. This is a widespread feature in the Member States that have been analysed. In the UK, no legal remedy is provided.

Another example of "regional blindness" is the direct challenge of EU measures by the national Government in cases of an encroachment on regional competences. There are Member States where the Regions have the right to compel the national Government to bring a challenge before the ECJ. This right is of the individual Regions or Communities in Belgium whereas it is cumulative (that is of the majority of the Regions) in Germany, Austria and Italy. Finally there are other countries where this right does not exist at all (Spain, France and UK).

A last example of "regional blindness" is the absence in a number of Member States (Austria, Italy and France) of a right of defence of the Regions in infringement proceedings arising from regional non-compliance with EU obligations. This position is justified from the European perspective. According to this perspective, only Member States can be held liable for non-compliance (principle of institutional and procedural autonomy).

The "regional blindness" of the Member States might prove extremely hard to tackle. It should not be forgotten that the EU is based upon national differences and that the motto of the EU is "united in diversity". Therefore, enhancement of participation rights of the Regions cannot be a sort of top-to-bottom process in which the EU enacts common rules. Each Member State has to find its own way and pace of reform. On the national level, there are a number of elements impairing the strengthening of the Regions. One element is certainly the existence of longstanding traditions. For example, France is still very centralised when compared to all other analysed Member States. This is the product of the Jacobin and Napoleonic traditions. Hence, the participation rights of the French Regions are almost non-existent.

A second element impairing reform is once again the supranational character of the Union. Some restrictions on regional participation rights appear justified in order to protect the prerogatives of the central government and the national interest. For example, in Austria and in Germany, the Federal Governments are allowed to depart from the common position reached by the *Länder*. This may happen in cases of imperative foreign and integration policy reasons (Austria) or when there are compelling reasons to believe that this is in the best interest of the Member State (Germany). In Belgium, the national government does not have the right to depart from an agreed common position. Given the principle of equality between the national level and the regional levels, the national interests of Belgium cannot prevail over the interests of the regions. It is questionable whether such a system would work in federal countries larger than Belgium. This system weakens the authority of the national government. At the same time, it reflects the strong centrifugal powers existing in Belgium.

Overall, the protection of national interests in combination with the involvement of sub-national entities in the decision-making process implies forms of collaboration and coordination between the levels of government concerned. Common positions and understandings need to be reached at any step, and loyal cooperation (the German "*Bundestreue*") is absolutely necessary in order to make the whole machinery work properly. This is further strengthening the cooperative character of federalism or regionalism in the countries that have been observed.

Overall, it emerges that Belgium is by far the forerunner in regional participation. The most specific aspect of Belgium is the absence of a chamber of the regions like the German *Bundesrat*. This might complicate Belgian Regions and Communities from benefiting in full from the rights that the ToL recognises to national parliaments. Belgium is followed by Germany, where regional participation in EU-related issues is strong and relies on a solid tradition. Coming behind these two Member States is a middle group including Austria, Spain and Italy. The members of this group are very advanced in some aspects of regional participation, whereas they only allow the Regions to play a limited role in other aspects. Finally, there is a group of two Member States at the bottom. The first is the UK, where the position of the devolved entities is not very strong in terms of legal power. However, the British system does not ignore political realities and therefore the voice of devolved entities in EU related issues. The second is France, which is not yet as strongly decentralised as the other examined national patterns.

Selected Bibliography

Birkinshaw PJ (2001) Does Europaen Public Law Exist? in Institute for European Studies Queen's University Belfast

Commission of the European Communities (2001) European governance: a white paper, 25 July 2001, COM(2001) 428. http://ec.europa.eu/governance/white_paper/en.pdf. Accessed 1 December 2009

Committee of the Regions (2009) White paper on multilevel governance, 17–18 June 2009. http://www.cor.europa.eu. Last accession on 30 June 2010

Craig P, De Búrca G (2008) EU Law. Text, cases, and materials, 4th edn. OUP, Oxford, p 525

Dani M (2004) Regions standing before the EU courts – towards a constitutional theory on "direct and individual" participation of the regions in the EU decision-making processes. In: Toniatti R et al (eds) An ever more complex union. Nomos, Baden-Baden, p 181

De Maio G (2006) Fonti regionali e direttive comunitarie in materia di appalti pubblici. Rassegna di diritto pubblico europeo:147–182

Degenhart C (2007) Art. 70 GG. In: Sachs M (ed) Grundgesetz-Kommentar. C.H. Beck, München, p 1424

Friedrich CJ (1968) Trends of federalism in theory and practice. Praeger, New York

García Roca J (2002) Conflictos entre el Estado y las Comunidades Autónomas ante el Tribunal Supremo: la competencia diferenciada entre las jurisdicciones constitucional y contencioso-administrativa. Revista Vasca de Administración Pública:89–110

Gatti-Montain J (1985) La region. In: Auby J-B (ed) Droit public. Economica, Paris, pp 285–320

Guillermin G (1992) Le principe de l'equilibre institutionnel dans la jurisprudence de la Cour de Justice des Communautés européennes. Journal de Droit International:319–346

Huber PM (2007) Die Europatauglichkeit des Art. 23 GG. In: Merten D (ed) Die Zukunft des Föderalismus in Deutschland und Europa. Duncker u. Humblot, Berlin, p 217

Ingelaere F (2005) De Belgische deelstaten en de Europese Unie. In: Judo F, Geudens G (eds) Internationale betrekkingen en federalisme. Larcier, Brussels, p 183

Ingelaere F (2006) De Belgische deelstaten en de Europese Unie. In: Judo F, Geudens G (eds) Internationale betrekkingen en federalisme. Larcier, Brussel, pp 173–174

Ipsen H-P (1966) Als Bundestaat in der Gemeinschaft. In: von Caemmerer E et al (eds) Probleme des Europäischen Rechts. Festschrift für Walter Hallstein. Klostermann, Frankfurt a.M., p 256

Konig C, Lorz RA (2003) Stärkung des Subsidiaritätsprinzip. Juristen-Zeitung:167–173

Korinek K (2004) Die doppelte Bedingtheit von gemeinschaftsrechts-ausführenden innerstaatlichen Rechtsvorschriften. In: Hammer S et al (eds) Demokratie und sozialer Rechtsstaat in Europa, Festschrift für Theo Öhlinger. WUV, Wien, p 137

Lenaerts K (2008) Access of the Regions with legislative power to the European Court of Justice. Speech at the Conference on subsidiarity organised by the CoR (25 August 2008). Last accession on 30 June 2010. p 10. http://cor.europa.eu/pages/EventTemplate.aspx?view=search&id=lenaerts

Lenaerts K, Van Nuffel P, Bray R (eds) (2005) Constitutional law of the European Union. Sweet and Maxwell, London

Louis JV, Alen A (1994) La Constitution et la participation à la Communauté européenne. Revue belge de droit international:100

Melchior M (1987) Constitution et organisations internationales. Le problème de la supranationalité. In: Delperee F (ed) Le noveau droit constitutionnel. Bruylant, Brussels, p 334

Müller-Graff P-Ch (2007) Die Europatauglichkeit der grundgesetzlichen Föderalismusreform. In: Pitschas R (ed) Wege gelebter Verfassung in Recht und Politik. Festschrift für Rupert Scholz zum 70. Geburtstag. Duncker u. Humblot, Berlin, p 717

Öhlinger T (1999) Art 23d B-VG, Rz. 32. In: Korinek K, Holoubek M (eds) Österreichisches Bundesverfassungsrecht, Kommentar. Wien-New York, Springer

Öhlinger T (2008) Vorrang des EU-Rechts. In: Schroeder W (ed) Europarecht als Mehrebenensystem. Nomos, Vienna, pp 11–23
Öhlinger T, Potacs M (2006) Gemeinschaftsrecht und staatliches Recht. Die Anwendung des Europarechts im innerstaatlichen Bereich, 3rd edn. LexisNexis, Wien
Panara C (2008) Offene Staatlichkeit: Italien. In: von Bogdandy A et al (eds) Ius Publicum Europaeum, vol II. C.F. Müller, Heidelberg, pp 158–159
Parodi G, Puoti ME (2006) L'attuazione del diritto comunitario nelle materie di competenza regionale dopo la legge n. 11 del 2005. http://www.issirfa.cnr.it (28–29 April 2006)
Rawlings R (2000) Concordats of the constitution. Law Q Rev:283–284
Rojahn O (2001) Art. 23 BL. In: von Münch I, Kunig Ph (eds) Grundgesetz-Kommentar, vol. II. C. H. Beck, München, p 169
Rozenberg O, Lequesne C (2000) La ratification du Traité de Amsterdam par la France. Annuaire français des relations internationales:451
Rubio Llorente F, Alvarez Junco J (eds) (2006) El informe del Consejo de Estado sobre la reforma constitucional: Texto del informe y debates academicos. Centro de Estudios Constitucionales, Madrid
Schaus A (1994) L'exécution des traités. Revue belge de droit international:79
Scholz R (1996) Art. 23 BL. In: Maunz T, Dürig G (eds) Grundgesetz-Kommentar, vol. III. C. H. Beck, München, pp 139–140
Scott A (2001) The role of concordats in the new governance of Britain: taking subsidiarity seriously? Edinburgh Law Rev:21–48
Sorrentino F (2002) Nuovi profili costituzionali dei rapporti tra diritto interno e diritto internazionale e comunitario. Diritto pubblico comparato ed europeo:1355–1361
Streinz R (2007) Art. 23 BL. In: Sachs M (ed) Grundgesetz-Kommentar, 4th edn. C. H. Beck, München, p 923
Tizzano A (2007) Ancora sui rapporti tra Corti europee: principi comunitari e c.d. controlimiti costituzionali. Il Diritto dell'Unione europea:734–744
Van Nuffel P (2000) De rechtsbescherming van de nationale overheden in het Europees recht. Kluwer, Deventer
Van Nuffel P (2001) What's in a member state? Central and decentralised authorities before the community courts. Common Market Law Rev:871–901
Velaers J (2006) In foro interno et in foro externo: de internationale bevoegdheden van de gemeenschappen en de gewesten. In: Judo F, Geudens G (eds) Internationale betrekkingen en federalisme. Larcier, Brussels, pp 66–67
Villamena S (2008) Contributo in tema di proporzionalità amministrativa. Giuffrè, Milano, p 127
Volpi M (1995) Stato federale e Stato regionale: due modelli a confronto. Quaderni costituzionali:367

The manufacturer's authorised representative in the EU is Springer
Nature Customer Service Centre GmbH, Europaplatz 3, 69115 Heidelberg,
Germany. If you have any concerns regarding our products, please
contact ProductSafety@springernature.com

Printed and bound by CPI Group (UK) Ltd, Croydon, CR0 4YY
30/09/2026
02225599-0013